CW00409769

# United Nations Conference on Environment & Development
## Rio de Janeiro, Brazil, 3 to 14 June 1992

## AGENDA 21

### CONTENTS

**SECTION IV**. <u>MEANS OF IMPLEMENTATION</u>

* * * * *

* For section I (Social and economic dimensions), see A/CONF.151/26 (Vol. I); for section III (Strengthening the role of major groups) and section IV (Means of implementation), see A.CONF/151/26 (Vol. III).

* For section II (Conservation and management of resources for development), see A/CONF.151/26 (Vol. II); for section III (Strengthening the role of major groups) and section IV (Means of implementation), see A/CONF.151/26 (Vol. III).

* For section I (Social and economic dimensions), see A/CONF.151/26 (Vol. I); for section II (Conservation and management of resources for development), see A/CONF.151/26 (Vol. II).

# Agenda 21 - Chapter 1
## PREAMBLE

1.1. Humanity stands at a defining moment in history. We are confronted with a perpetuation of disparities between and within nations, a worsening of poverty, hunger, ill health and illiteracy, and the continuing deterioration of the ecosystems on which we depend for our well-being. However, integration of environment and development concerns and greater attention to them will lead to the fulfilment of basic needs, improved living standards for all, better protected and managed ecosystems and a safer, more prosperous future. No nation can achieve this on its own; but together we can - in a global partnership for sustainable development.

1.2. This global partnership must build on the premises of General Assembly resolution 44/228 of 22 December 1989, which was adopted when the nations of the world called for the United Nations Conference on Environment and Development, and on the acceptance of the need to take a balanced and integrated approach to environment and development questions.

1.3. Agenda 21 addresses the pressing problems of today and also aims at preparing the world for the challenges of the next century. It reflects a global consensus and political commitment at the highest level on development and environment cooperation. Its successful implementation is first and foremost the responsibility of Governments. National strategies, plans, policies and processes are crucial in achieving this. International cooperation should support and supplement such national efforts. In this context, the United Nations system has a key role to play. Other international, regional and subregional organizations are also called upon to contribute to this effort. The broadest public participation and the active involvement of the non-governmental organizations and other groups should also be encouraged.

1.4. The developmental and environmental objectives of Agenda 21 will require a substantial flow of new and additional financial resources to developing countries, in order to cover the incremental costs for the actions they have to undertake to deal with global environmental problems and to accelerate sustainable development. Financial resources are also required for strengthening the capacity of international institutions for the implementation of Agenda 21. An indicative order-of-magnitude assessment of costs is included in each of the programme areas. This assessment will need to be examined and refined by the relevant implementing agencies and organizations.

1.5. In the implementation of the relevant programme areas identified in Agenda 21, special attention should be given to the particular circumstances facing the economies in transition. It must also be recognized that these countries are facing unprecedented challenges in transforming their economies, in some cases in the midst of considerable social and political tension.

1.6. The programme areas that constitute Agenda 21 are described in terms of the basis for action, objectives, activities and means of implementation. Agenda 21 is a dynamic programme. It will be carried out by the various actors according to the different situations, capacities and priorities of countries and regions in full respect of all the principles contained in the Rio Declaration on Environment and Development. It could evolve over time in the light of changing needs and circumstances. This process marks the beginning of a new global partnership for sustainable development.

* * * * *

* When the term "Governments" is used, it will be deemed to include the European Economic Community within its areas of competence. Throughout Agenda 21 the term "environmentally sound" means "environmentally safe and sound", in particular when applied to the terms "energy sources", "energy supplies", "energy systems" and "technology" or "technologies".

# Agenda 21 - Chapter 2
## INTERNATIONAL COOPERATION TO ACCELERATE SUSTAINABLE DEVELOPMENT IN DEVELOPING COUNTRIES AND RELATED DOMESTIC POLICIES

2.1. In order to meet the challenges of environment and development, States have decided to establish a new global partnership. This partnership commits all States to engage in a continuous and constructive dialogue, inspired by the need to achieve a more efficient and equitable world economy, keeping in view the increasing interdependence of the community of nations and that sustainable development should become a priority item on the agenda of the international community. It is recognized that, for the success of this new partnership, it is important to overcome confrontation and to foster a climate of genuine cooperation and solidarity. It is equally important to strengthen national and international policies and multinational cooperation to adapt to the new realities.

2.2. Economic policies of individual countries and international economic relations both have great relevance to sustainable development. The reactivation and acceleration of development requires both a dynamic and a supportive international economic environment and determined policies at the national level. It will be frustrated in the absence of either of these requirements. A supportive external economic environment is crucial. The development process will not gather momentum if the global economy lacks dynamism and stability and is beset with uncertainties. Neither will it gather momentum if the developing countries are weighted down by external indebtedness, if development finance is inadequate, if barriers restrict access to markets and if commodity prices and the terms of trade of developing countries remain depressed. The record of the 1980s was essentially negative on each of these counts and needs to be reversed. The policies and measures needed to create an international environment that is strongly supportive of national development efforts are thus vital. International cooperation in this area should be designed to complement and support - not to diminish or subsume - sound domestic economic policies, in both developed and developing countries, if global progress towards sustainable development is to be achieved.

2.3. The international economy should provide a supportive international climate for achieving environment and development goals by:

**PROGRAMME AREAS**

### A. Promoting sustainable development through trade Basis for action

2.5. An open, equitable, secure, non-discriminatory and predictable multilateral trading system that is consistent with the goals of sustainable development and leads to the optimal distribution of global production in accordance with comparative advantage is of benefit to all trading partners. Moreover, improved market access for developing countries' exports in conjunction with sound macroeconomic and environmental policies would have a positive environmental impact and therefore make an important contribution towards sustainable development.

2.6. Experience has shown that sustainable development requires a commitment to sound economic policies and management, an effective and predictable public administration, the integration of environmental concerns into decision-making and progress towards democratic government, in the light of country-specific conditions, which allows for full participation of all parties concerned. These attributes are essential for the fulfilment of the policy directions and objectives listed below.

2.7. The commodity sector dominates the economies of many developing countries in terms of production, employment and export earnings. An important feature of the world commodity economy in the 1980s was the prevalence of very low and declining real prices for most commodities in international markets and a resulting substantial contraction in commodity export earnings for many producing countries. The ability of those countries to mobilize, through international trade, the resources needed to finance investments required for sustainable development may be impaired by this development and by tariff and non-tariff impediments, including tariff escalation, limiting their access to export markets. The removal of existing distortions in international trade is essential. In particular, the achievement of this objective requires that there be substantial and progressive reduction in the support and protection of agriculture - covering internal regimes, market access and export subsidies - as well as of industry and other sectors, in order to avoid inflicting large losses on the more efficient producers, especially in developing countries. Thus, in agriculture, industry and other sectors, there is scope for initiatives aimed at trade liberalization and at policies to make production more responsive to environment and development needs. Trade liberalization should therefore be pursued on a global basis across economic sectors so as to contribute to sustainable develop ment.

2.8. The international trading environment has been affected by a number of developments that have created new challenges and opportunities and have made multilateral economic cooperation of even greater importance. World trade has continued to grow faster than world output in recent years. However, the expansion of world trade has been unevenly spread, and only a limited number of developing countries have been capable of achieving appreciable growth in their exports. Protectionist pressures and unilateral policy actions continue to endanger the functioning of an open multilateral trading system, affecting particularly the export interests of developing countries. Economic integration processes have intensified in recent years and should impart dynamism to global trade and enhance the trade and development possibilities for developing countries. In recent years, a growing number of these countries have adopted courageous policy reforms involving ambitious autonomous trade liberalization, while far-reaching reforms and profound restructuring processes are taking place in Central and Eastern European countries, paving the way for their integration into the world economy and the international trading system. Increased attention is being devoted to enhancing the role of enterprises and promoting competitive markets through adoption of competitive policies. The GSP has proved to be a useful trade policy instrument, although its objectives will have to be fulfilled, and trade facilitation strategies relating to electronic data interchange (EDI) have been effective in improving the trading efficiency of the public and private sectors. The interactions between environment policies and trade issues are manifold and have not yet been fully assessed. An early, balanced, comprehensive and successful outcome of the Uruguay Round of multilateral trade negotiations would bring about further liberalization and expansion of world trade, enhance the trade and development possibilities of developing countries and provide greater security and predictability to the international trading system.

## Objectives

2.9. In the years ahead, and taking into account the results of the Uruguay Round of multilateral trade negotiations, Governments should continue to strive to meet the following objectives:

a. To promote an open, non-discriminatory and equitable multilateral trading system that will enable all countries - in particular, the developing countries - to improve their economic structures and improve the standard of living of their populations through sustained economic development;

b. To improve access to markets for exports of developing countries;

c. To improve the functioning of commodity markets and achieve sound, compatible and consistent commodity policies at national and international levels with a view to optimizing the contribution of the commodity sector to sustainable development, taking into account environmental considerations;

d. To promote and support policies, domestic and international, that make economic growth and environmental protection mutually supportive.

## Activities

(a) International and regional cooperation and coordination Promoting an international trading system that takes account of the needs of developing countries

2.10.    Accordingly, the international community should:

a. Halt and reverse protectionism in order to bring about further liberalization and expansion of world trade, to the benefit of all countries, in particular the developing countries;

b. Provide for an equitable, secure, non-discriminatory and predictable international trading system;

c. Facilitate, in a timely way, the integration of all countries into the world economy and the international trading system;

d. Ensure that environment and trade policies are mutually supportive, with a view to achieving sustainable development;

e. Strengthen the international trade policies system through an early, balanced, comprehensive and successful outcome of the Uruguay Round of multilateral trade negotiations.

2.11. The international community should aim at finding ways and means of achieving a better functioning and enhanced transparency of commodity markets, greater diversification of the commodity sector in developing economies within a macroeconomic framework that takes into consideration a country's economic structure, resource endowments and market opportunities, and better management of natural resources that takes into account the necessities of sustainable development.

2.12. Therefore, all countries should implement previous commitments to halt and reverse protectionism and further expand market access, particularly in areas of interest to developing countries. This improvement of market access will be facilitated by appropriate structural adjustment in developed countries. Developing countries should continue the trade-policy reforms and structural adjustment they have undertaken. It is thus urgent to achieve an improvement in market access conditions for commodities, notably through the progressive removal of barriers that restrict imports, particularly from developing countries, of commodity products in primary and processed forms, as well as the substantial and progressive reduction of types of support that induce uncompetitive production, such as production and export subsidies. (b) Management related activities Developing domestic policies that maximize the benefits of trade liberalization for sustainable development

2.13. For developing countries to benefit from the liberalization of trading systems, they should implement the following policies, as appropriate:

a. Create a domestic environment supportive of an optimal balance between production for the domestic and export markets and remove biases against exports and discourage inefficient import-substitution;

b. Promote the policy framework and the infrastructure required to improve the efficiency of export and import trade as well as the functioning of domestic markets.

2.14. The following policies should be adopted by developing countries with respect to commodities consistent with market efficiency:

a. Expand processing, distribution and imp rove marketing practices and the competitiveness of the commodity sector;

b. Diversify in order to reduce dependence on commodity exports;

c. Reflect efficient and sustainable use of factors of production in the formation of commodity prices, including the reflection of environmental, social and resources costs.

(c) Data and information
Encouraging data collection and research

2.15.    GATT, UNCTAD and other relevant institutions should continue to collect appropriate trade data and information. The Secretary-General of the United Nations is requested to strengthen the Trade Control Measures Information System managed by UNCTAD.
Improving international cooperation in commodity trade and the diversification of the sector

2.16.    With regard to commodity trade, Governments should, directly or through appropriate international organizations, where appropriate:

a.    Seek optimal functioning of commodity markets, inter alia, through improved market transparency involving exchanges of views and information on investment plans, prospects and markets for individual commodities. Substantive negotiations between producers and consumers should be pursued with a view to achieving viable and more efficient international agreements that take into account market trends, or arrangements, as well as study groups. In this regard, particular attention should be paid to the agreements on cocoa, coffee, sugar and tropical timber. The importance of international commodity agreements and arrangements is underlined. Occupational health and safety matters, technology transfer and services associated with the production, marketing and promotion of commodities, as well as environmental considerations, should be taken into account;

b.    Continue to apply compensation mechanisms for shortfalls in commodity export earnings of developing countries in order to encourage diversification efforts;

c.    Provide assistance to developing countries upon request in the design and implementation of commodity policies and the gathering and utilization of information on commodity markets;

d.    Support the efforts of developing countries to promote the policy framework and infrastructure required to improve the efficiency of export and import trade;

e.    Support the diversification initiatives of the developing countries at the national, regional and international levels.

**Means of implementation**

a.    Financing and cost evaluation

2.17.    The Conference secretariat has estimated the average total annual cost (1993-2000) of implementing the activities in this programme area to be about $8.8 billion from the international community on grant or concessional terms. These are indicative and order-of-magnitude estimates only and have not been reviewed by Governments. Actual costs and financial terms, including any that are non-concessional, will depend upon, inter alia, the specific strategies and programmes Governments decide upon for implementation.

b.    Capacity-building 2.18. The above-mentioned technical cooperation activities aim at strengthening national capabilities for design and implementation of commodity policy, use and management of national resources and the gathering and utilization of information on commodity markets.

## B. Making trade and environment mutually supportive Basis for action

2.19. Environment and trade policies should be mutually supportive. An open, multilateral trading system makes possible a more efficient allocation and use of resources and thereby contributes to an increase in production and incomes and to lessening demands on the environment. It thus provides additional resources needed for economic growth and development and improved environmental protection. A sound environment, on the other hand, provides the ecological and other resources needed to sustain growth and underpin a continuing expansion of trade. An open, multilateral trading system, supported by the adoption of sound environmental policies, would have a positive impact on the environment and contribute to sustainable development.

2.20. International cooperation in the environmental field is growing, and in a number of cases trade provisions in multilateral environment agreements have played a role in tackling global environmental challenges. Trade measures have thus been used in certain specific instances, where considered necessary, to enhance the effectiveness of environmental regulations for the protection of the environment. Such regulations should address the root causes of environmental degradation so as not to result in unjustified restrictions on trade. The challenge is to ensure that trade and environment policies are consistent and reinforce the process of sustainable development. However, account should be taken of the fact that environmental standards valid for developed countries may have unwarranted social and economic costs in developing countries.

## Objectives

2.21. Governments should strive to meet the following objectives, through relevant multilateral forums, including GATT, UNCTAD and other international organizations:

    a. To make international trade and environment policies mutually supportive in favour of sustainable development;

    b. To clarify the role of GATT, UNCTAD and other international organizations in dealing with trade and environment -related issues, including, where relevant, conciliation procedure and dispute settlement;

    c. To encourage international productivity and competitiveness and encourage a constructive role on the part of industry in dealing with environment and development issues.

## Activities

Developing an environment/trade and development agenda

2.22. Governments should encourage GATT, UNCTAD and other relevant international and regional economic institutions to examine, in accordance with their respective mandates and competences, the following propositions and principles:

    a. Elaborate adequate studies for the better understanding of the relationship between trade and environment for the promotion of sustainable development;

    b. Promote a dialogue between trade, development and environment communities;

    c. In those cases when trade measures related to environment are used, ensure transparency and compatibility with international obligations;

    d. Deal with the root causes of environment and development problems in a manner that avoids the adoption of environmental measures resulting in unjustified restrictions on trade;

    e. Seek to avoid the use of trade restrictions or distortions as a means to offset differences in cost arising from differences in environmental standards and regulations, since their application could lead to trade distortions and increase protectionist tendencies;

    f. Ensure that environment -related regulations or standards, including those related to health and safety standards, do not constitute a means of arbitrary or unjustifiable discrimination or a disguised restriction on trade;

g.  Ensure that special factors affecting environment and trade policies in t he developing countries are borne in mind in the application of environmental standards, as well as in the use of any trade measures. It is worth noting that standards that are valid in the most advanced countries may be inappropriate and of unwarranted social cost for the developing countries;

h.  Encourage participation of developing countries in multilateral agreements through such mechanisms as special transitional rules;

i.  Avoid unilateral actions to deal with environmental challenges outside the jurisdiction of the importing country. Environmental measures addressing transborder or global environmental problems should, as far as possible, be based on an international consensus. Domestic measures targeted to achieve certain environmental objectives may need trade measures to render them effective. Should trade policy measures be found necessary for the enforcement of environmental policies, certain principles and rules should apply. These could include, inter alia, the principle of non-discrimination; the principle that the trade measure chosen should be the least trade-restrictive necessary to achieve the objectives; an obligation to ensure transparency in the use of trade measures related to the environment and to provide adequate notification of national regulations; and the need to give consideration to the special conditions and developmental requirements of developing countries as they move towards internationally agreed environmental objectives;

j.  Develop more precision, where necessary, and clarify the relationship between GATT provisions and some of the multilateral measures adopted in the environment area;

k.  Ensure public input in the formation, negotiation and implementation of trade policies as a means of fostering increased transparency in the light of country-specific conditions;

l.  Ensure that environmental policies provide the appropriate legal and institutional framework to respond to new needs for the protection of the environment that may result from changes in production and trade specialization.

### C. Providing adequate financial resources to developing countries

**Basis for action**

2.23. Investment is critical to the ability of developing countries to achieve needed economic growth to improve the welfare of their populations and to meet their basic needs in a sustainable manner, all without deteriorating or depleting the resource base that underpins development. Sustainable development requires increased investment, for which domestic and external financial resources are needed. Foreign private investment and the return of flight capital, which depend on a healthy investment climate, are an important source of financial resources. Many developing countries have experienced a decade-long situation of negative net transfer of financial resources, during which their financial receipts were exceeded by payments they had to make, in particular for debt-servicing. As a result, domestically mobilized resources had to be transferred abroad instead of being invested locally in order to promote sustainable economic development.

2.24. For many developing countries, the reactivation of development will not take place without an early and durable solution to the problems of external indebtedness, taking into account the fact that, for many developing countries, external debt burdens are a significant problem. The burden of debt-service payments on those countries has imposed severe constraints on their ability to accelerate growth and eradicate poverty and has led to a contraction in imports, investment and consumption. External indebtedness has emerged as a main factor in the economic stalemate in the developing countries. Continued vigorous implementation of the evolving international debt strategy is aimed at restoring debtor countries' external financial viability, and the resumption of their growth and development would assist in achieving sustainable growth and development. In this context, additional financial resources in favour of developing countries and the efficient utilization of such resources are essential.

**Objectives**

2.25. The specific requirements for the implementation of the sectoral and cross-sectoral programmes included in Agenda 21 are dealt with in the relevant programme areas and in chapter 33 (Financial resources and mechanisms).

**Activities**

(a) Meeting international targets of official development assistance funding

2.26. As discussed in chapter 33, new and additional resources should be provided to support Agenda 21 programmes.

(b) Addressing the debt issue

2.27. In regard to the external debt incurred with commercial banks, the progress being made under the strengthened debt strategy is recognized and a more rapid implementation of this strategy is encouraged. Some countries have already benefited from the combination of sound adjustment policies and commercial bank debt reduction or equivalent measures. The international community encourages:

    a.    Other countries with heavy debts to banks to negotiate similar commercial bank debt reduction with their creditors;

    b.    The parties to such a negotiation to take due account of both the medium-term debt reduction and new money requirements of the debtor country;

    c.    Multilateral institutions actively engaged in the strengthened international debt strategy to continue to support debt-reduction packages related to commercial bank debt with a view to ensuring that the magnitude of such financing is consonant with the evolving debt strategy;

    d.    Creditor banks to participate in debt and debt-service reduction;

    e.    Strengthened policies to attract direct investment, avoid unsustainable levels of debt and foster the return of flight capital.

2.28. With regard to debt owed to official bilateral creditors, the recent measures taken by the Paris Club with regard to more generous terms of relief to the poorest most indebted countries are welcomed. Ongoing efforts to implement these "Trinidad terms" measures in a manner commensurate with the payments capacity of those countries and in a way that gives additional support to their economic reform efforts are welcomed. The substantial bilateral debt reduction undertaken by some creditor countries is also welcomed, and others which are in a position to do so are encouraged to take similar action.

2.29. The actions of low-income countries with substantial debt burdens which continue, at great cost, to service their debt and safeguard their creditworthiness are commended. Particular attention should be paid to their resource needs. Other debt-distressed developing countries which are making great efforts to continue to service their debt and meet their external financial obligations also deserve due attention.

2.30. In connection with multilateral debt, it is urged that serious attention be given to continuing to work towards growth-oriented solutions to the problem of developing countries with serious debt-servicing problems, including those whose debt is mainly to official creditors or to multilateral financial institutions. Particularly in the case of low-income countries in the process of economic reform, the support of the multilateral financial institutions in the form of new disbursements and the use of their concessional funds is welcomed. The use of support groups should be continued in providing resources to clear arrears of countries embarking upon vigorous economic reform programmes supported by IMF and the World Bank. Measures by the multilateral financial institutions such as the refinancing of interest on non-concessional loans with IDA reflows - "fifth dimension" - are noted with appreciation.

**Means of implementation**

Financing and cost evaluation*

## D. Encouraging economic policies conducive to sustainable development

**Basis for action**

2.31. The unfavourable external environment facing developing countries makes domestic resource mobilization and efficient allocation and utilization of domestically mobilized resources all the more important for the promotion of sustainable development. In a number of countries, policies are necessary to correct misdirected public spending, large budget deficits and other macroeconomic imbalances, restrictive policies and distortions in the areas of exchange rates, investment and finance, and obstacles to entrepreneurship. In developed countries, continuing policy reform and adjustment, including appropriate savings rates, would help generate resources to support the transition to sustainable development both domestically and in developing countries.

* * * * *

* See chap. 33 (Financial resources and mechanisms).

* * * * *

2.32. Good management that fosters the association of effective, efficient, honest, equitable and accountable public administration with individual rights and opportunities is an essential element for sustainable, broadly based development and sound economic performance at all development levels. All countries should increase their efforts to eradicate mismanagement of public and private affairs, including corruption, taking into account the factors responsible for, and agents involved in, this phenomenon.

2.33. Many indebted developing countries are undergoing structural adjustment programmes relating to debt rescheduling or new loans. While such programmes are necessary for improving the balance in fiscal budgets and balance-of-payments accounts, in some cases they have resulted in adverse social and environmental effects, such as cuts in allocations for health care, education and environmental protection. It is important to ensure that structural adjustment programmes do not have negative impacts on the environment and social development so that such programmes can be more in line with the objectives of sustainable development.

**Objectives**

2.34. It is necessary to establish, in the light of the country-specific conditions, economic policy reforms that promote the efficient planning and utilization of resources for sustainable development through sound economic and social policies, foster entrepreneurship and the incorporation of social and environmental costs in resource pricing, and remove sources of distortion in the area of trade and investment.

**Activities**

(a) Management-related activities

Promoting sound economic policies

2.35. The industrialized countries and other countries in a position to do so should strengthen their efforts:
   a. To encourage a stable and predictable international economic environment, particularly with regard to monetary stability, real rates of interest and fluctuations in key exchange rates;

b. To stimulate savings and reduce fiscal deficits;

c. To ensure that the processes of policy coordination take into account the interests and concerns of the developing countries, including the need to promote positive action to support the efforts of the least developed countries to halt their marginalization in the world economy;

d. To undertake appropriate national macroeconomic and structural policies aimed at promoting non-inflationary growth, narrowing their major external imbalances and increasing the adjustment capacity of their economies.

2.36. Developing countries should consider strengthening their efforts to implement sound economic policies:

a. That maintain the monetary and fiscal discipline required to promote price stability and external balance;

b. That result in realistic exchange rates;

c. That raise domestic savings and investment, as well as improve returns to investment.

2.37. More specifically, all countries should develop policies that improve efficiency in the allocation of resources and take full advantage of the opportunities offered by the changing global economic environment. In particular, wherever appropriate, and taking into account national strategies and objectives, countries should:

a. Remove the barriers to progress caused by bureaucratic inefficiencies, administrative strains, unnecessary controls and the neglect of market conditions;

b. Promote transparency in administration and decision-making;

c. Encourage the private sector and foster entrepreneurship by improving institutional facilities for enterprise creation and market entry. The essential objective would be to simplify or remove the restrictions, regulations and formalities that make it more complicated, costly and time-consuming to set up and operate enterprises in many developing countries;

d. Promote and support the investment and infrastructure required for sustainable economic growth and diversification on an environmentally sound and sustainable basis;

e. Provide scope for appropriate economic instruments, including market mechanisms, in harmony with the objectives of sustainable development and fulfilment of basic needs;

f. Promote the operation of effective tax systems and financial sectors;

g. Provide opportunities for small-scale enterprises, both farm and non-farm, and for the indigenous population and local communities to contribute fully to the attainment of sustainable development;

h. Remove biases against exports and in favour of inefficient import substitution and establish policies that allow them to benefit fully from the flows of foreign investment, within the framework of national, social, economic and developmental goals;

i. Promote the creation of a domestic economic environment supportive of an optimal balance between production for the domestic and export markets.

(b) International and regional cooperation and coordination

2.38. Governments of developed countries and those of other countries in a position to do so should, directly or through appropriate international and regional organizations and international lending institutions, enhance their efforts to provide developing countries with increased technical assistance for the following:

a. Capacity-building in the nation's design and implementation of economic policies, upon request;

b.   Design and operation of efficient tax systems, accounting systems and financial sectors;

(c) Promotion of entrepreneurship.

2.39. International financial and development institutions should further review their policies and programmes in the light of the objective of sustainable development.

2.40. Stronger economic cooperation among developing countries has long been accepted as an important component of efforts to promote economic growth and technological capabilities and to accelerate development in the developing world. Therefore, the efforts of the developing countries to promote economic cooperation among themselves should be enhanced and continue to be supported by the international community.

**Means of implementation**

(a) Financing and cost evaluation

2.41. The Conference secretariat has estimated the average total annual cost (1993-2000) of implementing the activities in this programme area to be about $50 million from the international community on grant or concessional terms. These are indicative and order-of-magnitude estimates only and have not been reviewed by Governments. Actual costs and financial terms, including any that are non-concessional, will depend upon, inter alia, the specific strategies and programmes Governments decide upon for implementation.

(b) Capacity-building

2.42. The above-mentioned policy changes in developing countries involve substantial national efforts for capacity-building in the areas of public administration, central banking, tax administration, savings institutions and financial markets.

2.43. Particular efforts in the implementation of the four programme areas identified in this chapter are warranted in view of the especially acute environmental and developmental problems of the least developed countries.

# Agenda 21 - Chapter 3
# COMBATING POVERTY

## PROGRAMME AREA
Enabling the poor to achieve sustainable livelihoods

**Basis for action**

3.1. Poverty is a complex multidimensional problem with origins in both the national and international domains. No uniform solution can be found for global application. Rather, country-specific programmes to tackle poverty and international efforts supporting national efforts, as well as the parallel process of creating a supportive international environment, are crucial for a solution to this problem. The eradication of poverty and hunger, greater equity in income distribution and human resource development remain major challenges everywhere. The struggle against poverty is the shared responsibility of all countries.

3.2. While managing resources sustainably, an environmental policy that focuses mainly on the conservation and protection of resources must take due account of those who depend on the resources for their livelihoods. Otherwise it could have an adverse impact both on poverty and on chances for long-term success in resource and environmental conservation. Equally, a development policy that focuses mainly on increasing the production of goods without addressing the sustainability of the resources on which production is based will sooner or later run into declining productivity, which could also have an adverse impact on poverty. A specific anti-poverty strategy is therefore one of the basic conditions for ensuring sustainable development. An effective strategy for tackling the problems of poverty, development and environment simultaneously should begin by focusing on resources, production and people and should cover demographic issues, enhanced health care and education, the rights of women, the role of youth and of indigenous people and local communities and a democratic participation process in association with improved governance.

3.3. Integral to such action is, together with international support, the promotion of economic growth in developing countries that is both sustained and sustainable and direct action in eradicating poverty by strengthening employment and income-generating programmes.

**Objectives**

3.4. The long-term objective of enabling all people to achieve sustainable livelihoods should provide an integrating factor that allows policies to address issues of development, sustainable resource management and poverty eradication simultaneously. The objectives of this programme area are:

    a. To provide all persons urgently with the opportunity to earn a sustainable livelihood;

    b. To implement policies and strategies that promote adequate levels of funding and focus on integrated human development policies, including income generation, increased local control of resources, local institution-strengthening and capacity-building and greater involvement of non-governmental organizations and local levels of government as delivery mechanisms;

    c. To develop for all poverty-stricken areas integrated strategies and programmes of sound and sustainable management of the environment, resource mobilization, poverty eradication and alleviation, employment and income generation;

    d. To create a focus in national development plans and budgets on investment in human capital, with special policies and programmes directed at rural areas, the urban poor, women and children. Activities

3.5. Activities that will contribute to the integrated promotion of sustainable livelihoods and environmental protection cover a variety of sectoral interventions involving a range of actors, from local to global, and are essential at every level, especially the community and local levels. Enabling actions will be necessary at the national and international levels, taking full account of regional and subregional conditions to support a locally driven and country-specific approach. In general design, the programmes should:

a. Focus on the empowerment of local and community groups through the principle of delegating authority, accountability and resources to the most appropriate level to ensure that the programme will be geographically and ecologically specific;

b. Contain immediate measures to enable those groups to alleviate poverty and to develop sustainability;

c. Contain a long-term strategy aimed at establishing the best possible conditions for sustainable local, regional and national development that would eliminate poverty and reduce the inequalities between various population groups. It should assist the most disadvantaged groups - in particular, women, children and youth within those groups - and refugees. The groups will include poor smallholders, pastoralists, artisans, fishing communities, landless people, indigenous communities, migrants and the urban informal sector.

3.6. The focus here is on specific cross-cutting measures - in particular, in the areas of basic education, primary/maternal health care, and the advancement of women.

(a) Empowering communities

3.7. Sustainable development must be achieved at every level of society. Peoples' organizations, women's groups and non-governmental organizations are important sources of innovation and action at the local level and have a strong interest and proven ability to promote sustainable livelihoods. Governments, in cooperation with appropriate international and non-governmental organizations, should support a community-driven approach to sustainability, which would include, inter alia:

a. Empowering women through full participation in decision-making;

b. Respecting the cultural integrity and the rights of indigenous people and their communities;

c. Promoting or establishing grass-roots mechanisms to allow for the sharing of experience and knowledge between communities;

d. Giving communities a large measure of participation in the sustainable management and protection of the local natural resources in order to enhance their productive capacity;

e. Establishing a network of community-based learning centres for capacity-building and sustainable development.

(b) Management-related activities

3.8. Governments, with the assistance of and in cooperation with appropriate international, non-governmental and local community organizations, should establish measures that will directly or indirectly:

a. Generate remunerative employment and productive occupational opportunities compatible with country-specific factor endowments, on a scale sufficient to take care of prospective increases in the labour force and to cover backlogs;

b. With international support, where necessary, develop adequate infrastructure, marketing systems, technology systems, credit systems and the like and the human resources needed to support the above actions and to achieve a widening of options for resource-poor people. High priority should be given to basic education and professional training;

c. Provide substantial increases in economically efficient resource productivity and measures to ensure that the local population benefits in adequate measure from resource use;

d.	Empower community organizations and people to enable them to achieve sustainable livelihoods;

e.	Set up an effective primary health care and maternal health care system accessible to all;

f.	Consider strengthening/developing legal frameworks for land management, access to land resources and land ownership - in particular, for women - and for the protection of tenants;

g.	Rehabilitate degraded resources, to the extent practicable, and introduce policy measures to promote sustainable use of resources for basic human needs;

h.	Establish new community-based mechanisms and strengthen existing mechanisms to enable communities to gain sustained access to resources needed by the poor to overcome their poverty;

i.	Implement mechanisms for popular participation - particularly by poor people, especially women - in local community groups, to promote sustainable development;

j.	Implement, as a matter of urgency, in accordance with country-specific conditions and legal systems, measures to ensure that women and men have the same right to decide freely and responsibly on the number and spacing of their children and have access to the information, education and means, as appropriate, to enable them to exercise this right in keeping with their freedom, dignity and personally held values, taking into account ethical and cultural considerations. Governments should take active steps to implement programmes to establish and strengthen preventive and curative health facilities, which include women-centred, women-managed, safe and effective reproductive health care and affordable, accessible services, as appropriate, for the responsible planning of family size, in keeping with freedom, dignity and personally held values, taking into account ethical and cultural considerations. Programmes should focus on providing comprehensive health care, including pre-natal care, education and information on health and responsible parenthood and should provide the opportunity for all women to breast-feed fully, at least during the first four months post-partum. Programmes should fully support women's productive and reproductive roles and well-being, with special attention to the need for providing equal and improved health care for all children and the need to reduce the risk of maternal and child mortality and sickness;

k.	Adopt integrated policies aiming at sustainability in the management of urban centres;

l.	Undertake activities aimed at the promotion of food security and, where appropriate, food self-sufficiency within the context of sustainable agriculture;

m.	Support research on and integration of traditional methods of production that have been shown to be environmentally sustainable;

n.	Actively seek to recognize and integrate informal-sector activities into the economy by removing regulations and hindrances that discriminate against activities in those sectors;

o.	Consider making available lines of credit and other facilities for the informal sector and improved access to land for the landless poor so that they can acquire the means of production and reliable access to natural resources. In many instances special considerations for women are required. Strict feasibility appraisals are needed for borrowers to avoid debt crises;

p.	Provide the poor with access to fresh water and sanitation;

q.	Provide the poor with access to primary education.

(c) Data, information and evaluation

3.9. Governments should improve the collection of information on target groups and target areas in order to facilitate the design of focused programmes and activities, consistent with the target-group needs and aspirations. Evaluation of such programmes should be gender-specific, since women are a particularly disadvantaged group.

(d) International and regional cooperation and coordination

3.10. The United Nations system, through its relevant organs, organizations and bodies, in cooperation with Member States and with appropriate international and non-governmental organizations, should make poverty alleviation a major priority and should:

    a. Assist Governments, when requested, in the formulation and implementation of national action programmes on poverty alleviation and sustainable development. Action-oriented activities of relevance to the above objectives, such as poverty eradication, projects and programmes supplemented where relevant by food aid, and support and special emphasis on employment and income generation, should be given particular attention in this regard;

    b. Promote technical cooperation among developing countries for poverty eradication activities;

    c. Strengthen existing structures in the United Nations system for coordination of action relating to poverty eradication, including the establishment of a focal point for information exchange and the formulation and implementation of replicable pilot projects to combat poverty;

    d. In the follow-up of the implementation of Agenda 21, give high priority to the review of the progress made in eradicating poverty;

    e. Examine the international economic framework, including resource flows and structural adjustment programmes, to ensure that social and environmental concerns are addressed, and in this connection, conduct a review of the policies of international organizations, bodies and agencies, including financial institutions, to ensure the continued provision of basic services to the poor and needy;

    f. Promote international cooperation to address the root causes of poverty. The development process will not gather momentum if developing countries are weighted down by external indebtedness, if development finance is inadequate, if barriers restrict access to markets and if commodity prices and the terms of trade in developing countries remain depressed.

**Means of implementation**

(a) Financing and cost evaluation

3.11. The secretariat of the Conference has estimated the average total annual cost (1993-2000) of implementing the activities of this programme to be about $30 billion, including about $15 billion from the international community on grant or concessional terms. These are indicative and order-of-magnitude estimates only and have not been reviewed by Governments. This estimate overlaps estimates in other parts of Agenda 21. Actual costs and financial terms, including any that are non-concessional, will depend upon, inter alia, the specific strategies and programmes Governments decide upon for implementation.

(b) Capacity-building

3.12. National capacity-building for implementation of the above activities is crucial and should be given high priority. It is particularly important to focus capacity-building at the local community level in order to support a community-driven approach to sustainability and to establish and strengthen mechanisms to allow sharing of experience and knowledge between community groups at national and international levels. Requirements for such activities are considerable and are related to the various relevant sectors of Agenda 21 calling for requisite international, financial and technological support.

# Agenda 21 - Chapter 4
## CHANGING CONSUMPTION PATTERNS

4.1. This chapter contains the following programme areas:

    a. Focusing on unsustainable patterns of production and consumption;

    b. Developing national policies and strategies to encourage changes in unsustainable consumption patterns.

4.2. Since the issue of changing consumption patterns is very broad, it is addressed in several parts of Agenda 21, notably those dealing with energy, transportation and wastes, and in the chapters on economic instruments and the transfer of technology. The present chapter should also be read in conjunction with chapter 5 (Demographic dynamics and sustainability).

### PROGRAMME AREAS

### A. Focusing on unsustainable patterns of production and consumption

**Basis for action**

4.3. Poverty and environmental degradation are closely interrelated. While poverty results in certain kinds of environmental stress, the major cause of the continued deterioration of the global environment is the unsustainable pattern of consumption and production, particularly in industrialized countries, which is a matter of grave concern, aggravating poverty and imbalances.

4.4. Measures to be undertaken at the international level for the protection and enhancement of the environment must take fully into account the current imbalances in the global patterns of consumption and production.

4.5. Special attention should be paid to the demand for natural resources generated by unsustainable consumption and to the efficient use of those resources consistent with the goal of minimizing depletion and reducing pollution. Although consumption patterns are very high in certain parts of the world, the basic consumer needs of a large section of humanity are not being met. This results in excessive demands and unsustainable lifestyles among the richer segments, which place immense stress on the environment. The poorer segments, meanwhile, are unable to meet food, health care, shelter and educational needs. Changing consumption patterns will require a multipronged strategy focusing on demand, meeting the basic needs of the poor, and reducing wastage and the use of finite resources in the production process.

4.6. Growing recognition of the importance of addressing consumption has also not yet been matched by an understanding of its implications. Some economists are questioning traditional concepts of economic growth and underlining the importance of pursuing economic objectives that take account of the full value of natural resource capital. More needs to be known about the role of consumption in relation to economic growth and population dynamics in order to formulate coherent international and national policies.

**Objectives**

4.7. Action is needed to meet the following broad objectives:

    a.   To promote patterns of consumption and production that reduce environmental stress and will meet the basic needs of humanity;

    b.   To develop a better understanding of the role of consumption and how to bring about more sustainable consumption patterns.

**Activities**

(a) Management-related activities

Adopting an international approach to achieving sustainable consumption patterns

4.8. In principle, countries should be guided by the following basic objectives in their efforts to address consumption and lifestyles in the context of environment and development:

    a.   All countries should strive to promote sustainable consumption patterns;

    b.   Developed countries should take the lead in achieving sustainable consumption patterns;

    c.   Developing countries should seek to achieve sustainable consumption patterns in their development process, guaranteeing the provision of basic needs for the poor, while avoiding those unsustainable patterns, particularly in industrialized countries, generally recognized as unduly hazardous to the environment, inefficient and wasteful, in their development processes. This requires enhanced technological and other assistance from industrialized countries.

4.9. In the follow-up of the implementation of Agenda 21 the review of progress made in achieving sustainable consumption patterns should be given high priority.

(b) Data and information

Undertaking research on consumption

4.10.   In order to support this broad strategy, Governments, and/or private research and policy institutes, with the assistance of regional and international economic and environmental organizations, should make a concerted effort to:

    a.   Expand or promote databases on production and consumption and develop methodologies for analysing them;

    b.   Assess the relationship between production and consumption, environment, technological adaptation and innovation, economic growth and development, and demographic factors;

    c.   Examine the impact of ongoing changes in the structure of modern industrial economies away from material-intensive economic growth;

    d.   Consider how economies can grow and prosper while reducing the use of energy and materials and the production of harmful materials;

    e.   Identify balanced patterns of consumption worldwide which the Earth can support in the long term.

Developing new concepts of sustainable economic growth and prosperity

4.11.   Consideration should also be given to the present concepts of economic growth and the need for new concepts of wealth and prosperity which allow higher standards of living through changed lifestyles and are less dependent on the Earth's finite resources and more in harmony with the Earth's carrying capacity. This should be reflected in the evolution of new systems of national accounts and other indicators of sustainable development.

(c) International cooperation and coordination

4.12.     While international review processes exist for examining economic, development and demographic factors, more attention needs to be paid to issues related to consumption and production patterns and sustainable lifestyles and environment.

4.13.     In the follow-up of the implementation of Agenda 21, reviewing the role and impact of unsustainable production and consumption patterns and lifestyles and their relation to sustainable development should be given high priority.

Financing and cost evaluation

4.14.     The Conference secretariat has estimated that implementation of this programme is not likely to require significant new financial resources.

## B. Developing national policies and strategies to encourage changes in unsustainable consumption patterns

**Basis for action**

4.15.     Achieving the goals of environmental quality and sustainable development will require efficiency in production and changes in consumption patterns in order to emphasize optimization of resource use and minimization of waste. In many instances, this will require reorientation of existing production and consumption patterns that have developed in industrial societies and are in turn emulated in much of the world.

4.16.     Progress can be made by strengthening positive trends and directions that are emerging, as part of a process aimed at achieving significant changes in the consumption patterns of industries, Governments, households and individuals.

**Objectives**

4.17.     In the years ahead, Governments, working with appropriate organizations, should strive to meet the following broad objectives:

> a.   To promote efficiency in production processes and reduce wasteful consumption in the process of economic growth, taking into account the development needs of developing countries;

> b.   To develop a domestic policy framework that will encourage a shift to more sustainable patterns of production and consumption;

> c.   To reinforce both values that encourage sustainable production and consumption patterns and policies that encourage the transfer of environmentally sound technologies to developing countries.

**Activities**

(a) Encouraging greater efficiency in the use of energy and resources

4.18.     Reducing the amount of energy and materials used per unit in the production of goods and services can contribute both to the alleviation of environmental stress and to greater economic and industrial productivity and competitiveness. Governments, in cooperation with industry, should therefore intensify efforts to use energy and resources in an economically efficient and environmentally sound manner by:

    a. Encouraging the dissemination of existing environmentally sound technologies;

    b. Promoting research and development in environmentally sound technologies;

    c. Assisting developing countries to use these technologies efficiently and to develop technologies suited to their particular circumstances;

    d. Encouraging the environmentally sound use of new and renewable sources of energy;

    e. Encouraging the environmentally sound and sustainable use of renewable natural resources.

(b) Minimizing the generation of wastes

4.19.     At the same time, society needs to develop effective ways of dealing with the problem of disposing of mounting levels of waste products and materials. Governments, together with industry, households and the public, should make a concerted effort to reduce the generation of wastes and waste products by:

    a. Encouraging recycling in industrial processes and at the consumed level;

    b. Reducing wasteful packaging of products;

    c. Encouraging the introduction of more environmentally sound products.

(c) Assisting individuals and households to make environmentally sound purchasing decisions

4.20.     The recent emergence in many countries of a more environmentally conscious consumer public, combined with increased interest on the part of some industries in providing environmentally sound consumer products, is a significant development that should be encouraged. Governments and international organizations, together with the private sector, should develop criteria and methodologies for the assessment of environmental impacts and resource requirements throughout the full life cycle of products and processes. Results of those assessments should be transformed into clear indicators in order to inform consumers and decision makers.

4.21.     Governments, in cooperation with industry and other relevant groups, should encourage expansion of environmental labelling and other environmentally related product information programmes designed to assist consumers to make informed choices.

4.22.     They should also encourage the emergence of an informed consumer public and assist individuals and households to make environmentally informed choices by:

    a. Providing information on the consequences of consumption choices and behaviour so as to encourage demand for environmentally sound products and use of products;

    b. Making consumers aware of the health and environmental impact of products, through such means as consumer legislation and environmental labelling;

    c. Encouraging specific consumer-oriented programmes, such as recycling and deposit/refund systems.

(d) Exercising leadership through government purchasing

4.23.     Governments themselves also play a role in consumption, particularly in countries where the public sector plays a large role in the economy and can have a considerable influence on both corporate decisions and public perceptions. They should therefore review the purchasing policies of their agencies and departments so that they may improve, where possible, the environmental content of government procurement policies, without prejudice to international trade principles.

(e) Moving towards environmentally sound pricing

4.24. Without the stimulus of prices and market signals that make clear to producers and consumers the environmental costs of the consumption of energy, materials and natural resources and the generation of wastes, significant changes in consumption and production patterns seem unlikely to occur in the near future.

4.25. Some progress has begun in the use of appropriate economic instruments to influence consumer behaviour. These instruments include environmental charges and taxes, deposit/refund systems, etc. This process should be encouraged in the light of country-specific conditions.

(f) Reinforcing values that support sustainable consumption

4.26. Governments and private-sector organizations should promote more positive attitudes towards sustainable consumption through education, public awareness programmes and other means, such as positive advertising of products and services that utilize environmentally sound technologies or encourage sustainable production and consumption patterns. In the review of the implementation of Agenda 21, an assessment of the progress achieved in developing these national policies and strategies should be given due consideration.

**Means of implementation**

4.27. This programme is concerned primarily with changes in unsustainable patterns of consumption and production and values that encourage sustainable consumption patterns and lifestyles. It requires the combined efforts of Governments, consumers and producers. Particular attention should be paid to the significant role played by women and households as consumers and the potential impacts of their combined purchasing power on the economy.

# DEMOGRAPHIC DYNAMICS AND SUSTAINABILITY

5.1. This chapter contains the following programme areas:

    a. Developing and disseminating knowledge concerning the links between demographic trends and factors and sustainable development;

    b. Formulating integrated national policies for environment and development, taking into account demographic trends and factors;

    c. Implementing integrated, environment and development programmes at the local level, taking into account demographic trends and factors.

## PROGRAMME AREAS

### A. Developing and disseminating knowledge concerning the links between demographic trends and factors and sustainable development

**Basis for action**

5.2. Demographic trends and factors and sustainable development have a synergistic relationship.

5.3. The growth of world population and production combined with unsustainable consumption patterns places increasingly severe stress on the life-supporting capacities of our planet. These interactive processes affect the use of land, water, air, energy and other resources. Rapidly growing cities, unless well-managed, face major environmental problems. The increase in both the number and size of cities calls for greater attention to issues of local government and municipal management. The human dimensions are key elements to consider in this intricate set of relationships and they should be adequately taken into consideration in comprehensive policies for sustainable development. Such policies should address the linkages of demographic trends and factors, resource use, appropriate technology dissemination, and development. Population policy should also recognize the role played by human beings in environmental and development concerns. There is a need to increase awareness of this issue among decision makers at all levels and to provide both better information on which to base national and international policies and a framework against which to interpret this information.

5.4. There is a need to develop strategies to mitigate both the adverse impact on the environment of human activities and the adverse impact of environmental change on human populations. The world's population is expected to exceed 8 billion by the year 2020. Sixty per cent of the world's population already live in coastal areas, while 65 per cent of cities with populations above 2.5 million are located along the world coasts; several of them are already at or below the present sea level.

**Objectives**

5.5. The following objectives should be achieved as soon as practicable:

    a. To incorporate demographic trends and factors in the global analysis of environment and development issues;

    b. To develop a better understanding of the relationships among demographic dynamics, technology, cultural behaviour, natural resources and life support systems;

    c. To assess human vulnerability in ecologically sensitive areas and centres of population to determine the priorities for action at all levels, taking full account of community defined needs.

**Activities**

    Research on the interaction between demographic trends and factors and sustainable development

5.6. Relevant international, regional and national institutions should consider undertaking the following activities:

    a. Identifying the interactions between demographic processes, natural resources and life support systems, bearing in mind regional and subregional variations deriving from, inter alia, different levels of development;

    b. Integrating demographic trends and factors into the ongoing study of environmental change, using the expertise of international, regional and national research networks and of local communities, first, to study the human dimensions of environmental change and, second, to identify vulnerable areas;

    c. Identifying priority areas for action and developing strategies and programmes to mitigate the adverse impact of environmental change on human populations, and vice versa.

**Means of implementation**

(a) Financing and cost evaluation

5.7. The Conference secretariat has estimated the average total annual cost (1993-2000) of implementing the activities of this programme to be about $10 million from the international community on grant or concessional terms. These are indicative and order-of-magnitude estimates only and have not been reviewed by Governments. Actual costs and financial terms, including any that are non-concessional, will depend upon, inter alia, the specific strategies and programmes Governments decide upon for implementation.

(b) Strengthening research programmes that integrate population, environment and development

5.8. In order to integrate demographic analysis into a broader social science perspective on environment and development, interdisciplinary research should be increased. International institutions and networks of experts should enhance their scientific capacity, taking full account of community experience and knowledge, and should disseminate the experience gained in multidisciplinary approaches and in linking theory to action.

5.9. Better modelling capabilities should be developed, identifying the range of possible outcomes of current human activities, especially the interrelated impact of demographic trends and factors, per capita resource use and wealth distribution, as well as the major migration flows that may be expected with increasing climatic events and cumulative environmental change that may destroy people's local livelihoods.

(c) Developing information and public awareness

5.10. Socio-demographic information should be developed in a suitable format for interfacing with physical, biological and socio-economic data. Compatible spatial and temporal scales, cross-country and time-series information, as well as global behavioural indicators should be developed, learning from local communities' perceptions and attitudes.

5.11. Awareness should be increased at all levels concerning the need to optimize the sustainable use of resources through efficient resource management, taking into account the development needs of the populations of developing countries.

5.12. Awareness should be increased of the fundamental linkages between improving the status of women and demographic dynamics, particularly through women's access to education, primary and reproductive health care programmes, economic independence and their effective, equitable participation in all levels of decision-making.

5.13.    Results of research concerned with sustainable development issues should be disseminated through technical reports, scientific journals, the media, workshops, forums or other means so that the information can be used by decision makers at all levels and increase public awareness.

(d) Developing and/or enhancing institutional capacity and collaboration

5.14.    Collaboration and exchange of information should be increased between research institutions and international, regional and national agencies and all other sectors (including the private sector, local communities, non-governmental organizations and scientific institutions) from both the industrialized and developing countries, as appropriate.

5.15.    Efforts should be intensified to enhance the capacities of national and local governments, the private sector and non-governmental organizations in developing countries to meet the growing needs for improved management of rapidly growing urban areas.

## B. Formulating integrated national policies for environment and development, taking into account demographic trends and factors

**Basis for action**

5.16.    Existing plans for sustainable development have generally recognized demographic trends and factors as elements that have a critical influence on consumption patterns, production, lifestyles and long-term sustainability. But in future, more attention will have to be given to these issues in general policy formulation and the design of development plans. To do this, all countries will have to improve their own capacities to assess the environment and development implications of their demographic trends and factors. They will also need to formulate and implement policies and action programmes where appropriate. Policies should be designed to address the consequences of population growth built into population momentum, while at the same time incorporating measures to bring about demographic transition. They should combine environmental concerns and population issues within a holistic view of development whose primary goals include the alleviation of poverty; secure livelihoods; good health; quality of life; improvement of the status and income of women and their access to schooling and professional training, as well as fulfilment of their personal aspirations; and empowerment of individuals and communities. Recognizing that large increases in the size and number of cities will occur in developing countries under any likely population scenario, greater attention should be given to preparing for the needs, in particular of women and children, for improved municipal management and local government.

**Objective**

5.17.    Full integration of population concerns into national planning, policy and decision-making processes should continue. Population policies and programmes should be considered, with full recognition of women's rights.

**Activities**

5.18.    Governments and other relevant actors could, inter alia, undertake the following activities, with appropriate assistance from aid agencies, and report on their status of implementation to the International Conference on Population and Development to be held in 1994, especially to its committee on population and environment.

(a) Assessing the implications of national demographic trends and factors

5.19.    The relationships between demographic trends and factors and environmental change and between environmental degradation and the components of demographic change should be analysed.

5.20.    Research should be conducted on how environmental factors interact with socio-economic factors as a cause of migration.

5.21.    Vulnerable population groups (such as rural landless workers, ethnic minorities, refugees, migrants, displaced people, women heads of household) whose changes in demographic structure may have specific impacts on sustainable development should be identified.

5.22.　　An assessment should be made of the implications of the age structure of the population on resource demand and dependency burdens, ranging from educational expenses for the young to health care and support for the elderly, and on household income generation.

5.23.　　An assessment should also be made of national population carrying capacity in the context of satisfaction of human needs and sustainable development, and special attention should be given to critical resources, such as water and land, and environmental factors, such as ecosystem health and biodiversity.

5.24.　　The impact of national demographic trends and factors on the traditional livelihoods of indigenous groups and local communities, including changes in traditional land use because of internal population pressures, should be studied.

(b) Building and strengthening a national information base

5.25.　　National databases on demographic trends and factors and environment should be built and/or strengthened, disaggregating data by ecological region (ecosystem approach), and population/environment profiles should be established by region.

5.26.　　Methodologies and instruments should be developed to identify areas where sustainability is, or may be, threatened by the environmental effects of demographic trends and factors, incorporating both current and projected demographic data linked to natural environmental processes.

5.27.　　Case-studies of local level responses by different groups to demographic dynamics should be developed, particularly in areas subject to environmental stress and in deteriorating urban centres.

5.28.　　Population data should be disaggregated by, inter alia, sex and age in order to take into account the implications of the gender division of labour for the use and management of natural resources.

(c) Incorporating demographic features into policies and plans

5.29.　　In formulating human settlements policies, account should be taken of resource needs, waste production and ecosystem health.

5.30.　　5.30. The direct and induced effects of demographic changes on environment and development programmes should, where appropriate, be integrated, and the impact on demographic features assessed.

5.31.　　5.31. National population policy goals and programmes that are consistent with national environment and development plans for sustainability and in keeping with the freedom, dignity and personally held values of individuals should be established and implemented.

5.32.　　5.32. Appropriate socio-economic policies for the young and the elderly, both in terms of family and state support systems, should be developed.

5.33.　　5.33. Policies and programmes should be developed for handling the various types of migrations that result from or induce environmental disruptions, with special attention to women and vulnerable groups.

5.34.　　5.34. Demographic concerns, including concerns for environmental migrants and displaced people, should be incorporated in the programmes for sustainable development of relevant international and regional institutions.

5.35.     5.35. National reviews should be conducted and the integration of population policies in national development and environment strategies should be monitored nationally.

**Means of implementation**

(a) Financing and cost evaluation

5.36.     The Conference secretariat has estimated the average total annual cost (1993-2000) of implementing the activities of this programme to be about $90 million from the international community on grant or concessional terms. These are indicative and order-of-magnitude estimates only and have not been reviewed by Governments. Actual costs and financial terms, including any that are non-concessional, will depend upon, inter alia, the specific strategies and programmes Governments decide upon for implementation.

(b) Raising awareness of demographic and sustainable develop ment interactions

5.37.     Understanding of the interactions between demographic trends and factors and sustainable development should be increased in all sectors of society. Stress should be placed on local and national action. Demographic and sustainable development education should be coordinated and integrated in both the formal and non-formal education sectors. Particular attention should be given to population literacy programmes, notably for women. Special emphasis should be placed on the linkage between these programmes, primary environmental care and the provision of primary health care and services.

(c) Strengthening institutions

5.38.     The capacity of national, regional and local structures to deal with issues relating to demographic trends and factors and sustainable development should be enhanced. This would involve strengthening the relevant bodies responsible for population issues to enable them to elaborate policies consistent with the national prospects for sustainable development. Cooperation among government, national research institutions, non-governmental organizations and local communities in assessing problems and evaluating policies should also be enhanced.

5.39.     The capacity of the relevant United Nations organs, organizations and bodies, international and regional intergovernmental bodies, non-governmental organizations and local communities should, as appropriate, be enhanced to help countries develop sustainable development policies on request and, as appropriate, provide assistance to environmental migrants and displaced people.

5.40.     Inter-agency support for national sustainable development policies and programmes should be improved through better coordination of population and environment activities.

(d) Promoting human resource development

5.41.     The international and regional scientific institutions should assist Governments, upon request, to include concerns regarding the population/environment interactions at the global, ecosystem and micro-levels in the training of demographers and population and environment specialists. Training should include research on linkages and ways to design integrated strategies.

**C. Implementing integrated environment and development programmes at the local level, taking into account demographic trends and factors**

**Basis for action**

5.42.     Population programmes are more effective when implemented together with appropriate cross-sectoral policies. To attain sustainability at the local level, a new framework is needed that integrates demographic trends and factors with such factors as ecosystem health, technology and human settlements, and with socio-economic structures and access to resources. Population programmes should be consistent with socio-economic and environmental planning. Integrated sustainable development programmes should closely correlate action on demographic trends and factors with resource management activities and development goals that meet the needs of the people concerned.

**Objective**

5.43.    Population programmes should be implemented along with natural resource management and development programmes at the local level that will ensure sustainable use of natural resources, improve the quality of life of the people and enhance environmental quality.

**Activities**

5.44.    Governments and local communities, including community-based women's organizations and national non-governmental organizations, consistent with national plans, objectives, strategies and priorities, could, inter alia, undertake the activities set out below with the assistance and cooperation of international organizations, as appropriate. Governments could share their experience in the implementation of Agenda 21 at the International Conference on Population and Development, to be held in 1994, especially its committee on population and environment.

(a) Developing a framework for action

5.45.    An effective consultative process should be established and implemented with concerned groups of society where the formulation and decision-making of all components of the programmes are based on a nationwide consultative process drawing on community meetings, regional workshops and national seminars, as appropriate. This process should ensure that views of women and men on needs, perspective and constraints are equally well reflected in the design of programmes, and that solutions are rooted in specific experience. The poor and underprivileged should be priority groups in this process.

5.46.    Nationally determined policies for integrated and multifaceted programmes, with special attention to women, to the poorest people living in critical areas and to other vulnerable groups should be implemented, ensuring the involvement of groups with a special potential to act as agents for change and sustainable development. Special emphasis should be placed on those programmes that achieve multiple objectives, encouraging sustainable economic development, and mitigating adverse impacts of demographic trends and factors, and avoiding long-term environmental damage. Food security, access to secure tenure, basic shelter, and essential infrastructure, education, family welfare, women's reproductive health, family credit schemes, reforestation programmes, primary environmental care, women's employment should, as appropriate, be included among other factors.

5.47.    An analytical framework should be develop ed to identify complementary elements of sustainable development policies as well as the national mechanisms to monitor and evaluate their effects on population dynamics.

5.48.    Special attention should be given to the critical role of women in population/environment programmes and in achieving sustainable development. Projects should take advantage of opportunities to link social, economic and environmental gains for women and their families. Empowerment of women is essential and should be assured through education, training and policies to accord and improve women's right and access to assets, human and civil rights, labour-saving measures, job opportunities and participation in decision-making. Population/environment programmes must enable women to mobilize themselves to alleviate their burden and improve their capacity to participate in and benefit from socio-economic development. Specific measures should be undertaken to close the gap between female and male illiteracy rates.

(b) Supporting programmes that promote changes in demographic trends and factors towards sustainability

5.49.    Reproductive health programmes and services, should, as appropriate, be developed and enhanced to reduce maternal and infant mortality from all causes and enable women and men to fulfil their personal aspirations in terms of family size, in a way in keeping with their freedom and dignity and personally held values.

5.50. Governments should take active steps to implement, as a matter of urgency, in accordance with country-specific conditions and legal systems, measures to ensure that women and men have the same right to decide freely and responsibly on the number and spacing of their children, to have access to the information, education and means, as appropriate, to enable them to exercis e this right in keeping with their freedom, dignity and personally held values taking into account ethical and cultural considerations.

5.51. Governments should take active steps to implement programmes to establish and strengthen preventive and curative health facilities that include women-centred, women-managed, safe and effective reproductive health care and affordable, accessible services, as appropriate, for the responsible planning of family size, in keeping with freedom, dignity and personally held values and taking into account ethical and cultural considerations. Programmes should focus on providing comprehensive health care, including pre-natal care, education and information on health and responsible parenthood and should provide the opportunity for all women to breast-feed fully, at least during the first four months post-partum. Programmes should fully support women's productive and reproductive roles and well being, with special attention to the need for providing equal and improved health care for all children and the need to reduce the risk of maternal and child mortality and sickness.

5.52. Consistent with national priorities, culturally based information and education programmes that transmit reproductive health messages to men and women that are easily understood should be developed.

(c) Creating appropriate institutional conditions

5.53. Constituencies and institutional conditions to facilitate the implementation of demographic activities should, as appropriate, be fostered. This requires support and commitment from political, indigenous, religious and traditional authorities, the private sector and the national scientific community. In developing these appropriate institutional conditions, countries should closely involve established national machinery for women.

5.54. Population assistance should be coordinated with bilateral and multilateral donors to ensure that population needs and requirements of all developing countries are addressed, fully respecting the overall coordinating responsibility and the choice and strategies of the recipient countries.

5.55. Coordination should be improved at local and international levels. Working practices should be enhanced in order to make optimum use of resources, draw on collective experience and improve the implementation of programmes. UNFPA and other relevant agencies should strengthen the coordination of international cooperation activities with recipient and donor countries in order to ensure that adequate funding is available to respond to growing needs.

5.56. Proposals should be developed for local, national and international population/environment programmes in line with specific needs for achieving sustainability. Where appropriate, institutional changes must be implemented so that old-age security does not entirely depend on input from family members.

**Means of implementation**

(a) Financing and cost evaluation

5.57. The Conference secretariat has estimated the average total annual cost (1993-2000) of implementing the activities of this programme to be about $7 billion, including about $3.5 billion from the international community on grant or concessional terms. These are indicative and order-of-magnitude estimates only and have not been reviewed by Governments. Actual costs and financial

terms, including any that are non-concessional, will depend upon, inter alia, the specific strategies and programmes Governments decide upon for implementation.

(b) Research

5.58.    Research should be undertaken with a view to developing specific action programmes; it will be necessary to establish priorities between proposed areas of research.

5.59.    Socio-demographic research should be conducted on how populations respond to a changing environment.

5.60.    Understanding of socio-cultural and political factors that can positively influence acceptance of appropriate population policy instruments should be improved.

5.61.    Surveys of changes in needs for appropriate services relating to responsible planning of family size, reflecting variations among different socio-economic groups and variations in different geographical regions should be undertaken.

(c) Human resource development and capacity-building

5.62.    The areas of human resource development and capacity-building, with particular attention to the education and training of women, are areas of critical importance and are a very high priority in the implementation of population programmes.

5.63.    Workshops to help programme and projects managers to link population programmes to other development and environmental goals should be conducted.

5.64.     Educational materials, including guides/workbooks for planners and decision makers and other actors of population/environment/development programmes, should be developed.

5.65.    Cooperation should be developed between Governments, scientific institutions and non-governmental organizations within the region, and similar institutions outside the region. Cooperation with local organizations should be fostered in ordered to raise awareness, engage in demonstration projects and report on the experience gained.

5.66.    The recommendations contained in this chapter should in no way prejudice discussions at the International Conference on Population and Development in 1994, which will be the appropriate forum for dealing with population and development issues, taking into account the recommendations of the International Conference on Population, held in Mexico City in 1984, 1/ and the Forward-looking Strategies for the Advancement of Women, 2/ adopted by the World Conference to Review and Appraise the Achievements of the United Decade for Women: Equality, Development and Peace, held in Nairobi in 1985.

**Notes**

1/ Report of the International Conference on Population, Mexico City, 6-14 August 1984 (United Nations publication, Sales No. E.84.XIII.8), chap. I.

2/ Report of the World Conference to Review and Appraise the Achievements of the United Nations Decade for Women: Equality, Development and Peace, Nairobi, 15-26 July 1985 (United Nations publication, Sales No. E.84.IV.10), chap. I, sect. A.

# Agenda 21 – Chapter 6
## PROTECTING AND PROMOTING HUMAN HEALTH

6.1.  Health and development are intimately interconnected. Both insufficient development leading to poverty and inappropriate development resulting in overconsumption, coupled with an expanding world population, can result in severe environmental health p roblems in both developing and developed nations. Action items under Agenda 21 must address the primary health needs of the world's population, since they are integral to the achievement of the goals of sustainable development and primary environmental care. The linkage of health, environmental and socio-economic improvements requires intersectoral efforts. Such efforts, involving education, housing, public works and community groups, including businesses, schools and universities and religious, civic and cultural organizations, are aimed at enabling people in their communities to ensure sustainable development. Particularly relevant is the inclusion of prevention programmes rather than relying solely on remediation and treatment. Countries ought to develop plans for priority actions, drawing on the programme areas in this chapter, which are based on cooperative planning by the various levels of government, non-governmental organizations and local communities. An appropriate international organization, such as WHO, should coordinate these activities.

6.2.  The following programme areas are contained in this chapter:

    a.  Meeting primary health care needs, particularly in rural areas;

    b.  Control of communicable diseases;

    c.  Protecting vulnerable groups;

    d.  Meeting the urban health challenge;

    e.  Reducing health risks from environmental pollution and hazards.

### PROGRAMME AREAS

A. Meeting primary health care needs, particularly in rural areas Basis for action

6.3.  Health ultimately depends on the ability to manage successfully the interaction between the physical, spiritual, biological and economic/social environment. Sound development is not possible without a healthy population; yet most developmental activities affect the environment to some degree, which in turn causes or exacerbates many health problems. Conversely, it is the very lack of development that adversely affects the health condition of many people, which can be alleviated only through development. The health sector cannot meet basic needs and objectives on its own; it is dependent on social, economic and spiritual development, while directly contributing to such development. It is also dependent on a healthy environment, including the provision of a safe water supply and sanitation and the promotion of a safe food supply and proper nutrition. Particular attention should be directed towards food safety, with priority placed on the elimination of food contamination; comprehensive and sustainable water policies to ensure safe drinking water and sanitation to preclude both microbial and chemical contamination; and promotion of health education, immunization and provision of essential drugs. Education and appropriate services regarding responsible planning of family size, with respect for cultural, religious and social aspects, in keeping with freedom, dignity and personally held values and taking into account ethical and cultural considerations, also contribute to these intersectoral activities.

**Objectives**

6.4.  Within the overall strategy to achieve health for all by the year 2000, the objectives are to meet the basic health needs of rural peri-urban and urban populations; to provide the necessary specialized environmental health services; and to coordinate the involvement of citizens, the health sector, the health-related sectors and relevant non-health sectors (business, social, educational and religious institutions) in solutions to health problems. As a matter of priority, health service coverage should be achieved for population groups in greatest need, particularly those living in rural areas.

**Activities**

6.5. National Governments and local authorities, with the support of relevant non-governmental organizations and international organizations, in the light of countries' specific conditions and needs, should strengthen their health sector programmes, with special attention to rural needs, to:

(a) Build basic health infrastructures, monitoring and planning systems:

    i.    Develop and strengthen primary health care systems that are practical, community-based, scientifically sound, socially acceptable and appropriate to their needs and that meet basic health needs for clean water, safe food and sanitation;

    ii.    Support the use and strengthening of mechanisms that improve coordination between health and related sectors at all appropriate levels of government, and in communities and relevant organizations;

    iii.    Develop and implement rational and affordable approaches to the establishment and maintenance of health facilities;

    iv.    Ensure and, where appropriate, increase provision of social services support;

    v.    Develop strategies, including reliable health indicators, to monitor the progress and evaluate the effectiveness of health programmes;

    vi.    Explore ways to finance the health system based on the assessment of the resources needed and identify the various financing alternatives;

    vii.    Promote health education in schools, information exchange, technical support and training;

    viii.    Support initiatives for self-management of services by vulnerable groups;

    ix.    Integrate traditional knowledge and experience into national health systems, as appropriate;

    x.    Promote the provisions for necessary logistics for outreach activities, particularly in rural areas;

    xi.    Promote and strengthen community-based rehabilitation activities for the rural handicapped.

(b) Support research and methodology development:

    i.    Establish mechanisms for sustained community involvement in environmental health activities, including optimization of the appropriate use of community financial and human resources;

    ii.    Conduct environmental health research, including behaviour research and research on ways to increase coverage and ensure greater utilization of services by peripheral, underserved and vulnerable populations, as appropriate to good prevention services and health care;

    iii.    Conduct research into traditional knowledge of prevention and curative health practices.

**Means of implementation**

(a) Financing and cost evaluation

6.6. The Conference secretariat has estimated the average total annual cost (1993-2000) of implementing the activities of this programme to be about $40 billion, including about $5 billion from the international community on grant or concessional terms. These are indicative and order-of-magnitude estimates only and have not been reviewed by Governments. Actual costs and financial terms, including any that are non-concessional, will depend upon, inter alia, the specific strategies and programmes Governments decide upon for implementation.

### (b) Scientific and technological means

6.7. New approaches to planning and managing health care systems and facilities should be tested, and research on ways of integrating appropriate technologies into health infrastructures supported. The development of scientifically sound health technology should enhance adaptability to local needs and maintainability by community resources, including the maintenance and repair of equipment used in health care. Programmes to facilitate the transfer and sharing of information and expertise should be developed, including communication methods and educational materials.

### (c) Human resource development

6.8. Intersectoral approaches to the reform of health personnel development should be strengthened to ensure its relevance to the "Health for All" strategies. Efforts to enhance managerial skills at the district level should be supported, with the aim of ensuring the systematic development and efficient operation of the basic health system. Intensive, short, practical training programmes with emphasis on skills in effective communication, community organization and facilitation of behaviour change should be developed in order to prepare the local personnel of all sectors involved in social development for carrying out their respective roles. In cooperation with the education sector, special health education programmes should be developed focusing on the role of women in the health-care system.

### (d) Capacity-building

6.9. Governments should consider adopting enabling and facilitating strategies to promote the participation of communities in meeting their own needs, in addition to providing direct support to the provision of health-care services. A major focus should be the preparation of community-based health and health-related workers to assume an active role in community health education, with emphasis on team work, social mobilization and the support of other development workers. National programmes should cover district health systems in urban, peri-urban and rural areas, the delivery of health programmes at the district level, and the development and support of referral services.

## B. Control of communicable diseases

**Basis for action**

6.10. Advances in the development of vaccines and chemotherapeutic agents have brought many communicable diseases under control. However, there remain many important communicable diseases for which environmental control measures are indispensable, especially in the field of water supply and sanitation. Such diseases include cholera, diarrhoeal diseases, leishmaniasis, malaria and schistosomiasis. In all such instances, the environmental measures, either as an integral part of primary health care or undertaken outside the health sector, form an indispensable component of overall disease control strategies, together with health and hygiene education, and in some cases, are the only component.

6.11. With HIV infection levels estimated to increase to 30-40 million by the year 2000, the socio-economic impact of the pandemic is expected to be devastating for all countries, and increasingly for women and children. While direct health costs will be substantial, they will be dwarfed by the indirect costs of the pandemic - mainly costs associated with the loss of income and decreased productivity of the workforce. The pandemic will inhibit growth of the service and industrial sectors and significantly increase the costs of human capacity-building and retraining. The agricultural sector is particularly affected where production is labour-intensive.

**Objectives**

6.12.    A number of goals have been formulated through extensive consultations in various international forums attended by virtually all Governments, relevant United Nations organizations (including WHO, UNICEF, UNFPA, UNESCO, UNDP and the World Bank) and a number of non-governmental organizations. Goals (including but not limited to those listed below) are recommended for implementation by all countries where they are applicable, with appropriate adaptation to the specific situation of each country in terms of phasing, standards, priorities and availability of resources, with respect for cultural, religious and social aspects, in keeping with freedom, dignity and personally held values and taking into account ethical considerations. Additional goals that are particularly relevant to a country's specific situation should be added in the country's national plan of action (Plan of Action for Implementing the World Declaration on the Survival, Protection and Development of Children in the 1990s). 1/ Such national level action plans should be coordinated and monitored from within the public health sector. Some major goals are:

   a.   By the year 2000, to eliminate guinea worm disease (dracunculiasis);

   b.   By the year 2000, eradicate polio;

   c.   By the year 2000, to effectively control onchocerciasis (river blindness) and leprosy;

   d.   By 1995, to reduce measles deaths by 95 per cent and reduce measles cases by 90 per cent compared with pre-immunization levels;

   e.   By continued efforts, to provide health and hygiene education and to ensure universal access to safe drinking water and universal access to sanitary measures of excreta disposal, thereby markedly reducing waterborne diseases such as cholera and schistosomiasis and reducing:

        i.    By the year 2000, the number of deaths from childhood diarrhoea in developing countries by 50 to 70 per cent;

        ii.   By the year 2000, the incidence of childhood diarrhoea in developing countries by at least 25 to 50 per cent;

   f.   By the year 2000, to initiate comprehensive programmes to reduce mortality from acute respiratory infections in children under five years by at least one third, particularly in countries with high infant mortality;

   g.   By the year 2000, to provide 95 per cent of the world's child population with access to appropriate care for acute respiratory infections within the community and at first referral level;

   h.   By the year 2000, to institute anti-malaria programmes in all countries where malaria presents a significant health problem and maintain the transmission-free status of areas freed from endemic malaria;

   i.   By the year 2000, to implement control programmes in countries where major human parasitic infections are endemic and  achieve an overall reduction in the prevalence of schistosomiasis and of other trematode infections by 40 per cent and 25 per cent, respectively, from a 1984 baseline, as well as a marked reduction in incidence, prevalence and intensity of filarial infections;

j. To mobilize and unify national and international efforts against AIDS to prevent infection and to reduce the personal and social impact of HIV infection;

k. To contain the resurgence of tuberculosis, with particular emphasis on multiple antibiotic resistant forms;

l. To accelerate research on improved vaccines and implement to the fullest extent possible the use of vaccines in the prevention of disease.

**Activities**

6.13.  Each national Government, in accordance with national plans for public health, priorities and objectives, should consider developing a national health action plan with appropriate international assistance and support, including, at a minimum, the following components:

a. National public health systems:

  i. Programmes to identify environmental hazards in the causation of communicable diseases;

  ii. Monitoring systems of epidemiological data to ensure adequate forecasting of the introduction, spread or aggravation of communicable diseases;

  iii. Intervention programmes, including measures consistent with the principles of the global AIDS strategy;

  iv. Vaccines for the prevention of communicable diseases;

b. Public information and health education: Provide education and disseminate information on the risks of endemic communicable diseases and build awareness on environmental methods for control of communicable diseases to enable communities to play a role in the control of communicable diseases;

c. Intersectoral cooperation and coordination:

  i. Second experienced health professionals to relevant sectors, such as planning, housing and agriculture;

  ii. Develop guidelines for effective coordination in the areas of professional training, assessment of risks and development of control technology;

d. Control of environmental factors that influence the spread of communicable diseases: Apply methods for the prevention and control of communicable diseases, including water supply and sanitation control, water pollution control, food quality control, integrated vector control, garbage collection and disposal and environmentally sound irrigation practices;

e. Primary health care system:

  i. Strengthen prevention programmes, with particular emphasis on adequate and balanced nutrition;

  ii. Strengthen early diagnostic programmes and improve capacities for early preventative/treatment action;

  iii. Reduce the vulnerability to HIV infection of women and their offspring;

f. Support for research and methodology development:

   i.  Intensify and expand multidisciplinary research, including focused efforts on the mitigation and environmental control of tropical diseases;

   ii.  Carry out intervention studies to provide a solid epidemiological basis for control policies and to evaluate the efficiency of alternative approaches;

   iii.  Undertake studies in the population and among health workers to determine the influence of cultural, behavioural and social factors on control policies;

  g. Development and dissemination of technology:

   i.  Develop new technologies for the effective control of communicable diseases;

   ii.  Promote studies to determine how to optimally disseminate results from research;

   iii.  Ensure technical assistance, including the sharing of knowledge and know-how.

## Means of implementation

(a) Financing and cost evaluation

6.14.  The Conference secretariat has estimated the average total annual cost (1993-2000) of implementing the activities of this programme to be about \$4 billion, including about \$900 million from the international community on grant or concessional terms. These are indicative and order-of-magnitude estimates only and have not been reviewed by Governments. Actual costs and financial terms, including any that are non-concessional, will depend upon, inter alia, the specific strategies and programmes Governments decide upon for implementation.

(b) Scientific and technological means

6.15.  Efforts to prevent and control diseases should include investigations of the epidemiological, social and economic bases for the development of more effective national strategies for the integrated control of communicable diseases. Cost-effective methods of environmental control should be adapted to local developmental conditions.

(c) Human resource development

6.16.  National and regional training institutions should promote broad intersectoral approaches to prevention and control of communicable diseases, including training in epidemiology and community prevention and control, immunology, molecular biology and the application of new vaccines. Health education materials should be developed for use by community workers and for the education of mothers for the prevention and treatment of diarrhoeal diseases in the home.

(d) Capacity-building

6.17.  The health sector should develop adequate data on the distribution of communicable diseases, as well as the institutional capacity to respond and collaborate with other sectors for prevention, mitigation and correction of communicable disease hazards through environmental protection. The advocacy at policy- and decision-making levels should be gained, professional and societal support mobilized, and communities organized in developing self-reliance.

## C. Protecting vulnerable groups

## Basis for action

6.18.  In addition to meeting basic health needs, specific emphasis has to be given to protecting and educating vulnerable groups, particularly infants, youth, women, indigenous people and the very poor as a prerequisite for sustainable development. Special attention should also be paid to the health needs of the elderly and disabled population.

6.19.　　Infants and children. Approximately one third of the world's population are children under 15 years old. At least 15 million of these children die annually from such preventable causes as birth trauma, birth asphyxia, acute respiratory infections, malnutrition, communicable diseases and diarrhoea. The health of children is affected more severely than other population groups by malnutrition and adverse environmental factors, and many children risk exploitation as cheap labour or in prostitution.

6.20.　　Youth. As has been the historical experience of all countries, youth are particularly vulnerable to the problems associated with economic development, which often weakens traditional forms of social support essential for the healthy development, of young people. Urbanization and changes in social mores have increased substance abuse, unwanted pregnancy and sexually transmitted diseases, including AIDS. Currently more than half of all people alive are under the age of 25, and four of every five live in developing countries. Therefore it is important to ensure that historical experience is not replicated.

6.21.　　Women. In developing countries, the health status of women remains relatively low, and during the 1980s poverty, malnutrition and general ill-health in women were even rising. Most women in developing countries still do not have adequate basic educational opportunities and they lack the means of promoting their health, responsibly controlling their reproductive life and improving their socio-economic status. Particular attention should be given to the provision of pre-natal care to ensure healthy babies.

6.22.　　Indigenous people and their communities. Indigenous people had their communities make up a significant percentage of global population. The outcomes of their experience have tended to be very similar in that the basis of their relationship with traditional lands has been fundamentally changed. They tend to feature disproportionately in unemployment, lack of housing, poverty and poor health. In many countries the number of indigenous people is growing faster than the general population. Therefore it is important to target health initiatives for indigenous people.

**Objectives**

6.23.　　The general objectives of protecting vulnerable groups are to ensure that all such individuals should be allowed to develop to their full potential (including healthy physical, mental and spiritual development); to ensure that young people can develop, establish and maintain healthy lives; to allow women to perform their key role in society; and to support indigenous people through educational, economic and technical opportunities.

6.24.　　Specific major goals for child survival, development and protection were agreed upon at the World Summit for Children and remain valid also for Agenda 21. Supporting and sectoral goals cover women's health and education, nutrition, child health, water and sanitation, basic education and children in difficult circumstances.

6.25.　　Governments should take active steps to implement, as a matter of urgency, in accordance with country specific conditions and legal systems, measures to ensure that women and men have the same right to decide freely and responsibly on the number and spacing of their children, to have access to the information, education and means, as appropriate, to enable them to exercise this right in keeping with their freedom, dignity and personally held values, taking into account ethical and cultural considerations.

6.26.　　Governments should take active steps to implement programmes to establish and strengthen preventive and curative health facilities which include women-centred, women-managed, safe and effective reproductive health care and affordable, accessible services, as appropriate, for the responsible planning of family size, in keeping with freedom, dignity and personally held values and taking into account ethical and cultural considerations. Programmes should focus on providing comprehensive health care, including pre-natal care, education and information on health and responsible parenthood and should provide the opportunity for all women to breast-feed fully, at least during the first four months post-partum. Programmes should fully support women's productive and reproductive roles and well being, with special attention to the need for providing equal and improved health care for all children and the need to reduce the risk of maternal and child mortality and sickness.

**Activities**

6.27.     National Governments, in cooperation with local and non-governmental organizations, should initiate or enhance programmes in the following areas:

    a.     Infants and children:

        i.     Strengthen basic health-care services for children in the context of primary health-care delivery, including prenatal care, breast-feeding, immunization and nutrition programmes;

        ii.     Undertake widespread adult education on the use of oral rehydration therapy for diarrhoea, treatment of respiratory infections and prevention of communicable diseases;

        iii.     Promote the creation, amendment and enforcement of a legal framework protecting children from sexual and workplace exploitation;

        iv.     Protect children from the effects of environmental and occupational toxic compounds;

    b.     Youth: Strengthen services for youth in health, education and social sectors in order to provide better information, education, counselling and treatment for specific health problems, including drug abuse;

    c.     Women:

        i.     Involve women's groups in decision-making at the national and community levels to identify health risks and incorporate health issues in national action programmes on women and development;

        ii.     Provide concrete incentives to encourage and maintain attendance of women of all ages at school and adult education courses, including health education and training in primary, home and maternal health care;

        iii.     Carry out baseline surveys and knowledge, attitude and practice studies on the health and nutrition of women throughout their life cycle, especially as related to the impact of environmental degradation and adequate resources;

    d.     Indigenous people and their communities:

        i.     Strengthen, through resources and self-management, preventative and curative health services;

        ii.     Integrate traditional knowledge and experience into health systems.

**Means of implementation**

(a) Financing and cost evaluation

6.28.     The Conference secretariat has estimated the average total annual cost (1993-2000) of implementing the activities of this programme to be about $3.7 billion, including about $400 billion from the international community on grant or concessional terms. These are indicative and order-of-magnitude estimates only and have not been reviewed by Governments. Actual costs and financial terms, including any that are non-concessional, will depend upon, inter alia, the specific strategies and programmes Governments decide upon for implementation.

(b) Scientific and technological means

6.29.    Educational, health and research institutions should be strengthened to provide support to improve the health of vulnerable groups. Social research on the specific problems of these groups should be expanded and methods for implementing flexible pragmatic solutions explored, with emphasis on preventive measures. Technical support should be provided to Governments, institutions and non-governmental organizations for youth, women and indigenous people in the health sector.

(c) Human resources development

6.30.    The development of human resources for the health of children, youth and women should include reinforcement of educational instit utions, promotion of interactive methods of education for health and increased use of mass media in disseminating information to the target groups. This requires the training of more community health workers, nurses, midwives, physicians, social scientists and educators, the education of mothers, families and communities and the strengthening of ministries of education, health, population etc.

(d) Capacity-building

6.31.    Governments should promote, where necessary: (i) the organization of national, intercountry and interregional symposia and other meetings for the exchange of information among agencies and groups concerned with the health of children, youth, women and indigenous people, and (ii) women's organizations, youth groups and indigenous people's organizations to facilitate health and consult them on the creation, amendment and enforcement of legal frameworks to ensure a healthy environment for children, youth, women and indigenous peoples.

### D. Meeting the urban health challenge

**Basis for action**

6.32.    For hundreds of millions of people, the poor living conditions in urban and peri-urban areas are destroying lives, health, and social and moral values. Urban growth has outstripped society's capacity to meet human needs, leaving hundreds of millions of people with inadequate incomes, diets, housing and services. Urban growth exposes populations to serious environmental hazards and has outstripped the capacity of municipal and local governments to provide the environmental health services that the people need. All too often, urban development is associated with destructive effects on the physical environment and the resource base needed for sustainable development. Environmental pollution in urban areas is associated with excess morbidity and mortality. Overcrowding and inadequate housing contribute to respiratory diseases, tuberculosis, meningitis and other diseases. In urban environments, many factors that affect human health are outside the health sector. Improvements in urban health therefore will depend on coordinated action by all levels of government, health care providers, businesses, religious groups, social and educational institutions and citizens.

**Objectives**

6.33.    The health and well-being of all urban dwellers must be improved so that they can contribute to economic and social development. The global objective is to achieve a 10 to 40 per cent improvement in health indicators by the year 2000. The same rate of improvement should be achieved for environmental, housing and health service indicators. These include the development of quantitative objectives for infant mortality, maternal mortality, percentage of low birth weight newborns and specific indicators (e.g. tuberculosis as an indicator of crowded housing, diarrhoeal diseases as indicators of inadequate water and sanitation, rates of industrial and transportation accidents that indicate possible opportunities for prevention of injury, and social problems such as drug abuse, violence and crime that indicate underlying social disorders).

**Activities**

6.34.   Local authorities, with the appropriate support of national Governments and international organizations should be encouraged to take effective measures to initiate or strengthen the following activities:

   a.   Develop and implement municipal and local health plans:

   i.   Establish or strengthen intersectoral committees at both the political and technical level, including active collaboration on linkages with scientific, cultural, religious, medical, business, social and other city institutions, using networking arrangements;

   ii.   Adopt or strengthen municipal or local "enabling strategies" that emphasize "doing with" rather than "doing for" and create supportive environments for health;

   iii.   Ensure that public health education in schools, workplace, mass media etc. is provided or strengthened;

   iv.   Encourage communities to develop personal skills and awareness of primary health care;

   v.   Promote and strengthen community-based rehabilitation activities for the urban and peri-urban disabled and the elderly;

   b.   Survey, where necessary, the existing health, social and environmental conditions in cities, including documentation of intra-urban differences;

   c.   Strengthen environmental health services:

   i.   Adopt health impact and environmental impact assessment procedures;

   ii.   Provide basic and in-service training for new and existing personnel;

   d.   Establish and maintain city networks for collaboration and exchange of models of good practice.

**Means of implementation**

(a) Financing and cost evaluation

6.35.   The Conference secretariat has estimated the average total annual cost (1993-2000) of implementing the activities of this programme to be about $222 million, including about $22 million from the international community on grant or concessional terms. These are indicative and order-of-magnitude estimates only and have not been reviewed by Governments. Actual costs and financial terms, including any that are non-concessional, will depend upon, inter alia, the specific strategies and programmes Governments decide upon for implementation.

(b) Scientific and technological means

6.36.   Decision-making models should be further developed and more widely used to assess the costs and the health and environment impacts of alternative technologies and strategies. Improvement in urban development and management requires better national and municipal statistics based on practical, standardized indicators. Development of methods is a priority for the measurement of intra-urban and intra-district variations in health status and environmental conditions, and for the application of this information in planning and management.

(c) Human resources development

6.37.    Programmes must supply the orientation and basic training of municipal staff required for the healthy city processes. Basic and in-service training of environmental health personnel will also be needed.

(d) Capacity-building

6.38.    The programme is aimed towards improved planning and management capabilities in the municipal and local government and its partners in central Government, the private sector and universities. Capacity development should be focused on obtaining sufficient information, improving coordination mechanisms linking all the key actors, and making better use of available instruments and resources for implementation.

## E. Reducing health risks from environmental pollution and hazards

### Basis for action

6.39.    In many locations around the world the general environment (air, water and land), workplaces and even individual dwellings are so badly polluted that the health of hundreds of millions of people is adversely affected. This is, inter alia, due to past and present developments in consumption and production patterns and lifestyles, in energy production and use, in industry, in transportation etc., with little or no regard for environmental protection. There have been notable improvements in some countries, but deterioration of the environment continues. The ability of countries to tackle pollution and health problems is greatly restrained because of lack of resources. Pollution control and health protection measures have often not kept pace with economic development. Considerable development-related environmental health hazards exist in the newly industrializing countries. Furthermore, the recent analysis of WHO has clearly established the interdependence among the factors of health, environment and development and has revealed that most countries are lacking such integration as would lead to an effective pollution control mechanism. 2/ Without prejudice to such criteria as may be agreed upon by the international community, or to standards which will have to be determined nationally, it will be essential in all cases to consider the systems of values prevailing in each country and the extent of the applicability of standards that are valid for the most advanced countries but may be inappropriate and of unwarranted social cost for the developing countries.

### Objectives

6.40.    The overall objective is to minimize hazards and maintain the environment to a degree that human health and safety is not impaired or endangered and yet encourage development to proceed. Specific programme objectives are:

    a.    By the year 2000, to incorporate appropriate environmental and health safeguards as part of national development programmes in all countries;

    b.    By the year 2000, to establish, as appropriate, adequate national infrastructure and programmes for providing environmental injury, hazard surveillance and the basis for abatement in all countries;

    c.    By the year 2000, to establish, as appropriate, integrated programmes for tackling pollution at the source and at the disposal site, with a focus on abatement actions in all countries;

d. To identify and compile, as appropriate, the necessary statistical information on health effects to support cost/benefit analysis, including environmental health impact assessment for pollution control, prevention and abatement measures.

**Activities**

6.41. Nationally determined action programmes, with international assistance, support and coordination, where necessary, in this area should include:

a. Urban air pollution:

i. Develop appropriate pollution control technology on the basis of risk assessment and epidemiological research for the introduction of environmentally sound production processes and suitable safe mass transport;

ii. Develop air pollution control capacities in large cities, emphasizing enforcement programmes and using monitoring networks, as appropriate;

b. Indoor air pollution:

i. Support research and develop programmes for applying prevention and control methods to reducing indoor air pollution, including the provision of economic incentives for the installation of appropriate technology;

ii. Develop and implement health education campaigns, particularly in developing countries, to reduce the health impact of domestic use of biomass and coal;

c. Water pollution:

i. Develop appropriate water pollution control technologies on the basis of health risk assessment;

ii. Develop water pollution control capacities in large cities;

d. Pesticides: Develop mechanisms to control the distribution and use of pesticides in order to minimize the risks to human health by transportation, storage, application and residual effects of pesticides used in agriculture and preservation of wood;

e. Solid waste:

i. Develop appropriate solid waste disposal technologies on the basis of health risk assessment;

ii. Develop appropriate solid waste disposal capacities in large cities;

f. Human settlements: Develop programmes for improving health conditions in human settlements, in particular within slums and non-tenured settlements, on the basis of health risk assessment;

g. Noise: Develop criteria for maximum permitted safe noise exposure levels and promote noise assessment and control as part of environmental health programmes;

h. Ionizing and non-ionizing radiation: Develop and implement appropriate national legislation, standards and enforcement procedures on the basis of existing international guidelines;

      i.      Effects of ultraviolet radiation: Undertake, as a matter of urgency, research on the effects on human health of the increasing ultraviolet radiation reaching the earth's surface as a consequence of depletion of the stratospheric ozone layer;

      ii.     On the basis of the outcome of this research, consider taking appropriate remedial measures to mitigate the above-mentioned effects on human beings;

i.   Industry and energy production:

      i.      Establish environmental health impact assessment procedures for the planning and development of new industries and energy facilities;

      ii.     Incorporate appropriate health risk analysis in all national programmes for pollution control and management, with particular emphasis on toxic compounds such as lead;

      iii.    Establish industrial hygiene programmes in all major industries for the surveillance of workers' exposure to health hazards;

      iv.    Promote the introduction of environmentally sound technologies within the industry and energy sectors;

j.   Monitoring and assessment: Establish, as appropriate, adequate environmental monitoring capacities for the surveillance of environmental quality and the health status of populations;

k.   Injury monitoring and reduction:

      i.      Support, as appropriate, the development of systems to monitor the incidence and cause of injury to allow well-targeted intervention/prevention strategies;

      ii.     Develop, in accordance with national plans, strategies in all sectors (industry, traffic and others) consistent with t he WHO safe cities and safe communities programmes, to reduce the frequency and severity of injury;

      iii.    Emphasize preventive strategies to reduce occupationally derived diseases and diseases caused by environmental and occupational toxins to enhance worker safety;

l.   Research promotion and methodology development:

      i.      Support the development of new methods for the quantitative assessment of health benefits and cost associated with different pollution control strategies;

      ii.     Develop and carry out interdisciplinary research on the combined health effects of exposure to multiple environmental hazards, including epidemiological investigations of long-term exposures to low levels of pollutants and the use of biological markers capable of estimating human exposures, adverse effects and susceptibility to environmental agents.

**Means of implementation**

(a) Financing and cost evaluation

6.42.    The Conference secretariat has estimated the average total annual cost (1993-2000) of implementing the activities of this programme to be about $3 billion, including about $115 million from the international community on grant or concessional terms. These are indicative and order-of-magnitude estimates only and have not been reviewed by Governments. Actual costs and financial terms, including any that are non-concessional, will depend upon, inter alia, the specific strategies and programmes Governments decide upon for implementation.

(b) Scientific and technological means

6.43.    Although technology to prevent or abate pollution is readily available for a large number of problems, for programme and policy development countries should undertake research within an intersectoral framework. Such efforts should include collaboration with the business sector. Cost/effect analysis and environmental impact assessment methods should be developed through cooperative international programmes and applied to the setting of priorities and strategies in relation to health and development.

6.44.    In the activities listed in paragraph 6.41 (a) to (m) above, developing country efforts should be facilitated by access to and transfer of technology, know-how and information, from the repositories of such knowledge and technologies, in conformity with chapter 34.

(c) Human resource development

6.45.    Comprehensive national strategies should be designed to overcome the lack of qualified human resources, which is a major impediment to progress in dealing with environmental health hazards. Training should include environmental and health officials at all levels from managers to inspect ors. More emphasis needs to be placed on including the subject of environmental health in the curricula of secondary schools and universities and on educating the public.

(d) Capacity-building

6.46.    Each country should develop the knowledge and practical skills to foresee and identify environmental health hazards, and the capacity to reduce the risks. Basic capacity requirements must include knowledge about environmental health problems and awareness on the part of leaders, citizens and specialists; operational mechanisms for intersectoral and intergovernmental cooperation in development planning and management and in combating pollution; arrangements for involving private and community interests in dealing with social issues; delegation of authority and distribution of resources to intermediate and local levels of government to provide front-line capabilities to meet environmental health needs.

**Notes**

1/ A/45/625, annex.

2/ Report of the WHO Commission on Health and Environment (Geneva, forthcoming).

# Agenda 21 – Chapter 7
## PROMOTING SUSTAINABLE HUMAN SETTLEMENT DEVELOPMENT

7.1.  In industrialized countries, the consumption patterns of cities are severely stressing the global ecosystem, while settlements in the developing world need more raw material, energy, and economic development simply to overcome basic economic and social problems. Human settlement conditions in many parts of the world, particularly the developing countries, are deteriorating mainly as a result of the low levels of investment in the sector attributable to the overall resource constraints in these countries. In the low-income countries for which recent data are available, an average of only 5.6 per cent of central government expenditure went to housing, amenities, social security and welfare. 1/ Expenditure by international support and finance organizations is equally low. For example, only 1 per cent of the United Nations system's total grant-financed expenditures in 1988 went to human settlements, 2/ while in 1991, loans from the World Bank and the International Development Association (IDA) for urban development and water supply and sewerage amounted to 5.5 and 5.4 per cent, respectively, of their total lending. 3/

7.2.  On the other hand, available information indicates that technical cooperation activities in the human settlement sector generate considerable public and private sector investment. For example, every dollar of UNDP technical cooperation expenditure on human settlements in 1988 generated a follow-up investment of $122, t he highest of all UNDP sectors of assistance. 4/

7.3.  This is the foundation of the "enabling approach" advocated for the human settlement sector. External assistance will help to generate the internal resources needed to improve the living and working environments of all people by the year 2000 and beyond, including the growing number of unemployed - the no-income group. At the same time the environmental implications of urban development should be recognized and addressed in an integrated fashion by all countries, with high priority being given to the needs of the urban and rural poor, the unemployed and the growing number of people without any source of income.

Human settlement objective

7.4.  The overall human settlement objective is to improve the social, economic and environmental quality of human settlements and the living and working environments of all people, in particular the urban and rural poor. Such improvement should be based on technical cooperation activities, partnerships among the public, private and community sectors and participation in the decision-making process by community groups and special interest groups such as women, indigenous people, the elderly and the disabled. These approaches should form the core principles of national settlement strategies. In developing these strategies, countries will need to set priorities among the eight programme areas in this chapter in accordance with their national plans and objectives, taking fully into account their social and cultural capabilities. Furthermore, countries should make appropriate provision to monitor the impact of their strategies on marginalized and disenfranchised groups, with particular reference to the needs of women.

7.5.  The programme areas included in this chapter are:

    a.  Providing adequate shelter for all;

    b.  Improving human settlement management;

    c.  Promoting sustainable land-use planning and management;

    d.  Promoting the integrated provision of environmental infrastructure: water, sanitation, drainage and solid-waste management;

    e.  Promoting sustainable energy and transport systems in human settlements;

    f.  Promoting human settlement planning and management in disaster-prone areas;

g.   Promoting sustainable construction industry activities;

h.   Promoting human resource development and capacity-building for human settlement development.

## PROGRAMME AREAS

### A. Providing adequate shelter for all

**Basis for action**

7.6.  Access to safe and healthy shelter is essential to a person's physical, psychological, social and economic well-being and should be a fundamental part of national and international action. The right to adequate housing as a basic human right is enshrined in the Universal Declaration of Human Rights and the International Covenant on Economic, Social and Cultural Rights. Despite this, it is estimated that at the present time, at least 1 billion people do not have access to safe and healthy shelter and that if appropriate action is not taken, this number will increase dramatically by the end of the century and beyond.

7.7.  A major global programme to address this problem is the Global Strategy for Shelter to the Year 2000, adopted by the General Assembly in December 1988 (resolution 43/181, annex). Despite its widespread endorsement, the Strategy needs a much greater level of political and financial support to enable it to reach its goal of facilitating adequate shelter for all by the end of the century and beyond.

**Objective**

7.8.  The objective is to achieve adequate shelter for rapidly growing populations and for the currently deprived urban and rural poor through an enabling approach to shelter development and improvement that is environmentally sound.

**Activities**

7.9.  The following activities should be undertaken:

a.   As a first step towards the goal of providing adequate shelter for all, all countries should take immediate measures to provide shelter to their homeless poor, while the international community and financial institutions should undertake actions to support the efforts of the developing countries to provide shelter to the poor;

b.   All countries should adopt and/or strengthen national shelter strategies, with targets based, as appropriate, on the principles and recommendations contained in the Global Strategy for Shelter to the Year 2000. People should be protected by law against unfair eviction from their homes or land;

c.   All countries should, as appropriate, support the shelter efforts of the urban and rural poor, the unemployed and the no-income group by adopting and/or adapting existing codes and regulations, to facilitate their access to land, finance and low-cost building materials and by actively promoting the regularization and upgrading of informal settlements and urban slums as an expedient measure and pragmatic solution to the urban shelter deficit;

d.   All countries should, as appropriate, facilitate access of urban and rural poor to shelter by adopting and utilizing housing and finance schemes and new innovative mechanisms adapted to their circumstances;

e.   All countries should support and develop environmentally compatible shelter strategies at national, state/provincial and municipal levels through partnerships among the private, public and community sectors and with the support of community-based organizations;

f. All countries, especially developing ones, should, as appropriate, formulate and implement programmes to reduce the impact of the phenomenon of rural to urban drift by improving rural living conditions;

g. All countries, where appropriate, should develop and implement resettlement programmes that address the specific problems of displaced populations in their respective countries;

h. All countries should, as appropriate, document and monitor the implementation of their national shelter strategies by using, inter alia, the monitoring guidelines adopted by the Commission on Human Settlements and the shelter performance indicators being produced jointly by the United Nations Centre for Human Settlements (Habitat) and the World Bank;

i. Bilateral and multilateral cooperation should be strengthened in order to support the implementation of the national shelter strategies of developing countries;

j. Global progress reports covering national action and the support activities of international organizations and bilateral donors should be produced and disseminated on a biennial basis, as requested in the Global Strategy for Shelter to the Year 2000.

## Means of implementation

(a) Financing and cost evaluation

7.10. The Conference secretariat has estimated the average total annual cost (1993-2000) of implementing the activities of this programme to be about $75 billion, including about $10 billion from the international community on grant or concessional terms. These are indicative and order-of-magnitude estimates only and have not been reviewed by Governments. Actual costs and financial terms, including any that are non-concessional, will depend upon, inter alia, the specific strategies and programmes Governments decide upon for implementation.

(b) Scientific and technological means

7.11. The requirements under this heading are addressed in each of the other programme areas included in the present chapter.

(c) Human resource development and capacity-building

7.12. Developed countries and funding agencies should provide specific assistance to developing countries in adopting an enabling approach to the provision of shelter for all, including the no-income group, and covering research institutions and training activities for government officials, professionals, communities and non-governmental organizations and by strengthening local capacity for the development of appropriate technologies.

### B. Improving human settlement management

## Basis for action

7.13. By the turn of the century, the majority of the world's population will be living in cities. While urban settlements, particularly in developing countries, are showing many of the symptoms of the global environment and development crisis, they nevertheless generate 60 per cent of gross national product and, if properly managed, can develop the capacity to sustain their productivity, improve the living conditions of their residents and manage natural resources in a sustainable way.

7.14. Some metropolitan areas extend over the boundaries of several political and/or administrative entities (counties and municipalities) even though they conform to a continuous urban system. In many cases this political heterogeneity hinders the implementation of comprehensive environmental management programmes.

## Objective

7.15.    The objective is to ensure sustainable management of all urban settlements, particularly in developing countries, in order to enhance their ability to improve the living conditions of residents, especially the marginalized and disenfranchised, thereby contributing to the achievement of national economic development goals.

## Activities

(a) Improving urban management

7.16.    One existing framework for strengthening management is in the United Nations Development Programme/World Bank/United Nations Centre for Human Settlements (Habitat) Urban Management Programme (UMP), a concerted global effort to assist developing countries in addressing urban management issues. Its coverage should be extended to all interested countries during the period 1993-2000. All countries should, as appropriate and in accordance with national plans, objectives and priorities and with the assistance of non-governmental organizations and representatives of local authorities, undertake the following activities at the national, state/provincial and local levels, with the assistance of relevant programmes and support agencies:

a.    Adopting and applying urban management guidelines in the areas of land management, urban environmental management, infrastructure management and municipal finance and administration;

b.    Accelerating efforts to reduce urban poverty through a number of actions, including:

i.    Generating employment for the urban poor, particularly women, through the provision, improvement and maintenance of urban infrastructure and services and the support of economic activities in the informal sector, such as repairs, recycling, services and small commerce;

ii.    Providing specific assistance to the poorest of the urban poor through, inter alia, the creation of social infrastructure in order to reduce hunger and homelessness, and the provision of adequate community services;

iii.    Encouraging the establishment of indigenous community-based organizations, private voluntary organizations and other forms of non-governmental entities that can contribute to the efforts to reduce poverty and improve the quality of life for low-income families;

c.    Adopting innovative city planning strategies to address environmental and social issues by:

i.    Reducing subsidies on, and recovering the full costs of, environmental and other services of high standard (e.g. water supply, sanitation, waste collection, roads, telecommunications) provided to higher income neighbourhoods;

ii.    Improving the level of infrastructure and service provision in poorer urban areas;

d.    Developing local strategies for improving the quality of life and the environment, integrating decisions on land use and land management, investing in the public and private sectors and mobilizing human and material resources, thereby promoting employment generation that is environmentally sound and protective of human health.

(b) Strengthening urban data systems

7.17.    During the period 1993-2000 all countries should undertake, with the active participation of the business sector as appropriate, pilot projects in selected cities for the collection, analysis and subsequent dissemination of urban data, including environmental impact analysis, at the local, state/provincial, national and international levels and the establishment of city data management capabilities. 5/ United Nations organizations, such as Habitat, UNEP and UNDP, could provide technical advice and model data management systems.

(c) Encouraging int ermediate city development

7.18.    In order to relieve pressure on large urban agglomerations of developing countries, policies and strategies should be implemented towards the development of intermediate cities that create employment opportunities for unemployed labour in the rural areas and support rural-based economic activities, although sound urban management is essential to ensure that urban sprawl does not expand resource degradation over an ever wider land area and increase pressures to convert open space and agricultural/buffer lands for development.

7.19.    Therefore all countries should, as appropriate, conduct reviews of urbanization processes and policies in order to assess the environmental impacts of growth and apply urban planning and management approaches specifically suited to the needs, resource capabilities and characteristics of their growing intermediate-sized cities. As appropriate, they should also concentrate on activities aimed at facilitating the transition from rural to urban lifestyles and settlement patterns and at promoting the development of small-scale economic activities, particularly the production of food, to support local income generation and the production of intermediate goods and services for rural hinterlands.

7.20.    All cities, particularly those characterized by severe sustainable development problems, should, in accordance with national laws, rules and regulations, develop and strengthen programmes aimed at addressing such problems and guiding their development along a sustainable path. Some international initiatives in support of such efforts, as in the Sustainable Cities Programme of Habitat and the Healthy Cities Programme of WHO, should be intensified. Additional initiatives involving the World Bank, the regional development banks and bilateral agencies, as well as other interested stakeholders, particularly international and national representatives of local authorities, should be strengthened and coordinated. Individual cities should, as appropriate:

   a.    Institutionalize a participatory approach to sustainable urban development, based on a continuous dialogue between the actors involved in urban development (the public sector, private sector and communities), especially women and indigenous people;

   b.    Improve the urban environment by promoting social organization and environmental awareness through the participation of local communities in the identification of public services needs, the provision of urban infrastructure, the enhancement of public amenities and the protection and/or rehabilitation of older buildings, historic precincts and other cultural artifacts. In addition, "green works" programmes should be activated to create self-sustaining human development activities and both formal and informal employment opportunities for low-income urban residents;

   c.    Strengthen the capacities of their local governing bodies to deal more effectively with the broad range of developmental and environmental challenges associated with rapid and sound urban growth through comprehensive approaches to planning that recognize the individual needs of cities and are based on ecologically sound urban design practices;

   d.    Participate in international "sustainable city networks" to exchange experiences and mobilize national and international technical and financial support;

e. Promote the formulation of environmentally sound and culturally sensitive tourism programmes as a strategy for sustainable development of urban and rural settlements and as a way of decentralizing urban development and reducing discrepancies among regions;

f. Establish mechanisms, with the assistance of relevant international agencies, to mobilize resources for local initiatives to improve environmental quality;

g. Empower community groups, non-governmental organizations and individuals to assume the authority and responsibility for managing and enhancing their immediate environment through participatory tools, techniques and approaches embodied in the concept of environmental care.

7.21.    Cities of all countries should reinforce cooperation among themselves and cities of the developed countries, under the aegis of non-governmental organizations active in this field, such as the International Union of Local Authorities (IULA), the International Council for Local Environmental Initiatives (ICLEI) and the World Federation of Twin Cities.

**Means of implementation**

(a) Financing and cost evaluation

7.22.    The Conference secretariat has estimated the average total annual cost (1993-2000) of implementing the activities of this programme to be about $100 billion, including about $15 billion from the international community on grant or concessional terms. These are indicative and order-of-magnitude estimates only and have not been reviewed by Governments. Actual costs and financial terms, including any that are non-concessional, will depend upon, inter alia, the specific strategies and programmes Governments decide upon for implementation.

(b) Human resource development and capacity-building

7.23.    Developing countries should, with appropriate international assistance, consider focusing on training and developing a cadre of urban managers, technicians, administrators and other relevant stakeholders who can successfully manage environmentally sound urban development and growth and are equipped with the skills necessary to analyse and adapt the innovative experiences of other cities. For this purpose, the full range of training methods - from formal education to the use of the mass media - should be utilized, as well as the "learning by doing" option.

7.24.    Developing countries should also encourage technological training and research through joint efforts by donors, non-governmental organizations and private business in such areas as the reduction of waste, water quality, saving of energy, safe production of chemicals and less polluting transportation.

7.25.    Capacity-building activities carried out by all countries, assisted as suggested above, should go beyond the training of individuals and functional groups to include institutional arrangements, administrative routines, inter-agency linkages, information flows and consultative processes.

7.26.    In addition, international efforts, such as the Urban Management Programme, in cooperation with multilateral and bilateral agencies, should continue to assist the developing countries in their efforts to develop a participatory structure by mobilizing the human resources of the private sector, non-governmental organizations and the poor, particularly women and the disadvantaged.

### C. Promoting sustainable land-use planning and management

**Basis for action**

7.27.    Access to land resources is an essential component of sustainable low-impact lifestyles. Land resources are the basis for (human) living systems and provide soil, energy, water and the opportunity for all human activity. In rapidly growing urban areas, access to land is rendered increasingly difficult by the conflicting demands of industry, housing, commerce, agriculture, land tenure structures and the need for open spaces. Furthermore, the rising costs of urban land prevent the poor from gaining access to suitable land. In rural areas, unsustainable practices, such as the exploitation of marginal lands and the encroachment on forests and ecologically fragile areas by commercial interests and landless rural populations, result in environmental degradation, as well as in diminishing returns for impoverished rural settlers.

## Objective

7.28.    The objective is to provide for the land requirements of human settlement development through environmentally sound physical planning and land use so as to ensure access to land to all households and, where appropriate, the encouragement of communally and collectively owned and managed land. 6/ Particular attention should be paid to the needs of women and indigenous people for economic and cultural reasons.

## Activi ties

7.29.    All countries should consider, as appropriate, undertaking a comprehensive national inventory of their land resources in order to establish a land information system in which land resources will be classified according to their most appropriate uses and environmentally fragile or disaster-prone areas will be identified for special protection measures.

7.30.    Subsequently, all countries should consider developing national land-resource management plans to guide land-resource development and utilization and, to that end, should:

a. Establish, as appropriate, national legislation to guide the implementation of public policies for environmentally sound urban development, land utilization, housing and for the improved management of urban expansion;

b. Create, where appropriate, efficient and accessible land markets that meet community development needs by, inter alia, improving land registry systems and streamlining procedures in land transactions;

c. Develop fiscal incentives and land-use control measures, including land-use planning solutions for a more rational and environmentally sound use of limited land resources;

d. Encourage partnerships among the public, private and community sectors in managing land resources for human settlements development;

e. Strengthen community-based land-resource protection practices in existing urban and rural settlements;

f. Establish appropriate forms of land tenure that provide security of tenure for all land-users, especially indigenous people, women, local communities, the low-income urban dwellers and the rural poor;

g. Accelerate efforts to promote access to land by the urban and rural poor, including credit schemes for the purchase of land and for building/acquiring or improving safe and healthy shelter and infrastructure services;

h. Develop and support the implementation of improved land-management practices that deal comprehensively with potentially competing land requirements for agriculture, industry, transport, urban development, green spaces, preserves and other vital needs;

  i. Promote understanding among policy makers of the adverse consequences of unplanned settlements in environmentally vulnerable areas and of the appropriate national and local land-use and settlements policies required for this purpose.

7.31. At the international level, global coordination of land-resource management activities should be strengthened by the various bilateral and multilateral agencies and programmes, such as UNDP, FAO, the World Bank, the regional development banks, other interested organizations and the UNDP/World Bank/Habitat Urban Management Programme, and action should be taken to promote the transfer of applicable experience on sustainable land-management practices to and among developing countries.

**Means of implementation**

(a) Financing and cost evaluation

7.32. The Conference secretariat has estimated the average total annual cost (1993-2000) of implementing the activities of this programme to be about $3 billion, including about $300 million from the international community on grant or concessional t erms. These are indicative and order-of-magnitude estimates only and have not been reviewed by Governments. Actual costs and financial terms, including any that are non-concessional, will depend upon, inter alia, the specific strategies and programmes Governments decide upon for implementation.

(b) Scientific and technological means

7.33. All countries, particularly developing countries, alone or in regional or subregional groupings, should be given access to modern techniques of land-resource management, such as geographical information systems, satellite photography/imagery and other remote-sensing technologies.

(c) Human resource development and capacity-building

7.34. Environmentally focused training activities in sustainable land-resources planning and management should be undertaken in all countries, with developing countries being given assistance through international support and funding agencies in order to:

  a. Strengthen the capacity of national, state/provincial and local educational research and training institutions to provide formal training of land-management technicians and professionals;

  b. Facilitate the organizational review of government ministries and agencies responsible for land questions, in order to devise more efficient mechanisms of land-resource management, and carry out periodic in-service refresher courses for the managers and staff of such ministries and agencies in order to familiarize them with up-to-date land-resource-management technologies;

  c. Where appropriate, provide such agencies with modern equipment, such as computer hardware and software and survey equipment;

  d. Strengthen existing programmes and promote an international and interregional exchange of information and experience in land management through the establishment of professional associations in land-management sciences and related activities, such as workshops and seminars.

### D. Promoting the integrated provision of environmental infrastructure: water, sanitation, drainage and solid-waste management

**Basis for action**

7.35. The sustainability of urban development is defined by many parameters relating to the availability of water supplies, air quality and the provision of environmental infrastructure for sanitation and waste management. As a result of the density of users, urbanization, if properly managed, offers unique opportunities for the supply of sustainable environmental infrastructure through adequate pricing policies, educational programmes and equitable access mechanisms that are economically and environmentally sound. In most developing countries, however, the inadequacy and lack of environmental infrastructure is responsible for widespread ill-health and a large number of preventable deaths each year. In those countries conditions are set to worsen due to growing needs that exceed the capacity of Governments to respond adequately.

7.36.    An integrated approach to the provision of environmentally sound infrastructure in human settlements, in particular for the urban and rural poor, is an investment in sustainable development that can improve the quality of life, increase productivity, improve health and reduce the burden of investments in curative medicine and poverty alleviation.

7.37.    Most of the activities whose management would be improved by an integrated approach, are covered in Agenda 21 as follows: chapter 6 (Protecting and promoting human health conditions), chapters 9 (Protecting the atmosphere), 18 (Protecting the quality and supply of freshwater resources) and 21 (Environmentally sound management of solid wastes and sewage-related issues).


## Objective

7.38.    The objective is to ensure the provision of adequate environmental infrastructure facilities in all settlements by the year 2025. The achievement of this objective would require that all developing countries incorporate in their national strategies programmes to build the necessary technical, financial and human resource capacity aimed at ensuring better integration of infrastructure and environmental planning by the year 2000.

## Activities

7.39.    All countries should assess the environmental suitability of infrastructure in human settlements, develop national goals for sustainable management of waste, and implement environmentally sound technology to ensure that the environment, human health and quality of life are protected. Settlement infrastructure and environmental programmes designed to promote an integrated human settlements approach to the planning, development, maintenance and management of environmental infrastructure (water supply, sanitation, drainage, solid-waste management) should be strengthened with the assistance of bilateral and multilateral agencies. Coordination among these agencies and with collaboration from international and national representatives of local authorities, the private sector and community groups should also be strengthened. The activities of all agencies engaged in providing environmental infrastructure should, where possible, reflect an ecosystem or metropolitan area approach to settlements and should include monitoring, applied research, capacity-building, transfer of appropriate technology and technical cooperation among the range of programme activities.

7.40.    Developing countries should be assisted at the national and local levels in adopting an integrated approach to the provision of water supply, energy, sanitation, drainage and solid-waste management, and external funding agencies should ensure that this approach is applied in particular to environmental infrastructure improvement in informal settlements based on regulations and standards that take into account the living conditions and resources of the communities to be served.

7.41.    All countries should, as appropriate, adopt the following principles for the provision of environmental infrastructure:

        a.    Adopt policies that minimize if not altogether avoid environmental damage, whenever possible;

        b.    Ensure that relevant decisions are preceded by environmental impact assessments and also take into account the costs of any ecological consequences;

    c.   Promote development in accordance with indigenous practices and adopt technologies appropriate to local conditions;

    d.   Promote policies aimed at recovering the actual cost of infrastructure services, while at the same time recognizing the need to find suitable approaches (including subsidies) to extend basic services to all households;

    e.   Seek joint solutions to environmental problems that affect several localities.

7.42.    The dissemination of information from existing programmes should be facilitated and encouraged among interested countries and local institutions.

**Means of implementation**

(a) Financing and cost evaluation

7.43.    The Conference secretariat has estimated most of the costs of implementing the activities of this programme in other chapters. The secretariat estimates the average total annual cost (1993-2000) of technical assistance from the international community grant or concessional terms to be about $50 million. These are indicative and order-of-magnitude estimates only and have not been reviewed by Governments. Actual costs and financial terms, including any that are non-concessional, will depend upon, inter alia, the specific strategies and programmes Governments decide upon for implementation.

(b) Scientific and technological means

7.44.    Scientific and technological means within the existing programmes should be coordinated wherever possible and should:

    a.   Accelerate research in the area of integrated policies of environmental infrastructure programmes and projects based on cost/benefit analysis and overall environmental impact;

    b.   Promote methods of assessing "effective demand", utilizing environment and development data as criteria for selecting technology.

(c) Human resource development and capacity-building

7.45.    With the assistance and support of funding agencies, all countries should, as appropriate, undertake training and popular participation programmes aimed at:

    a.   Raising awareness of the means, approaches and benefits of the provision of environmental infrastructure facilities, especially among indigenous people, women, low-income groups and the poor;

    b.   Developing a cadre of professionals with adequate skills in integrated infrastructural service planning and maintenance of resource-efficient, environmentally sound and socially acceptable systems;

    c.   Strengthening the institutional capacity of local authorities and administrators in the integrated provision of adequate infrastructure services in partnership with local communities and the private sector;

    d.   Adopting appropriate legal and regulatory instruments, including cross-subsidy arrangements, to extend the benefits of adequate and affordable environmental infrastructure to unserved population groups, especially the poor.

### E. Promoting sustainable energy and transport systems in human settlements

**Basis for action**

7.46. Most of the commercial and non-commercial energy produced today is used in and for human settlements, and a substantial percentage of it is used by the household sector. Developing countries are at present faced with the need to increase their energy production to accelerate development and raise the living standards of their populations, while at the same time reducing energy production costs and energy-related pollution. Increasing the efficiency of energy use to reduce its polluting effects and to promote the use of renewable energies must be a priority in any action taken to protect the urban environment.

7.47. Developed countries, as the largest consumers of energy, are faced with the need for energy planning and management, promoting renewable and alternate sources of energy, and evaluating the life-cycle costs of current systems and practices as a result of which many metropolitan areas are suffering from pervasive air quality problems related to ozone, particulate matters and carbon monoxide. The causes have much to do with technological inadequacies and with an increasing fuel consumption generated by inefficiencies, high demographic and industrial concentrations and a rapid expansion in the number of motor vehicles.

7.48. Transport accounts for about 30 per cent of commercial energy consumption and for about 60 per cent of total global consumption of liquid petroleum. In developing countries, rapid motorization and insufficient investments in urban-transport planning, traffic management and infrastructure, are creating increasing problems in terms of accidents and injury, health, noise, congestion and loss of productivity similar to those occurring in many developed countries. All of these problems have a severe impact on urban populations, particularly the low-income and no-income groups.

**Objectives**

7.49. The objectives are to extend the provision of more energy-efficient technology and alternative/renewable energy for human settlements and to reduce negative impacts of energy production and use on human health and on the environment.

**Activities**

7.50. The principal activities relevant to this programme area are included in chapter 9 (Protection of the atmosphere), programme area B, subprogramme 1 (Energy development, efficiency and consumption) and subprogramme 2 (Transportation).

7.51. A comprehensive approach to human settlements development should include the promotion of sustainable energy development in all countries, as follows:

    a. Developing countries, in particular, should:

        i. Formulate national action programmes to promote and support reafforestation and national forest regeneration with a view to achieving sustained provision of the biomass energy needs of the low-income groups in urban areas and the rural poor, in particular women and children;

        ii. Formulate national action programmes to promote integrated development of energy-saving and renewable energy technologies, particularly for the use of solar, hydro, wind and biomass sources;

        iii. Promote wide dissemination and commercialization of renewable energy technologies through suitable measures, inter alia, fiscal and technology transfer mechanisms;

iv.    Carry out information and training programmes directed at manufacturers and users in order to promote energy -saving techniques and energy -efficient appliances;

b.    International organizations and bilateral donors should:

i.    Support developing countries in implementing national energy programmes in order to achieve widespread use of energy -saving and renewable energy technologies, particularly the use of solar, wind, biomass and hydro sources;

ii.    Provide access to research and development results to increase energy-use efficiency levels in human settlements.

7.52.    Promoting efficient and environmentally sound urban transport systems in all countries should be a comprehensive approach to urban-transport planning and management. To this end, all countries should:

a.    Integrate land-use and transportation planning to encourage development patterns that reduce transport demand;

b.    Adopt urban-transport programmes favouring high-occupancy public transport in countries, as appropriate;

c.    Encourage non-motorized modes of transport by providing safe cycleways and footways in urban and suburban centres in countries, as appropriate;

d.    Devote particular attention to effective traffic management, efficient operation of public transport and maintenance of transport infrastructure;

e.    Promote the exchange of information among countries and representatives of local and metropolitan areas;

f.    Re-evaluate the present consumption and production patterns in order to reduce the use of energy and national resources.

**Means of implementation**

(a) Financing and cost evaluation

7.53.    The Conference secretariat has estimated the costs of implementing the activities of this programme in chapter 9 (Protection of the atmosphere).

(b) Human resource development and capacity-building

7.54.    In order to enhance the skills of energy service and transport professionals and institutions, all countries should, as appropriate:

a.    Provide on-the-job and other training of government officials, planners, traffic engineers and managers involved in the energy -service and transport section;

b.    Raise public awareness of the environmental impacts of transport and travel behaviour through mass media campaigns and support for non-governmental and community initiatives promoting the use of non-motorized transport, shared driving and improved traffic safety measures;

c.    Strengthen regional, national, state/provincial, and private sector institutions that provide education and training on energy service and urban transport planning and management.

**F. Promoting human settlement planning and management in disaster-prone areas**

**Basis for action**

7.55.    Natural disasters cause loss of life, disruption of economic activities and urban productivity, particularly for highly susceptible low-income groups, and environmental damage, such as loss of fertile agricultural land and contamination of water resources, and can lead to major resettlement of populations. Over the past two decades, they are estimated to have caused some 3 million deaths and affected 800 million people. Global economic losses have been estimated by the Office of the United Nations Disaster Relief Coordinator to be in the range of $30-50 billion per year.

7.56.    The General Assembly, in resolution 44/236, proclaimed the 1990s as the International Decade for Natural Disaster Reduction. The goals of the Decade 7/ bear relevance to the objectives of the present programme area.

7.57.    In addition, there is an urgent need to address the prevention and reduction of man-made disasters and/or disasters caused by, inter alia, industries, unsafe nuclear power generation and toxic wastes (see chapter 6 of Agenda 21).

**Objective**

7.58.    The objective is to enable all countries, in particular those that are disaster-prone, to mitigate the negative impact of natural and man-made disasters on human settlements, national economies and the environment.

**Activities**

7.59.    Three distinct areas of activity are foreseen under this programme area, namely, the development of a "culture of safety", pre-disaster planning and post-disaster reconstruction.
(a) Developing a culture of safety

7.60.    To promote a "culture of safety" in all countries, especially those that are disaster-prone, the following activities should be carried out:

    a.   Completing national and local studies on the nature and occurrence of natural disasters, their impact on people and economic activities, the effects of inadequate construction and land use in hazard-prone areas, and the social and economic advantages of adequate pre-disaster planning;

    b.   Implementing nationwide and local awareness campaigns through all available media, translating the above knowledge into information easily comprehensible to the general public and to the populations directly exposed to hazards;

    c.   Strengthening, and/or developing global, regional, national and local early warning systems to alert populations to impending disasters;

    d.   Identifying industrially based environmental disaster areas at the national and international levels and implementing strategies aimed at the rehabilitation of these areas through, inter alia:

        i.   Restructuring of the economic activities and promoting new job opportunities in environmentally sound sectors;

        ii.   Promoting close collaboration between governmental and local authorities, local communities and non-governmental organizations and private business;

        iii.   Developing and enforcing strict environmental control standards.

(b) Developing pre-disaster planning

7.61.    Pre-disaster planning should form an integral part of human settlement planning in all countries. The following should be included:

a.    Undertaking complete multi-hazard research into risk and vulnerability of human settlements and settlement infrastructure, including water and sewerage, communication and transportation networks, as one type of risk reduction may increase vulnerability to another (e.g., an earthquake-resistant house made of wood will be more vulnerable to wind storms);

b.    Developing methodologies for determining risk and vulnerability within specific human settlements and incorporating risk and vulnerability reduction into the human settlement planning and management process;

c.    Redirecting inappropriate new development and human settlements to areas not prone to hazards;

d.    Preparing guidelines on location, design and operation of potentially hazardous industries and activities;

e.    Developing tools (legal, economic etc.) to encourage disaster-sensitive development, including means of ensuring that limitations on development options are not punitive to owners, or incorporate alternative means of compensation;

f.    Further developing and disseminating information on disaster-resistant building materials and construction technologies for buildings and public works in general;

g.    Developing training programmes for contractors and builders on disaster-resistant construction methods. Some programmes should be directed particularly to small enterprises, which build the great majority of housing and other small buildings in the developing countries, as well as to the rural populations, which build their own houses;

h.    Developing training programmes for emergency site managers, non-governmental organizations and community groups which cover all aspects of disaster mitigation, including urban search and rescue, emergency communications, early warning techniques, and pre-disaster planning;

i.    Developing procedures and practices to enable local communities to receive information about hazardous installations or situations in these areas, and facilitate their participation in early warning and disaster abatement and response procedures and plans;

j.    Preparing action plans for the reconstruction of settlements, especially the reconstruction of community life-lines.

(c) Initiating post-disaster reconstruction and rehabilitation planning

7.62.    The international community, as a major partner in post-reconstruction and rehabilitation, should ensure that the countries involved derive the greatest benefits from the funds allocated by undertaking the following activities:

a.    Carrying out research on past experiences on the social and economic aspects of post-disaster reconstruction and adopting effective strategies and guidelines for post-disaster reconstruction, with particular focus on development-focused strategies in the allocation of scarce reconstruction resources, and on the opportunities that post-disaster reconstruction provides to introduce sustainable settlement patterns;

      b.     Preparing and disseminating international guidelines for adaptation to national and local needs;

      c.     Supporting efforts of national Governments to initiate contingency planning, with participation of affected communities, for post-disaster reconstruction and rehabilitation.

**Means of implementation**

(a) Financing and cost evaluation

7.63.     The Conference secretariat has estimated the average total annual cost (1993-2000) of implementing the activities of this programme to be about $50 million from the international community on grant or concessional terms. These are indicative and order-of-magnitude estimates only and have not been reviewed by Governments. Actual costs and financial terms, including any that are non-concessional, will depend upon, inter alia, the specific strategies and programmes Governments decide upon for implementation.

(b) Scientific and technological means

7.64.     Scientists and engineers specializing in this field in both developing and developed countries should collaborate with urban and regional planners in order to provide the basic knowledge and means to mitigate losses owing to disasters as well as environmentally inappropriate development.

(c) Human resource development and capacity-building

7.65.     Developing countries should conduct training programmes on disaster-resistant construction methods for contractors and builders, who build the majority of housing in the developing countries. This should focus on the small business enterprises, which build the majority of housing in the developing countries.

7.66.     Training programmes should be extended to government officials and planners and community and non-governmental organizations to cover all aspects of disaster mitigation, such as early warning techniques, pre-disaster planning and construction, post-disaster construction and rehabilitation.

### G. Promoting sustainable construction industry activities

**Basis for action**

7.67.     The activities of the construction sector are vital to the achievement of the national socio-economic development goals of providing shelter, infrastructure and employment. However, they can be a major source of environmental damage through depletion of the natural resource base, degradation of fragile eco-zones, chemical pollution and the use of building materials harmful to human health.

**Objectives**

7.68.     The objectives are, first, to adopt policies and technologies and to exchange information on them in order to enable the construction sector to meet human settlement development goals, while avoiding harmful side-effects on human health and on the biosphere, and, second, to enhance the employment-generation capacity of the construction sector. Governments should work in close collaboration with the private sector in achieving these objectives.

**Activities**

7.69.    All countries should, as appropriate and in accordance with national plans, objectives and
priorities:

  a.    Establish and strengthen indigenous building materials industry, based, as much as
possible, on inputs of locally available natural resources;

  b.    Formulate programmes to enhance the utilization of local materials by the construction
sector by expanding technical support and incentive schemes for increasing the
capabilities and economic viability of small-scale and informal operatives which make
use of these materials and traditional construction techniques;

  c.    Adopt standards and other regulatory measures which promote the increased use of
energy -efficient designs and technologies and sustainable utilization of natural resources
in an economically and environmentally appropriate way;

  d.    Formulate appropriate land-use policies and introduce planning regulations specially
aimed at the protection of eco-sensitive zones against physical disruption by construction
and construction-related activities;

  e.    Promote the use of labour-intensive construction and maintenance technologies which
generate employment in the construction sector for the underemployed labour force
found in most large cities, while at the same time promoting the development of skills in
the construction sector;

  f.    Develop policies and practices to reach the informal sector and self-help housing builders
by adopting measures to increase the affordability of building materials on the part of the
urban and rural poor, through, inter alia, credit schemes and bulk procurement of building
materials for sale to small-scale builders and communities.

7.70.    All countries should:

  a.    Promote the free exchange of information on the entire range of environmental and health
aspects of construction, including the development and dissemination of databases on the
adverse environmental effects of building materials through the collaborative efforts of
the private and public sectors;

  b.    Promote the development and dissemination of databases on the adverse environmental
and health effects of building materials and introduce legislation and financial incentives
to promote recycling of energy -intensive materials in the construction industry and
conservation of waste energy in building-materials production methods;

  c.    Promote the use of economic instruments, such as product charges, to discourage the use
of construction materials and products that create pollution during their life cycle;

  d.    Promote information exchange and appropriate technology transfer among all countries,
with particular attention to developing countries, for resource management in
construction, particularly for non-renewable resources;

  e.    Promote research in construction industries and related activities, and establish and
strengthen institutions in this sector.

**Means of implementation**

(a) Financing and cost evaluation

7.71.    The Conference secretariat has estimated the average total annual cost (1993-2000) of
implementing the activities of this programme to be about $40 billion, including about $4 billion from

the international community on grant or concessional terms. These are indicative and order-of-magnitude estimates only and have not been reviewed by Governments. Actual costs and financial terms, including any that are non-concessional, will depend upon, inter alia, the specific strategies and programmes Governments decide upon for implementation.

(b) Human resource development and capacity-building

7.72.    Developing countries should be assisted by international support and funding agencies in upgrading the technical and managerial capacities of the small entrepreneur and the vocational skills of operatives and supervisors in the building materials industry, using a variety of training methods. These countries should also be assisted in developing programmes to encourage the use of non-waste and clean technologies through appropriate transfer of technology.

7.73.    General education programmes should be developed in all countries, as appropriate, to increase builder awareness of available sustainable technologies.

7.74.    Local authorities are called upon to play a pioneering role in promoting the increased use of environmentally sound building materials and construction technologies, e.g., by pursuing an innovative procurement policy.

## H. Promoting human resource development and capacity-building for human settlements development

**Basis for action**

7.75.    Most countries, in addition to shortcomings in the availability of specialized expertise in the areas of housing, settlement management, land management, infrastructure, construction, energy, transport, and pre-disaster planning and reconstruction, face three cross-sectoral human resource development and capacity-building shortfalls. First is the absence of an enabling policy environment capable of integrating the resources and activities of the public sector, the private sector and the community, or social sector; second is the weakness of specialized training and research institutions; and third is the insufficient capacity for technical training and assistance for low-income communities, both urban and rural.

**Objective**

7.76.    The objective is to improve human resource development and capacity-building in all countries by enhancing the personal and institutional capacity of all actors, particularly indigenous people and women, involved in human settlement development. In this regard, account should be taken of traditional cultural practices of indigenous people and their relationship to the environment.

**Activities**

7.77.    Specific human resource development and capacity-building activities have been built into each of the programme areas of this chapter. More generally, however, additional steps should be taken to reinforce those activities. In order to do so, all countries, as appropriate, should take the following action:

> a.    Strengthening the development of human resources and of capacities of public sector institutions through technical assistance and international cooperation so as to achieve by the year 2000 substantial improvement in the efficiency of governmental activities;

    b.    Creating an enabling policy environment supportive of the partnership between the public, private and community sectors;

    c.    Providing enhanced training and technical assistance to institutions providing training for technicians, professionals and administrators, and appointed, elected and professional members of local governments and strengthening their capacity to address priority training needs, particularly in regard to social, economic and environmental aspects of human settlements development;

    d.    Providing direct assistance for human settlement development at the community level, inter alia, by:

        i.    Strengthening and promoting programmes for social mobilization and raising awareness of the potential of women and youth in human settlements activities;

        ii.    Facilitating coordination of the activities of women, youth, community groups and non-governmental organizations in human settlements development;

        iii.    Promoting research on women's programmes and other groups, and evaluating progress made with a view to identifying bottlenecks and needed assistance;

    e.    Promoting the inclusion of integrated environmental management into general local government activities.

7.78.    Both international organizations and non-governmental organizations should support the above activities by, inter alia, strengthening subregional training institutions, providing updated training materials and disseminating the results of successful human resource and capacity-building activities, programmes and projects.

**Means of implementation**

(a) Financing and cost evaluation

7.79.    The Conference secretariat has estimated the average total annual cost (1993-2000) of implementing the activities of this programme to be about $65 million from the international community on grant or concessional terms. These are indicative and order-of-magnitude estimates only and have not been reviewed by Governments. Actual costs and financial terms, including any that are non-concessional, will depend upon, inter alia, the specific strategies and programmes Governments decide upon for implementation.

(b) Scientific and technological means

7.80.    Both formal training and non-formal types of human resource development and capacity-building programmes should be combined, and use should be made of user-oriented training methods, up -to-date training materials and modern audio-visual communication systems.

**Notes**

1/ No aggregate figures are available on internal expenditure or official development assistance on human settlements. However, data available in the World Development Report, 1991, for 16 low-income developing countries show that the percentage of central government expenditure on housing, amenities and social security and welfare for 1989 averaged 5.6 per cent, with a high of 15.1 per cent in the case of

Sri Lanka, which has embarked on a vigorous housing programme. In OECD industrialized countries, during the same year, the percentage of central government expenditure on housing, amenities and social security and welfare ranged from a minimum of 29.3 per cent to a maximum of 49.4 per cent, with an average of 39 per cent (World Bank, World Development Report, 1991, World Development Indicators, table 11 (Washington, D.C., 1991)).

2/ See the report of the Director-General for Development and International Economic Cooperation containing preliminary statistical data on operational activities of the United Nations system for 1988 (A/44/324-E/1989/106/Add.4, annex).

3/ World Bank, Annual Report, 1991 (Washington, D.C., 1991).

4/ UNDP, "Reported investment commitments related to UNDP-assisted projects, 1988", table 1, "Sectoral distribution of investment commitment in 1988-1989".

5/ A pilot programme of this type, the City Data Programme (CDP), is already in operation in the United Nations Centre on Human Settlements (Habitat) aimed at the production and dissemination to participating cities of microcomputer application software designed to store, process and retrieve city data for local, national and international exchange and dissemination.

6/ This calls for integrated land-resource management policies, which are also addressed in chapter 10 of Agenda 21 (Integrated approach to planning and management of land resources).

7/ The goals of the International Decade for Natural Disaster Reduction, set out in the annex to General Assembly resolution 44/236, are as follows:

    a.    To improve the capacity of each country to mitigate the effects of natural disasters expeditiously and effectively, paying special attention to assisting developing countries in the assessment of disaster damage potential and in the establishment of early warning systems and disaster-resistant structures when and where needed;

    b.    To devise appropriate guidelines and strategies for applying existing scientific and technical knowledge, taking into account the cultural and economic diversity among nations;

    c.    To foster scientific and engineering endeavours aimed at closing critical gaps in knowledge in order to reduce loss of life and property;

    d.    To disseminate existing and new technical information related to measures for the assessment, prediction and mitigation of natural disasters;

    e.    To develop measures for the assessment, prediction, prevention and mitigation of natural disasters through programmes of technical assistance and technology transfer, demonstration projects, and education and training, tailored to specific disasters and locations, and to evaluate the effectiveness of those programmes.

# Agenda 21 – Chapter 8
## INTEGRATING ENVIRONMENT AND DEVELOPMENT IN DECISION-MAKING

8.1. This chapter contains the following programme areas:

- a. Integrating environment and development at the policy, planning and management levels;

- b. Providing an effective legal and regulatory framework;

- c. Making effective use of economic instruments and market and other incentives;

- d. Establishing systems for integrated environmental and economic accounting.

### PROGRAMME AREAS

### A. Integrating environment and development at the policy, planning and management levels

**Basis for action**

8.2. Prevailing systems for decision-making in many countries tend to separate economic, social and environmental factors at the policy, planning and management levels. This influences the actions of all groups in society, including Governments, industry and individuals, and has important implications for the efficiency and sustainability of development. An adjustment or even a fundamental reshaping of decision-making, in the light of country-specific conditions, may be necessary if environment and development is to be put at the centre of economic and political decision-making, in effect achieving a full integration of these factors. In recent years, some Governments have also begun to make significant changes in the institutional structures of government in order to enable more systematic consideration of the environment when decisions are made on economic, social, fiscal, energy, agricultural, transportation, trade and other policies, as well as the implications of policies in these areas for the environment. New forms of dialogue are also being developed for achieving better integration among national and local government, industry, science, environmental groups and the public in the process of developing effective approaches to environment and development. The responsibility for bringing about changes lies with Governments in partnership with the private sector and local authorities, and in collaboration with national, regional and international organizations, including in particular UNEP, UNDP and the World Bank. Exchange of experience between countries can also be significant. National plans, goals and objectives, national rules, regulations and law, and the specific situation in which different countries are placed are the overall framework in which such integration takes place. In this context, it must be borne in mind that environmental standards may pose severe economic and social costs if they are uniformly applied in developing countries.

**Objectives**

8.3. The overall objective is to improve or restructure the decision-making process so that consideration of socio-economic and environmental issues is fully integrated and a broader range of public participation assured. Recognizing that countries will develop their own priorities in accordance with their prevailing conditions, needs, national plans, policies and programmes, the following objectives are proposed:

- a. To conduct a national review of economic, sectoral and environmental policies, strategies and plans to ensure the progressive integration of environmental and developmental issues;

- b. To strengthen institutional structures to allow the full integration of environmental and developmental issues, at all levels of decision-making;

- c. To develop or improve mechanisms to facilitate the involvement of concerned individuals, groups and organizations in decision-making at all levels;

        d.    To establish domestically determined procedures to integrate environment and development issues in decision-making.

**Activities**

(a) Improving decision-making processes

8.4.  The primary need is to integrate environmental and developmental decision-making processes. To do this, Governments should conduct a national review and, where appropriate, improve the processes of decision-making so as to achieve the progressive integration of economic, social and environmental issues in the pursuit of development that is economically efficient, socially equitable and responsible and environmentally sound. Countries will develop their own priorities in accordance with their national plans, policies and programmes for the following activities:

        a.    Ensuring the integration of economic, social and environmental considerations in decision-making at all levels and in all ministries;

        b.    Adopting a domestically formulated policy framework that reflects a long-term perspective and cross-sectoral approach as the basis for decisions, taking account of the linkages between and within the various political, economic, social and environmental issues involved in the development process;

        c.    Establishing domestically determined ways and means to ensure the coherence of sectoral, economic, social and environmental policies, plans and policy instruments, including fiscal measures and the budget; these mechanisms should apply at various levels and bring together those interested in the development process;

        d.    Monitoring and evaluating the development process systematically, conducting regular reviews of the state of human resources development, economic and social conditions and trends, the state of the environment and natural resources; this could be complemented by annual environment and development reviews, with a view to assessing sustainable development achievements by the various sectors and departments of government;

        e.    Ensuring transparency of, and accountability for, the environmental implications of economic and sectoral policies;

        f.    Ensuring access by the public to relevant information, facilitating the reception of public views and allowing for effective participation.

(b) Improving planning and management systems

8.5.  To support a more integrated approach to decision-making, the data systems and analytical methods used to support such decision-making processes may need to be improved. Governments, in collaboration, where appropriate, with national and international organizations, should review the status of the planning and management system and, where necessary, modify and strengthen procedures so as to facilitate the integrated consideration of social, economic and environmental issues. Countries will develop their own priorities in accordance with their national plans, policies and programmes for the following activities:

        a.    Improving the use of data and information at all stages of planning and management, making systematic and simultaneous use of social, economic, developmental, ecological and environmental data; analysis should stress interactions and synergisms; a broad range of analytical methods should be encouraged so as to provide various points of view;

        b.    Adopting comprehensive analytical procedures for prior and simultaneous assessment of the impacts of decisions, including the impacts within and among the economic, social and environmental spheres; these procedures should extend beyond the project level to policies and programmes; analysis should also include assessment of costs, benefits and risks;

c.   Adopting flexible and integrative planning approaches that allow the consideration of multiple goals and enable adjustment of changing needs; integrative area approaches at the ecosystem or watershed level can assist in this approach;

d.   Adopting integrated management systems, particularly for the management of natural resources; traditional or indigenous methods should be studied and considered wherever they have proved effective; women's traditional roles should not be marginalized as a result of the introduction of new management systems;

e.   Adopting integrated approaches to sustainable development at the regional level, including transboundary areas, subject to the requirements of particular circumstances and needs;

f.   Using policy instruments (legal/regulatory and economic) as a tool for planning and management, seeking incorporation of efficiency criteria in decisions; instruments should be regularly reviewed and adapted to ensure that they continue to be effective;

g.   Delegating planning and management responsibilities to the lowest level of public authority consistent with effective action; in particular the advantages of effective and equitable opportunities for participation by women should be discussed;

h.   Establishing procedures for involving local communities in contingency planning for environmental and industrial accidents, and maintaining an open exchange of information on local hazards.

(c) Data and information

8.6. Countries could develop systems for monitoring and evaluation of progress towards achieving sustainable development by adopting indicators that measure changes across economic, social and environmental dimensions.

(d) Adopting a national strategy for sustainable development

8.7. Governments, in cooperation, where appropriate, with international organizations, should adopt a national strategy for sustainable development based on, inter alia, the implementation of decisions taken at the Conference, particularly in respect of Agenda 21. This strategy should build upon and harmonize the various sectoral economic, social and environmental policies and plans that are operating in the country. The experience gained through existing planning exercises such as national reports for the Conference, national conservation strategies and environment action plans should be fully used and incorporated into a country-driven sustainable development strategy. Its goals should be to ensure socially responsible economic development while protecting the resource base and the environment for the benefit of future generations. It should be developed through the widest possible participation. It should be based on a thorough assessment of the current situation and initiatives.

**Means of implementation**
(a) Financing and cost evaluation

8.8. The Conference secretariat has estimated the average total annual cost (1993-2000) of implementing the activities of this programme to be about $50 million from the international community on grant or concessional terms. These are indicative and order-of-magnitude estimates only and have not been reviewed by Governments. Actual costs and financial terms, including any that are non-concessional, will depend upon, inter alia, the specific strategies and programmes Governments decide upon for implementation.

(b) Researching environment and development interactions

8.9. Governments, in collaboration with the national and international scientific community and in cooperation with international organizations, as appropriate, should intensify efforts to clarify the interactions between and within social, economic and environmental considerations. Research should be undertaken with the explicit objective of assisting policy decisions and providing recommendations on improving management practices.

(c) Enhancing education and training

8.10. Countries, in cooperation, where appropriate, with national, regional or international organizations, should ensure that essential human resources exist, or be developed, to undertake the integration of environment and development at various stages of the decision-making and implementation process. To do this, they should improve education and technical training, particularly for women and girls, by including interdisciplinary approaches, as appropriate, in technical, vocational, university and other curricula. They should also undertake systematic training of government personnel, planners and managers on a regular basis, giving priority to the requisite integrative approaches and planning and management techniques that are suited to country-specific conditions.

(d) Promoting public awareness

8.11. Countries, in cooperation with national institutions and groups, the media and the international community, should promote awareness in the public at large, as well as in specialized circles, of the importance of considering environment and development in an integrated manner, and should establish mechanisms for facilitating a direct exchange of information and views with the public. Priority should be given to highlighting the responsibilities and potential contributions of different social groups.

(e) Strengthen national institutional capacity

8.12. Governments, in cooperation, where appropriate, with international organizations, should strengthen national institutional capability and capacity to integrate social, economic, developmental and environmental issues at all levels of development decision-making and implementation. Attention should be given to moving away from narrow sectoral approaches, progressing towards full cross-sectoral coordination and cooperation.

## B. Providing an effective legal and regulatory framework

**Basis for action**

8.13. Laws and regulations suited to country -specific conditions are among the most important instruments for transforming environment and development policies into action, not only through "command and control" methods, but also as a normative framework for economic planning and market instruments. Yet, although the volume of legal texts in this field is steadily increasing, much of the law-making in many countries seems to be ad hoc and piecemeal, or has not been endowed with the necessary institutional machinery and authority for enforcement and timely adjustment.

8.14. While there is continuous need for law improvement in all countries, many developing countries have been affected by shortcomings of laws and regulations. To effectively integrate environment and development in the policies and practices of each country, it is essential to develop and implement integrated, enforceable and effective laws and regulations that are based upon sound social, ecological, economic and scientific principles. It is equally critical to develop workable programmes to review and enforce compliance with the laws, regulations and standards that are adopted. Technical support may be needed for many countries to accomplish these goals. Technical cooperation requirements in this field include legal information, advisory services and specialized training and institutional capacity-building.

8.15.     The enactment and enforcement of laws and regulations (at the regional, national, state/provincial or local/municipal level) are also essential for the implementation of most international agreements in the field of environment and development, as illustrated by the frequent treaty obligation to report on legislative measures. The survey of existing agreements undertaken in the context of conference preparations has indicated problems of compliance in this respect, and the need for improved national implementation and, where appropriate, related technical assistance. In developing their national priorities, countries should take account of their international obligations.

**Objectives**

8.16.     The overall objective is to promote, in the light of country -specific conditions, the integration of environment and development policies through appropriate legal and regulatory policies, instruments and enforcement mechanisms at the national, state, provincial and local level. Recognizing that countries will develop their own priorities in accordance with their needs and national and, where appropriate, regional plans, policies and programmes, the following objectives are proposed:

> a.     To disseminate information on effective legal and regulatory innovations in the field of environment and development, including appropriate instruments and compliance incentives, with a view to encouraging their wider use and adoption at the national, state, provincial and local level;

> b.     To support countries that request it in their national efforts to modernize and strengthen the policy and legal framework of governance for sustainable development, having due regard for local social values and infrastructures;

> c.     To encourage the development and implementation of national, state, provincial and local programmes that assess and promote compliance and respond appropriately to non-compliance.

**Activities**

(a) Making laws and regulations more effective

8.17.     Governments, with the support, where appropriate, of competent international organizations, should regularly assess the laws and regulations enacted and the related institutional/administrative machinery established at t he national/state and local/municipal level in the field of environment and sustainable development, with a view to rendering them effective in practice. Programmes for this purpose could include the promotion of public awareness, preparation and distribution of guidance material, and specialized training, including workshops, seminars, education programmes and conferences, for public officials who design, implement, monitor and enforce laws and regulations.

(b) Establishing judicial and administrative procedures

8.18.     Governments and legislators, with the support, where appropriate, of competent international organizations, should establish judicial and administrative procedures for legal redress and remedy of actions affecting environment and development that may be unlawful or infringe on rights under the law, and should provide access to individuals, groups and organizations with a recognized legal interest.

(c) Providing legal reference and support services

8.19.     Competent intergovernmental and non-governmental organizations could cooperate to provide Governments and legislators, upon request, with an integrated programme of environment and development law (sustainable development law) services, carefully adapted to the specific requirements of the recipient legal and administrative systems. Such systems could usefully include assistance in the preparation of comprehensive inventories and reviews of national legal systems. Past experience has demonstrated the usefulness of combining specialized legal information services with legal expert advice. Within the United Nations system, closer cooperation among all agencies concerned would avoid duplication of databases and facilitate division of labour. These agencies could examine the possibility and merit of performing reviews of selected national legal systems.

(d) Establishing a cooperative training network for sustainable development law

8.20.    Competent international and academic institutions could, within agreed frameworks, cooperate to provide, especially for trainees from developing countries, postgraduate programmes and in-service training facilities in environment and development law. Such training should address both the effective application and the progressive improvement of applicable laws, the related skills of negotiating, drafting and mediation, and the training of trainers. Intergovernmental and non-governmental organizations already active in this field could cooperate with related university programmes to harmonize curriculum planning and to offer an optimal range of options to interested Governments and potential sponsors.

(e) Developing effective national programmes for reviewing and enforcing compliance with national, state, provincial and local laws on environment and development

8.21.    Each country should develop integrated strategies to maximize compliance with its laws and regulations relating to sustainable development, with assistance from international organizations and other countries as appropriate. The strategies could include:

    a.    Enforceable, effective laws, regulations and standards that are based on sound economic, social and environmental principles and appropriate risk assessment, incorporating sanctions designed to punish violations, obtain redress and deter future violations;

    b.    Mechanisms for promoting compliance;

    c.    Institutional capacity for collecting compliance data, regularly reviewing compliance, detecting violations, establishing enforcement priorities, undertaking effective enforcement, and conducting periodic evaluations of the effectiveness of compliance and enforcement programmes;

    d.    Mechanisms for appropriate involvement of individuals and groups in the development and enforcement of laws and regulations on environment and development.

    e.    National monitoring of legal follow-up to international instruments

8.22.    Contracting parties to international agreements, in consultation with the appropriate secretariats of relevant international conventions as appropriate, should improve practices and procedures for collecting information on legal and regulatory measures taken. Contracting parties to international agreements could undertake sample surveys of domestic follow-up action subject to agreement by the sovereign States concerned.

**Means of implementation**

(a) Financing and cost evaluation

8.23.    The Conference secretariat has estimated the average total annual cost (1993-2000) of implementing the activities of this programme to be about $6 million from the international community on grant or concessional terms. These are indicative and order-of-magnitude estimates only and have not been reviewed by Governments. Actual costs and financial terms, including any that are non-concessional, will depend upon, inter alia, the specific strategies and programmes Governments decide upon for implementation.

(b) Scientific and technological means

8.24.    The programme relies essentially on a continuation of ongoing work for legal data collection, translation and assessment. Closer cooperation between existing databases may be expected to lead to better division of labour (e.g., in geographical coverage of national legislative gazettes and other reference sources) and to improved standardization and compatibility of data, as appropriate.

(c) Human resource development

8.25.    Participation in training is expected to benefit practitioners from developing countries and to enhance training opportunities for women. Demand for this type of postgraduate and in-service training is known to be high. The seminars, workshops and conferences on review and enforcement that have been held to dat e have been very successful and well attended. The purpose of these efforts is to develop resources (both human and institutional) to design and implement effective programmes to continuously review and enforce national and local laws, regulations and standards on sustainable development.

(d) Strengthening legal and institutional capacity

8.26.    A major part of the programme should be oriented towards improving the legal-institutional capacities of countries to cope with national problems of governance and effective law-making and law-applying in the field of environment and sustainable development. Regional centres of excellence could be designated and supported to build up specialized databases and training facilities for linguistic/cultural groups of legal systems.

## C. Making effective use of economic instruments and market and other incentives

**Basis for action**

8.27.    Environmental law and regulation are important but cannot alone be expected to deal with the problems of environment and development. Prices, markets and governmental fiscal and economic policies also play a complementary role in shaping attitudes and behaviour towards the environment.

8.28.    During the past several years, many Governments, primarily in industrialized countries but also in Central and Eastern Europe and in developing countries, have been making increasing use of economic approaches, including those that are market -oriented. Examples include the polluter-pays principle and the more recent natural-resource-user-pays concept.

8.29.    Within a supportive international and national economic context and given the necessary legal and regulatory framework, economic and market -oriented approaches can in many cases enhance capacity to deal with the issues of environment and development. This would be achieved by providing cost-effective solutions, applying integrated pollution prevention control, promoting technological innovation and influencing environmental behaviour, as well as providing financial resources to meet sustainable development objectives.

8.30.    What is needed is an appropriate effort to explore and make more effective and widespread use of economic and market-oriented approaches within a broad framework of development policies, law and regulation suited to country -specific conditions as part of a general transition to economic and environmental policies that are supportive and mutually reinforcing.

**Objectives**

8.31.    Recognizing that countries will develop their own priorities in accordance with their needs and national plans, policies and programmes, the challenge is to achieve significant progress in the years ahead in meeting three fundamental objectives:

          a.    To incorporate environmental costs in the decisions of producers and consumers, to reverse the tendency to treat the environment as a "free good" and to pass these costs on to other parts of society, other countries, or to future generations;

          b.    To move more fully towards integration of social and environmental costs into economic activities, so that prices will appropriately reflect the relative scarcity and total value of resources and contribute towards the prevention of environmental degradation;

          c.    To include, wherever appropriate, the use of market principles in the framing of economic instruments and policies to pursue sustainable development.

**Activities**

(a) Improving or reorienting governmental policies

8.32.    In the near term, Governments should consider gradually building on experience with economic instruments and market mechanisms by undertaking to reorient their policies, keeping in mind national plans, priorities and objectives, in order to:

          a.    Establish effective combinations of economic, regulatory and voluntary (self-regulatory) approaches;

          b.    Remove or reduce those subsidies that do not conform with sustainable development objectives;

          c.    Reform or recast existing structures of economic and fiscal incentives to meet environment and development objectives;

          d.    Establish a policy framework that encourages the creation of new markets in pollution control and environmentally sounder resource management;

          e.    Move towards pricing consistent with sustainable development objectives.

8.33.    In particular, Governments should explore, in cooperation with business and industry, as appropriate, how effective use can be made of economic instruments and market mechanisms in the following areas:

          a.    Issues related to energy, transportation, agriculture and forestry, water, wastes, health, tourism and tertiary services;

          b.    Global and transboundary issues;

          c.    The development and introduction of environmentally sound technology and its adaptation, diffusion and transfer to developing countries in conformity with chapter 34.

(b) Taking account of the particular circumstances of developing countries and countries with economies in transition

8.34.    A special effort should be made to develop applications of the use of economic instruments and market mechanisms geared to the particular needs of developing countries and countries with economies in transition, with the assistance of regional and international economic and environmental organizations and, as appropriate, non-governmental research institutes, by:

          a.    Providing technical support to those countries on issues relating to the application of economic instruments and market mechanisms;

    b.   Encouraging regional seminars and, possibly, the development of regional centres of expertise.

(c) Creating an inventory of effective uses of economic instruments and market mechanisms

8.35.     Given the recognition that the use of economic instruments and market mechanisms is relatively recent, exchange of information about different countries' experiences with such approaches should be actively encouraged. In this regard, Governments should encourage the use of existing means of information exchange to look at effective uses of economic instruments.

(d) Increasing understanding of the role of economic instruments and market mechanisms

8.36.     Governments should encourage research and analysis on effective uses of economic instruments and incentives with the assistance and support of regional and international economic and environmental organizations, as well as non-governmental research institutes, with a focus on such key issues as:

    a.   The role of environmental taxation suited to national conditions;

    b.   The implications of economic instruments and incentives for competitiveness and international trade, and potential needs for appropriate future international cooperation and coordination;

    c.   The possible social and distributive implications of using various instruments.

(e) Establishing a process for focusing on pricing

8.37.     The theoretical advantages of using pricing policies, where appropriate, need to be better understood, and accompanied by greater understanding of what it means to take significant steps in this direction. Processes should therefore be initiated, in cooperation with business, industry, large enterprises, transnational corporations, as well as other social groups, as appropriate, at both the national and international levels, to examine:

    a.   The practical implications of moving towards greater reliance on pricing that internalize environmental costs appropriate to help achieve sustainable development objectives;

    b.   The implications for resource pricing in the case of resource-exporting countries, including the implications of such pricing policies for developing countries;

    c.   The methodologies used in valuing environmental costs.

(f) Enhancing understanding of sustainable development economics

8.38.     Increased interest in economic instruments, including market mechanisms, also requires a concerted effort to improve understanding of sustainable development economics by:

    a.   Encouraging institutions of higher learning to review their curricula and strengthen studies in sustainable development economics;

    b.   Encouraging regional and international economic organizations and non-governmental research institutes with expertise in this area to provide training sessions and seminars for government officials;

    c.   Encouraging business and industry, including large industrial enterprises and transnational corporations with expertise in environmental matters, to organize training programmes for the private sector and other groups.

**Means of implementation**

8.39.    This programme involves adjustments or reorientation of policies on the part of Governments. It also involves international and regional economic and environmental organizations and agencies with expertise in this area, including transnational corporations.

(a) Financing and cost evaluation

8.40.    The Conference secretariat has estimated the average total annual cost (1993-2000) of implementing the activities of this programme to be about $5 million from the international community on grant or concessional terms. These are indicative and order-of-magnitude estimates only and have not been reviewed by Governments. Actual costs and financial terms, including any that are non-concessional, will depend upon, inter alia, the specific strategies and programmes Governments decide upon for implementation.

## D. Establishing systems for integrated environmental and economic accounting

### Basis for action

8.41.    A first step towards the integration of sustainability into economic management is the establishment of better measurement of the crucial role of the environment as a source of natural capital and as a sink for by-products generated during the production of man-made capital and other human activities. As sustainable development encompasses social, economic and environmental dimensions, it is also important that national accounting procedures are not restricted to measuring the production of goods and services that are conventionally remunerated. A common framework needs to be developed whereby the contributions made by all sectors and activities of society, that are not included in the conventional national accounts, are included, to the extent consistent with sound theory and practicability, in satellite accounts. A programme to develop national systems of integrated environmental and economic accounting in all countries is proposed.

### Objectives

8.42.    The main objective is to expand existing systems of national economic accounts in order t o integrate environment and social dimensions in the accounting framework, including at least satellite systems of accounts for natural resources in all member States. The resulting systems of integrated environmental and economic accounting (IEEA) to be established in all member States at the earliest date should be seen as a complement to, rather than a substitute for, traditional national accounting practices for the foreseeable future. IEEAs would be designed to play an integral part in the national development decision-making process. National accounting agencies should work in close collaboration with national environmental statistics as well as the geographic and natural resource departments. The definition of economically active could be expanded to include people performing productive but unpaid tasks in all countries. This would enable their contribution to be adequately measured and taken into account in decision-making.

### Activities

(a) Strengthening international cooperation

8.43.    The Statistical Office of the United Nations Secretariat should:

    a.    Make available to all member States the methodologies contained in the SNA Handbook on Integrated Environmental and Economic Accounting;

    b.    In collaboration with other relevant United Nations organizations, further develop, test, refine and then standardize the provisional concepts and methods such as those proposed by the SNA Handbook, keeping member States informed of the status of the work throughout this process;

    c.    Coordinate, in close cooperation with other international organizations, the training of national accountants, environmental statisticians and national technical staff in small groups for the establishment, adaptation and development of national IEEAs.

8.44.    The Department of Economic and Social Development of the United Nations Secretariat, in close collaboration with other relevant United Nations organizations, should:

    a.    Support, in all member States, the utilization of sustainable development indicators in national economic and social planning and decision-making practices, with a view to ensuring that IEEAs are usefully integrated in economic development planning at the national level;

b. Promote improved environmental and economic and social data collection.

(b) Strengthening national accounting systems

8.45. At the national level, the programme could be adopted mainly by the agencies dealing with national accounts, in close cooperation with environmental statistics and natural resource departments, with a view to assisting national economic analysts and decision makers in charge of national economic planning. National institutions should play a crucial role not only as the depositary of the system but also in its adaptation, establishment and continuous use. Unpaid productive work such as domestic work and child care should be included, where appropriate, in satellite national accounts and economic statistics. Time-use surveys could be a first step in the process of developing these satellite accounts.

(c) Establishing an assessment process

8.46. At the international level, the Statistical Commission should assemble and review experience and advise member States on technical and methodological issues related to the further development and implementation of IEEAs in member States.

8.47. Governments should seek to identify and consider measures to correct price distortions arising from environmental programmes affecting land, water, energy and other natural resources.

8.48. Governments should encourage corporations:

a. To provide relevant environmental information through transparent reporting to shareholders, creditors, employees, governmental authorities, consumers and the public;

b. To develop and implement methods and rules for accounting for sustaining development.

(d) Strengthening data and information collection

8.49. National Governments could consider implementing the necessary enhancement in data collection to set in place national IEEAs with a view to contributing pragmatically to sound economic management. Major efforts should be made to augment the capacity to collect and analyse environmental data and information and to integrate it with economic data, including gender disaggregated data. Efforts should also be made to develop physical environmental accounts. International donor agencies should consider financing the development of intersectoral data banks to help ensure that national planning for sustainable development is based on precise, reliable and effective information and is suited to national conditions.

(e) Strengthening technical cooperation

8.50. The Statistical Office of the United Nations Secretariat, in close collaboration with relevant United Nations organizations, should strengthen existing mechanisms for technical cooperation among countries. This should also include exchange of experience in the establishment of IEEAs, particularly in connection with the valuation of non-marketed natural resources and standardization in data collection. The cooperation of business and industry, including large industrial enterprises and transnational corporations with experience in valuation of such resources, should also be sought.

**Means of implementation**

(a) Financing and cost evaluation

8.51. The Conference secretariat has estimated the average total annual cost (1993-2000) of implementing the activities of this programme to be about $2 million from the international community on grant or concessional terms. These are indicative and order-of-magnitude estimates only and have not been reviewed by Governments. Actual costs and financial terms, including any that are non-concessional, will depend upon, inter alia, the specific strategies and programmes Governments decide upon for implementation.

(b) Strengthening institutions

8.52. To ensure the application of IEEAs:

a. National institutions in developing countries could be strengthened to ensure the effective integration of environment and development at the planning and decision-making levels;

    b.    The Statistical Office should provide the necessary technical support to member States, in close collaboration with the assessment process to be established by the Statistical Commission; the Statistical Office should provide appropriate support for establishing IEEAs, in collaboration with relevant United Nations agencies.

(c) Enhancing the use of information technology

8.53.    Guidelines and mechanisms could be developed and agreed upon for the adaptation and diffusion of information technologies to developing countries. State-of-the-art data management technologies should be adopted for the most efficient and widespread use of IEEAs.

(d) Strengthening national capacity

8.54.    Governments, with the support of the international community, should strengthen national institutional capacity to collect, store, organize, assess and use data in decision-making. Training in all areas related to the establishment of IEEAs, and at all levels, will be required, especially in developing countries. This should include technical training of those involved in economic and environmental analysis, data collection and national accounting, as well as training decision makers to use such information in a pragmatic and appropriate way.

# Agenda 21 – Chapter 9
# PROTECTION OF THE ATMOSPHERE

## INTRODUCTION

9.1. Protection of the atmosphere is a broad and multidimensional endeavour involving various sectors of economic activity. The options and measures described in the present chapter are recommended for consideration and, as appropriate, implementation by Governments and other bodies in their efforts to protect the atmosphere.

9.2. It is recognized that many of the issues discussed in this chapter are also addressed in such international agreements as the 1985 Vienna Convention for the Protection of the Ozone Layer, the 1987 Montreal Protocol on Substances that Deplete the Ozone Layer as amended, the 1992 United Nations Framework Convention on Climate Change and other international, including regional, instruments. In the case of activities covered by such agreements, it is understood that the recommendations contained in this chapter do not oblige any Government to take measures which exceed the provisions of these legal instruments. However, within the framework of this chapter, Governments are free to carry out additional measures which are consistent with those legal instruments.

9.3. It is also recognized that activities that may be undertaken in pursuit of the objectives of this chapter should be coordinated with social and economic development in an integrated manner with a view to avoiding adverse impacts on the latter, taking into full account the legitimate priority needs of developing countries for the achievement of sustained economic growth and the eradication of poverty.

9.4. In this context particular reference is also made to programme area A of chapter 2 of Agenda 21 (Promoting sustainable development through trade).

9.5. The present chapter includes the following four programme areas:

    a. Addressing the uncertainties: improving the scientific basis for decision-making;

    b. Promoting sustainable development:

        i. Energy development, efficiency and consumption;

        ii. Transportation;

        iii. Industrial development;

        iv. Terrestrial and marine resource development and land use;

    c. Preventing stratospheric ozone depletion;

    d. Transboundary atmospheric pollution.

## PROGRAMME AREAS

### A. Addressing the uncertainties: improving the scientific basis for decision-making

**Basis for action**

9.6. Concern about climate change and climate variability, air pollution and ozone depletion has created new demands for scientific, economic and social information to reduce the remaining uncertainties in these fields. Better understanding and prediction of the various properties of the atmosphere and of the affected ecosystems, as well as health impacts and their interactions with socio-economic factors, are needed.

## Objectives

9.7. The basic objective of this programme area is to improve the understanding of processes that influence and are influenced by the Earth's atmosphere on a global, regional and local scale, including, inter alia, physical, chemical, geological, biological, oceanic, hydrological, economic and social processes; to build capacity and enhance international cooperation; and to improve understanding of the economic and social consequences of atmospheric changes and of mitigation and response measures addressing such changes.

## Activities

9.8. Governments at the appropriate level, with the cooperation of the relevant United Nations bodies and, as appropriate, intergovernmental and non-governmental organizations, and the private sector, should:

    a. Promote research related to the natural processes affecting and being affected by the atmosphere, as well as the critical linkages between sustainable development and atmospheric changes, including impacts on human health, ecosystems, economic sectors and society;

    b. Ensure a more balanced geographical coverage of the Global Climate Observing System and its components, including the Global Atmosphere Watch, by facilitating, inter alia, the establishment and operation of additional systematic observation stations, and by contributing to the development, utilization and accessibility of these databases;

    c. Promote cooperation in:

        i. The development of early detection systems concerning changes and fluctuations in the atmosphere;

        ii. The establishment and improvement of capabilities to predict such changes and fluctuations and to assess the resulting environmental and socio-economic impacts;

    d. Cooperate in research to develop methodologies and identify threshold levels of atmospheric pollutants, as well as atmospheric levels of greenhouse gas concentrations, that would cause dangerous anthropogenic interference with the climate system and the environment as a whole, and the associated rates of change that would not allow ecosystems to adapt naturally;

    e. Promote, and cooperate in the building of scientific capacities, the exchange of scientific data and information, and the facilitation of the participation and training of experts and technical staff, particularly of developing countries, in the fields of research, data assembly, collection and assessment, and systematic observation related to the atmosphere.

### B. Promoting sustainable development

### 1. Energy development, efficiency and consumption

**Basis for action**

9.9. Energy is essential to economic and social development and improved quality of life. Much of the world's energy, however, is currently produced and consumed in ways that could not be sustained if technology were to remain constant and if overall quantities were to increase substantially. The need to control atmospheric emissions of greenhouse and other gases and substances will increasingly need to be based on efficiency in energy production, transmission, distribution and consumption, and on growing reliance on environmentally sound energy systems, particularly new and renewable sources of energy. 1/ All energy sources will need to be used in ways that respect the atmosphere, human health and the environment as a whole.

9.10.    The existing constraints to increasing the environmentally sound energy supplies required for pursuing the path towards sustainable development, particularly in developing countries, need to be removed.

**Objectives**

9.11.    The basic and ultimate objective of this programme area is to reduce adverse effects on the atmosphere from the energy sector by promoting policies or programmes, as appropriate, to increase the contribution of environmentally sound and cost-effective energy systems, particularly new and renewable ones, through less polluting and more efficient energy production, transmission, distribution and use. This objective should reflect the need for equity, adequate energy supplies and increasing energy consumption in developing countries, and should take into consideration the situations of countries that are highly dependent on income generated from the production, processing and export, and/or consumption of fossil fuels and associated energy-intensive products and/or the use of fossil fuels for which countries have serious difficulties in switching to alternatives, and the situations of countries highly vulnerable to adverse effects of climate change.

**Activities**

9.12.    Governments at the appropriate level, with the cooperation of the relevant United Nations bodies and, as appropriate, intergovernmental and non-governmental organizations, and the private sector, should:

a.   Cooperate in identifying and developing economically viable, environmentally sound energy sources to promote the availability of increased energy supplies to support sustainable development efforts, in particular in developing countries;

b.   Promote the development at the national level of appropriate methodologies for making integrated energy, environment and economic policy decisions for sustainable development, inter alia, through environmental impact assessments;

c.   Promote the research, development, transfer and use of improved energy-efficient technologies and practices, including endogenous technologies in all relevant sectors, giving special attention to the rehabilitation and modernization of power systems, with particular attention to developing countries;

d.   Promote the research, development, transfer and use of technologies and practices for environmentally sound energy systems, including new and renewable energy systems, with particular attention to developing countries;

e.   Promote the development of institutional, scientific, planning and management capacities, particularly in developing countries, to develop, produce and use increasingly efficient and less polluting forms of energy;

f.   Review current energy supply mixes to determine how the contribution of environmentally sound energy systems as a whole, particularly new and renewable energy systems, could be increased in an economically efficient manner, taking into account respective countries' unique social, physical, economic and political characteristics, and examining and implementing, where appropriate, measures to overcome any barriers to their development and use;

g.   Coordinate energy plans regionally and subregionally, where applicable, and study the feasibility of efficient distribution of environmentally sound energy from new and renewable energy sources;

h.  In accordance with national socio-economic development and environment priorities, evaluate and, as appropriate, promote cost-effective policies or programmes, including administrative, social and economic measures, in order to improve energy efficiency;

i.  Build capacity for energy planning and programme management in energy efficiency, as well as for the development, introduction, and promotion of new and renewable sources of energy;

j.  Promote appropriate energy efficiency and emission standards or recommendations at the national level, 2/ aimed at the development and use of technologies that minimize adverse impacts on the environment;

k.  Encourage education and awareness-raising programmes at the local, national, subregional and regional levels concerning energy efficiency and environmentally sound energy systems;

l.  Establish or enhance, as appropriate, in cooperation with the private sector, labelling programmes for products to provide decision makers and consumers with information on opportunities for energy efficiency.

## 2. Transportation

### Basis for action

9.13.   The transport sector has an essential and positive role to play in economic and social development, and transportation needs will undoubtedly increase. However, since the transport sector is also a source of atmospheric emissions, there is need for a review of existing transport systems and for more effective design and management of traffic and transport systems.

### Objectives

9.14.   The basic objective of this programme area is to develop and promote cost-effective policies or programmes, as appropriate, to limit, reduce or control, as appropriate, harmful emissions into the atmosphere and other adverse environmental effects of the transport sector, taking into account development priorities as well as the specific local and national circumstances and safety aspects.

### Activities

9.15.   Governments at the appropriate level, with the cooperation of the relevant United Nations bodies and, as appropriate, intergovernmental and non-governmental organizations, and the private sector, should:

a.  Develop and promote, as appropriate, cost-effective, more efficient, less polluting and safer transport systems, particularly integrated rural and urban mass transit, as well as environmentally sound road networks, taking into account the needs for sustainable social, economic and development priorities, particularly in developing countries;

b.  Facilitate at the international, regional, subregional and national levels access to and the transfer of safe, efficient, including resource-efficient, and less polluting transport technologies, particularly to the developing countries, including the implementation of appropriate training programmes;

c.  Strengthen, as appropriate, their efforts at collecting, analysing and exchanging relevant information on the relation between environment and transport, with particular emphasis on the systematic observation of emissions and the development of a transport database;

d.  In accordance with national socio-economic development and environment priorities, evaluate and, as appropriate, promote cost-effective policies or programmes, including administrative, social and economic measures, in order to encourage use of transportation modes that minimize adverse impacts on the atmosphere;

e.   Develop or enhance, as appropriate, mechanisms to integrate transport planning strategies and urban and regional settlement planning strategies, with a view to reducing the environmental impacts of transport;

f.   Study, within the framework of the United Nations and its regional commissions, the feasibility of convening regional conferences on transport and the environment.

### 3. Industrial development

**Basis for action**

9.16.   Industry is essential for the production of goods and services and is a major source of employment and income, and industrial development as such is essential for economic growth. At the same time, industry is a major resource and materials user and consequently industrial activities result in emissions into the atmosphere and the environment as a whole. Protection of the atmosphere can be enhanced, inter alia, by increasing resource and materials efficiency in industry, installing or improving pollution abatement technologies and replacing chlorofluorocarbons (CFCs) and other ozone-depleting substances with appropriate substitutes, as well as by reducing wastes and by-products.

**Objectives**

9.17.   The basic objective of this programme area is to encourage industrial development in ways that minimize adverse impacts on the atmosphere by, inter alia, increasing efficiency in the production and consumption by industry of all resources and materials, by improving pollution-abatement technologies and by developing new environmentally sound technologies.

**Activities**

9.18.   Governments at the appropriate level, with the cooperation of the relevant United Nations bodies and, as appropriate, intergovernmental and non-governmental organizations, and the private sector, should:

a.   In accordance with national socio-economic development and environment priorities, evaluate and, as appropriate, promote cost-effective policies or programmes, including administrative, social and economic measures, in order to minimize industrial pollution and adverse impacts on the atmosphere;

b.   Encourage industry to increase and strengthen its capacity to develop technologies, products and processes that are safe, less polluting and make more efficient use of all resources and materials, including energy;

c.   Cooperate in the development and transfer of such industrial technologies and in the development of capacities to manage and use such technologies, particularly with respect to developing countries;

d.   Develop, improve and apply environmental impact assessments to foster sustainable industrial development;

e.   Promote efficient use of materials and resources, taking into account the life cycles of products, in order to realize the economic and environmental benefits of using resources more efficiently and producing fewer wastes;

f.   Support the promotion of less polluting and more efficient technologies and processes in industries, taking into account area-specific accessible potentials for energy, particularly safe and renewable sources of energy, with a view to limiting industrial pollution, and adverse impacts on the atmosphere.

## 4. Terrestrial and marine resource development and land use

**Basis for action**

9.19.    Land-use and resource policies will both affect and be affected by changes in the atmosphere. Certain practices related to terrestrial and marine resources and land use can decrease greenhouse gas sinks and increase atmospheric emissions. The loss of biological diversity may reduce the resilience of ecosystems to climatic variations and air pollution damage. Atmospheric changes can have important impacts on forests, biodiversity, and freshwater and marine ecosystems, as well as on economic activities, such as agriculture. Policy objectives in different sectors may often diverge and will need to be handled in an integrated manner.

**Objectives**

9.20.    The objectives of this programme area are:

a.    To promote terrestrial and marine resource utilization and appropriate land-use practices that contribute to:

   i.    The reduction of atmospheric pollution and/or the limitation of anthropogenic emissions of greenhouse gases;

   ii.    The conservation, sustainable management and enhancement, where appropriate, of all sinks for greenhouse gases;

   iii.    The conservation and sustainable use of natural and environmental resources;

b.    To ensure that actual and potential atmospheric changes and their socio-economic and ecological impacts are fully taken into account in planning and implementing policies and programmes concerning terrestrial and marine resources utilization and land-use practices.

**Activities**

9.21.    Governments at the appropriate level, with the cooperation of the relevant United Nations bodies and, as appropriate, intergovernmental and non-governmental organizations, and the private sector, should:

a.    In accordance with national socio-economic development and environment priorities, evaluate and, as appropriate, promote cost-effective policies or programmes, including administrative, social and economic measures, in order to encourage environmentally sound land-use practices;

b.    Implement policies and programmes that will discourage inappropriate and polluting land-use practices and promote sustainable utilization of terrestrial and marine resources;

c.    Consider promoting the development and use of terrestrial and marine resources and land-use practices that will be more resilient to atmospheric changes and fluctuations;

d.    Promote sustainable management and cooperation in the conservation and enhancement, as appropriate, of sinks and reservoirs of greenhouse gases, including biomass, forests and oceans, as well as other terrestrial, coastal and marine ecosystems.

## C. Preventing stratospheric ozone depletion

**Basis for action**

9.22.    Analysis of recent scientific data has confirmed the growing concern about the continuing depletion of the Earth's stratospheric ozone layer by reactive chlorine and bromine from man-made CFCs, halons and related substances. While the 1985 Vienna Convention for the Protection of the

Ozone Layer and the 1987 Montreal Protocol on Substances that Deplete the Ozone Layer (as amended in London in 1990) were important steps in international action, the total chlorine loading of the atmosphere of ozone-depleting substances has continued to rise. This can be changed through compliance with the control measures identified within the Protocol.

**Objectives**

9.23.    The objectives of this programme area are:

    a.    To realize the objectives defined in the Vienna Convention and the Montreal Protocol and its 1990 amendments, including the consideration in those instruments of the special needs and conditions of the developing countries and the availability to them of alternatives to substances that deplete the ozone layer. Technologies and natural products that reduce demand for these substances should be encouraged;

    b.    To develop strategies aimed at mitigating the adverse effects of ultraviolet radiation reaching the Earth's surface as a consequence of depletion and modification of the stratospheric ozone layer.

**Activities**

9.24.    Governments at the appropriate level, with the cooperation of the relevant United Nations bodies and, as appropriate, intergovernmental and non-governmental organizations, and the private sector, should:

    a.    Ratify, accept or approve the Montreal Protocol and its 1990 amendments; pay their contributions towards the Vienna/Montreal trust funds and the interim multilateral ozone fund promptly; and contribute, as appropriate, towards ongoing efforts under the Montreal Protocol and its implementing mechanisms, including making available substitutes for CFCs and other ozone-depleting substances and facilitating the transfer of the corresponding technologies to developing countries in order to enable them to comply with the obligations of the Protocol;

    b.    Support further expansion of the Global Ozone Observing System by facilitating - through bilateral and multilateral funding - the establishment and operation of additional systematic observation stations, especially in the tropical belt in the southern hemisphere;

    c.    Participate actively in the continuous assessment of scientific information and the health and environmental effects, as well as of the technological/economic implications of stratospheric ozone depletion; and consider further actions that prove warranted and feasible on the basis of these assessments;

    d.    Based on the results of research on the effects of the additional ultraviolet radiation reaching the Earth's surface, consider taking appropriate remedial measures in the fields of human health, agriculture and marine environment;

    e.    Replace CFCs and other ozone-depleting substances, consistent with the Montreal Protocol, recognizing that a replacement's suitability should be evaluated holistically and not simply based on its contribution to solving one atmospheric or environmental problem.

### D. Transboundary atmospheric pollution

**Basis for action**

9.25.    Transboundary air pollution has adverse health impacts on humans and other detrimental environmental impacts, such as tree and forest loss and the acidification of water bodies. The geographical distribution of atmospheric pollution monitoring networks is uneven, with the developing countries severely underrepresented. The lack of reliable emissions data outside Europe and North America is a major constraint to measuring transboundary air pollution. There is also insufficient information on the environmental and health effects of air pollution in other regions.

9.26. The 1979 Convention on Long-range Transboundary Air Pollution, and its protocols, have established a regional regime in Europe and North America, based on a review process and cooperative programmes for systematic observation of air pollution, assessment and information exchange. These programmes need to be continued and enhanced, and their experience needs to be shared with other regions of the world.

**Objectives**

9.27. The objectives of this programme area are:

    a. To develop and apply pollution control and measurement technologies for stationary and mobile sources of air pollution and to develop alternative environmentally sound technologies;

    b. To observe and assess systematically the sources and extent of transboundary air pollution resulting from natural processes and anthropogenic activities;

    c. To strengthen the capabilities, particularly of developing countries, to measure, model and assess the fate and impacts of transboundary air pollution, through, inter alia, exchange of information and training of experts;

    d. To develop capabilities to assess and mitigate transboundary air pollution resulting from industrial and nuclear accidents, natural disasters and the deliberate and/or accidental destruction of natural resources;

    e. To encourage the establishment of new and the implementation of existing regional agreements for limiting transboundary air pollution;

    f. To develop strategies aiming at the reduction of emissions causing transboundary air pollution and their effects.

**Activities**

9.28. Governments at the appropriate level, with the cooperation of the relevant United Nations bodies and, as appropriate, intergovernmental and non-governmental organizations, the private sector and financial institutions, should:

    a. Establish and/or strengthen regional agreements for transboundary air pollution control and cooperate, particularly with developing countries, in the areas of systematic observation and assessment, modelling and the development and exchange of emission control technologies for mobile and stationary sources of air pollution. In this context, greater emphasis should be put on addressing the extent, causes, health and socio-economic impacts of ultraviolet radiation, acidification of the environment and photo-oxidant damage to forests and other vegetation;

    b. Establish or strengthen early warning systems and response mechanisms for transboundary air pollution resulting from industrial accidents and natural disasters and the deliberate and/or accidental destruction of natural resources;

    c. Facilitate training opportunities and exchange of data, information and national and/or regional experiences;

    d. Cooperate on regional, multilateral and bilateral bases to assess transboundary air pollution, and elaborate and implement programmes identifying specific actions to reduce atmospheric emissions and to address their environmental, economic, social and other effects.

**Means of implementation**

International and regional cooperation

9.29.    Existing legal instruments have created institutional structures which relate to the purposes of these instruments, and relevant work should primarily continue in those contexts. Governments should continue to cooperate and enhance their cooperation at the regional and global levels, including cooperation within the United Nations system. In this context reference is made to the recommendations in chapter 38 of Agenda 21 (International institutional arrangements).

Capacity-building

9.30.    Countries, in cooperation with the relevant United Nations bodies, international donors and non-governmental organizations, should mobilize technical and financial resources and facilitate technical cooperation with developing countries to reinforce their technical, managerial, planning and administrative capacities to promote sustainable development and the protection of the atmosphere, in all relevant sectors.

Human resource development

9.31.    Education and awareness-raising programmes concerning the promotion of sustainable development and the protection of the atmosphere need to be introduced and strengthened at the local, national and international levels in all relevant sectors.

Financial and cost evaluation

9.32.    The Conference secretariat has estimated the average total annual cost (1993-2000) of implementing the activities under programme area A to be about $640 million from the international community on grant or concessional terms. These are indicative and order-of-magnitude estimates only and have not been reviewed by Governments. Actual costs and financial terms, including any that are non-concessional, will depend upon, inter alia, the specific strategies and programmes Governments decide upon for implementation.

9.33.    The Conference secretariat has estimated the average total annual cost (1993-2000) of implementing the activities of the four-part programme under programme area B to be about $20 billion from the international community on grant or concessional terms. These are indicative and order-of-magnitude estimates only and have not been reviewed by Governments. Actual costs and financial terms, including any that are non-concessional, will depend upon, inter alia, the specific strategies and programmes Governments decide upon for implementation.

9.34.    The Conference secretariat has estimated the average total annual cost (1993-2000) of implementing the activities under programme area C to be in the range of $160-590 million on grant or concessional terms. These are indicative and order-of-magnitude estimates only and have not been reviewed by Governments. Actual costs and financial terms, including any that are non-concessional, will depend upon, inter alia, the specific strategies and programmes Governments decide upon for implementation.

9.35.    The Conference secretariat has included costing for technical assistance and pilot programmes under paragraphs 9.32 and 9.33.

**Notes**

1/ New and renewable energy sources are solar thermal, solar photovoltaic, wind, hydro, biomass, geothermal, ocean, animal and human power, as referred to in the reports of the Committee on the Development and Utilization of New and Renewable Sources of Energy, prepared specifically for the Conference (see A/CONF.151/PC/119 and A/AC.218/1992/5).

2/ This includes standards or recommendations promoted by regional economic integration organizations.

# Agenda 21 – Chapter 10
## INTEGRATED APPROACH TO THE PLANNING AND MANAGEMENT OF LAND RESOURCES

10.1. Land is normally defined as a physical entity in terms of its topography and spatial nature; a broader integrative view also includes natural resources: the soils, minerals, water and biota that the land comprises. These components are organized in ecosystems which provide a variety of services essential to the maintenance of the integrity of life-support systems and the productive capacity of the environment. Land resources are used in ways that take advantage of all these characteristics. Land is a finite resource, while the natural resources it supports can vary over time and according to management conditions and uses. Expanding human requirements and economic activities are placing ever increasing pressures on land resources, creating competition and conflicts and resulting in suboptimal use of both land and land resources. If, in the future, human requirements are to be met in a sustainable manner, it is now essential to resolve these conflicts and move towards more effective and efficient use of land and its natural resources. Integrated physical and land-use planning and management is an eminently practical way to achieve this. By examining all uses of land in an integrated manner, it makes it possible to minimize conflicts, to make the most efficient trade-offs and to link social and economic development with environmental protection and enhancement, thus helping to achieve the objectives of sustainable development. The essence of the integrated approach finds expression in the coordination of the sectoral planning and management activities concerned with the various aspects of land use and land resources.

10.2. The present chapter consists of one programme area, the integrated approach to the planning and management of land resources, which deals with the reorganization and, where necessary, some strengthening of the decision-making structure, including existing policies, planning and management procedures and methods that can assist in putting in place an integrated approach to land resources. It does not deal with the operational aspects of planning and management, which are more appropriately dealt with under the relevant sectoral programmes. Since the programme deals with an important cross-sectoral aspect of decision-making for sustainable development, it is closely related to a number of other programmes that deal with that issue directly.

## PROGRAMME AREA

### Integrated approach to the planning and management of land resources

**Basis for action**

10.3. Land resources are used for a variety of purposes which interact and may compete with one another; therefore, it is desirable to plan and manage all uses in an integrated manner. Integration should take place at two levels, considering, on the one hand, all environmental, social and economic factors (including, for example, impacts of the various economic and social sectors on the environment and natural resources) and, on the other, all environmental and resource components together (i.e., air, water, biota, land, geological and natural resources). Integrated consideration facilitates appropriate choices and trade-offs, thus maximizing sustainable productivity and use. Opportunities to allocate land to different uses arise in the course of major settlement or development projects or in a sequential fashion as lands become available on the market. This in turn provides opportunities to support traditional patterns of sustainable land management or to assign protected status for conservation of biological diversity or critical ecological services.

10.4. A number of techniques, frameworks and processes can be combined to facilitate an integrated approach. They are the indispensable support for the planning and management process, at the national and local level, ecosystem or area levels and for the development of specific plans of action. Many of its elements are already in place but need to be more widely applied, further developed and strengthened. This programme area is concerned primarily with providing a framework that will coordinate decision-making; the content and operational functions are therefore not included here but are dealt with in the relevant sectoral programmes of Agenda 21.

**Objectives**

10.5. The broad objective is to facilitate allocation of land to the uses that provide the greatest sustainable benefits and to promote the transition to a sustainable and integrated management of land resources. In doing so, environmental, social and economic issues should be taken into consideration. Protected areas, private property rights, the rights of indigenous people and their communities and other local communities and the economic role of women in agriculture and rural development, among other issues, should be taken into account. In more specific terms, the objectives are as follows:

    a. To review and develop policies to support the best possible use of land and the sustainable management of land resources, by not later than 1996;

    b. To improve and strengthen planning, management and evaluation systems for land and land resources, by not later than 2000;

    c. To strengthen institutions and coordinating mechanisms for land and land resources, by not later than 1998;

    d. To create mechanisms to facilitate the active involvement and participation of all concerned, particularly communities and people at the local level, in decision-making on land use and management, by not later than 1996.

**Activities**

(a) Management-related activities

Developing supportive policies and policy instruments

10.6. Governments at the appropriate level, with the support of regional and international organizations, should ensure that policies and policy instruments support the best possible land use and sustainable management of land resources. Particular attention should be given to the role of agricultural land. To do this, they should:

    a. Develop integrated goal-setting and policy formulation at the national, regional and local levels that takes into account environmental, social, demographic and economic issues;

    b. Develop policies that encourage sustainable land use and management of land resources and take the land resource base, demographic issues and the interests of the local population into account;

    c. Review the regulatory framework, including laws, regulations and enforcement procedures, in order to identify improvements needed to support sustainable land use and management of land resources and restricts the transfer of productive arable land to other uses;

    d. Apply economic instruments and develop institutional mechanisms and incentives to encourage the best possible land use and sustainable management of land resources;

    e. Encourage the principle of delegating policy-making to the lowest level of public authority consistent with effective action and a locally driven approach.

Strengthening planning and management systems

10.7. Governments at the appropriate level, with the support of regional and international organizations, should review and, if appropiate, revise planning and management systems to facilitate an integrated approach. To do this, they should:

   a. Adopt planning and management systems that facilitate the integration of environmental components such as air, water, land and other natural resources, using landscape ecological planning (LANDEP) or other approaches that focus on, for example, an ecosystem or a watershed;

   b. Adopt strategic frameworks that allow the integration of both developmental and environmental goals; examples of these frameworks include sustainable livelihood systems, rural development, the World Conservation Strategy/Caring for the Earth, primary environmental care (PEC) and others;

   c. Establish a general framework for land-use and physical planning within which specialized and more detailed sectoral plans (e.g., for protected areas, agriculture, forests, human settlements, rural development) can be developed; establish intersectoral consultative bodies to streamline project planning and implementation;

   d. Strengthen management systems for land and natural resources by including appropriate traditional and indigenous methods; examples of these practices include pastoralism, Hema reserves (traditional Islamic land reserves) and terraced agriculture;

   e. Examine and, if necessary, establish innovative and flexible approaches to programme funding;

   f. Compile detailed land capability inventories to guide sustainable land resources allocation, management and use at the national and local levels.

Promoting application of appropriate tools for planning and management

10.8. Governments at the appropriate level, with the support of national and international organizations, should promote the improvement, further development and widespread application of planning and management tools that facilitate an integrated and sustainable approach to land and resources. To do this, they should:

   a. Adopt improved systems for the interpretation and integrated analysis of data on land use and land resources;

   b. Systematically apply techniques and procedures for assessing the environmental, social and economic impacts, risks, costs and benefits of specific actions;

   c. Analyse and test methods to include land and ecosystem functions and land resources values in national accounts.

Raising awareness

10.9. Governments at the appropriate level, in collaboration with national institutions and interest groups and with the support of regional and international organizations, should launch awareness-raising campaigns to alert and educate people on the importance of integrated land and land resources management and the role that individuals and social groups can play in it. This should be accompanied by provision of the means to adopt improved practices for land use and sustainable management.

Promoting public participation

10.10. Governments at the appropriate level, in collaboration with national organizations and with the support of regional and international organizations, should establish innovative procedures, programmes, projects and services that facilitate and encourage the active participation of those affected in the decision-making and implementation process, especially of groups that have, hitherto, often been excluded, such as women, youth, indigenous people and their communities and other local communities.

(b) Data and information

Strengthening information systems

10.11.    Governments at the appropriate level, in collaboration with national institutions and the private sector and with the support of regional and international organizations, should strengthen the information systems necessary for making decisions and evaluating future changes on land use and management. The needs of both men and women should be taken into account. To do this, they should:

a.    Strengthen information, systematic observation and assessment systems for environmental, economic and social data related to land resources at the global, regional, national and local levels and for land capability and land-use and management patterns;

b.    Strengthen coordination between existing sectoral data systems on land and land resources and strengthen national capacity to gather and assess data;

c.    Provide the appropriate technical information necessary for informed decision-making on land use and management in an accessible form to all sectors of the population, especially to local communities and women;

d.    Support low-cost, community-managed systems for the collection of comparable information on the status and processes of change of land resources, including soils, forest cover, wildlife, climate and other elements.

(c) International and regional coordination and cooperation Establishing regional machinery

10.12.    Governments at the appropriate level, with the support of regional and international organizations, should strengthen regional cooperation and exchange of information on land resources. To do this, they should:

a.    Study and design regional policies to support programmes for land-use and physical planning;

b.    Promote the development of land-use and physical plans in the countries of the region;

c.    Design information systems and promote training;

d.    Exchange, through networks and other appropriate means, information on experiences with the process and results of integrated and participatory planning and management of land resources at the national and local levels.

**Means of implementation**

(a) Financing and cost evaluation

10.13.    The Conference secretariat has estimated the average total annual cost (1993-2000) of implementing the activities of this programme to be about $50 million from the international community on grant or concessional terms. These are indicative and order-of-magnitude estimates only and have not been reviewed by Governments. Actual costs and financial terms, including any that are non-concessional, will depend upon, inter alia, the specific strategies and programmes Governments decide upon for implementation.

(b) Scientific and technological means

Enhancing scientific understanding of the land resources system

10.14.     Governments at the appropriate level, in collaboration wit h the national and international scientific community and with the support of appropriate national and international organizations, should promote and support research, tailored to local environments, on the land resources system and the implications for sustainable development and management practices. Priority should be given, as appropriate, to:

      a. Assessment of land potential capability and ecosystem functions;

      b. Ecosystemic interactions and interactions between land resources and social, economic and environmental systems;

      c. Developing indicators of sustainability for land resources, taking into account environmental, economic, social, demographic, cultural and political factors.

Testing research findings through pilot projects

10.15.     Governments at the appropriate level, in collaboration with the national and international scientific community and with the support of the relevant international organizations, should research and test, through pilot projects, the applicability of improved approaches to the integrated planning and management of land resources, including technical, social and institutional factors.

(c) Human resource development

Enhancing education and training

10.16.     Governments at the appropriate level, in collaboration with the appropriate local authorities, non-governmental organizations and international institutions, should promote the development of the human resources that are required to plan and manage land and land resources sustainably. This should be done by providing incentives for local initiatives and by enhancing local management capacity, particularly of women, through:

      a. Emphasizing interdisciplinary and integrative approaches in the curricula of schools and technical, vocational and university training;

      b. Training all relevant sectors concerned to deal with land resources in an integrated and sustainable manner;

      c. Training communities, relevant extension services, community-based groups and non-governmental organizations on land management techniques and approaches applied successfully elsewhere.

(d) Capacity-building Strengthening technological capacity

10.17.     Governments at the appropriate level, in cooperation with other Governments and with the support of relevant international organizations, should promote focused and concerted efforts for education and training and the transfer of techniques and technologies that support the various aspects of the sustainable planning and management process at the national, state/provincial and local levels.

Strengthening institutions

10.18.     Governments at t he appropriate level, with the support of appropriate international organizations, should:

      a. Review and, where appropriate, revise the mandates of institutions that deal with land and natural resources to include explicitly the interdisciplinary integration of environmental, social and economic issues;

b. Strengthen coordinating mechanisms between institutions that deal with land-use and resources management to facilitate integration of sectoral concerns and strategies;

c. Strengthen local decision-making capacity and improve coordination with higher levels.

# Agenda 21 – Chapter 11
# COMBATING DEFORESTATION

## PROGRAMME AREAS
## A. Sustaining the multiple roles and functions of all types of forests, forest lands and woodlands

### Basis for action

11.1. There are major weaknesses in the policies, methods and mechanisms adopted to support and develop the multiple ecological, economic, social and cultural roles of trees, forests and forest lands. Many developed countries are confronted with the effects of air pollution and fire damage on their forests. More effective measures and approaches are often required at the national level to improve and harmonize policy formulation, planning and programming; legislative measures and instruments; development patterns; participation of the general public, especially women and indigenous people; involvement of youth; roles of the private sector, local organizations, non-governmental organizations and cooperatives; development of technical and multidisciplinary skills and quality of human resources; forestry extension and public education; research capability and support; administrative structures and mechanisms, including intersectoral coordination, decentralization and responsibility and incentive systems; and dissemination of information and public relations. This is especially important to ensure a rational and holistic approach to the sustainable and environmentally sound development of forests. The need for securing the multiple roles of forests and forest lands through adequate and appropriate institutional strengthening has been repeatedly emphasized in many of the reports, decisions and recommendations of FAO, ITTO, UNEP, the World Bank, IUCN and other organizations.

### Objectives

11.2. The objectives of this programme area are as follows:

   a. To strengthen forest-related national institutions, to enhance the scope and effectiveness of activities related to the management, conservation and sustainable development of forests, and to effectively ensure the sustainable utilization and production of forests' goods and services in both the developed and the developing countries; by the year 2000, to strengthen the capacities and capabilities of national institutions to enable them to acquire the necessary knowledge for the protection and conservation of forests, as well as to expand their scope and, correspondingly, enhance the effectiveness of programmes and activities related to the management and development of forests;

   b. To strengthen and improve human, technical and professional skills, as well as expertise and capabilities to effectively formulate and implement policies, plans, programmes, research and projects on management, conservation and sustainable development of all types of forests and forest-based resources, and forest lands inclusive, as well as other areas from which forest benefits can be derived.

### Activities
(a) Management-related activities

11.3 Governments at the appropriate level, with the support of regional, subregional and international organizations, should, where necessary, enhance institutional capability to promote the multiple roles and functions of all types of forests and vegetation inclusive of other related lands and forest-based resources in supporting sustainable development and environmental conservation in all sectors. This should be done, wherever possible and necessary, by strengthening and/or modifying the existing structures and arrangements, and by improving cooperation and coordination of their respective roles. Some of the major activities in this regard are as follows:

   a. Rationalizing and strengthening administrative structures and mechanisms, including provision of adequate levels of staff and allocation of responsibilities, decentralization of decision-making, provision of infrastructural facilities and equipment, intersectoral coordination and an effective system of communication;

b. Promoting participation of the private sector, labour unions, rural cooperatives, local communities, indigenous people, youth, women, user groups and non-governmental organizations in forest-related activities, and access to information and training programmes within the national context;

c. Reviewing and, if necessary, revising measures and programmes relevant to all types of forests and vegetation, inclusive of other related lands and forest-based resources, and relating them to other land uses and development policies and legislation; promoting adequate legislation and other measures as a basis against uncontrolled conversion to other types of land uses;

d. Developing and implementing plans and programmes, including definition of national and, if necessary, regional and subregional goals, programmes and criteria for their implementation and subsequent improvement;

e. Establishing, developing and sustaining an effective system of forest extension and public education to ensure better awareness, appreciation and management of forests with regard to the multiple roles and values of trees, forests and forest lands;

f. Establishing and/or strengthening institutions for forest education and training, as well as forestry industries, for developing an adequate cadre of trained and skilled staff at the professional, technical and vocational levels, with emphasis on youth and women;

g. Establishing and strengthening capabilities for research related to the different aspects of forests and forest products, for example, on the sustainable management of forests, research on biodiversity, on the effects of air-borne pollutants, on traditional uses of forest resources by local populations and indigenous people, and on improving market returns and other non-market values from the management of forests.

(b) Data and information

11.4. Governments at the appropriate level, with the assistance and cooperation of international, regional, subregional and bilateral agencies, where relevant, should develop adequate databases and baseline information necessary for planning and programme evaluation. Some of the more specific activities include the following:

a. Collecting, compiling and regularly updating and distributing information on land classification and land use, including data on forest cover, areas suitable for afforestation, endangered species, ecological values, traditional/indigenous land use values, biomass and productivity, correlating demographic, socio-economic and forest resources information at the micro- and macro-levels, and undertaking periodic analyses of forest programmes;

b. Establishing linkages with other data systems and sources relevant to supporting forest management, conservation and development, while further developing or reinforcing existing systems such as geographic information systems, as appropriate;

c. Creating mechanisms to ensure public access to this information.

(c) International and regional cooperation and coordination

11.5. Governments at the appropriate level and institutions should cooperate in the provision of expertise and other support and the promotion of international research efforts, in particular with a view to enhancing transfer of technology and specialized training and ensuring access to experiences and research results. There is need for strengthening coordination and improving the performance of existing forest-related international organizations in providing technical cooperation and support to interested countries for the management, conservation and sustainable development of forests.

**Means of implementation**

(a) Financial and cost evaluation

11.6. The secretariat of the Conference has estimated the average total annual cost (1993-2000) of implementing the activities of this programme to be about $2.5 billion, including about $860 million from the international community on grant or concessional terms. These are indicative and order-of-magnitude estimates only and have not been reviewed by Governments. Actual costs and financial terms, including any that are non-concessional, will depend upon, inter alia, the specific strategies and programmes Governments decide upon for implementation.

(b) Scientific and technological means

11.7. The planning, research and training activities specified will form the scientific and technological means for implementing the programme, as well as its output. The systems, methodology and know-how generated by the programme will help improve efficiency. Some of the specific steps involved should include:

    a. Analysing achievements, constraints and social issues for supporting programme formulation and implementation;

    b. Analysing research problems and research needs, research planning and implementation of specific research projects;

    c. Assessing needs for human resources, skill development and training;

    d. Developing, testing and applying appropriate methodologies/approaches in implementing forest programmes and plans.

(c) Human resource development

11.8. The specific components of forest education and training will effectively contribute to human resource development. These include:

    a. Launching of graduate and post-graduate degree, specialization and research programmes;

    b. Strengthening of pre-service, in-service and extension service training programmes at the technical and vocational levels, including training of trainers/teachers, and developing curriculum and teaching materials/methods;

    c. Special training for staff of national forest-related organizations in aspects such as project formulation, evaluation and periodical evaluations.

(d) Capacity-building

11.9. This programme area is specifically concerned with capacity-building in the forest sector and all programme activities specified contribute to that end. In building new and strengthened capacities, full advantage should be taken of the existing systems and experience.

**B. Enhancing the protection, sustainable management and conservation of all forests, and the greening of degraded areas, through forest rehabilitation, afforestation, reforestation and other rehabilitative means**

**Basis for action**

11.10.    Forests world wide have been and are being threatened by uncontrolled degradation and conversion to other types of land uses, influenced by increasing human needs; agricultural expansion; and environmentally harmful mismanagement, including, for example, lack of adequate forest-fire control and anti-poaching measures, unsustainable commercial logging, overgrazing and unregulated browsing, harmful effects of airborne pollutants, economic incentives and other measures taken by other sectors of the economy. The impacts of loss and degradation of forests are in the form of soil erosion; loss of biological diversity, damage to wildlife habitats and degradation of watershed areas, deterioration of the quality of life and reduction of the options for development.

11.11.    The present situation calls for urgent and consistent action for conserving and sustaining forest resources. The greening of suitable areas, in all its component activities, is an effective way of increasing public awareness and participation in protecting and managing forest resources. It should include the consideration of land use and tenure patterns and local needs and should spell out and clarify the specific objectives of the different types of greening activities.

**Objectives**

11.12.    The objectives of this programme area are as follows:

a.    To maintain existing forests through conservation and management, and sustain and expand areas under forest and tree cover, in appropriate areas of both developed and developing countries, through the conservation of natural forests, protection, forest rehabilitation, regeneration, afforestation, reforestation and tree planting, with a view to maintaining or restoring the ecological balance and expanding the contribution of forests to human needs and welfare;

b.    To prepare and implement, as appropriate, national forestry action programmes and/or plans for the management, conservation and sustainable development of forests. These programmes and/or plans should be integrated with other land uses. In this context, country-driven national forestry action programmes and/or plans under the Tropical Forestry Action Programme are currently being implemented in more than 80 countries, with the support of the international community;

c.    To ensure sustainable management and, where appropriate, conservation of existing and future forest resources;

d.    To maintain and increase the ecological, biological, climatic, socio-cultural and economic contributions of forest resources;

e.    To facilitate and support the effective implementation of the non-legally binding authoritative statement of principles for a global consensus on the management, conservation and sustainable development of all types of forests, adopted by the United Nations Conference on Environment and Development, and on the basis of the implementation of these principles to consider the need for and the feasibility of all kinds of appropriate internationally agreed arrangements to promote international cooperation on forest management, conservation and sustainable development of all types of forests, including afforestation, reforestation and rehabilitation.

**Activities**

(a) Management-related activities

11.13.    Governments should recognize the importance of categorizing forests, within the framework of long-t erm forest conservation and management policies, into different forest types and setting up sustainable units in every region/watershed with a view to securing the conservation of forests. Governments, with the participation of the private sector, non-governmental organizations, local community groups, indigenous people, women, local government units and the public at large, should act to maintain and expand the existing vegetative cover wherever ecologically, socially and economically feasible, through technical cooperation and other forms of support. Major activities to be considered include:

a. Ensuring the sustainable management of all forest ecosystems and woodlands, through improved proper planning, management and timely implementation of silvicultural operations, including inventory and relevant research, as well as rehabilitation of degraded natural forests to restore productivity and environmental contributions, giving particular attention to human needs for economic and ecological services, wood-based energy, agroforestry, non-timber forest products and services, watershed and soil protection, wildlife management, and forest genetic resources;

b. Establishing, expanding and managing, as appropriate to each national context, protected area systems, which includes systems of conservation units for their environmental, social and spiritual functions and values, including conservation of forests in representative ecological systems and landscapes, primary old-growth forests, conservation and management of wildlife, nomination of World Heritage Sites under the World Heritage Convention, as appropriate, conservation of genetic resources, involving in situ and ex situ measures and undertaking supportive measures to ensure sustainable utilization of biological resources and conservation of biological diversity and the traditional forest habitats of indigenous people, forest dwellers and local communities;

c. Undertaking and promoting buffer and transition zone management;

d. Carrying out revegetation in appropriate mountain areas, highlands, bare lands, degraded farm lands, arid and semi-arid lands and coastal areas for combating desertification and preventing erosion problems and for other protective functions and national programmes for rehabilitation of degraded lands, including community forestry, social forestry, agroforestry and silvipasture, while also taking into account the role of forests as national carbon reservoirs and sinks;

e. Developing industrial and non-industrial planted forests in order to support and promote national ecologically sound afforestation and reforestation/regeneration programmes in suitable sites, including upgrading of existing planted forests of both industrial and non-industrial and commercial purpose to increase their contribution to human needs and to offset pressure on primary/old growth forests. Measures should be taken to promote and provide intermediate yields and to improve the rate of returns on investments in planted forests, through interplanting and underplanting valuable crops;

f. Developing/strengthening a national and/or master plan for planted forests as a priority, indicating, inter alia, the location, scope and species, and specifying areas of existing planted forests requiring rehabilitation, taking into account the economic aspect for future planted forest development, giving emphasis to native species;

g. Increasing the protection of forests from pollutants, fire, pests and diseases and other human-made interferences such as forest poaching, mining and unmitigated shifting cultivation, the uncontrolled introduction of exotic plant and animal species, as well as developing and accelerating research for a better understanding of problems relating to the management and regeneration of all types of forests; strengthening and/or establishing appropriate measures to assess and/or check inter-border movement of plants and related materials;

h. Stimulating development of urban forestry for the greening of urban, peri-urban and rural human settlements for amenity, recreation and production purposes and for protecting trees and groves;

i. Launching or improving opportunities for particpation of all people, including youth, women, indigenous people and local communities in the formulation, development and implementation of forest-related programmes and other activities, taking due account of the local needs and cultural values;

j.    Limiting and aiming to halt destructive shifting cultivation by addressing the underlying social and ecological causes.

(b) Data and information

11.14.   Management-related activities should involve collection, compilation and analysis of data/information, including baseline surveys. Some of the specific activities include the following:

a.    Carrying out surveys and developing and implementing land-use plans for appropriate greening/planting/afforestation/reforestation/forest rehabilitation;

b.    Consolidating and updating land-use and forest inventory and management information for management and land-use planning of wood and non-wood resources, including data on shifting cultivation and other agents of forest destruction;

c.    Consolidating information on genetic resources and related biotechnology, including surveys and studies, as necessary;

d.    Carrying out surveys and research on local/indigenous knowledge of trees and forests and their uses to improve the planning and implementation of sustainable forest management;

e.    Compiling and analysing research data on species/site interaction of species used in planted forests and assessing the potential impact on forests of climatic change, as well as effects of forests on climate, and initiating in-depth studies on the carbon cycle relating to different forest types to provide scientific advice and technical support;

f.    Establishing linkages with other data/information sources that relate to sustainable management and use of forests and improving access to data and information;

g.    Developing and intensifying research to improve knowledge and understanding of problems and natural mechanisms related to the management and rehabilitation of forests, including research on fauna and its interrelation with forests;

h.    Consolidating information on forest conditions and site-influencing immissions and emissions.

(c) International and regional cooperation and coordination

11.15.   The greening of appropriate areas is a task of global importance and impact. The international and regional community should provide technical cooperation and other means for this programme area. Specific activities of an international nature, in support of national efforts, should include the following:

a.    Increasing cooperative actions to reduce pollutants and trans-boundary impacts affecting the health of trees and forests and conservation of representative ecosystems;

b.    Coordinating regional and subregional research on carbon sequestration, air pollution and other environmental issues;

c.    Documenting and exchanging information/experience for the benefit of countries with similar problems and prospects;

d.    Strengthening the coordination and improving the capacity and ability of intergovernmental organizations such as FAO, ITTO, UNEP and UNESCO to provide technical support for the management, conservation and sustainable development of forests, including support for the negotiation of the International Tropical Timber Agreement of 1983, due in 1992/93.

**Means of implementation**

(a) Financial and cost evaluation

11.16.    The secretariat of the Conference has estimated the average total annual cost (1993-2000) of implementing the activities of this programme to be about $10 billion, including about $3.7 billion from the international community on grant or concessional terms. These are indicative and order-of-magnitude estimates only and have not been reviewed by Governments. Actual costs and financial terms, including any that are non-concessional, will depend upon, inter alia, the specific strategies and programmes Governments decide upon for implementation.

(b) Scientific and technological means

11.17.    Data analysis, planning, research, transfer/development of technology and/or training activities form an integral part of the programme activities, providing the scientific and technological means of implementation. National institutions should:

    a.    Develop feasibility studies and operational planning related to major forest activities;

    b.    Develop and apply environmentally sound technology relevant to the various activities listed;

    c.    Increase action related to genetic improvement and application of biotechnology for improving productivity and tolerance to environmental stress and including, for example, tree breeding, seed t echnology, seed procurement networks, germ-plasm banks, "in vitro" techniques, and in situ and ex situ conservation.

(c) Human resource development

11.18.    Essential means for effectively implementing the activities include training and development of appropriate skills, working facilities and conditions, public motivation and awareness. Specific activities include:

    a.    Providing specialized training in planning, management, environmental conservation, biotechnology etc.;

    b.    Establishing demonstration areas to serve as models and training facilities;

    c.    Supporting local organizations, communities, non-governmental organizations and private land owners, in particular women, youth, farmers and indigenous people/shifting cultivators, through extension and provision of inputs and training.

(d) Capacity-building

11.19.    National Governments, the private sector, local organizations/communities, indigenous people, labour unions and non-governmental organizations should develop capacities, duly supported by relevant international organizations, to implement the programme activities. Such capacities should be developed and strengthened in harmony with the programme activities. Capacity-building activities include policy and legal frameworks, national institution building, human resource development, development of research and technology, development of infrastructure, enhancement of public awareness etc.

### C. Promoting efficient utilization and assessment to recover the full valuation of the goods and services provided by forests, forest lands and woodlands

**Basis for action**

11.20.    The vast potential of forests and forest lands as a major resource for development is not yet fully realized. The improved management of forests can increase the production of goods and services and, in particular, the yield of wood and non-wood forest products, thus helping to generate additional employment and income, additional value through processing and trade of forest products, increased contribution to foreign exchange earnings, and increased return on investment. Forest resources, being renewable, can be sustainably managed in a manner that is compatible with environmental conservation. The implications of the harvesting of forest resources for the other values of the forest should be taken fully into consideration in the development of forest policies. It is also possible to increase the value of forests through non-damaging uses such as eco-tourism and the managed supply of genetic materials. Concerted action is needed in order to increase people's perception of the value of forests and of the benefits they provide. The survival of forests and their continued contribution to human welfare depends to a great extent on succeeding in this endeavour.

## Objectives

11.21.　The objectives of this programme area are as follows:

    a.　To improve recognition of the social, economic and ecological values of trees, forests and forest lands, including the consequences of the damage caused by the lack of forests; to promote methodologies with a view to incorporating social, economic and ecological values of trees, forests and forest lands into the national economic accounting systems; to ensure their sustainable management in a way that is consistent with land use, environmental considerations and development needs;

    b.　To promote efficient, rational and sustainable utilization of all types of forests and vegetation inclusive of other related lands and forest-based resources, through the development of efficient forest-based processing industries, value-adding secondary processing and trade in forest products, based on sustainably managed forest resources and in accordance with plans that integrate all wood and non-wood values of forests;

    c.　To promote more efficient and sustainable use of forests and trees for fuelwood and energy supplies;

    d.　To promote more comprehensive use and economic contributions of forest areas by incorporating eco-tourism into forest management and planning.

## Activities

(a) Management-related activities

11.22.　Governments, with the support of the private sector, scientific institutions, indigenous people, non-governmental organizations, cooperatives and entrepreneurs, where appropriate, should undertake the following activities, properly coordinated at the national level, with financial and technical cooperation from int ernational organizations:

    a.　Carrying out detailed investment studies, supply-demand harmonization and environmental impact analysis to rationalize and improve trees and forest utilization and to develop and establish appropriate incentive schemes and regulatory measures, including tenurial arrangements, to provide a favourable investment climate and promote better management;

    b.　Formulating scientifically sound criteria and guidelines for the management, conservation and sustainable development of all types of forests;

    c.　Improving environmentally sound methods and practices of forest harvesting, which are ecologically sound and economically viable, including planning and management, improved use of equipment, storage and transportation to reduce and, if possible, maximize the use of waste and improve value of both wood and non-wood forest products;

    d.　Promoting the better use and development of natural forests and woodlands, including planted forests, wherever possible, through appropriate and environmentally sound and economically viable activities, including silvicultural practices and management of other plant and animal species;

e. Promoting and supporting the downstream processing of forest products to increase retained value and other benefits;

f. Promoting/popularizing non-wood forest products and other forms of forest resources, apart from fuelwood (e.g., medicinal plants, dyes, fibres, gums, resins, fodder, cultural products, rattan, bamboo) through programmes and social forestry/participatory forest activities, including research on their processing and uses;

g. Developing, expanding and/or improving the effectiveness and efficiency of forest-based processing industries, both wood and non-wood based, involving such aspects as efficient conversion technology and improved sustainable utilization of harvesting and process residues; promoting underutilized species in natural forests through research, demonstration and commercialization; promoting value-adding secondary processing for improved employment, income and ret ained value; and promoting/improving markets for, and trade in, forest products through relevant institutions, policies and facilities;

h. Promoting and supporting the management of wildlife, as well as eco-tourism, including farming, and encouraging and supporting the husbandry and cultivation of wild species, for improved rural income and employment, ensuring economic and social benefits without harmful ecological impacts;

i. Promoting appropriate small-scale forest-based enterprises for supporting rural development and local entrepreneurship;

j. Improving and promoting methodologies for a comprehensive assessment that will capture the full value of forests, with a view to including that value in the market-based pricing structure of wood and non-wood based products;

k. Harmonizing sustainable development of forests with national development needs and trade policies that are compatible with the ecologically sound use of forest resources, using, for example, the ITTO Guidelines for Sustainable Management of Tropical Forests;

l. Developing, adopting and strengthening national programmes for accounting the economic and non-economic value of forests.

(b) Data and information

11.23. The objectives and management -related activities presuppose data and information analysis, feas ibility studies, market surveys and review of technological information. Some of the relevant activities include:

a. Undertaking analysis of supply and demand for forest products and services, to ensure efficiency in their utilization, wherever necessary;

b. Carrying out investment analysis and feasibility studies, including environmental impact assessment, for establishing forest-based processing enterprises;

c. Conducting research on the properties of currently underutilized species for their promotion and commercialization;

d. Supporting market surveys of forest products for trade promotion and intelligence;

e. Facilitating the provision of adequate technological information as a measure to promote better utilization of forest resources.

(c) International and regional cooperation and coordination

11.24. Cooperation and assistance of international organizations and the international community in technology transfer, specialization and promotion of fair terms of trade, without resorting to unilateral restrictions and/or bans on forest products contrary to GATT and other multilateral trade agreements, the application of appropriate market mechanisms and incentives will help in addressing global environmental concerns. Strengthening the coordination and performance of existing international organizations, in particular FAO, UNIDO, UNESCO, UNEP, ITC/UNCTAD/GATT, ITTO and ILO, for providing technical assistance and guidance in this programme area is another specific activity.

**Means of implementation**

(a) Financial and cost evaluation

11.25. The secretariat of the Conference has estimated the average total annual cost (1993-2000) of implementing the activities of this programme to be about $18 billion, including about $880 million from the international community on grant or concessional terms. These are indicative and order-of-magnitude estimates only and have not been reviewed by Governments. Actual costs and financial terms, including any that are non-concessional, will depend upon, inter alia, the specific strategies and programmes Governments decide upon for implementation.

(b) Scientific and technological means

11.26. The programme activities presuppose major research efforts and studies, as well as improvement of technology. This should be coordinated by national Governments, in collaboration with and supported by relevant international organizations and institutions. Some of the specific components include:

    a. Research on properties of wood and non-wood products and their uses, to promote improved utilization;

    b. Development and application of environmentally sound and less-polluting technology for forest utilization;

    c. Models and techniques of outlook analysis and development planning;

    d. Scientific investigations on the development and utilization of non-timber forest products;

    e. Appropriate methodologies to comprehensively assess the value of forests.

(c) Human resource development

11.27. The success and effectiveness of the programme area depends on the availability of skilled personnel. Specialized training is an important factor in this regard. New emphasis should be given to the incorporation of women. Human resource development for programme implementation, in quantitative and qualitative terms, should include:

    a. Developing required specialized skills to implement the programme, including establishing special training facilities at all levels;

    b. Introducing/strengthening refresher training courses, including fellowships and study tours, to update skills and technological know-how and improve productivity;

    c. Strengthening capability for research, planning, economic analysis, periodical evaluations and evaluation, relevant to improved utilization of forest resources;

    d. Promoting efficiency and capability of private and cooperative sectors through provision of facilities and incentives.

(d) Capacity-building

11.28.    Capacity-building, including strengthening of existing capacity, is implicit in the programme activities. Improving administration, policy and plans, national institutions, human resources, research and scientific capabilities, technology development, and periodical evaluations and evaluation are important components of capacity-building.

## D. Establishing and/or strengthening capacities for the planning, assessment and systematic observations of forests and related programmes, projects and activities, including commercial trade and processes

**Basis for action**

11.29.    Assessment and systematic observations are essential components of long-term planning, for evaluating effects, quantitatively and qualitatively, and for rectifying inadequacies. This mechanism, however, is one of the often neglected aspects of forest resources, management, conservation and development. In many cases, even the basic information related to the area and type of forests, existing potential and volume of harvest is lacking. In many developing countries, there is a lack of structures and mechanisms to carry out these functions. There is an urgent need to rectify this situation for a better understanding of the role and importance of forests and to realistically plan for their effective conservation, management, regeneration, and sustainable development.

**Objectives**

11.30.    The objectives of this programme area are as follows:

a.    To strengthen or establish systems for the assessment and systematic observations of forests and forest lands with a view to assessing the impacts of programmes, projects and activities on the quality and extent of forest resources, land available for afforestation, and land tenure, and to integrate the systems in a continuing process of research and in-depth analysis, while ensuring necessary modifications and improvements for planning and decision-making. Specific emphasis should be given to the participation of rural people in these processes;

b.    To provide economists, planners, decision makers and local communities with sound and adequate updated information on forests and forest land resources.

**Activities**

(a) Management-related activities

11.31.    Governments and institutions, in collaboration, where necessary, with appropriate international agencies and organizations, universities and non-governmental organizations, should undertake assessments and systematic observations of forests and related programmes and processes with a view to their continuous improvement. This should be linked to related activities of research and management and, wherever possible, be built upon existing systems. Major activities to be considered are:

a.    Assessing and carrying out systematic observations of the quantitative and qualitative situation and changes of forest cover and forest resources endowments, including land classification, land use and updates of its status, at the appropriate national level, and linking this activity, as appropriate, with planning as a basis for policy and programme formulation;

b.    Establishing national assessment and systematic observation systems and evaluation of programmes and processes, including establishment of definitions, standards, norms and intercalibration methods, and the capability for initiating corrective actions as well as improving the formulation and implementation of programmes and projects;

      c.    Making estimates of impacts of activities affecting forestry developments and conservation proposals, in terms of key variables such as developmental goals, benefits and costs, contributions of forests to other sectors, community welfare, environmental conditions and biological diversity and their impacts at the local, regional and global levels, where appropriate, to assess the changing technological and financial needs of countries;

      d.    Developing national systems of forest resource assessment and valuation, including necessary research and data analysis, which account for, where possible, the full range of wood and non-wood forest products and services, and incorporating results in plans and strategies and, where feasible, in national systems of accounts and planning;

      e.    Establishing necessary intersectoral and programme linkages, including improved access to information, in order to support a holistic approach to planning and programming.

(b) Data and information

11.32.    Reliable data and information are vital to this programme area. National Governments, in collaboration, where necessary, with relevant international organizations, should, as appropriate, undertake to improve data and information continuously and to ensure its exchange. Major activities to be considered are as follows:

      a.    Collecting, consolidating and exchanging existing information and establishing baseline information on aspects relevant to this programme area;

      b.    Harmonizing the methodologies for programmes involving data and information activities to ensure accuracy and consistency;

      c.    Undertaking special surveys on, for example, land capability and suitability for afforestation action;

      d.    Enhancing research support and improving access to and exchange of research results.

(c) International and regional cooperation and coordination

11.33.    The international community should extend to the Governments concerned necessary technical and financial support for implementing this programme area, including consideration of the following activities:

      a.    Establishing conceptual framework and formulating acceptable criteria, norms and definitions for systematic observations and assessment of forest resources;

      b.    Establishing and strengthening national institutional coordination mechanisms for forest assessment and systematic observation activities;

      c.    Strengthening existing regional and global networks for the exchange of relevant information;

      d.    Strengthening the capacity and ability and improving the performance of existing international organizations, such as the Consultative Group on International Agricultural Research (CGIAR), FAO, ITTO, UNEP, UNESCO and UNIDO, to provide technical support and guidance in this programme area.

**Means of implementation**

(a) Financial and cost evaluation

11.34.    The secretariat of the Conference has estimated the average total annual cost (1993-2000) of implementing the activities of this programme to be about $750 million, including about $230 million from the international community on grant or concessional terms. These are indicative and order-of-magnitude estimates only and have not been reviewed by Governments. Actual costs and financial terms, including any that are non-concessional, will depend upon, inter alia, the specific strategies and programmes Governments decide upon for implementation.

11.35.    Accelerating development consists of implementing the management-related and data/information activities cited above. Activities related to global environmental issues are those that will contribute to global information for assessing/evaluating/addressing environmental issues on a worldwide basis. Strengthening the capacity of international institutions consists of enhancing the technical staff and the executing capacity of several international organizat ions in order to meet the requirements of countries.

(b) Scientific and technological means

11.36.    Assessment and systematic observation activities involve major research efforts, statistical modelling and technological innovation. These have been internalized into the management -related activities. The activities in turn will improve the technological and scientific content of assessment and periodical evaluations. Some of the specific scientific and technological components included under these activities are:

    a.   Developing technical, ecological and economic methods and models related to periodical evaluations and evaluation;

    b.   Developing data systems, data processing and statistical modelling;

    c.   Remote sensing and ground surveys;

    d.   Developing geographic information systems;

    e.   Assessing and improving technology.

11.37.    These are to be linked and harmonized with similar activities and components in the other programme areas.

(c) Human resource development

11.38.    The programme activities foresee the need and include provision for human resource development in terms of specialization (e.g., the use of remote-sensing, mapping and statistical modelling), training, technology transfer, fellowships and field demonstrations.

(d) Capacity-building

11.39.    National Governments, in collaboration with appropriate international organizations and institutions, should develop the necessary capacity for implementing this programme area. This should be harmonized with capacity-building for other programme areas. Capacity-building should cover such aspects as policies, public administration, national-level institutions, human resource and skill development, research capability, technology development, information systems, programme evaluation, intersectoral coordination and international cooperation.

(e) Funding of international and regional cooperation

11.40.    The secretariat of the Conference has estimated the average total annual cost (1993-2000) of implementing the activities of this programme to be about $750 million, including about $530 million from the international community on grant or concessional terms. These are indicative and order-of-magnitude estimates only and have not been reviewed by Governments. Actual costs and financial terms, including any that are non-concessional, will depend upon, inter alia, the specific strategies and programmes Governments decide upon for implementation.

# Agenda 21 – Chapter 12
## MANAGING FRAGILE ECOSYSTEMS: COMBATING DESERTIFICATION AND DROUGHT

12.1. Fragile ecosystems are important ecosystems, with unique features and resources. Fragile ecosystems include deserts, semi-arid lands, mountains, wetlands, small islands and certain coastal areas. Most of these ecosystems are regional in scope, as they transcend national boundaries. This chapter addresses land resource issues in deserts, as well as arid, semi-arid and dry sub-humid areas. Sustainable mountain development is addressed in chapter 13; small islands and coastal areas are discussed in chapter 17.

12.2. Desertification is land degradation in arid, semi-arid and dry sub-humid areas resulting from various factors, including climatic variations and human activities. Desertification affects about one sixth of the world's population, 70 per cent of all drylands, amounting to 3.6 billion hectares, and one quarter of the total land area of the world. The most obvious impact of desertification, in addition to widespread poverty, is the degradation of 3.3 billion hectares of the total area of rangeland, constituting 73 per cent of the rangeland with a low potential for human and animal carrying capacity; decline in soil fertility and soil structure on about 47 per cent of the dryland areas constituting marginal rainfed cropland; and the degradation of irrigated cropland, amounting to 30 per cent of the dryland areas with a high population density and agricultural potential.

12.3. The priority in combating desertification should be the implementation of preventive measures for lands that are not yet degraded, or which are only slightly degraded. However, the severely degraded areas should not be neglected. In combating desertification and drought, the participation of local communities, rural organizations, national Governments, non-governmental organizations and international and regional organizations is essential.

12.4. The following programme areas are included in this chapter:

 a. Strengthening the knowledge base and developing information and monitoring systems for regions prone to desertification and drought, including the economic and social aspects of these ecosystems;

 b. Combating land degradation through, inter alia, intensified soil conservation, afforestation and reforestation activities;

 c. Developing and strengthening integrated development programmes for the eradication of poverty and promotion of alternative livelihood systems in areas prone to desertification;

 d. Developing comprehensive anti-desertification programmes and integrating them into national development plans and national environmental planning;

 e. Developing comprehensive drought preparedness and drought-relief schemes, including self-help arrangements, for drought-prone areas and designing programmes to cope with environmental refugees;

 f. Encouraging and promoting popular participation and environmental education, focusing on desertification control and management of the effects of drought.

### PROGRAMME AREAS

**A. Strengthening the knowledge base and developing information and monitoring systems for regions prone to desertification and drought, including the economic and social aspects of these ecosystems**

**Basis for action**

12.5. The global assessments of the status and rate of desertification conducted by the United Nations Environment Programme (UNEP) in 1977, 1984 and 1991 have revealed insufficient basic knowledge of desertification processes. Adequate world-wide systematic observation systems are helpful for the development and implementation of effective anti-desertification programmes. The capacity of existing international, regional and national institutions, particularly in developing countries, to generate and exchange relevant information is limited. An integrated and coordinated information and systematic observation system based on appropriate technology and embracing global, regional, national and local levels is essential for understanding the dynamics of desertification and drought processes. It is also important for developing adequate measures to deal with desertification and drought and improving socio-economic conditions.

**Objectives**

12.6. The objectives of this programme area are:

    a. To promote the establishment and/or strengthening of national environmental information coordination centres that will act as focal points within Governments for sectoral ministries and provide the necessary standardization and back-up services; to ensure also that national environmental information systems on desertification and drought are linked together through a network at subregional, regional and interregional levels;

    b. To strengthen regional and global systematic observation networks linked to the development of national systems for the observation of land degradation and desertification caused both by climate fluctuations and by human impact, and to identify priority areas for action;

    c. To establish a permanent system at both national and international levels for monitoring desertification and land degradation with the aim of improving living conditions in the affected areas.

**Activities**

(a) Management-related activities

12.7. Governments at the appropriate level, with the support of the relevant international and regional organizations, should:

    a. Establish and/or strengthen environmental information systems at the national level;

    b. Strengthen national, state/provincial and local assessment and ensure cooperation/networking between existing environmental information and monitoring systems, such as Earthwatch and the Sahara and Sahel Observatory;

    c. Strengthen the capacity of national institutions to analyse environmental data so that ecological change can be monitored and environmental information obtained on a continuing basis at the national level.

(b) Data and information

12.8. Governments at the appropriate level, with the support of the relevant international and regional organizations, should:

    a. Review and study the means for measuring the ecological, economic and social consequences of desertification and land degradation and introduce the results of these studies internationally into desertification and land degradation assessment practices;

    b. Review and study the interactions between the socio-economic impacts of climate, drought and desertification and utilize the results of these studies to secure concrete action.

12.9. Governments at the appropriate level, with the support of the relevant international and regional organizations, should:

a. Support the integrated data collection and research work of programmes related to desertification and drought problems;

b. Support national, regional and global programmes for integrated data collection and research networks carrying out assessment of soil and land degradation;

c. Strengthen national and regional meteorological and hydrological networks and monitoring systems to ensure adequate collection of basic information and communication among national, regional and international centres.

(c) International and regional cooperation and coordination

12.10. Governments at the appropriate level, with the support of the relevant international and regional organizations, should:

a. Strengthen regional programmes and international cooperation, such as the Permanent Inter-State Committee on Drought Control in the Sahel (CILSS), the Intergovernmental Authority for Drought and Development (IGADD), the Southern African Development Coordination Conference (SADCC), the Arab Maghreb Union and other regional organizations, as well as such organizations as the Sahara and Sahel Observatory;

b. Establish and/or develop a comprehensive desertification, land degradation and human condition database component that incorporates both physical and socio-economic parameters. This should be based on existing and, where necessary, additional facilities, such as those of Earthwatch and other information systems of international, regional and national institutions strengthened for this purpose;

c. Determine benchmarks and define indicators of progress that facilitate the work of local and regional organizations in tracking progress in the fight for anti-desertification. Particular attention should be paid to indicators of local participation.

**Means of implementation**

(a) Financing and cost evaluation

12.11. The Conference secretariat has estimated the average total annual cost (1993-2000) of implementing the activities of this programme to be about $350 million, including about $175 million from the international community on grant or concessional terms. These are indicative and order-of-magnitude estimates only and have not been reviewed by Governments. Actual costs and financial terms, including any that are non-concessional, will depend upon, inter alia, the specific strategies and programmes Governments decide upon for implementation.

(b) Scientific and technological means

12.12. Governments at the appropriate level, with the support of the relevant international and regional organizations working on the issue of desertification and drought, should:

a. Undertake and update existing inventories of natural resources, such as energy, water, soil, minerals, plant and animal access to food, as well as other resources, such as housing, employment, health, education and demographic distribution in time and space;

b. Develop integrated information systems for environmental monitoring, accounting and impact assessment;

c. International bodies should cooperate with national Governments to facilitate the acquisition and development of appropriate technology for monitoring and combating drought and desertification.

(c) Human resource development

12.13.    Governments at the appropriate level, with the support of the relevant international and regional organizations working on the issue of desertification and drought, should develop the technical and professional skills of people engaged in monitoring and assessing the issue of desertification and drought.

(d) Capacity-building

12.14.    Governments at the appropriate level, with the support of the relevant international and regional organizations working on the issue of desertification and drought, should:

   a.    Strengthen national and local institutions by providing adequate staff equipment and finance for assessing desertification;

   b.    Promote the involvement of the local population, particularly women and youth, in the collection and utilization of environmental information through education and awareness-building.

## B. Combating land degradation through, inter alia, intensified soil conservation, afforestation and reforestation activities

### Basis for action

12.15.    Desertification affects about 3.6 billion hectares, which is about 70 per cent of the total area of the world's drylands or nearly one quarter of the global land area. In combating desertification on rangeland, rainfed cropland and irrigated land, preventative measures should be launched in areas which are not yet affected or are only slightly affected by desertification; corrective measures should be implemented to sustain the productivity of moderately desertified land; and rehabilitative measures should be taken to recover severely or very severely desertified drylands.

12.16.    An increasing vegetation cover would promote and stabilize the hydrological balance in the dryland areas and maintain land quality and land productivity. Prevention of not yet degraded land and application of corrective measures and rehabilitation of moderate and severely degraded drylands, including areas affected by sand dune movements, through the introduction of environmentally sound, socially acceptable, fair and economically feasible land-use systems. This will enhance the land carrying capacity and maintenance of biotic resources in fragile ecosystems.

### Objectives

12.17.    The objectives of this programme area are:

   a.    As regards areas not yet affected or only slightly affected by desertification, to ensure appropriate management of existing natural formations (including forests) for the conservation of biodiversity, watershed protection, sustainability of their production and agricultural development, and other purposes, with the full participation of indigenous people;

   b.    To rehabilitate moderately to severely desertified drylands for productive utilization and sustain their productivity for agropastoral/agroforestry development through, inter alia, soil and water conservation;

   c.    To increase the vegetation cover and support management of biotic resources in regions affected or prone to desertification and drought, notably through such activities as afforestation/reforestation, agroforestry, community forestry and vegetation retention schemes;

d.  To improve management of forest resources, including woodfuel, and to reduce woodfuel consumption through more efficient utilization, conservation and the enhancement, development and use of other sources of energy, including alternative sources of energy.

**Activities**

(a) Management-related activities

12.18.  Governments at the appropriate level, and with the support of the relevant international and regional organizations, should:

    a.  Implement urgent direct preventive measures in drylands that are vulnerable but not yet affected, or only slightly desertified drylands, by introducing (i) improved land-use policies and practices for more sustainable land productivity; (ii) appropriate, environmentally sound and economically feasible agricultural and pastoral technologies; and (iii) improved management of soil and water resources;

    b.  Carry out accelerated afforestation and reforestation programmes, using drought-resistant, fast-growing species, in particular native ones, including legumes and other species, combined with community-based agroforestry schemes. In this regard, creation of large-scale reforestation and afforestation schemes, particularly through the establishment of green belts, should be considered, bearing in mind the multiple benefits of such measures;

    c.  Implement urgent direct corrective measures in moderately to severely desertified drylands, in addition to the measures listed in paragraph 19 (a) above, with a view to restoring and sustaining their productivity;

    d.  Promote improved land/water/crop-management systems, making it possible to combat salinization in existing irrigated croplands; and to stabilize rainfed croplands and introduce improved soil/crop-management systems into land-use practice;

    e.  Promote participatory management of natural resources, including rangeland, to meet both the needs of rural populations and conservation purposes, based on innovative or adapted indigenous technologies;

    f.  Promote in situ protection and conservation of special ecological areas through legislation and other means for the purpose of combating desertification while ensuring the protection of biodiversity;

    g.  Promote and encourage investment in forestry development in drylands through various incentives, including legislative measures;

    h.  Promote the development and use of sources of energy which will lessen pressure on ligneous resources, including alternative sources of energy and improved stoves.

(b) Data and information

12.19.  Governments at the appropriate level, with the support of the relevant international and regional organizations, should:

    a.  Develop land-use models based on local practices for the improvement of such practices, with a focus on preventing land degradation. The models should give a better understanding of the variety of natural and human-induced factors that may contribute to desertification. Models should incorporate the interaction of both new and traditional practices to prevent land degradation and reflect the resilience of the whole ecological and social system;

      b.    Develop, test and introduce, with due regard to environmental security considerations, drought resistant, fast-growing and productive plant species appropriate to the environment of the regions concerned.

(c) International and regional cooperation and coordination

12.20.    The appropriate United Nations agencies, international and regional organizations, non-governmental organizations and bilateral agencies should:

      a.    Coordinate their roles in combating land degradation and promoting reforestation, agroforestry and land-management systems in affected countries;

      b.    Support regional and subregional activities in technology development and dissemination, training and programme implementation to arrest dryland degradation.

12.21.    The national Governments concerned, the appropriate United Nations agencies and bilateral agencies should strengthen the coordinating role in dryland degradation of subregional intergovernmental organizations set up to cover these activities, such as CILSS, IGADD, SADCC and the Arab Maghreb Union.

**Means of implementation**

(a) Financing and cost evaluation

12.22.    The Conference secretariat has estimated the average total annual cost (1993-2000) of implementing the activities of this programme to be about $6 billion, including about $3 billion from the international community on grant or concessional terms. These are indicative and order-of-magnitude estimates only and have not been reviewed by Governments. Actual costs and financial terms, including any that are non-concessional, will depend upon, inter alia, the specific strategies and programmes Governments decide upon for implementation.

(b) Scientific and technological means

12.23.    Governments at the appropriate level and local communities, with the support of the relevant international and regional organizations, should:

      a.    Integrate indigenous knowledge related to forests, forest lands, rangeland and natural vegetation into research activities on desertification and drought;

      b.    Promote integrated research programmes on the protection, restoration and conservation of water and land resources and land-use management based on traditional approaches, where feasible.

(c) Human resource development

12.24.    Governments at the appropriate level and local communities, with the support of the relevant international and regional organizations, should:

      a.    Establish mechanisms to ensure that land users, particularly women, are the main actors in implementing improved land use, including agroforestry systems, in combating land degradation;

      b.    Promote efficient extension-service facilities in areas prone to desertification and drought, particularly for training farmers and pastoralists in the improved management of land and water resources in drylands.

(d) Capacity-building

12.25.    Governments at the appropriate level and local communities, with the support of the relevant international and regional organizations, should:

a.  Develop and adopt, through appropriate national legislation, and introduce institutionally, new and environmentally sound development-oriented land-use policies;

b.  Support community-based people's organizations, especially farmers and pastoralists.

## C. Developing and strengthening integrated development programmes for the eradication of poverty and promotion of alternative livelihood systems in areas prone to desertification

**Basis for action**

12.26.   In areas prone to desertification and drought, current livelihood and resource-use systems are not able to maintain living standards. In most of the arid and semi-arid areas, the traditional livelihood systems based on agropastoral systems are often inadequate and unsustainable, particularly in view of the effects of drought and increasing demographic pressure. Poverty is a major factor in accelerating the rate of degradation and desertification. Action is therefore needed to rehabilitate and improve the agropastoral systems for sustainable management of rangelands, as well as alternative livelihood systems.

**Objectives**

12.27.   The objectives of this programme area are:

a.  To create the capacity of village communities and pastoral groups to take charge of their development and the management of their land resources on a socially equitable and ecologically sound basis;

b.  To improve production systems in order to achieve greater productivity within approved programmes for conservation of national resources and in the framework of an integrated approach to rural development;

c.  To provide opportunities for alternative livelihoods as a basis for reducing pressure on land resources while at the same time providing additional sources of income, particularly for rural populations, thereby improving their standard of living.

**Activi ties**

(a) Management-related activities

12.28.   Governments at the appropriate level, with the support of the relevant international and regional organizations, should:

a.  Adopt policies at the national level regarding a decentralized approach to land-resource management, delegating responsibility to rural organizations;

b.  Create or strengthen rural organizations in charge of village and pastoral land management;

c.  Establish and develop local, national and intersectoral mechanisms to handle environmental and develop mental consequences of land tenure expressed in terms of land use and land ownership. Particular attention should be given to protecting the property rights of women and pastoral and nomadic groups living in rural areas;

d.  Create or strengthen village associations focused on economic activities of common pastoral interest (market gardening, transformation of agricultural products, livestock, herding, etc.);

e.  Promote rural credit and mobilization of rural savings through the establishment of rural banking systems;

    f.    Develop infrastructure, as well as local production and marketing capacity, by involving the local people to promote alternative livelihood systems and alleviate poverty;

    g.    Establish a revolving fund for credit to rural entrepreneurs and local groups to facilitate the establishment of cottage industries/business ventures and credit for input to agropastoral activities.

(b) Data and information

12.29.    Governments at the appropriate level, with the support of the relevant international and regional organizations, should:

    a.    Conduct socio-economic baseline studies in order to have a good understanding of the situation in the programme area regarding, particularly, resource and land tenure issues, traditional land-management practices and characteristics of production systems;

    b.    Conduct inventory of natural resources (soil, water and vegetation) and their state of degradation, based primarily on the knowledge of the local population (e.g., rapid rural appraisal);

    c.    Disseminate information on technical packages adapted to the social, economic and ecological conditions of each;

    d.    Promote exchange and sharing of information concerning the development of alternative livelihoods with other agro-ecological regions.

(c) International and regional cooperation and coordination

12.30.    Governments at the appropriate level, and with the support of the relevant international and regional organizations, should:

    a.    Promote cooperation and exchange of information among the arid and semi-arid land research institutions concerning techniques and technologies to improve land and labour productivity, as well as viable production systems;

    b.    Coordinate and harmonize the implementation of programmes and projects funded by the international organization communities and non-governmental organizations that are directed towards the alleviation of poverty and promotion of an alternative livelihood system.

**Means of implementation**

(a) Financing and cost evaluation

12.31.    The Conference secretariat has estimated the costs for this programme area in chapter 3 (Combating poverty) and chapter 14 (Promoting sustainable agriculture and rural development).

(b) Scientific and technological means

12.32.    Governments at the appropriate level, and with the support of the relevant international and regional organizations, should:

    a.    Undertake applied research in land use with the support of local research institutions;

    b.    Facilitate regular national, regional and interregional communication on and exchange of information and experience between extension officers and researchers;

    c.    Support and encourage the introduction and use of technologies for the generation of alternative sources of incomes.

(c) Human resource development

12.33.    Governments at the appropriate level, with the support of the relevant international and regional organizations, should:

    a.    Train members of rural organizations in management skills and train agropastoralists in such special techniques as soil and water conservation, water harvesting, agroforestry and small-scale irrigation;

    b.    Train extension agents and officers in the participatory approach to integrated land management.

(d) Capacity-building

12.34.    Governments at the appropriate level, with the support of the relevant international and regional organizations, should establish and maintain mechanisms to ensure the integration into sectoral and national development plans and programmes of strategies for poverty alleviation among the inhabitants of lands prone to desertification.

## D. Developing comprehensive anti-desertification programmes and integrating them into national development plans and national environmental planning

**Basis for action**

12.35.    In a number of developing countries affected by desertification, the natural resource base is the main resource upon which the development process must rely. The social systems interacting with land resources make the problem much more complex, requiring an integrated approach to the planning and management of land resources. Action plans to combat desertification and drought should include management aspects of the environment and development, thus conforming with the approach of integrating national development plans and national environmental action plans.

**Objectives**

12.36.    The objectives of this programme area are:

    a.    To strengthen national institutional capabilities to develop appropriate anti-desertification programmes and to integrate them into national development planning;

    b.    To develop and integrate strategic planning frameworks for the development, protection and management of natural resources in dryland areas into national development plans, including national plans to combat desertification, and environmental action plans in countries most prone to desertification;

    c.    To initiate a long-term process for implementing and monitoring strategies related to natural resources management;

    d.    To strengthen regional and international cooperation for combating desertification through, inter alia, the adoption of legal and other instruments.

**Activities**

(a) Management-related activities

12.37.    Governments at the appropriate level, and with the support of the relevant international and regional organizations, should:

    a.    Establish or strengthen, national and local anti-desertification authorities within government and local executive bodies, as well as local committees/associations of land users, in all rural communities affected, with a view to organizing working cooperation between all actors concerned, from the grass-roots level (farmers and pastoralists) to the higher levels of government;

b. Develop national plans of action to combat desertification and as appropriate, make them integral parts of national development plans and national environmental action plans;

c. Implement policies directed towards improving land use, managing common lands appropriately, providing incentives to small farmers and pastoralists, involving women and encouraging private investment in the development of drylands;

d. Ensure coordination among ministries and institutions working on anti-desertification programmes at national and local levels.

(b) Data and information

12.38.   Governments at the appropriate level, and with the support of the relevant international and regional organizations, should promote information exchange and cooperation with respect to national planning and programming among affected countries, inter alia, through networking.

(c) International and regional cooperation and coordination

12.39.   The relevant international organizations, multilateral financial institutions, non-governmental organizations and bilateral agencies should strengthen their cooperation in assisting with the preparation of desertification control programmes and their integration into national planning strategies, with the establishment of national coordinating and systematic observation mechanisms and with the regional and global networking of these plans and mechanisms.

12.40.   The General Assembly, at its forty-seventh session, should be requested to establish, under the aegis of the General Assembly, an intergovernmental negotiating committee for the elaboration of an international convention to combat desertification in in those countries experiencing serious drought and/or desertification, particularly in Africa, with a view to finalizing such a convention by June 1994.

**Means of implementation**

(a) Financing and cost evaluation

12.41.   The Conference secretariat has estimated the average total annual cost (1993-2000) of implementing the activities of this programme to be about $180 million, including about $90 million from the international community on grant or concessional terms. These are indicative and order-of-magnitude estimates only and have not been reviewed by Governments. Actual costs and financial terms, including any that are non-concessional, will depend upon, inter alia, the specific strategies and programmes Governments decide upon for implementation.

(b) Scientific and technological means

12.42.   Governments at the appropriate level, with the support of the relevant international and regional organizations, should:

a. Develop and introduce appropriate improved sustainable agricultural and pastoral technologies that are socially and environmentally acceptable and economically feasible;

b. Undertake applied study on the integration of environmental and developmental activities into national development plans.

(c) Human resource development

12.43.    Governments at the appropriate level, with the support of the relevant international and regional organizations, should undertake nationwide major anti-desertification awareness/training campaigns within countries affected through existing national mass media facilities, educational networks and newly created or strengthened extension services. This should ensure people's access to knowledge of desertification and drought and to national plans of action to combat desertification.

(d) Capacity-building

12.44.    Governments at the appropriate level, with the support of the relevant international and regional organizations, should establish and maintain mechanisms to ensure coordination of sectoral ministries and institutions, including local-level institutions and appropriate non-governmental organizations, in integrating anti-desertification programmes into national development plans and national environmental action plans.

## E. Developing comprehensive drought preparedness and drought-relief schemes, including self-help arrangements, for drought-prone areas and designing programmes to cope with environmental refugees

**Basis for action**

12.45.    Drought, in differing degrees of frequency and severity, is a recurring phenomenon throughout much of the developing world, especially Africa. Apart from the human toll - an estimated 3 million people died in the mid-1980s because of drought in sub-Saharan Africa - the economic costs of drought -related disasters are also high in terms of lost production, misused inputs and diversion of development resources.

12.46.    Early-warning systems to forecast drought will make possible the implementation of drought - preparedness schemes. Integrated packages at the farm and watershed level, such as alternative cropping strategies, soil and water conservation and promotion of water harvesting techniques, could enhance the capacity of land to cope with drought and provide basic necessities, thereby minimizing the number of environmental refugees and the need for emergency drought relief. At the same time, contingency arrangements for relief are needed for periods of acute scarcity.

**Objectives**

12.47.    The objectives of this programme area are:

a.    To develop national strategies for drought preparedness in both the short and long term, aimed at reducing the vulnerability of production systems to drought;

b.    To strengthen the flow of early-warning information to decision makers and land users to enable nations to implement strategies for drought intervention;

c.    To develop and integrate drought-relief schemes and means of coping with environmental refugees into national and regional development planning.

**Activities**

(a) Management-related activities

12.48.    In drought-prone areas, Governments at the appropriate level, with the support of the relevant international and regional organizations, should:

a.    Design strategies to deal with national food deficiencies in periods of production shortfall. These strategies should deal with issues of storage and stocks, imports, port facilities, food storage, transport and distribution;

b.  Improve national and regional capacity for agrometeorology and contingency crop planning. Agrometeorology links the frequency, content and regional coverage of weather forecasts with the requirements of crop planning and agricultural extension;

c.  Prepare rural projects for providing short-term rural employment to drought-affected households. The loss of income and entitlement to food is a common source of distress in times of drought. Rural works help to generate the income required to buy food for poor households;

d.  Establish contingency arrangements, where necessary, for food and fodder distribution and water supply;

e.  Establish budgetary mechanisms for providing, at short notice, resources for drought relief;

f.  Establish safety nets for the most vulnerable households.

(b) Data and information

12.49.    Governments of affected countries, at the appropriate level, with the support of the relevant international and regional organizations, should:

a.  Implement research on seasonal forecasts to improve contingency planning and relief operations and allow preventive measures to be taken at the farm level, such as the selection of appropriate varieties and farming practices, in times of drought;

b.  Support applied research on ways of reducing water loss from soils, on ways of increasing the water absorption capacities of soils and on water harvesting techniques in drought -prone areas;

c.  Strengthen national early -warning systems, with particular emphasis on the area of risk-mapping, remote-sensing, agrometeorological modelling, integrated multidisciplinary crop-forecasting techniques and computerized food supply/demand analysis.

(c) International and regional cooperation and coordination

12.50.    Governments at the appropriate level, with the support of the relevant international and regional organizations, should:

a.  Establish a system of stand-by capacities in terms of foodstock, logistical support, personnel and finance for a speedy international response to drought-related emergencies;

b.  Support programmes of the World Meteorological Organization (WMO) on agrohydrology and agrometeorology, the Programme of the Regional Training Centre for Agrometeorology and Operational Hydrology and their Applications (AGRHYMET), drought -monitoring centres and the African Centre of Meteorological Applications for Development (ACMAD), as well as the efforts of the Permanent Inter-State Committee on Drought Control in the Sahel (CILSS) and the Intergovernmental Authority for Drought and Development (IGADD);

c.  Support FAO programmes and other programmes for the development of national early -warning systems and food security assistance schemes;

d.  Strengthen and expand the scope of existing regional programmes and the activities of appropriate United Nations organs and organizations, such as the World Food Programme (WFP), the Office of the United Nations Disaster Relief Coordinator (UNDRO) and the United Nations Sudano-Sahelian Office as well as of non-governmental organizations, aimed at mitigating the effects of drought and emergencies.

**Means of implementation**

(a) Financing and cost evaluation

12.51.    The Conference secretariat has estimated the average total annual cost (1993-2000) of implementing the activities of this programme to be about $1.2 billion, including about $1.1 billion from the international community on grant or concessional terms. These are indicative and order-of-magnitude estimates only and have not been reviewed by Governments. Actual costs and financial terms, including any that are non-concessional, will depend upon, inter alia, the specific strategies and programmes Governments decide upon for implementation.

(b) Scientific and technological means

12.52.    Governments at the appropriate level and drought -prone communities, with the support of the relevant international and regional organizations, should:

   a.    Use traditional mechanisms to cope with hunger as a means of channelling relief and development assistance;

   b.    Strengthen and develop national, regional and local interdisciplinary research and training capabilities for drought -prevention strategies.

(c) Human resource development

12.53.    Governments at the appropriate level, with the support of the relevant international and regional organizations, should:

   a.    Promote the training of decision makers and land users in the effective utilization of information from early-warning systems;

   b.    Strengthen research and national training capabilities to assess the impact of drought and to develop methodologies to forecast drought.

(d) Capacity-building

12.54.    Governments at the appropriate level, with the support of the relevant international and regional organizations, should:

   a.    Improve and maintain mechanisms with adequate staff, equipment and finances for monitoring drought parameters to take preventive measures at regional, national and local levels;

   b.    Establish interministerial linkages and coordinating units for drought monitoring, impact assessment and management of drought-relief schemes.

## F. Encouraging and promoting popular participation and environmental education, focusing on desertification control and management of the effects of drought

**Basis for action**

12.55.    The experience to date on the successes and failures of programmes and projects points to the need for popular support to sustain activities related to desertification and drought control. But it is necessary to go beyond the theoretical ideal of popular participation and to focus on obtaining actual active popular involvement, rooted in the concept of partnership. This implies the sharing of responsibilities and the mutual involvement of all parties. In this context, this programme area should be considered an essential supporting component of all desertification-control and drought -related activities.

**Objectives**

12.56.    The objectives of this programme area are:

    a.    To develop and increase public awareness and knowledge concerning desertification and drought, including the integration of environmental education in the curriculum of primary and secondary schools;

    b.    To establish and promote true partnership between government authorities, at both the national and local levels, other executing agencies, non-governmental organizations and land users stricken by drought and desertification, giving land users a responsible role in the planning and execution processes in order to benefit fully from development projects;

    c.    To ensure that the partners understand one another's needs, objectives and points of view by providing a variety of means such as training, public awareness and open dialogue;

    d.    To support local communities in their own efforts in combating desertification, and to draw on the knowledge and experience of the populations concerned, ensuring the full participation of women and indigenous populations.

**Activities**

(a) Management-related activities

12.57.    Governments at the appropriate level, with the support of the relevant international and regional organizations, should:

    a.    Adopt policies and establish administrative structures for more decentralized decision-making and implementation;

    b.    Establish and utilize mechanisms for the consultation and involvement of land users and for enhancing capability at the grass-roots level to identify and/or contribute to the identification and planning of action;

    c.    Define specific programme/project objectives in cooperation with local communities; design local management plans to include such measures of progress, thereby providing a means of altering project design or changing management practices, as appropriate;

    d.    Introduce legislative, institutional/organizational and financial measures to secure user involvement and access to land resources;

    e.    Establish and/or expand favourable conditions for the provision of services, such as credit facilities and marketing outlets for rural populations;

    f.    Develop training programmes to increase the level of education and participation of people, particularly women and indigenous groups, through, inter alia, literacy and the development of technical skills;

    g.    Create rural banking systems to facilitate access to credit for rural populations, particularly women and indigenous groups, and to promote rural savings;

    h.    Adopt appropriate policies to stimulate private and public investment.

(b) Data and information

12.58.    Governments at the appropriate level, with the support of the relevant international and regional organizations, should:

    a.    Review, develop and disseminate gender-disaggregated information, skills and know-how at all levels on ways of organizing and promoting popular participation;

b.  Accelerate the development of technological know-how, focusing on appropriate and intermediate technology;

c.  Disseminate knowledge about applied research results on soil and water issues, appropriate species, agricultural techniques and technological know-how.

(c) International and regional cooperation and coordination

12.59.   Governments at the appropriate level, and with the support of the relevant international and regional organizations, should:

a.  Develop programmes of support to regional organizations such as CILSS, IGADD, SADCC and the Arab Maghreb Union and other intergovernmental organizations in Africa and other parts of the world, to strengthen outreach programmes and increase the participation of non-governmental organizations together with rural populations;

b.  Develop mechanisms for facilitating cooperation in technology and promote such cooperation as an element of all external assistance and activities related to technical assistance projects in the public or private sector;

c.  Promote collaboration among different actors in environment and development programmes;

d.  Encourage the emergence of representative organizational structures to foster and sustain interorganizational cooperation.

**Means of implementation**

(a) Financing and cost evaluation

12.60.   The Conference secretariat has estimated the average total annual cost (1993-2000) of implementing the activities of this programme to be about $1.0 billion, including about $500 million from the international community on grant or concessional terms. These are indicative and order-of-magnitude estimates only and have not been reviewed by Governments. Actual costs and financial terms, including any that are non-concessional, will depend upon, inter alia, the specific strategies and programmes Governments decide upon for implementation.

(b) Scientific and technological means

12.61.   Governments at the appropriate level, and with the support of the relevant international and regional organizations, should promote the development of indigenous know-how and technology transfer.

(c) Human resource development

12.62.   Governments, at the appropriate level, and with the support of the relevant international and regional organizations, should:

a.  Support and/or strengthen institutions involved in public education, including the local media, schools and community groups;

b.  Increase the level of public education.

(d) Capacity-building

12.63.   Governments at the appropriate level, and with the support of the relevant international and regional organizations, should promote members of local rural organizations and train and appoint more extension officers working at the local level.

# Agenda 21 – Chapter 13
# MANAGING FRAGILE ECOSYSTEMS: SUSTAINABLE MOUNTAIN DEVELOPMENT

13.1. Mountains are an important source of water, energy and biological diversity. Furthermore, they are a source of such key resources as minerals, forest products and agricultural products and of recreation. As a major ecosystem representing the complex and interrelated ecology of our planet, mountain environments are essential to the survival of the global ecosystem. Mountain ecosystems are, however, rapidly changing. They are susceptible to accelerated soil erosion, landslides and rapid loss of habitat and genetic diversity. On the human side, there is widespread poverty among mountain inhabitants and loss of indigenous knowledge. As a result, most global mountain areas are experiencing environmental degradation. Hence, the proper management of mountain resources and socio-economic development of the people deserves immediate action.

13.2. About 10 per cent of the world's population depends on mountain resources. A much larger percentage draws on other mountain resources, including and especially water. Mountains are a storehouse of biological diversity and endangered species.

13.3. Two programme areas are included in this chapter to further elaborate the problem of fragile ecosystems with regard to all mountains of the world. These are:

    a. Generating and strengthening knowledge about the ecology and sustainable development of mountain ecosystems;

    b. Promoting integrated watershed development and alternative livelihood opportunities.

## PROGRAMME AREAS

## A. Generating and strengthening knowledge about the ecology and sustainable development of mountain ecosystems

### Basis for action

13.4. Mountains are highly vulnerable to human and natural ecological imbalance. Mountains are the areas most sensitive to all climatic changes in the atmosphere. Specific information on ecology, natural resource potential and socio-economic activities is essential. Mountain and hillside areas hold a rich variety of ecological systems. Because of their vertical dimensions, mountains create gradients of temperature, precipitation and insolation. A given mountain slope may include several climatic systems - such as tropical, subtropical, temperate and alpine - each of which represents a microcosm of a larger habitat diversity. There is, however, a lack of knowledge of mountain ecosystems. The creation of a global mountain database is therefore vital for launching programmes that contribute to the sustainable development of mountain ecosystems.

### Objectives

13.5. The objectives of this programme area are:

    a. To undertake a survey of the different forms of soils, forest, water use, crop, plant and animal resources of mountain ecosystems, taking into account the work of existing international and regional organizations;

    b. To maintain and generate database and information systems to facilitate the integrated management and environmental assessment of mountain ecosystems, taking into account the work of existing international and regional organizations;

    c.    To improve and build the existing land/water ecological knowledge base regarding technologies and agricultural and conservation practices in the mountain regions of the world, with the participation of local communities;

    d.    To create and strengthen the communications network and information clearing-house for existing organizations concerned with mountain issues;

    e.    To improve coordination of regional efforts to protect fragile mountain ecosystems through the consideration of appropriate mechanisms, including regional legal and other instruments;

    f.    To generate information to establish databases and information systems to facilitate an evaluation of environmental risks and natural disasters in mountain ecosystems.

**Activities**

(a) Management-related activities

13.6. Governments at the appropriate level, with the support of the relevant international and regional organizations, should:

    a.    Strengthen existing institutions or establish new ones at local, national and regional levels to generate a multidisciplinary land/water ecological knowledge base on mountain ecosystems;

    b.    Promote national policies that would provide incentives to local people for the use and transfer of environment-friendly technologies and farming and conservation practices;

    c.    Build up the knowledge base and understanding by creating mechanisms for cooperation and information exchange among national and regional institutions working on fragile ecosystems;

    d.    Encourage policies that would provide incentives to farmers and local people to undertake conservation and regenerative measures;

    e.    Diversify mountain economies, inter alia, by creating and/or strengthening tourism, in accordance with integrated management of mountain areas;

    f.    Integrate all forest, rangeland and wildlife activities in such a way that specific mountain ecosystems are maintained;

    g.    Establish appropriate natural reserves in representative species -rich sites and areas.

(b) Data and information

13.7. Governments at the appropriate level, with the support of the relevant international and regional organizations, should:

    a.    Maintain and establish meteorological, hydrological and physical monitoring analysis and capabilities that would encompass the climatic diversity as well as water distribution of various mountain regions of the world;

    b.    Build an inventory of different forms of soils, forests, water use, and crop, plant and animal genetic resources, giving priority to those under threat of extinction. Genetic resources should be protected in situ by maintaining and establishing protected areas and improving traditional farming and animal husbandry activities and establishing programmes for evaluating the potential value of the resources;

    c.    Identify hazardous areas that are most vulnerable to erosion, floods, landslides, earthquakes, snow avalanches and other natural hazards;

        d.    Identify mountain areas threatened by air pollution from neighbouring industrial and urban areas.

(c) International and regional cooperation

13.8. National Governments and intergovernmental organizations should:

        a.    Coordinate regional and international cooperation and facilitate an exchange of information and experience among the specialized agencies, the World Bank, IFAD and other international and regional organizations, national Governments, research institutions and non-governmental organizations working on mountain development;

        b.    Encourage regional, national and international networking of people's initiatives and the activities of international, regional and local non-governmental organizations working on mountain development, such as the United Nations University (UNU), the Woodland Mountain Institutes (WMI), the International Center for Integrated Mountain Development (ICIMOD), the International Mountain Society (IMS), the African Mountain Association and the Andean Mountain Association, besides supporting those organizations in exchange of information and experience;

        c.    Protect Fragile Mountain Ecosystem through the consideration of appropriate mechanisms including regional legal and other instruments.

**Means of implementation**

(a) Financing and cost evaluation

13.9. The Conference secretariat has estimated the average total annual cost (1993-2000) of implementing the activities of this programme to be about $50 million from the international community on grant or concessional terms. These are indicative and order-of-magnitude estimates only and have not been reviewed by Governments. Actual costs and financial terms, including any that are non-concessional, will depend upon, inter alia, the specific strategies and programmes Governments decide upon for implementation.

(b) Scientific and technological means 13.10. Governments at the appropriate level, with the support of the relevant international and regional organizations, should strengthen scientific research and technological development programmes, including diffusion through national and regional institutions, particularly in meteorology, hydrology, forestry, soil sciences and plant sciences.

(c) Human resource development

13.10. Governments at the appropriate level, and with the support of the relevant international and regional organizations, should:

        a.    Launch training and extension programmes in environmentally appropriate technologies and practices that would be suitable to mountain ecosystems;

        b.    Support higher education through fellowships and research grants for environmental studies in mountains and hill areas, particularly for candidates from indigenous mountain populations;

        c.    Undertake environmental education for farmers, in particular for women, to help the rural population better understand the ecological issues regarding the sustainable development of mountain ecosystems.

(d) Capacity-building

13.11. Governments at the appropriate level, with the support of the relevant international and regional organizations, should build up national and regional institutional bases that could carry out research, training and dissemination of information on the sustainable development of the economies of fragile ecosystems.

## B. Promoting integrated watershed development and alternative livelihood opportunities

**Basis for action**

13.13.    Nearly half of the world's population is affected in various ways by mountain ecology and the degradation of watershed areas. About 10 per cent of the Earth's population lives in mountain areas with higher slopes, while about 40 per cent occupies the adjacent medium- and lower-watershed areas. There are serious problems of ecological deterioration in these watershed areas. For example, in the hillside areas of the Andean countries of South America a large portion of the farming population is now faced with a rapid deterioration of land resources. Similarly, the mountain and upland areas of the Himalayas, South-East Asia and East and Central Africa, which make vital contributions to agricultural production, are threatened by cultivation of marginal lands due to expanding population. In many areas this is accompanied by excessive livestock grazing, deforestation and loss of biomass cover.

13.14.    Soil erosion can have a devastating impact on the vast numbers of rural people who depend on rainfed agriculture in the mountain and hillside areas. Poverty, unemployment, poor health and bad sanitation are widespread. Promoting integrated watershed development programmes through effective participation of local people is a key to preventing further ecological imbalance. An integrated approach is needed for conserving, upgrading and using the natural resource base of land, water, plant, animal and human resources. In addition, promoting alternative livelihood opportunities, particularly through development of employment schemes that increase the productive base, will have a significant role in improving the standard of living among the large rural population living in mountain ecosystems.

Objectives

13.15.    The objectives of this programme area are:

      a.    By the year 2000, to develop appropriate land-use planning and management for both arable and non-arable land in mountain-fed watershed areas to prevent soil erosion, increase biomass production and maintain the ecological balance;

      b.    To promote income-generating activities, such as sustainable tourism, fisheries and environmentally sound mining, and to improve infrastructure and social services, in particular to protect the livelihoods of local communities and indigenous people;

      c.    To develop technical and institutional arrangements for affected countries to mitigate the effects of natural disasters through hazard-prevention measures, risk zoning, early-warning systems, evacuation plans and emergency supplies.

**Activities**

(a) Management-related activities

13.16.    Governments at the appropriate level, with the support of the relevant international and regional organizations, should:

      a.    Undertake measures to prevent soil erosion and promote erosion-control activities in all sectors;

b.    Establish task forces or watershed development committees, complementing existing institutions, to coordinate integrated services to support local initiatives in animal husbandry, forestry, horticulture and rural development at all administrative levels;

c.    Enhance popular participation in the management of local resources through appropriate legislation;

d.    Support non-governmental organizations and other private groups assisting local organizations and communities in the preparation of projects that would enhance participatory development of local people;

e.    Provide mechanisms to preserve threatened areas that could protect wildlife, conserve biological diversity or serve as national parks;

f.    Develop national policies that would provide incentives to farmers and local people to undertake conservation measures and to use environment-friendly technologies;

g.    Undertake income-generating activities in cottage and agro-processing industries, such as the cultivation and processing of medicinal and aromatic plants;

h.    Undertake the above activities, taking into account the need for full participation of women, including indigenous people and local communities, in development.

(b) Data and information

13.17.    Governments at the appropriate level, with the support of the relevant international and regional organizations, should:

a.    Maintain and establish systematic observation and evaluation capacities at the national, state or provincial level to generate information for daily operations and to assess the environmental and socio-economic impacts of projects;

b.    Generate data on alternative livelihoods and diversified production systems at the village level on annual and tree crops, livestock, poultry, beekeeping, fisheries, village industries, markets, transport and income-earning opportunities, taking fully into account the role of women and integrating them into the planning and implementation process.

(c) International and regional cooperation

13.18.    Governments at the appropriate level, with the support of the relevant international and regional organizations, should:

a.    Strengthen the role of appropriate international research and training institutes such as the Consultative Group on International Agricultural Research Centers (CGIAR) and the International Board for Soil Research and Management (IBSRAM), as well as regional research centres, such as the Woodland Mountain Institutes and the International Center for Integrated Mountain Development, in undertaking applied research relevant to watershed development;

b.    Promote regional cooperation and exchange of data and information among countries sharing the same mountain ranges and river basins, particularly those affected by mountain disasters and floods;

c.    Maintain and establish partnerships with non-governmental organizations and other private groups working in watershed development.

**Means of implementation**

(a) Financial and cost evaluation

13.19.    The Conference secretariat has estimated the average total annual cost (1993-2000) of implementing the activities of this programme to be about $13 billion, including about $1.9 billion from the international community on grant or concessional terms. These are indicative and order-of-magnitude estimates only and have not been reviewed by Governments. Actual costs and financial terms, including any that are non-concessional, will depend upon, inter alia, the specific strategies and programmes Governments decide upon for implementation.

13.20.    Financing for the promotion of alternative livelihoods in mountain ecosystems should be viewed as part of a country's anti-poverty or alternative livelihoods programme, which is also discussed in chapter 3 (Combating poverty) and chapter 14 (Promoting sustainable agriculture and rural development) of Agenda 21.

(b) Scientific and technical means

13.21.    Governments at the appropriate level, with the support of the relevant international and regional organizations, should:

- Consider undertaking pilot projects that combine environmental protection and development functions with particular emphasis on some of the traditional environmental management practices or systems that have a good impact on the environment;

- Generate technologies for specific watershed and farm conditions through a participatory approach involving local men and women, researchers and extension agents who will carry out experiments and trials on farm conditions;

- Promote technologies of vegetative conservation measures for erosion prevention, in situ moisture management, improved cropping technology, fodder production and agroforestry that are low-cost, simple and easily adopted by local people.

(c) Human resource development

13.22.    Governments at the appropriate level, with the support of the relevant international and regional organizations, should:

a. Promote a multidisciplinary and cross-sectoral approach in training and the dissemination of knowledge to local people on a wide range of issues, such as household production systems, conservation and utilization of arable and non-arable land, treatment of drainage lines and recharging of groundwater, livestock management, fisheries, agroforestry and horticulture;

b. Develop human resources by providing access to education, health, energy and infrastructure;

c. Promote local awareness and preparedness for disaster prevention and mitigation, combined with the latest available technology for early warning and forecasting.

(d) Capacity-building

13.23.    Governments at the appropriate level, with the support of the relevant international and regional organizations, should develop and strengthen national centres for watershed management to encourage a comprehensive approach to the environmental, socio-economic, technological, legislative, financial and administrative aspects and provide support to policy makers, administrators, field staff and farmers for watershed development.

13.24.    The private sector and local communities, in cooperation with national Governments, should promote local infrastructure development, including communication networks, mini- or micro-hydro development to support cottage industries, and access to markets.

# Agenda 21 – Chapter 14
# PROMOTING SUSTAINABLE AGRICULTURE AND RURAL DEVELOPMENT

14.1. By the year 2025, 83 per cent of the expected global population of 8.5 billion will be living in developing countries. Yet the capacity of available resources and technologies to satisfy the demands of this growing population for food and other agricultural commodities remains uncertain. Agriculture has to meet this challenge, mainly by increasing production on land already in use and by avoiding further encroachment on land that is only marginally suitable for cultivation.

14.2. Major adjustments are needed in agricultural, environmental and macroeconomic policy, at both national and international levels, in developed as well as developing countries, to create the conditions for sustainable agriculture and rural development (SARD). The major objective of SARD is to increase food production in a sustainable way and enhance food security. This will involve education initiatives, utilization of economic incentives and the development of appropriate and new technologies, thus ensuring stable supplies of nutritionally adequate food, access to those supplies by vulnerable groups, and production for markets; employment and income generation to alleviate poverty; and natural resource management and environmental protection.

14.3. The priority must be on maintaining and improving the capacity of the higher potential agricultural lands to support an expanding population. However, conserving and rehabilitating the natural resources on lower potential lands in order to maintain sustainable man/land ratios is also necessary. The main tools of SARD are policy and agrarian reform, participation, income diversification, land conservation and improved management of inputs. The success of SARD will depend largely on the support and participation of rural people, national Governments, the private sector and international cooperation, including technical and scientific cooperation.

14.4. The following programme areas are included in this chapter:

    a. Agricultural policy review, planning and integrated programming in the light of the multifunctional aspect of agriculture, particularly with regard to food security and sustainable development;

    b. Ensuring people's participation and promoting human resource development for sustainable agriculture;

    c. Improving farm production and farming systems through diversification of farm and non-farm employment and infrastructure development;

    d. Land-resource planning information and education for agriculture;

    e. Land conservation and rehabilitation;

    f. Water for sustainable food production and sustainable rural development;

    g. Conservation and sustainable utilization of plant genetic resources for food and sustainable agriculture;

    h. Conservation and sustainable utilization of animal genetic resources for sustainable agriculture;

    i. Integrated pest management and control in agriculture;

    j. Sustainable plant nutrition to increase food production;

    k. Rural energy transition to enhance productivity;

    l. Evaluation of the effects of ultraviolet radiation on plants and animals caused by the depletion of the stratospheric ozone layer.

## PROGRAMME AREAS

### A. Agricultural policy re view, planning and integrated programmes in the light of the multifunctional aspect of agriculture, particularly with regard to food security and sustainable development

**Basis for action**

14.5. There is a need to integrate sustainable development considerations with agricultural policy analysis and planning in all countries, particularly in developing countries. Recommendations should contribute directly to development of realistic and operational medium- to long-term plans and programmes, and thus to concrete actions. Support to and monitoring of implementation should follow.

14.6. The absence of a coherent national policy framework for sustainable agriculture and rural development (SARD) is widespread and is not limited to the developing countries. In particular t he economies in transition from planned to market-oriented systems need such a framework to incorporate environmental considerations into economic activities, including agriculture. All countries need to assess comprehensively the impacts of such policies on food and agriculture sector performance, food security, rural welfare and international trading relations as a means for identifying appropriate offsetting measures. The major thrust of food security in this case is to bring about a significant increase in agricultural production in a sustainable way and to achieve a substantial improvement in people's entitlement to adequate food and culturally appropriate food supplies.

14.7. Sound policy decisions pertaining to international trade and capital flows also necessitate action to overcome: (a) a lack of awareness of the environmental costs incurred by sectoral and macroeconomic policies and hence their threat to sustainability; (b) insufficient skills and experience in incorporating issues of sustainability into policies and programmes; and (c) inadequacy of tools of analysis and monitoring. 1/

**Objectives**

14.8. The objectives of this Programme area are:

    a. By 1995, to review and, where appropriate, establish a programme to integrate environmental and sustainable development with policy analysis for the food and agriculture sector and relevant macroeconomic policy analysis, formulation and implementation;

    b. To maintain and develop, as appropriate, operational multisectoral plans, programmes and policy measures, including programmes and measures to enhance sustainable food production and food security within the framework of sustainable development, not later than 1998;

    c. To maintain and enhance the ability of developing countries, particularly the least developed ones, to themselves manage policy, programming and planning activities, not later than 2005.

**Activities**

(a) Management-related activities

14.9. Governments at the appropriate level, with the support of the relevant international and regional organizations, should:

    a. Carry out national policy reviews related to food security, including adequate levels and stability of food supply and access to food by all households;

b. Review national and regional agricultural policy in relation, inter alia, to foreign trade, price policy, exchange rate policies, agricultural subsidies and taxes, as well as organization for regional economic integration;

c. Implement policies to influence land tenure and property rights positively with due recognition of the minimum size of land-holding required to maintain production and check further fragmentation;

d. Consider demographic trends and population movements and identify critical areas for agricultural production;

e. Formulate, introduce and monitor policies, laws and regulations and incentives leading to sustainable agricultural and rural development and improved food security and to the development and transfer of appropriate farm technologies, including, where appropriate, low-input sustainable agricultural (LISA) systems;

f. Support national and regional early warning systems through food-security assistance schemes that monitor food supply and demand and factors affecting household access to food;

g. Review policies with respect to improving harvesting, storage, processing, distribution and marketing of products at the local, national and regional levels;

h. Formulate and implement integrated agricultural projects that include other natural resource activities, such as management of rangelands, forests, and wildlife, as appropriate;

i. Promote social and economic research and policies that encourage sustainable agriculture development, particularly in fragile ecosystems and densely populated areas;

j. Identify storage and distribution problems affecting food availability; support research, where necessary, to overcome these problems and cooperate with producers and distributors to implement improved practices and systems.

## (b) Data and information

14.10. Governments at the appropriate level, with the support of the relevant international and regional organizations, should:

a. Cooperate actively to expand and improve the information on early warning systems on food and agriculture at both regional and national levels;

b. Examine and undertake surveys and research to establish baseline information on the status of natural resources relating to food and agricultural production and planning in order to assess the impacts of various uses on these resources, and develop methodologies and tools of analysis, such as environmental accounting.

## (c) International and regional cooperation and coordination

14.11. United Nations agencies, such as FAO, the World Bank, IFAD and GATT, and regional organizations, bilateral donor agencies and other bodies should, within their respective mandates, assume a role in working with national Governments in the following activities:

a. Implement integrated and sustainable agricultural development and food security strategies at the subregional level that use regional production and trade potentials, including organizations for regional economic integration, to promote food security;

b. Encourage, in the context of achieving sustainable agricultural development and consistent with relevant internationally agreed principles on trade and environment, a more open and non-discriminatory trading system and the avoidance of unjustifiable trade barriers which together with other policies will facilitate the further integration of agricultural and environmental policies so as to make them mutually supportive;

c. Strengthen and establish national, regional and international systems and networks to increase the understanding of the interaction between agriculture and the state of the environment, identify ecologically sound technologies and facilitate the exchange information on data sources, policies, and techniques and tools of analysis.

**Means of implementation**

(a) Financing and cost evaluation

14.12. The Conference secretariat has estimated the average total annual cost (1993-2000) on implementing the activities of this programme to be about $3 billion, including about $450 million from the international community on grant or concessional terms. These are indicative and order-of-magnitude estimates only and have not been reviewed by Governments. Actual costs and financial terms, including any that are non-concessional, will depend upon, inter alia, the specific strategies and programmes Governments decide upon for implementation.

(b) Scientific and technological means

14.13. Governments at the appropriate level and with the support of the relevant international and regional organizations should assist farming households and communities to apply technologies related to improved food production and security, including storage, monitoring of production and distribution.

(c) Human resource development

14.14. Governments at the appropriate level, with the support of the relevant international and regional organizations, should:

a. Involve and train local economists, planners and analysts to initiate national and international policy reviews and develop frameworks for sustainable agriculture;

b. Establish legal measures to promote access of women to land and remove biases in their involvement in rural development.

(d) Capacity-building

14.15. Governments at the appropriate level, with the support of the relevant international and regional organizations, should strengthen ministries for agriculture, natural resources and planning.

### B. Ensuring people's participation and promoting human resource development for sustainable agriculture

**Basis for action**

14.16. This component bridges policy and integrated resource management. The greater the degree of community control over the resources on which it relies, the greater will be the incentive for economic and human resources development. At the same time, policy instruments to reconcile long-run and short-run requirements must be set by national Governments. The approaches focus on fostering self-reliance and cooperation, providing information and supporting user-based organizations. Emphasis should be on management practices, building agreements for changes in resource utilization, the rights and duties associated with use of land, water and forests, the functioning of markets, prices, and the access to information, capital and inputs. This would require training and capacity-building to assume greater responsibilities in sustainable development efforts. 2/

## Objectives

14.17.    The objectives of this programme area are:

      a.   To promote greater public awareness of the role of people's participation and people's organizations, especially women's groups, youth, indigenous people, local communities and small farmers, in sustainable agriculture and rural development;

      b.   To ensure equitable access of rural people, particularly women, small farmers, landless and indigenous people, to land, water and forest resources and to t echnologies, financing, marketing, processing and distribution;

      c.   To strengthen and develop the management and the internal capacities of rural people's organizations and extension services and to decentralize decision-making to the lowest community level.

## Activities

(a) Management-related activities

14.18.    Governments at the appropriate level, with the support of the relevant international and regional organizations, should:

      a.   Develop and improve integrated agricultural extension services and facilities and rural organizations and undertake natural resource management and food security activities, taking into account the different needs of subsistence agriculture as well as market - oriented crops;

      b.   Review and refocus existing measures to achieve wider access to  land, water and forest resources and ensure equal rights of women and other disadvantaged groups, with particular emphasis on rural populations, indigenous people and local communities;

      c.   Assign clear titles, rights and responsibilities for land and for individuals or communities to encourage investment in land resources;

      d.   Develop guidelines for decentralization policies for rural development through reorganization and strengthening of rural institutions;

      e.   Develop policies in extension, training, pricing, input distribution, credit and taxation to ensure necessary incentives and equitable access by the poor to production-support services;

      f.   Provide support services and training, recognizing the variation in agricultural circumstances and practices by location; the optimal use of on-farm inputs and the minimal use of external inputs; optimal use of local natural resources and management of renewable energy sources; and the establishment of networks that deal with the exchange of information on alternative forms of agriculture.

(b) Data and information

14.19.    Governments at the appropriate level, and with the support of the relevant international and regional organizations, should collect, analyse, and disseminate information on human resources, the role of Governments, local communities and non-governmental organizations in social innovation and strategies for rural development.

(c) International and regional cooperation and coordination

14.20.    Appropriate international and regional agencies should:

    a.    Reinforce their work with non-governmental organizations in collecting and disseminating information on people's participation and people's organizations, testing participatory development methods, training and education for human resource development and strengthening the management structures of rural organizations;

    b.    Help develop information available through non-governmental organizations and promote an international ecological agricultural network to accelerate the development and implementation of ecological agriculture practices.

**Means of implementation**

(a) Financing and cost evaluation

14.21.    The Conference secretariat has estimated the average total annual cost (1993-2000) of implementing the activities of this programme to be about $4.4 billion, including about $650 million from the international community on grant or concessional terms. These are indicative and order-of-magnitude estimates only and have not been reviewed by Governments. Actual costs and financial terms, including any that are non-concessional, will depend upon, inter alia, the specific strategies and programmes Governments decide upon for implementation.

(b) Scientific and technological means

14.22.    Governments at the appropriate level, with the support of the relevant international and regional organizations, should:

    a.    Encourage people's participation on farm technology development and transfer, incorporating indigenous ecological knowledge and practices;

    b.    Launch applied research on participatory methodologies, management strategies and local organizations.

(c) Human resource development

14.23.    Governments at the appropriate level, with the support of the relevant international and regional organizations, should provide management and technical training to government administrators and members of resource-user groups in the principles, practice and benefits of people's participation in rural development.

(d) Capacity-building

14.24.    Governments at the appropriate level, with the support of the relevant international and regional organizations, should introduce management strategies and mechanisms, such as accounting and audit services for rural people's organizations and institutions for human resource development, and delegate administrative and financial responsibilities to local levels for decision-making, revenue-raising and expenditure.

## C. Improving farm production and farming systems through diversification of farm and non-farm employment and infrastructure development

**Basis for action**

14.25.    Agriculture needs to be intensified to meet future demands for commodities and to avoid further expansion onto marginal lands and encroachment on fragile ecosystems. Increased use of external inputs and development of specialized production and farming systems tend to increase vulnerability to environmental stresses and market fluctuations. There is, therefore, a need to intensify agriculture by diversifying the production systems for maximum efficiency in the utilization of local resources, while minimizing environmental and economic risks. Where intensification of farming systems is not possible, other on-farm and off-farm employment opportunities should be identified and developed, such as cottage industries, wildlife utilization, aquaculture and fisheries, non-farm activities, such as light village-based manufacturing, farm commodity processing, agribusiness, recreation and tourism, etc.

## Objectives

14.26. The objectives of this programme area are:

    a. To improve farm productivity in a sustainable manner, as well as to increase diversification, efficiency, food security and rural incomes, while ensuring that risks to the ecosystem are minimized;

    b. To enhance the self-reliance of farmers in developing and improving rural infrastructure, and to facilitate the transfer of environmentally sound technologies for integrated production and farming systems, including indigenous technologies and the sustainable use of biological and ecological processes, including agroforestry, sustainable wildlife conservation and management, aquaculture, inland fisheries and animal husbandry;

    c. To create farm and non-farm employment opportunities, particularly among the poor and those living in marginal areas, taking into account the alternative livelihood proposal inter alia in dryland areas.

## Activities

(a) Management-related activities

14.27. Governments at the appropriate level, with the support of the relevant international and regional organizations, should:

    a. Develop and disseminate to farming households integrated farm management technologies, such as crop rotation, organic manuring and other techniques involving reduced use of agricultural chemicals, multiple techniques for sources of nutrients and the efficient utilization of external inputs, while enhancing techniques for waste and by-product utilization and prevention of pre- and post-harvest losses, taking particular note of the role of women;

    b. Create non-farm employment opportunities through private small-scale agro-processing units, rural service centres and related infrastructural improvements;

    c. Promote and improve rural financial networks that utilize investment capital resources raised locally;

    d. Provide the essential rural infrastructure for access to agricultural inputs and services, as well as to national and local markets, and reduce food losses;

    e. Initiate and maintain farm surveys, on-farm testing of appropriate technologies and dialogue with rural communities to identify constraints and bottlenecks and find solutions;

    f. Analyse and identify possibilities for economic integration of agricultural and forestry activities, as well as water and fisheries, and to take effective measures to encourage forest management and growing of trees by farmers (farm forestry) as an option for resource development.

(b) Data and information

14.28.    Governments at the appropriate level, with the support of the relevant international and regional organizations, should:

      a.    Analyse the effects of technical innovations and incentives on farm-household income and well-being;

      b.    Initiate and maintain on-farm and off-farm programmes to collect and record indigenous knowledge.

(c) International and regional cooperation and coordination

14.29    International institutions, such as FAO and IFAD, international agricultural research centres, such as CGIAR, and regional centres should diagnose the world's major agro-ecosystems, their extension, ecological and socio-economic characteristics, their susceptibility to deterioration and their productive potential. This could form the basis for technology development and exchange and for regional research collaboration.

**Means of implementation**

(a) Financing and cost evaluation

14.29.    The Conference secretariat has estimated the average total annual cost (1993-2000) of implementing the activities of this programme to be about $10 billion, including about $1.5 billion from the international community on grant or concessional terms. These are indicative and order-of-magnitude estimates only and have not been reviewed by Governments. Actual costs and financial terms, including any that are non-concessional, will depend upon, inter alia, the specific strategies and programmes Governments decide upon for implementation.

(b) Scientific and technological means

14.30.    Governments at the appropriate level, with the support of the relevant international and regional organizations, should strengthen research on agricultural production systems in areas with different endowments and agro-ecological zones, including comparative analysis of the intensification, diversification and different levels of external and internal inputs.

(c) Human resource development

14.31.    Governments at t he appropriate level, with the support of the relevant international and regional organizations, should:

      a.    Promote educational and vocational training for farmers and rural communities through formal and non-formal education;

      b.    Launch awareness and training programmes for entrepreneurs, managers, bankers and traders in rural servicing and small-scale agro-processing techniques.

(d) Capacity-building

14.32.    Governments at the appropriate level, with the support of the relevant international and regional organizations, should:

      a.    Improve their organizational capacity to deal with issues related to off-farm activities and rural industry development;

      b.    Expand credit facilities and rural infrastructure related to processing, transportation and marketing.

**D. Land-resource planning, information and education for agriculture**

**Basis for action**

14.33.  Inappropriate and uncontrolled land uses are a major cause of degradation and depletion of land resources. Present land use often disregards the actual potentials, carrying capacities and limitations of land resources, as well as their diversity in space. It is estimated that the world's population, now at 5.4 billion, will be 6.25 billion by the turn of the century. The need to increase food production to meet the expanding needs of the population will put enormous pressure on all natural resources, including land.

14.34.  Poverty and malnutrition are already endemic in many regions. The destruction and degradation of agricultural and environmental resources is a major issue. Techniques for increasing production and conserving soil and water resources are already available but are not widely or systematically applied. A systematic approach is needed for identifying land uses and production systems that are sustainable in each land and climat e zone, including the economic, social and institutional mechanisms necessary for their implementation. 3/

**Objectives**

14.35.  The objectives of this programme area are:

a.  To harmonize planning procedures, involve farmers in the planning process, collect land-resource data, design and establish databases, define land areas of similar capability, identify resource problems and values that need to be taken into account to establish mechanisms to encourage efficient and environmentally sound use of resources;

b.  To establish agricultural planning bodies at national and local levels to decide priorities, channel resources and implement programmes.

**Activities**

(a) Management-related activities

14.36.  Governments at the appropriate level, with the support of the relevant int ernational and regional organizations, should:

a.  Establish and strengthen agricultural land-use and land-resource planning, management, education and information at national and local levels;

b.  Initiate and maintain district and village agricultural land-res ource planning, management and conservation groups to assist in problem identification, development of technical and management solutions, and project implementation.

(b) Data and information

14.37.  Governments at the appropriate level, with the support of the relevant international and regional organizations, should:

a.  Collect, continuously monitor, update and disseminate information, whenever possible, on the utilization of natural resources and living conditions, climate, water and soil factors, and on land use, distribution of vegetation cover and animal species, utilization of wild plants, production systems and yields, costs and prices, and social and cultural considerations that affect agricultural and adjacent land use;

b.  Establish programmes to provide information, promote discussion and encourage the formation of management groups.

(c) International and regional cooperation and coordination

14.38.  The appropriate United Nations agencies and regional organizations should:

a. Strengthen or establish international, regional and subregional technical working groups with specific terms of reference and budgets to promote the integrated use of land resources for agriculture, planning, data collection and diffusion of simulation models of production and information dissemination;

b. Develop internationally acceptable methodologies for the establishment of databases, description of land uses and multiple goal optimization.

**Means of implementation**

(a) Financing and cost evaluation

14.39. The Conference secretariat has estimat ed the average total annual cost (1993-2000) of implementing the activities of this programme to be about $1.7 billion, including about $250 million from the international community on grant or concessional terms. These are indicative and order-of-magnitude estimates only and have not been reviewed by Governments. Actual costs and financial terms, including any that are non-concessional, will depend upon, inter alia, the specific strategies and programmes Governments decide upon for implementation.

(b) Scientific and technological means

14.40. Governments at the appropriate level, with the support of the relevant international and regional organizations, should:

a. Develop databases and geographical information systems to store and display physical, social and economic information pertaining to agriculture, and the definition of ecological zones and development areas;

b. Select combinations of land uses and production systems appropriate to land units through multiple goal optimization procedures, and strengthen delivery systems and local community participation;

c. Encourage integrated planning at the watershed and landscape level to reduce soil loss and protect surface and groundwater resources from chemical pollution.

(c) Human resource development

14.41. Governments at the appropriate level, with the support of the relevant international and regional organizations, should:

a. Train professionals and planning groups at national, district and village levels through formal and informal instructional courses, travel and interaction;

b. Generate discussion at all levels on policy, development and environmental issues related to agricultural land use and management, through media programmes, conferences and seminars.

(d) Capacity-building

14.42. Governments at the appropriate level, with the support of the relevant international and regional organizations, should:

a. Establish land-resource mapping and planning units at national, district and village levels to act as focal points and links between institutions and disciplines, and between Governments and people;

b. Establish or strengthen Governments and international institutions with responsibility for agricultural resource survey, management and development; rationalize and strengthen legal frameworks; and provide equipment and technical assistance.

## E. Land conservation and rehabilitation

**Basis for action**

14.43.   Land degradation is the most important environmental problem affecting extensive areas of land in both developed and developing countries. The problem of soil erosion is particularly acute in developing countries, while problems of salinization, waterlogging, soil pollution and loss of soil fertility are increasing in all countries. Land degradation is serious because the productivity of huge areas of land is declining just when populations are increasing rapidly and the demand on the land is growing to produce more food, fibre and fuel. Efforts to control land degradation, particularly in developing countries, have had limited success to date. Well planned, long-term national and regional land conservation and rehabilitation programmes, with strong political support and adequate funding, are now needed. While land-use planning and land zoning, combined with better land management, should provide long-term solutions, it is urgent to arrest land degradation and launch conservation and rehabilitation programmes in the most critically affected and vulnerable areas.

**Objectives**

14.44.   The objectives of this programme area are:

    a.   By the year 2000, to review and initiate, as appropriate, national land-resource surveys, detailing the location, extent and severity of land degradation;

    b.   To prepare and implement comprehensive policies and programmes leading to the reclamation of degraded lands and the conservation of areas at risk, as well as improve the general planning, management and utilization of land resources and preserve soil fertility for sustainable agricultural development.

**Activities**

(a) Management-related activities

14.45.   Governments at the appropriate level, with the support of the relevant international and regional organizations, should:

    a.   Develop and implement programmes to remove and resolve the physical, social and economic causes of land degradation, such as land tenure, appropriate trading systems and agricultural pricing structures, which lead to inappropriate land-use management;

    b.   Provide incentives and, where appropriate and possible, resources for the participation of local communities in the planning, implementation and maintenance of their own conservation and reclamation programmes;

    c.   Develop and implement programmes for the rehabilitation of land degraded by water-logging and salinity;

    d.   Develop and implement programmes for the progressive use of non-cultivated land with agricultural potential in a sustainable way.

(b) Data and information

14.46.   Governments, at the appropriate level, with the support of the relevant international and regional organizations, should:

    a.   Conduct periodic surveys to assess the extent and state of its land resources;

    b.   Strengthen and establish national land-resource data banks, including identification of the location, extent and severity of existing land degradation, as well as areas at risk, and evaluate the progress of the conservation and rehabilitation programmes launched in this regard;

c.  Collect and record information on indigenous conservation and rehabilitation practices and farming systems as a basis for research and extension programmes.

(c) International and regional cooperation and coordination

14.47.  The appropriate United Nations agencies, regional organizations and non-governmental organizations should:

a.  Develop priority conservation and rehabilitation programmes with advisory services to Governments and regional organizations;

b.  Establish regional and subregional networks for scientists and technicians to exchange experiences, develop joint programmes and spread successful technologies on land conservation and rehabilitation.

## Means of implementation

(a) Financing and cost evaluation

14.48.  The Conference secretariat has estimated the average total annual cost (1993-2000) of implementing the activities of this programme to be about $5 billion, including about $800 million from the international community on grant or concessional terms. These are indicative and order-of-magnitude estimates only and have not been reviewed by Governments. Actual costs and financial terms, including any that are non-concessional, will depend upon, inter alia, the specific strategies and programmes Governments decide upon for implementation.

(b) Scientific and technological means

14.49.  Governments at the appropriate level, with the support of the relevant international and regional organizations, should help farming household communities to investigate and promote site-specific technologies and farming systems that conserve and rehabilitate land, while increasing agricultural production, including conservation tillage agroforestry, terracing and mixed cropping.

(c) Human resource development

14.50.  Governments at the appropriate level, with the support of the relevant international and regional organizations, should train field staff and land users in indigenous and modern techniques of conservation and rehabilitation and should establish training facilities for extension staff and land users.

(d) Capacity-building

14.51.  Governments at the appropriate level, with the support of the relevant international and regional organizations, should:

a.  Develop and strengthen national research institutional capacity to identify and implement effective conservation and rehabilitation practices that are appropriate to the existing socio-economic physical conditions of the land users;

b.  Coordinate all land conservation and rehabilitation policies, strategies and programmes with related ongoing programmes, such as national environment action plans, the Tropical Forestry Action Plan and national development programmes.

## F. Water for sustainable food production and sustainable rural development

14.52.    This programme area is included in chapter 18 (Protection of the quality and supply of freshwater resources), programme area F.

## G. Conservation and sustainable utilization of plant genetic resources for food and sustainable agriculture

**Basis for action**

14.53.    Plant genetic resources for agriculture (PGRFA) are an essential resource to meet future needs for food. Threats t o the security of these resources are growing, and efforts to conserve, develop and use genetic diversity are underfunded and understaffed. Many existing gene banks provide inadequate security and, in some instances, the loss of plant genetic diversity in gene banks is as great as it is in the field.

14.54.    The primary objective is to safeguard the world's genetic resources while preserving them to use sustainably. This includes the development of measures to facilitate the conservation and use of plant genetic resources, networks of in situ conservation areas and use of tools such as ex situ collections and germ plasma banks. Special emphasis could be placed on the building of endogenous capacity for characterization, evaluation and utilization of PGRFA, particularly for the minor crops and other underutilized or non-utilized species of food and agriculture, including tree species for agro-forestry. Subsequent action could be aimed at consolidation and efficient management of networks of in situ conservation areas and use of tools such as ex situ collections and germ plasma banks.

14.55.    Major gaps and weaknesses exist in the capacity of existing national and international mechanisms to assess, study, monitor and use plant genetic resources to increase food production. Existing institutional capacity, structures and programmes are generally inadequate and largely underfunded. There is genetic erosion of invaluable crop species. Existing diversity in crop species is not used to the extent possible for increased food production in a sustainable way. 4/

**Objectives**

14.56.    The objectives of this programme area are:

a.    To complete the first regeneration and safe duplication of existing ex situ collections on a world-wide basis as soon as possible;

b.    To collect and study plants useful for increasing food production through joint activities, including training, within the framework of networks of collaborating institutions;

c.    Not later than the year 2000, to adopt policies and strengthen or establish programmes for in situ on-farm and ex situ conservation and sustainable use of plant genetic resources for food and agriculture, integrated into strategies and programmes for sustainable agriculture;

d.    To take appropriate measures for the fair and equitable sharing of benefits and results of research and development in plant breeding between the sources and users of plant genetic resources.

**Activities**

(a) Management-related activities

14.57.    Governments at the appropriate level, with the support of the relevant international and regional organiz ations, should:

a.    Develop and strengthen institutional capacity, structures and programmes for conservation and use of PGRFA;

b. Strengthen and establish research in the public domain on PGRFA evaluation and utilization, with the objectives of sustainable agriculture and rural development in view;

c. Develop multiplication/propagation, exchange and dissemination facilities for PGRFAs (seeds and planting materials), particularly in developing countries and monitor, control and evaluate plant introductions;

d. Prepare plans or programmes of priority action on conservation and sustainable use of PGRFA, based, as appropriate, on country studies on PGRFA;

e. Promote crop diversification in agricultural systems where appropriate, including new plants with potential value as food crops;

f. Promote utilization as well as research on poorly known, but potentially useful, plants and crops, where appropriate;

g. Strengthen national capabilities for utilization of PGRFA, plant breeding and seed production capabilities, both by specialized institutions and farming communities.

(b) Data and information

14.58.  Governments at the appropriate level, with the support of the relevant international and regional organizations, should:

a. Develop strategies for networks of in situ conservation areas and use of tools such as on-farm ex situ collections, germplasm banks and related technologies;

b. Establish ex situ base collection networks;

c. Review periodically and report on the situation on PGRFA, using existing systems and procedures;

d. Characterize and evaluate PGRFA material collected, disseminate information to facilitate the use of PGRFA collections and assess genetic variation in collections.

(c) International and regional cooperation and coordination

14.59.  The appropriate United Nations agencies and regional organizations should:

a. Strengthen the Global System on the Conservation and Sustainable Use of PGRFA by, inter alia, accelerating the development of the Global Information and Early Warning System to facilitate the exchange of information; developing ways to promote the transfer of environmentally sound technologies, in particular to developing countries; and taking further steps to realize farmers' rights;

b. Develop subregional, regional and global networks of PGRFA in situ in protected areas;

c. Prepare periodic state of the world reports on PGRFA;

d. Prepare a rolling global cooperative plan of action on PGRFA;

e. Promote, for 1994, the Fourth International Technical Conference on the Conservation and Sustainable Use of PGRFA, which is to adopt the first state of the world report and the first global plan of action on the conservation and sustainable use of PGRFA;

f. Adjust the Global System for the Conservation and Sustainable Use of PGRFA in line with the outcome of the negotiations of a convention on biological diversity.

**Means of implementation**

(a) Financing and cost evaluation

14.60.    The Conference secretariat has estimated the average total annual cost (1993-2000) of implementing the activities of this programme to be about $600 million, including about $300 million from the international community on grant or concessional terms. These are indicative and order-of-magnitude estimates only and have not been reviewed by Governments. Actual costs and financial terms, including any that are non-concessional, will depend upon, inter alia, the specific strategies and programmes Governments decide upon for implementation.

(b) Scientific and technological means

14.61.    Governments, at the appropriate level, with the support of the relevant international and regional organizations, should:

      a.    Develop basic science research in such areas as plant taxonomy and phytogeography, utilizing recent developments, such as computer sciences, molecular genetics and in vitro cryopreservation;

      b.    Develop major collaborative projects between research programmes in developed and developing countries, particularly for the enhancement of poorly known or neglected crops;

      c.    Promote cost-effective technologies for keeping duplicate sets of ex situ collections (which can also be used by local communities);

      d.    Develop further conservation sciences in relation to in situ conservation and technical means to link it with ex situ conservation efforts.

(c) Human resource development

14.62.    Governments at the appropriate level and with the support of the relevant international and regional organizations should:

      a.    Promote training programmes at both undergraduate and post-graduate levels in conservation sciences for running PGRFA facilities and for the design and implementation of national programmes in PGRFA;

      b.    Raise the awareness of agricultural extension services in order to link PGRFA activities with user communities;

      c.    Develop training materials to promote conservation and utilization of PGRFA at the local level.

(d) Capacity-building

14.63.    Governments at the appropriate level, with the support of the relevant international and regional organizations, should establish national policies to provide legal status for and strengthen legal aspects of PGRFA, including long-term financial commitments for germplasm collections and implementation of activities in PGRFA.

**H. Conservation and sustainable utilization of animal genetic resources for sustainable agriculture**

**Basis for action**

14.64.    The need for increased quantity and quality of animal products and for draught animals calls for conservation of the existing diversity of animal breeds to meet future requirements, including those for use in biotechnology. Some local animal breeds, in addition to their socio-cultural value, have unique attributes for adaptation, disease resistance and specific uses and should be preserved. These local breeds are threatened by extinction as a result of the introduction of exotic breeds and of changes in livestock production systems.

**Objectives**

14.65.   The objectives of this programme area are:

     a.   To enumerate and describe all breeds of livestock used in animal agriculture in as broad a way as possible and begin a 10-year programme of action;

     b.   To establish and implement action programmes to identify breeds at risk, together with the nature of the risk  and appropriate preservation measures;

     c.   To establish and implement development programmes for indigenous breeds in order to guarantee their survival, avoiding the risk of their being replaced by breed substitution or cross-breeding programmes.

**Activities**

(a) Management-related activities

14.66.   Governments at the appropriate level, with the support of the relevant international and regional organizations, should:

     a.   Draw up breed preservation plans, for endangered populations, including semen/embryo collection and storage, farm-based conservation of indigenous stock or in situ preservation;

     b.   Plan and initiate breed development strategies;

     c.   Select indigenous populations on the basis of regional importance and genetic uniqueness, for a 10-year programme, followed by selection of an additional cohort of indigenous breeds for development.

(b) Data and information

14.67.   Governments at the appropriate level, with the support of the relevant international and regional organizations, should prepare and complete national inventories of available animal genetic resources. Cryogenic storage could be given priority over characterization and evaluation. Training of nationals in conservation and assessment techniques would be given special attention.

(c) International and regional cooperation and coordination

14.68.   The appropriate United Nations and other international and regional agencies should:

     a.   Promote the establishment of regional gene banks to the extent that they are justified, based on principles of technical cooperation among developing countries;

     b.   Process, store and analyse animal genetic data at the global level, including the establishment of a world watch list and an early warning system for endangered breeds; global assessment of scientific and intergovernmental guidance of the programme and review of regional and national activities; development of methodologies, norms and standards (including international agreements); monitoring of their implementation; and related technical and financial assistance;

     c.   Prepare and publish a comprehensive database of animal genetic resources, describing each breed, its derivation, its relationship with other breeds, effective population size and a concise set of biological and production characteristics;

d.　Prepare and publish a world watch list on farm animal species at risk to enable national Governments to take action to preserve endangered breeds and to seek technical assistance, where necessary.

**Means of implementation**

(a) Financing and cost evaluation

14.69.　The Conference secretariat has estimated the average total annual cost (1993-2000) of implementing the activities of this programme to be about $200 million, including about $100 million from the international community on grant or concessional terms. These are indicative and order-of-magnitude estimates only and have not been reviewed by Governments. Actual costs and financial terms, including any that are non-concessional, will depend upon, inter alia, the specific strategies and programmes Governments decide upon for implementation.

(b) Scientific and technological means

14.70.　Governments at the appropriate level, with the support of the relevant international and regional organizations, should:

　a.　Use computer-based data banks and questionnaires to prepare a global inventory/world watch list;

　b.　Using cryogenic storage of germplasm, preserve breeds at serious risk and other material from which genes can be reconstructed.

(c) Human resource development

14.71.　Governments at the appropriate level, with the support of the relevant international and regional organizations, should:

　a.　Sponsor training courses for nationals to obtain the necessary expertise for data collection and handling and for the sampling of genetic material;

　b.　Enable scientists and managers to establish an information base for indigenous livestock breeds and promote programmes to develop and conserve essential livestock genetic material.

(d) Capacity-building

14.72.　Governments at the appropriate level, with the support of the relevant international and regional organizations, should:

　a.　Establish in-country facilities for artificial insemination centres and in situ breeding farms;

　b.　Promote in-country programmes and related physical infrastructure for animal livestock conservation and breed development, as well as for strengthening national capacities to take preventive action when breeds are endangered.

### I. Integrated pest management and control in agriculture

**Basis for action**

14.73.　World food demand projections indicate an increase of 50 per cent by the year 2000 which will more than double again by 2050. Conservative estimates put pre-harvest and post-harvest losses caused by pests between 25 and 50 per cent. Pests affecting animal health also cause heavy losses and in many areas prevent livestock development. Chemical control of agricultural pests has dominated the scene, but its overuse has adverse effects on farm budgets, human health and the environment, as well as on international trade. New pest problems continue to develop. Integrated pest management, which combines biological control, host plant resistance and appropriate farming practices and minimizes the use of pesticides, is the best option for the future, as it guarantees yields, reduces costs, is environmentally friendly and contributes to the sustainability of agriculture. Integrated pest management should go hand in hand with appropriate pesticide management to allow for pesticide regulation and control, including trade, and for the safe handling and disposal of pesticides, particularly those that are toxic and persistent.

**Objectives**

14.74. The objectives of this programme area are:

    a. Not later than the year 2000, to improve and implement plant protection and animal health services, including mechanisms to control the distribution and use of pesticides, and to implement the International Code of Conduct on the Distribution and Use of Pesticides;

    b. To improve and implement programmes to put integrated pest-management practices within the reach of farmers through farmer networks, extension services and research institutions;

    c. Not later than the year 1998, to establish operational and interactive networks among farmers, researchers and extension services to promote and develop integrated pest management.

**Activities**

(a) Management-related activities

14.75. Governments at the appropriate level, with the support of the relevant international and regional organizations, should:

    a. Review and reform national policies and the mechanisms that would ensure the safe and appropriate use of pesticides - for example, pesticide pricing, pest control brigades, price-structure of inputs and outputs and integrated pest-management policies and action plans;

    b. Develop and adopt efficient management systems to control and monitor the incidence of pests and disease in agriculture and the distribution and use of pesticides at the country level;

    c. Encourage research and development into pesticides that are target -specific and readily degrade into harmless constituent parts after use;

    d. Ensure that pesticide labels provide farmers with understandable information about safe handling, application and disposal.

(b) Data and information

14.76. Governments at the appropriate level, with the support of the relevant international and regional organizations, should:

    a. Consolidate and harmonize existing information and programmes on the use of pesticides that have been banned or severely restricted in different countries;

    b. Consolidate, document and disseminate information on biological control agents and organic pesticides, as well as on traditional and other relevant knowledge and skills regarding alternative non-chemical ways of controlling pests;

    c. Undertake national surveys to establish baseline information on the use of pesticides in each country and the side-effects on human health and environment, and also undertake appropriate education.

(c) International and regional cooperation and coordination

14.77.    Appropriate United Nations agencies and regional organizations should:

     a.   Establish a system for collecting, analysing and disseminating data on the quantity and quality of pesticides used every year and their impact on human health and the environment;

     b.   Strengthen regional interdisciplinary projects and establish integrated pest management (IPM) networks to demonstrate the social, economic and environmental benefits of IPM for food and cash crops in agriculture;

     c.   Develop proper IPM, comprising the selection of the variety of biological, physical and cultural controls, as well as chemical controls, taking into account specific regional conditions.

**Means of implementation**

(a) Financing and cost evaluation

14.78.    The Conference secretariat has estimated the average total annual cost (1993-2000) of implementing the activities of this programme to be about $1.9 billion, including about $285 million from the international community on grant or concessional terms. These are indicative and order-of-magnitude estimates only and have not been reviewed by Governments. Actual costs and financial terms, including any that are non-concessional, will depend upon, inter alia, the specific strategies and programmes Governments decide upon for implementation.

(b) Scientific and technological means

14.79.    Governments at the appropriate level, with the support of the relevant international and regional organizations, should launch on-farm research in the development of non-chemical alternative pest management technologies.

(c) Human resource development

14.80.    Governments at the appropriate level, with the support of the relevant international and regional organizations, should:

     a.   Prepare and conduct training programmes on approaches and techniques for integrated pest management and control of pesticide use, to inform policy makers, researchers, non-governmental organizations and farmers;

     b.   Train extension agents and involve farmers and women's groups in crop health and alternative non-chemical ways of controlling pests in agriculture.

(d) Capacity-building

14.81.    Governments at the appropriate level, with the support of the relevant international and regional organizations, should strengthen national public administrations and regulatory bodies in the control of pesticides and the transfer of technology for integrated pest management.

### J. Sustainable plant nutrition to increase food production

**Basis for action**

14.82.    Plant nutrient depletion is a serious problem resulting in loss of soil fertility, particularly in developing countries. To maintain soil productivity, the FAO sustainable plant nutrition programmes could be helpful. In sub-Saharan Africa, nutrient output from all sources currently exceeds inputs by a factor of three or four, the net loss being estimated at some 10 million metric tons per year. As a result, more marginal lands and fragile natural ecosystems are put under agricultural use, thus creating further land degradation and other environmental problems. The int egrated plant nutrition approach aims at ensuring a sustainable supply of plant nutrients to increase future yields without harming the environment and soil productivity.

14.83. In many developing countries, population growth rates exceed 3 per cent a year, and national agricultural production has fallen behind food demand. In these countries the goal should be to increase agricultural production by at least 4 per cent a year, without destroying the soil fertility. This will require increasing agricultural production in high-potential areas through efficiency in the use of inputs. Trained labour, energy supply, adapted tools and technologies, plant nutrients and soil enrichment will all be essential.

## Objectives

14.84. The objectives of this programme area are:

a. Not later than the year 2000, to develop and maintain in all countries the integrated plant nutrition approach, and to optimize availability of fertilizer and other plant nutrient sources;

b. Not later than the year 2000, to establish and maintain institutional and human infrastructure to enhance effective decision-making on soil productivity;

c. To develop and make available national and international know-how to farmers, extension agents, planners and policy makers on environmentally sound new and existing technologies and soil-fertility management strategies for application in promoting sustainable agriculture.

## Activities

(a) Management-related activities

14.85. Governments at the appropriate level, with the support of the relevant international and regional organizations, should:

a. Formulate and apply strategies that will enhance soil fertility maintenance to meet sustainable agricultural production and adjust the relevant agricultural policy instruments accordingly;

b. Integrate organic and inorganic sources of plant nutrients in a system to sustain soil fertility and determine mineral fertilizer needs;

c. Determine plant nutrient requirements and supply strategies and optimize the use of both organic and inorganic sources, as appropriate, to increase farming efficiency and production;

d. Develop and encourage processes for the recycling of organic and inorganic waste into the soil structure, without harming the environment, plant growth and human health.

(b) Data and information

14.86. Governments at the appropriate level, with the support of the relevant international and regional organizations, should:

a. Assess "national accounts" for plant nutrients, including supplies (inputs) and losses (outputs) and prepare balance sheets and projections by cropping systems;

b. Review technical and economic potentials of plant nutrient sources, including national deposits, improved organic supplies, recycling, wastes, topsoil produced from discarded organic matter and biological nitrogen fixation.

(c) International and regional cooperation and coordination

14.87. The appropriate United Nations agencies, such as FAO, the international agricultural research institutes, and non-governmental organizations should collaborate in carrying out information and publicity campaigns about the integrated plant nutrients approach, efficiency of soil productivity and their relationship to the environment.

**Means of implementation**

(a) Financing and cost evaluation

14.88. The Conference secretariat has estimated the average total annual cost (1993-2000) of implementing the activities of this programme to be about $3.2 billion, including about $475 million from the international community on grant or concessional terms. These are indicative and order-of-magnitude estimates only and have not been reviewed by Governments. Actual costs and financial terms, including any that are non-concessional, will depend upon, inter alia, the specific strategies and programmes Governments decide upon for implementation.

(b) Scientific and technological means

14.89. Governments at the appropriate level, with the support of the relevant international and regional organizations, should:

a. Develop site-specific technologies at benchmark sites and farmers' fields that fit prevailing socio-economic and ecological conditions through research that involves the full collaboration of local populations;

b. Reinforce interdisciplinary international research and transfer of technology in cropping and farming systems research, improved in situ biomass production techniques, organic residue management and agroforestry technologies.

(c) Human resource development

14.90. Governments at the appropriate level, with the support of the relevant international and regional organizations, should:

a. Train extension officers and researchers in plant nutrient management, cropping systems and farming systems, and in economic evaluation of plant nutrient impact;

b. Train farmers and women's groups in plant nutrition management, with special emphasis on topsoil conservation and production.

(d) Capacity-building

14.91. Governments at the appropriate level, with the support of the relevant international and regional organizations, should:

a. Develop suitable institutional mechanisms for policy formulation to monitor and guide the implementation of integrated plant nutrition programmes through an interactive process involving farmers, research, extension services and other sectors of society;

b. Where appropriate, strengthen existing advisory services and train staff, develop and test new technologies and facilitate the adoption of practices to upgrade and maintain full productivity of the land.

## K. Rural energy transition to enhance productivity

**Basis for action**

14.92.    Energy supplies in many countries are not commensurate with their development needs and are highly priced and unstable. In rural areas of the developing countries, the chief sources of energy are fuelwood, crop residues and manure, together with animal and human energy. More intensive energy inputs are required for increased productivity of human labour and for income-generation. To this end, rural energy policies and technologies should promote a mix of cost-effective fossil and renewable energy sources that is itself sustainable and ensures sustainable agricultural development. Rural areas provide energy supplies in the form of wood. The full potential of agriculture and agroforestry, as well as common property resources, as sources of renewable energy, is far from being realized. The attainment of sustainable rural development is intimately linked with energy demand and supply patterns. 5/

**Objectives**

14.93.    The objectives of this programme area are:

    a.    Not later than the year 2000, to initiate and encourage a process of environmentally sound energy transition in rural communities, from unsustainable energy sources, to structured and diversified energy sources by making available alternative new and renewable sources of energy;

    b.    To increase the energy inputs available for rural household and agro-industrial needs through planning and appropriate technology transfer and development;

    c.    To imp lement self-reliant rural programmes favouring sustainable development of renewable energy sources and improved energy efficiency.

**Activities**

(a) Management-related activities

14.94.    Governments at the appropriate level, with the support of the relevant international and regional organizations, should:

    a.    Promote pilot plans and projects consisting of electrical, mechanical and thermal power (gasifiers, biomass, solar driers, wind-pumps and combustion systems) that are appropriate and likely to be adequately maintained;

    b.    Initiate and promote rural energy programmes supported by technical training, banking and related infrastructure;

    c.    Intensify research and the development, diversification and conservation of energy, taking into account the need for efficient use and environmentally sound technology.

(b) Data and information

14.95.    Governments at the appropriate level, with the support of the relevant international and regional organizations, should:

    a.    Collect and disseminate data on rural energy supply and demand patterns related to energy needs for households, agriculture and agro-industry;

    b.    Analyse sectoral energy and production data in order to identify rural energy requirements.

(c) International and regional cooperation and coordination

14.96.   The appropriate United Nations agencies and regional organizations should, drawing on the experience and available information of non-governmental organizations in this field, exchange country and regional experience on rural energy planning methodologies in order to promote efficient planning and select cost-effective technologies.

**Means of implementation**

(a) Financing and cost evaluation

14.97.   The Conference secretariat has estimated the average total annual cost (1993-2000) of implementing the activities of this programme to be about $1.8 billion per year, including about $265 million from the international community on grant or concessional terms. These are indicative and order-of-magnitude estimates only and have not been reviewed by Governments. Actual costs and financial terms, including any that are non-concessional, will depend upon, inter alia, the specific strategies and programmes Governments decide upon for implementation.

(b) Scientific and technological means

14.98.   Governments at the appropriate level, with the support of the relevant international and regional organizations, should:

      a.   Intensify public and private sector research in developing and industrialized countries on renewable sources of energy for agriculture;

      b.   Undertake research and transfer of energy technologies in biomass and solar energy to agricultural production and post-harvest activities.

(c) Human resource development

14.99.   Governments at the appropriate level, with the support of the relevant international and regional organizations, should enhance public awareness of rural energy problems, stressing the economic and environmental advantages of renewable energy sources.

(d) Capacity-building

14.100.   Governments at the appropriate level, with the support of the relevant international and regional organizations, should:

      a.   Establish national institutional mechanisms for rural energy planning and management that would improve efficiency in agricultural productivity and reach the village and household level;

      b.   Strengthen extension services and local organizations to implement plans and programmes for new and renewable sources of energy at the village level.

### L. Evaluation of the effects of ultraviolet radiation on plants and animals caused by the depletion of the stratospheric ozone layer

**Basis for action**

14.101.   The increase of ultraviolet radiation as a consequence of the depletion of the stratospheric ozone layer is a phenomenon that has been recorded in different regions of the world, particularly in the southern hemisphere. Consequently, it is important to evaluate its effects on plant and animal life, as well as on sustainable agricultural development.

**Objective**

14.102.  The objective of this programme area is to undertake research to determine the effects of increased ultraviolet radiation resulting from stratospheric ozone layer depletion on the Earth's surface, and on plant and animal life in affected regions, as well as its impact on agriculture, and to develop, as appropriate, strategies aimed at mitigating its adverse effects.

**Activities**

Management-related activities

14.103.  In affected regions, Governments at the appropriate level, with the support of the relevant international and regional organizations, should take the necessary measures, through institutional cooperation, to facilitate the implementation of research and evaluation regarding the effects of enhanced ultraviolet radiation on plant and animal life, as well as on agricultural activities, and consider taking appropriate remedial measures.

**Notes**

1/ Some of the issues in this programme area are presented in chapter 3 of Agenda 21 (Combating poverty).

2/ Some of the issues in this programme area are discussed in chapter 8 of Agenda 21 (Integrating environment and development in decision-making) and in chapter 37 (National mechanisms and international cooperation for capacity-building in developing countries).

3/ Some of the issues are presented in chapter 10 of Agenda 21 (Integrated approach to the planning and management of land resources).

4/ The activities of this programme area are related to some of the activities in chapter 15 of Agenda 21 (Conservation of biological diversity).

5/ The activities of this programme area are related to some of the activities in chapter 9 of Agenda 21 (Protection of the atmosphere).

# Agenda 21 – Chapter 15
## CONSERVATION OF BIOLOGICAL DIVERSITY

15.1. The objectives and activities in this chapter of Agenda 21 are intended to improve the conservation of biological diversity and the sustainable use of biological resources, as well as to support the Convention on Biological Diversity.

15.2. Our planet's essential goods and services depend on the variety and variability of genes, species, populations and ecosystems. Biological resources feed and clothe us and provide housing, medicines and spiritual nourishment. The natural ecosystems of forests, savannahs, pastures and rangelands, deserts, tundras, rivers, lakes and seas contain most of the Earth's biodiversity. Farmers' fields and gardens are also of great importance as repositories, while gene banks, botanical gardens, zoos and other germplasm repositories make a small but significant contribution. The current decline in biodiversity is largely the result of human activity and represents a serious threat to human development.

## PROGRAMME AREA

### Conservation of biological diversity

**Basis for action**

15.3. Despite mounting efforts over the past 20 years, the loss of the world's biological diversity, mainly from habitat destruction, over-harvesting, pollution and the inappropriate introduction of foreign plants and animals, has continued. Biological resources constitute a capital asset with great potential for yielding sustainable benefits. Urgent and decisive action is needed to conserve and maintain genes, species and ecosystems, with a view to the sustainable management and use of biological resources. Capacities for the assessment, study and systematic observation and evaluation of biodiversity need to be reinforced at national and international levels. Effective national action and international cooperation is required for the in situ protection of ecosystems, for the ex situ conservation of biological and genetic resources and for the enhancement of ecosystem functions. The participation and support of local communities are elements essential to the success of such an approach. Recent advances in biotechnology have pointed up the likely potential for agriculture, health and welfare and for the environmental purposes of the genetic material contained in plants, animals and micro-organisms. At the same time, it is particularly important in this context to stress that States have the sovereign right to exploit their own biological resources pursuant to their environmental policies, as well as the responsibility to conserve their biodiversity and use their biological resources sustainably, and to ensure that activities within their jurisdiction or control do not cause damage to the biological diversity of other States or of areas beyond the limits of national jurisdiction.

**Objectives**

15.4. Governments at the appropriate level, with the cooperation of the relevant United Nations bodies and regional, intergovernmental and non-governmental organizations, the private sector and financial institutions, and taking into consideration indigenous people and their communities, as well as social and economic factors, should:

    a.    Press for the early entry into force of the Convention on Biological Diversity, with the widest possible participation;

    b.    Develop national strategies for the conservation of biological diversity and the sustainable use of biological resources;

    c.    Integrate strategies for the conservation of biological diversity and the sustainable use of biological resources into national development strategies and/or plans;

    d.    Take appropriate measures for the fair and equitable sharing of benefits derived from research and development and use of biological and genetic resources, including biotechnology, between the sources of those resources and those who use them;

    e.    Carry out country studies, as appropriate, on the conservation of biological diversity and the sustainable use of biological resources, including analyses of relevant costs and benefits, with particular reference to socio-economic aspects;

f.    Produce regularly updated world reports on biodiversity based upon national assessments;

g.    Recognize and foster the traditional methods and the knowledge of indigenous people and their communities, emphasizing the particular role of women, relevant to the conservation of biological diversity and the sustainable use of biological resources, and ensure the opportunity for the participation of those groups in the economic and commercial benefits derived from the use of such traditional methods and knowledge; 1/

h.    Implement mechanisms for the improvement, generation, development and sustainable use of biotechnology and its safe transfer, particularly to developing countries, taking account the potential contribution of biotechnology to the conservation of biological diversity and the sustainable use of biological resources; 2/

i.    Promote broader international and regional cooperation in furthering scientific and economic understanding of the importance of biodiversity and its functions in ecosystems;

j.    Develop measures and arrangements to implement the rights of countries of origin of genetic resources or countries providing genetic resources, as defined in the Convention on Biological Diversity, particularly developing countries, to benefit from the biotechnological development and the commercial utilization of products derived from such resources. 2/ 3/

**Activities**

(a) Management-related activities

15.5. Governments at the appropriate levels, consistent with national policies and practices, with the cooperation of the relevant United Nations bodies and, as appropriate, intergovernmental organizations and, with the support of indigenous people and their communities, non-governmental organizations and other groups, including the business and scientific communities, and consistent with the requirements of international law, should, as appropriate:

a.    Develop new or strengthen existing strategies, plans or programmes of action for the conservation of biological diversity and the sustainable use of biological resources, taking account of education and training needs; 4/

b.    Integrate strategies for the conservation of biological diversity and the sustainable use of biological and genetic resources into relevant sectoral or cross-sectoral plans, programmes and policies, with particular reference to the special importance of terrestrial and aquatic biological and genetic resources for food and agriculture; 5/

c.    Undertake country studies or use other methods to identify components of biological diversity important for its conservation and for the sustainable use of biological resources, ascribe values to biological and genetic resources, identify processes and activities with significant impacts upon biological diversity, evaluate the potential economic implications of the conservation of biological diversity and the sustainable use of biological and genetic resources, and suggest priority action;

d.    Take effective economic, social and other appropriate incentive measures to encourage the conservation of biological diversity and the sustainable use of biological resources, including the promotion of sustainable production systems, such as traditional methods of agriculture, agroforestry, forestry, range and wildlife management, which use, maintain or increase biodiversity; 5/

e.    Subject to national legislation, take action to respect, record, protect and promote the wider application of the knowledge, innovations and practices of indigenous and local communities embodying traditional lifestyles for the conservation of biological diversity and the sustainable use of biological resources, with a view to the fair and equitable sharing of the benefits arising, and promote mechanisms to involve those communities, including women, in the conservation and management of ecosystems; 1/

f.  Undertake long-term research into the importance of biodiversity for the functioning of ecosystems and the role of ecosystems in producing goods, environmental services and other values supporting sustainable development, with particular reference to the biology and reproductive capacities of key terrestrial and aquatic species, including native, cultivated and cultured species; new observation and inventory techniques; ecological conditions necessary for biodiversity conservation and continued evolution; and social behaviour and nutrition habits dependent on natural ecosystems, where women play key roles. The work should be undertaken with the widest possible participation, especially of indigenous people and their communities, including women; 1/

g.  Take action where necessary for the conservation of biological diversity through the in situ conservation of ecosystems and natural habitats, as well as primitive cultivars and their wild relatives, and the maintenance and recovery of viable populations of species in their natural surroundings, and implement ex situ measures, preferably in the source country. In situ measures should include the reinforcement of terrestrial, marine and aquatic protected area systems and embrace, inter alia, vulnerable freshwater and other wetlands and coastal ecosystems, such as estuaries, coral reefs and mangroves; 6/

h.  Promote the rehabilitation and restoration of damaged ecosystems and the recovery of threatened and endangered species;

i.  Develop policies to encourage the conservation of biodiversity and the sustainable use of biological and genetic resources on private lands;

j.  Promote environmentally sound and sustainable development in areas adjacent to protected areas with a view to furthering protection of these areas;

k.  Introduce appropriate environmental impact assessment procedures for proposed projects likely to have significant impacts upon biological diversity, providing for suitable information to be made widely available and for public participation, where appropriate, and encourage the assessment of the impacts of relevant policies and programmes on biological diversity;

l.  Promote, where appropriate, the establishment and strengthening of national inventory, regulation or management and control systems related to biological resources, at the appropriate level;

m.  Take measures to encourage a greater understanding and appreciation of the value of biological diversity, as manifested both in its component parts and in the ecosystem services provided.

(b) Data and information

15.6. Governments at the appropriate level, consistent with national policies and practices, with the cooperation of the relevant United Nations bodies and, as appropriate, intergovernmental organizations, and with the support of indigenous people and their communities, non-governmental organizations and other groups, including the business and scientific communities, and consistent with the requirements of international law, should, as appropriate: 7/

a.  Regularly collate, evaluate and exchange information on the conservation of biological diversity and the sustainable use of biological resources;

b.  Develop methodologies with a view to undertaking systematic sampling and evaluation on a national basis of the components of biological diversity identified by means of country studies;

c.  Initiate or further develop methodologies and begin or continue work on surveys at the appropriate level on the status of ecosystems and establish baseline information on biological and genetic resources, including those in terrestrial, aquatic, coastal and marine ecosystems, as well as inventories undertaken with the participation of local and indigenous people and their communities;

d.  Identify and evaluate the potential economic and social implications and benefits of the conservation and sustainable use of terrestrial and aquatic species in each country, building upon the results of country studies;

e.  Undertake the updating, analysis and interpretation of data derived from the identification, sampling and evaluation activities described above;

f.  Collect, assess and make available relevant and reliable information in a timely manner and in a form suitable for decision-making at all levels, with the full support and participation of local and indigenous people and their communities.

(c) International and regional cooperation and coordination

15.7. Governments at the appropriate level, with the cooperation of the relevant United Nations bodies and, as appropriate, intergovernmental organizations, and, with the support of indigenous people and their communities, non-governmental organizations and other groups, including the business and scientific communities, and consistent with the requirements of international law, should, as appropriate:

a.  Consider the establishment or strengthening of national or international capabilities and networks for the exchange of data and information of relevance to the conservation of biological diversity and the sustainable use of biological and genetic resources; 7/

b.  Produce regularly updated world reports on biodiversity based upon national assessments in all countries;

c.  Promote technical and scientific cooperation in the field of conservation of biological diversity and the sustainable use of biological and genetic resources. Special attention should be given to the development and strengthening of national capabilities by means of human resource development and institution-building, including the transfer of technology and/or development of research and management facilities, such as herbaria, museums, gene banks, and laboratories, related to the conservation of biodiversity; 8/

d.  Without prejudice to the relevant provisions of the Convention on Biological Diversity, facilitate for this chapter the transfer of technologies relevant to the conservation of biological diversity and the sustainable use of biological resources or technologies that make use of genetic resources and cause no significant damage to the environment, in conformity with chapter 34, and recognizing that technology includes biotechnology; 2/ 8/

e.  Promote cooperation between the parties to relevant international conventions and action plans with the aim of strengthening and coordinating efforts to conserve biological diversity and the sustainable use of biological resources;

f.  Strengthen support for international and regional instruments, programmes and action plans concerned with the conservation of biological diversity and the sustainable use of biological resources;

g.  Promote improved international coordination of measures for the effective conservation and management of endangered/non-pest migratory species, including appropriate levels of support for the establishment and management of protected areas in transboundary locations;

h.  Promote national efforts with respect to surveys, data collection, sampling and evaluation, and the maintenance of gene banks.

**Means of implementation**

(a) Financing and cost evaluation

15.8. The Conference secretariat has estimated the average total annual cost (1993-2000) of implementing the activities of this chapter to be about $3.5 billion, including about $1.75 billion from the international community on grant or concessional terms. These are indicative and order-of-magnitude estimates only and have not been reviewed by Governments. Actual costs and financial terms, including any that are non-concessional, will depend upon, inter alia, the specific strategies and programmes Governments decide upon for implementation.

(b) Scientific and technological means

15.9.  Specific aspects to be addressed include the need to develop:

  a.  Efficient methodologies for baseline surveys and inventories, as well as for the systematic sampling and evaluation of biological resources;

  b.  Methods and technologies for the conservation of biological diversity and the sustainable use of biological resources;

  c.  Improved and diversified methods for ex situ conservation with a view tothe long-term conservation of genetic resources of importance for research and development.

(c) Human resource development

15.10.  There is a need, where appropriate, to:

  a.  Increase the number and/or make more efficient use of trained personnel in scientific and technological fields relevant to the conservation of biological diversity and the sustainable use of biological resources;

  b.  Maintain or establish programmes for scientific and technical education and training of managers and professionals, especially in developing countries, on measures for the identification, conservation of biological diversity and the sustainable use of biological resources;

  c.  Promote and encourage understanding of the importance of the measures required for the conservation of biological diversity and the sustainable use of biological resources at all policy-making and decision-making levels in Governments, business enterprises and lending institutions, and promote and encourage the inclusion of these topics in educational programmes.

(d) Capacity-building

15.11.  There is a need, where appropriate, to:

  a.  Strengthen existing institutions and/or establish new ones responsible for the conservation of biological diversity and to consider the development of mechanisms such as national biodiversity institutes or centres;

  b.  Continue to build capacity for the conservation of biological diversity and the sustainable use of biological resources in all relevant sectors;

  c.  Build capacity, especially within Governments, business enterprises and bilateral and multilateral development agencies, for integrating biodiversity concerns, potential benefits and opportunity cost calculations into project design, implementation and evaluation processes, as well as for evaluating the impact on biological diversity of proposed development projects;

  d.  Enhance the capacity of governmental and private institutions, at the appropriate level, responsible for protected area planning and management to undertake intersectoral coordination and planning with other governmental institutions, non-governmental organizations and, where appropriate, indigenous people and their communities.

# Agenda 21 – Chapter 16
## ENVIRONMENTALLY SOUND MANAGEMENT OF BIOTECHNOLOGY

16.1. Biotechnology is the integration of the new techniques emerging from modern biotechnology with the well-established approaches of traditional biotechnology. Biotechnology, an emerging knowledge-intensive field, is a set of enabling techniques for bringing about specific man-made changes in deoxyribonucleic acid (DNA), or genetic material, in plants, animals and microbial systems, leading to useful products and technologies. By itself, biotechnology cannot resolve all the fundamental problems of environment and development, so expectations need to be tempered by realism. Nevertheless, it promises to make a significant contribution in enabling the development of, for example, better health care, enhanced food security through sustainable agricultural practices, improved supplies of potable water, more efficient industrial development processes for transforming raw materials, support for sustainable methods of afforestation and reforestation, and detoxification of hazardous wastes. Biotechnology also offers new opportunities for global partnerships, especially between the countries rich in biological resources (which include genetic resources) but lacking the expertise and investments needed to apply such resources through biotechnology and the countries that have developed the technological expertise to transform biological resources so that they serve the needs of sustainable development. 1/ Biotechnology can assist in the conservation of those resources through, for example, ex situ techniques. The programme areas set out below seek to foster internationally agreed principles to be applied to ensure the environmentally sound management of biotechnology, to engender public trust and confidence, to promote the development of sustainable applications of biotechnology and to establish appropriate enabling mechanisms, especially within developing countries, through the following activities:

   a. Increasing the availability of food, feed and renewable raw materials;

   b. Improving human health;

   c. Enhancing protection of the environment;

   d. Enhancing safety and developing international mechanisms for cooperation;

   e. Establishing enabling mechanisms for the development and the environmentally sound application of biotechnology.

### PROGRAMME AREAS

### A. Increasing the availability of food, feed and renewable raw materials

**Basis for action**

16.2. To meet the growing consumption needs of the global population, the challenge is not only to increase food supply, but also to improve food distribution significantly while simultaneously developing more sustainable agricultural systems. Much of this increased productivity will need to take place in developing countries. It will require the successful and environmentally safe application of biotechnology in agriculture, in the environment and in human health care. Most of the investment in modern biotechnology has been in the industrialized world. Significant new investments and human resource development will be required in biotechnology, especially in the developing world.

**Objectives**

16.3. The following objectives are proposed, keeping in mind the need to promote the use of appropriate safety measures based on programme area D:

   a. To increase to the optimum possible extent the yield of major crops, livestock, and aquaculture species, by using the combined resources of modern biotechnology and conventional plant/animal/micro-organism improvement, including the more diverse use of genetic material resources, both hybrid and original. 2/ Forest product yields should similarly be increased, to ensure the sustainable use of forests; 3/

b. To reduce the need for volume increases of food, feed and raw materials by improving the nutritional value (composition) of the source crops, animals and micro-organisms, and to reduce post-harvest losses of plant and animal products;

c. To increase the use of integrated pest, disease and crop management t echniques to eliminate overdependence on agrochemicals, thereby encouraging environmentally sustainable agricultural practices;

d. To evaluate the agricultural potential of marginal lands in comparison with other potential uses and to develop, where appropriate, systems allowing for sustainable productivity increases;

e. To expand the applications of biotechnology in forestry, both for increasing yields and more efficient utilization of forest products and for improving afforestation and reforestation techniques. Efforts should be concentrated on species and products that are grown in and are of value particularly for developing countries;

f. To increase the efficiency of nitrogen fixation and mineral absorption by the symbiosis of higher plants with micro-organis ms;

g. To improve capabilities in basic and applied sciences and in the management of complex interdisciplinary research projects.

## Activities

(a) Management-related activities

16.4. Governments at the appropriate level, with the assistance of international and regional organizations and with the support of non-governmental organizations, the private sector and academic and scientific institutions, should improve both plant and animal breeding and micro-organisms through the use of traditional and modern biotechnologies, to enhance sustainable agricultural output to achieve food security, particularly in developing countries, with due regard to the prior identification of desired characteristics before modification, taking into account the needs of farmers, the socio-economic, cultural and environmental impacts of modifications and the need to promote sustainable social and economic development, paying particular attention to how the use of biotechnology will impact on the maintenance of environmental integrity.

16.5. More specifically, these entities should:

a. Improve productivity, nutritional quality and shelf-life of food and animal feed products, with efforts including work on pre- and post-harvest losses;

b. Further develop resistance to diseases and pests;

c. Develop plant cultivars tolerant and/or resistant to stress from factors such as pests and diseases and from abiotic causes;

d. Promote the use of underutilized crops of possible future importance for human nutrition and industrial supply of raw materials;

e. Increase the efficiency of symbiotic processes that assist sustainable agricultural production;

f.   Facilitate the conservation and safe exchange of plant, animal and microbial germ plasm by applying risk assessment and management procedures, including improved diagnostic techniques for detection of pests and diseases by better methods of rapid propagation;

g.   Develop improved diagnostic techniques and vaccines for the prevention and spread of diseases and for rapid assessment of toxins or infectious organisms in products for human use or livestock feed;

h.   Identify more productive strains of fast-growing trees, especially for fuel wood, and develop rapid propagation methods to aid their wider dissemination and use;

i.   Evaluate the use of various biotechnology techniques to improve the yields of fish, algal and other aquatic species;

j.   Promote sustainable agricultural output by strengthening and broadening the capacity and scope of existing research centres to achieve the necessary critical mass through encouragement and monitoring of research into the development of biological products and processes of productive and environmental value that are economically and socially feasible, while taking safety considerations into account;

k.   Promote the integration of appropriate and traditional biotechnologies for the purposes of cultivating genetically modified plants, rearing healthy animals and protecting forest genetic resources;

l.   Develop processes to increase the availability of materials derived from biotechnology for use in food, feed and renewable raw materials production.

(b) Data and information

16.6.  The following activities should be undertaken:

a.   Consideration of comparative assessments of the potential of the different technologies for food production, together with a system for assessing the possible effects of biotechnologies on international trade in agricultural products;

b.   Examination of the implications of the withdrawal of subsidies and the possible use of other economic instruments to reflect the environmental costs associated with the unsustainable use of agrochemicals;

c.   Maintenance and development of data banks of information on environmental and health impacts of organisms to facilitate risk assessment;

d.   Acceleration of technology acquisition, transfer and adaptation by developing countries to support national activities that promote food security.

(c) International and regional cooperation and coordination

16.7.  Governments at the appropriate level, with the support of relevant international and regional organizations, should promote the following activities in conformity with international agreements or arrangements on biological diversity, as appropriate:

a.   Cooperation on issues related to conservation of, access to and exchange of germ plasm; rights associated with intellectual property and informal innovations, including farmers' and breeders' rights; access to the benefits of biotechnology; and bio-safety;

b.   Promotion of collaborative research programmes, especially in developing countries, to support activities outlined in this programme area, with particular reference to cooperation with local and indigenous people and their communities in the conservation of biological diversity and sustainable use of biological resources, as well as the fostering of traditional methods and knowledge of such groups in connection with these activities;

    c.    Acceleration of technology acquisition, transfer and adaptation by developing countries to support national activities that promote food security, through the development of systems for substantial and sustainable productivity increases that do not damage or endanger local ecosystems; 4/

    d.    Development of appropriate safety procedures based on programme area D, taking account of ethical considerations.

**Means of implementation**

(a) Financing and cost evaluation

16.8.  The Conference secretariat has estimated the average total annual cost (1993-2000) of implementing the activities of this programme to be about $5 billion, including about $50 million from the international community on grant or concessional terms. These are indicative and order-of-magnitude estimates only and have not been reviewed by Governments. Actual costs and financial terms, including any that are non-concessional, will depend upon, inter alia, the specific strategies and programmes Governments decide upon for implementation.

(b) Scientific and technological means*

(c) Human resource development

16.9.  Training of competent professionals in the basic and applied sciences at all levels (including scientific personnel, technical staff and extension workers) is one of the most essential components of any programme of this kind. Creating awareness of the benefits and risks of biotechnology is essential. Given the importance of good management of research resources for the successful completion of large multidisciplinary projects, continuing programmes of formal training for scientists should include managerial training. Training programmes should also be developed, within the context of specific projects, to meet regional or national needs for comprehensively trained personnel capable of using advanced technology to reduce the "brain drain" from developing to developed countries. Emphasis should be given to

\* \* \* \*
\* See paras. 16.6 and 16.7.
\* \* \* \*

encouraging collaboration between and training of scientists, extension workers and users to produce integrated systems. Additionally, special consideration should be given to the execution of programmes for training and exchange of knowledge on traditional biotechnologies and for training on safety procedures.

(d) Capacity-building

16.10.    Institutional upgrading or other appropriate measures will be needed to build up technical, managerial, planning and administrative capacities at the national level to support the activities in this programme area. Such measures should be backed up by international, scientific, technical and financial assistance adequate to facilitate technical cooperation and raise the capacities of the developing countries. Programme area E contains further details.

## B. Improving human health

**Basis for action**

16.11.    The improvement of human health is one of the most important objectives of development. The deterioration of environmental quality, notably air, water and soil pollution owing to toxic chemicals, hazardous wastes, radiation and other sources, is a matter of growing concern. This degradation of the environment resulting from inadequate or inappropriate development has a direct negative effect on human health. Malnutrition, poverty, poor human settlements, lack of good-quality potable water and inadequate sanitation facilities add to the problems of communicable and non-communicable diseases. As a consequence, the health and well-being of people are exposed to increasing pressures.

**Objectives**

16.12.   The main objective of this programme area is to contribute, through the environmentally sound application of biotechnology to an overall health programme, to: 5/

    a.   Reinforce or inaugurate (as a matter of urgency) programmes to help combat major communicable diseases;

    b.   Promote good general health among people of all ages;

    c.   Develop and improve programmes to assist in specific treatment of and protection from major non-communicable diseases;

    d.   Develop and strengthen appropriate safety procedures based on programme area D, taking account of ethical considerations;

    e.   Create enhanced capabilities for carrying out basic and applied research and for managing interdisciplinary research.

**Activities**

(a) Management-related activities

16.13.   Governments at the appropriate level, with the assistance of international and regional organizations, academic and scientific institutions, and the pharmaceutical industry, should, taking into account appropriate safety and ethical considerations:

    a.   Develop national and international programmes for identifying and targeting those populations of the world most in need of improvement in general health and protection from diseases;

    b.   Develop criteria for evaluating the effectiveness and the benefits and risks of the proposed activities;

    c.   Establish and enforce screening, systematic sampling and evaluation procedures for drugs and medical technologies, with a view to barring the use of those that are unsafe for the purposes of experimentation; ensure that drugs and technologies relating to reproductive health are safe and effective and take account of ethical considerations;

    d.   Improve, systematically sample and evaluate drinking-water quality by introducing appropriate specific measures, including diagnosis of water-borne pathogens and pollutants;

    e.   Develop and make widely available new and improved vaccines against major communicable diseases that are efficient and safe and offer protection with a minimum number of doses, including intensifying efforts directed at the vaccines needed to combat common diseases of children;

    f.   Develop biodegradable delivery systems for vaccines that eliminate the need for present multiple-dose schedules, facilitate better coverage of the population and reduce the costs of immunization;

g. Develop effective biological control agents against dis ease-transmitting vectors, such as mosquitoes and resistant variants, taking account of environmental protection considerations;

h. Using the tools provided by modern biotechnology, develop, inter alia, improved diagnostics, new drugs and improved treatments and delivery systems;

i. Develop the improvement and more effective utilization of medicinal plants and other related sources;

j. Develop processes to increase the availability of materials derived from biotechnology, for use in improving human health.

(b) Data and information

16.14. The following activities should be undertaken:

a. Research to assess the comparative social, environmental and financial costs and benefits of different technologies for basic and reproductive health care within a framework of universal safety and ethical considerations;

b. Development of public education programmes directed at decision makers and the general public to encourage awareness and understanding of the relative benefits and risks of modern biotechnology, according to ethical and cultural considerations.

(c) International and regional cooperation and coordination

16.15. Governments at the appropriate levels, with the support of relevant international and regional organizations, should:

a. Develop and strengthen appropriate safety procedures based on programme area D, taking account of ethical considerations;

b. Support the development of national programmes, particularly in developing countries, for improvements in general health, especially protection from major communicable diseases, common diseases of children and disease-transmitting factors.

**Means of implementation**

16.16. To achieve the above goals, the activities need to be implemented with urgency if progress towards the control of major communicable diseases is to be achieved by the beginning of the next century. The spread of some diseases to all regions of the world calls for global measures. For more localized diseases, regional or national policies will be more appropriate. The achievement of goals calls for:

a. Continuous international commitment;

b. National priorities with a defined time-frame;

c. Scientific and financial input at global and national levels.

(a) Financing and cost evaluation

16.17. The Conference secretariat has estimated the average total annual cost (1993-2000) of implement ing the activities of this programme to be about $14 billion, including about $130 million from the international community on grant or concessional terms. These are indicative and order-of-magnitude estimates only and have not been reviewed by Governments. Actual costs and financial terms, including any that are non-concessional, will depend upon, inter alia, the specific strategies and programmes Governments decide upon for implementation.

(b) Scientific and technological means

16.18.    Well-coordinated multidisciplinary efforts involving cooperation between scientists, financial institutions and industries will be required. At the global level, this may mean collaboration between research institutions in different countries, with funding at the intergovernment al level, possibly supported by similar collaboration at the national level. Research and development support will also need to be strengthened, together with the mechanisms for providing the transfer of relevant technology.

(c) Human resource development

16.19.    Training and technology transfer is needed at the global level, with regions and countries having access to, and participation in exchange of, information and expertise, particularly indigenous or traditional knowledge and related biotechnology. It is essential to create or enhance endogenous capabilities in developing countries to enable them to participate actively in the processes of biotechnology production. The training of personnel could be undertaken at three levels:

      a.    That of scientists required for basic and product-oriented research;

      b.    That of health personnel (to be trained in the safe use of new products) and of science managers required for complex intermultidisciplinary research;

      c.    That of tertiary-level technical workers required for delivery in the field.

(d) Capacity-building*

## C. Enhancing protection of the environment

**Basis for action**

16.20.    Environmental protection is an integral component of sustainable development. The environment is threatened in all its biotic and abiotic components: animals, plants, microbes and ecosystems comprising biological diversity; water, soil and air, which form the physical components of habitats and ecosystems; and all the interactions between the components of biodiversity and their sustaining habitats and ecosystems. With the continued increase in the use of chemicals, energy and non-renewable resources by an

* * * *

* See programme area E.

* * * *

expanding global population, associated environmental problems will also increase. Despite increasing efforts to prevent waste accumulation and to promote recycling, the amount of environmental damage caused by overconsumption, the quantities of waste generated and the degree of unsustainable land use appear likely to continue growing.

16.21.    The need for a diverse genetic pool of plant, animal and microbial germ plasm for sustainable development is well established. Biotechnology is one of many tools that can play an important role in supporting the rehabilitation of degraded ecosystems and landscapes. This may be done through the development of new techniques for reforestation and afforestation, germ plasm conservation, and cultivation of new plant varieties. Biotechnology can also contribute to the study of the effects exerted on the remaining organisms and on ot her organisms by organisms introduced into ecosystems.

**Objectives**

16.22.    The aim of this programme is to prevent, halt and reverse environmental degradation through the appropriate use of biotechnology in conjunction with other technologies, while supporting safety procedures as an integral component of the programme. Specific objectives include the inauguration as soon as possible of specific programmes with specific targets:

a. To adopt production processes making optimal use of natural resources, by recycling biomass, recovering energy and minimizing waste generation; 6/

b. To promote the use of biotechnologies, with emphasis on bio-remediation of land and water, waste treatment, soil conservation, reforestation, afforestation and land rehabilitation; 7/ 8/

c. To apply biotechnologies and their products to protect environmental integrity with a view to long-term ecological security.

**Activities**

(a) Management-related activities

16.23.    Governments at the appropriate level, with the support of relevant international and regional organizations, the private sector, non-governmental organizations and academic and scientific institutions, should:

a. Develop environmentally sound alternatives and improvements for environmentally damaging production processes;

b. Develop applications to minimize the requirement for unsustainable synthetic chemical input and to maximize the use of environmentally appropriate products, including natural products (see programme area A);

c. Develop processes to reduce waste generation, treat waste before disposal and make use of biodegradable materials;

d. Develop processes to recover energy and provide renewable energy sources, animal feed and raw materials from recycling organic waste and biomass;

e. Develop processes to remove pollutants from the environment, including accidental oil spills, where conventional techniques are not available or are expensive, inefficient or inadequate;

f. Develop processes to increase the availability of planting materials, particularly indigenous varieties, for use in afforestation and reforestation and to improve sustainable yields from forests;

g. Develop applications to increase the availability of stress-tolerant planting material for land rehabilitation and soil conservation;

h. Promote the use of integrated pest management based on the judicious use of bio-control agents;

i. Promote the appropriate use of bio-fertilizers within national fertilizer programmes;

j. Promote the use of biotechnologies relevant to the conservation and scientific study of biological diversity and the sustainable use of biological resources;

k. Develop easily applicable technologies for the treatment of sewage and organic waste;

l. Develop new technologies for rapid screening of organisms for useful biological properties;

m. Promote new biotechnologies for tapping mineral resources in an environmentally sustainable manner.

(b) Data and information

16.24. Steps should be taken to increase access both to existing information about biotechnology and to facilities based on global databases.

(c) International and regional cooperation and coordination

16.25. Governments at the appropriate level, with the support of relevant international and regional organizations, should:

a. Strengthen research, training and development capabilities, particularly in developing countries, to support the activities outlined in this programme area;

b. Develop mechanisms for scaling up and disseminating environmentally sound biotechnologies of high environmental importance, especially in the short term, even though those biotechnologies may have limited commercial potential;

c. Enhance cooperation, including transfer of biotechnology, between participating countries for capacity-building;

d. Develop appropriate safety procedures based on programme area D, taking account of ethical considerations.

**Means of implementation**

(a) Financing and cost evaluation

16.26. The Conference secretariat has estimated the average total annual cost (1993-2000) of implementing the activities of this programme to be about $1 billion, including about $10 million from the international community on grant or concessional terms. These are indicative and order-of-magnitude estimates only and have not been reviewed by Governments. Actual costs and financial terms, including any that are non-concessional, will depend upon, inter alia, the specific strategies and programmes Governments decide upon for implementation.

(b) Scientific and technological means*
(c) Human resource development

16.27. The activities for this programme area will increase the demand for trained personnel. Support for existing training programmes needs to be increased, for example, at the university and technical institute level, as well as the exchange of trained personnel between countries and regions. New and additional training programmes also need to be developed, for example, for technical and support personnel. There is also an urgent need to improve the level of understanding of biological principles and their policy implications among decision makers in Governments, and financial and other institutions.

(d) Capacity-building

16.28. Relevant institutions will need to have the responsibility for undertaking, and the capacity (political, financial and workforce) to undertake, the above-mentioned activities and to be dynamic in response to new biotechnological developments (see programme area E).

* * * *
* See paras. 16.23-16.25 above.
* * * *

**D. Enhancing safety and developing international mechanisms for cooperation**

**Basis for action**

16.29.　There is a need for further development of internationally agreed principles on risk assessment and management of all aspects of biotechnology, which should build upon those developed at the national level. Only when adequate and transparent safety and border-control procedures are in place will the community at large be able to derive maximum benefit from, and be in a much better position to accept the potential benefits and risks of, biotechnology. Several fundamental principles could underlie many of these safety procedures, including primary consideration of the organism, building on the principle of familiarity, applied in a flexible framework, taking into account national requirements and recognizing that the logical progression is to start with a step -by-step and case-by-case approach, but also recognizing that experience has shown that in many instances a more comprehensive approach should be used, based on the experiences of the first period, leading, inter alia, to streamlining and categorizing; complementary consideration of risk assessment and risk management; and classification into contained use or release to the environment.

**Objectives**

16.30.　The aim of this programme area is to ensure safety in biotechnology development, application, exchange and transfer through international agreement on principles to be applied on risk assessment and management, with particular reference to health and environmental considerations, including the widest possible public participation and taking account of ethical considerations.

**Activities**

16.31.　The proposed activities for this programme area call for close international cooperation. They should build upon planned or existing activities to accelerate the environmentally sound application of biotechnology, especially in developing countries.

(a) Management-related activities

16.32.　Governments at the appropriate level, with the support of relevant international and regional organizations, the private sector, non-governmental organizations and academic and scientific institutions, should:

　　　a.　Make the existing safety procedures widely available by collecting the existing information and adapting it to the specific needs of different countries and regions;

　　　b.　Further develop, as necessary, the existing safety procedures to promote scientific development and categorization in the areas of risk assessment and risk management (information requirements; databases; procedures for assessing risks and conditions of release; establishment of safety conditions; monitoring and inspections, taking account of ongoing national, regional and international initiatives and avoiding duplication wherever possible);

　　　c.　Compile, update and develop compatible safety procedures into a framework of internationally agreed principles as a basis for guidelines to be applied on safety in biotechnology, including consideration of the need for and feasibility of an international agreement, and promote information exchange as a basis for further development, drawing on the work already undertaken by international or other expert bodies;

　　　d.　Undertake training programmes at the national and regional levels on the application of the proposed technical guidelines;

　　　e.　Assist in exchanging information about the procedures required for safe handling and risk management and about the conditions of release of the products of biotechnology, and cooperate in providing immediate assistance in cases of emergencies that may arise in conjunction with the use of biotechnology products.

(b) Data and information*

(c) International and regional cooperation and coordination

16.33. Governments at the appropriate level, with the support of the relevant international and regional organizations, should raise awareness of the relative benefits and risks of biotechnology.

16.34. Further activities should include the following (see also para. 16.32):

a. Organizing one or more regional meetings between countries to identify further practical steps to facilitate international cooperation in bio-safety;

b. Establishing an international network incorporating national, regional and global contact points;

c. Providing direct assistance upon request through the international network, using information networks, databases and information procedures;

d. Considering the need for and feasibility of internationally agreed guidelines on safety in biotechnology releases, including risk assessment and risk management, and considering studying the feasibility of guidelines which could facilitate national legislation on liability and compensation.

* * * *

* See paras. 16.32 and 16.33.

* * * *


**Means of implementation**

(a) Financing and cost evaluation

16.35. The UNCED secretariat has estimated the average total annual cost (1993-2000) of implementing the activities of this programmes to be about $2 million from the international community on grant or concessional terms. These are indicative and order-of-magnitude estimates only and have not been reviewed by Governments. Actual costs and financial terms, including any that are non-concessional, will depend upon, inter alia, the specific strategies and programmes Governments decide upon for implementation.

(b) Scientific and technological means*

(c) Human resource development*

(d) Capacity-building

16.36. Adequate international technical and financial assistance should be provided and technical cooperation to developing countries facilitated in order to build up technical, managerial, planning and administrative capacities at the national level to support the activities in this programme area (see also programme area E).

**E. Establishing enabling mechanisms for the development and the environmentally sound application of biotechnology**

**Basis for action**

16.37. The accelerated development and application of biotechnologies, particularly in developing countries, will require a major effort to build up institutional capacities at the national and regional levels. In developing countries, enabling factors such as training capacity, know-how, research and development facilities and funds, industrial building capacity, capital (including venture capital) protection of intellectual property rights, and expertise in areas including marketing research, technology assessment, socio-economic assessment and safety assessment are frequently inadequate. Efforts will therefore need to be made to build up capacities in these and other areas and to match such efforts with appropriate levels of financial support. There is therefore a need to strengthen the endogenous capacities of developing countries by means of new international initiatives to support research in order to speed up the development and application of both new and conventional biotechnologies to serve the needs of sustainable development at the local, national and regional levels. National mechanisms to allow for informed comment by the public with regard to biotechnology research and application should be part of the process.

\* \* \* \*

\* See para. 16.32.

\* \* \* \*

16.38. Some activities at the national, regional and global levels already address the issues outlined in programme areas A, B, C and D, as well as the provisioin of advice to individual countries on the development of national guidelines and systems for the implementation of those guidelines. These activities are generally uncoordinated, however, involving many different organizations, priorities, constituencies, time-scales, funding sources and resource constraints. There is a need for a much more cohesive and coordinated approach to harness available resources in the most effective manner. As with most new technologies, research in biotechnology and the application of its findings could have significant positive and negative socio-economic as well as cultural impacts. These impacts should be carefully identified in the earliest phases of the development of biotechnology in order to enable appropriate management of the consequences of transferring biotechnology.

## Objectives

16.39. The objectives are as follows:

a. To promote the development and application of biotechnologies, with special emphasis on developing countries, by:

    i. Enhancing existing efforts at the national, regional and global levels;

    ii. Providing the necessary support for biotechnology, particularly research and product development, at the national, regional and international levels;

    iii. Raising public awareness regarding the relative beneficial aspects of and risks related to biotechnology, to contribute to sustainable development;

    iv. Helping to create a favourable climate for investments, industrial capacity-building and distribution/marketing;

    v. Encouraging the exchange of scientists among all countries and discouraging the "brain drain";

    vi. Recognizing and fostering the traditional methods and knowledge of indigenous peoples and their communities and ensuring the opportunity for their participation in the economic and commercial benefits arising from developments in biotechnology; 9/

b. To identify ways and means of enhancing current efforts, building wherever possible on existing enabling mechanisms, particularly regional, to determine the precise nature of the needs for additional initiatives, particularly in respect of developing countries, and to develop appropriate response strategies, including proposals for any new international mechanisms;

c. To establish or adapt appropriate mechanisms for safety appraisal and risk assessment at the local, regional and international levels, as appropriate.

## Activities

(a) Management-related activities

16.40. Governments at the appropriate level, with the support of international and regional organizations, the private sector, non-governmental organizations and academic and scientific institutions, should:

   a.   Develop policies and mobilize additional resources to facilitate greater access to the new biotechnologies, particularly by and among developing countries;

   b.   Implement programmes to create greater awareness of the potential and relative benefits and risks of the environmentally sound application of biotechnology among the public and key decision makers;

   c.   Undertake an urgent review of existing enabling mechanisms, programmes and activities at the national, regional and global levels to identify strengths, weaknesses and gaps, and to assess the priority needs of developing countries;

   d.   Undertake an urgent follow-up and critical review to identify ways and means of strengthening endogenous capacities within and among developing countries for the environmentally sound application of biot echnology, including, as a first step, ways to improve existing mechanisms, particularly at the regional level, and, as a subsequent step, the consideration of possible new international mechanisms, such as regional biotechnology centres;

   e.   Develop strategic plans for overcoming targeted constraints by means of appropriate research, product development and marketing;

   f.   Establish additional quality-assurance standards for biotechnology applications and products, where necessary.

(b) Data and information

16.40. The following activities should be undertaken: facilitation of access to existing information dissemination systems, especially among developing countries; improvement of such access where appropriate; and consideration of the development of a directory of information.

(c) International and regional cooperation and coordination

16.41. Governments at the appropriate level, with the assistance of international and regional organizations, should develop appropriate new initiatives to identify priority areas for research based on specific problems and facilitate access to new biotechnologies, particularly by and among developing countries, among relevant undertakings within those countries, in order to strengthen endogenous capacities and to support the building of research and institutional capacity in those countries.

**Means of implementation**

(a) Financing and cost evaluation

16.42. The Conference secretariat has estimated the average total annual cost (1993-2000) of implementing the activities of this programme to be about $5 million from the international community on grant or concessional terms. These are indicative and order-of-magnitude estimates only and have not been reviewed by Governments. Actual costs and financial terms, including any that are non-concessional, will depend upon, inter alia, the specific strategies and programmes Governments decide upon for implementation.

(b) Scientific and technological means

16.43. Workshops, symposia, seminars and other exchanges among the scientific community at the regional and global levels, on specific priority themes, will need to be organized, making full use of the existing scientific and technological manpower in each country for bringing about such exchanges.

(c) Human resource development

16.44. Personnel development needs will need to be identified and additional training programmes developed at the national, regional and global levels, especially in developing countries. These should be supported by increased training at all levels, graduate, postgraduate and post-doctoral, as well as by the training of technicians and support staff, with particular reference to the generation of trained manpower in consultant services, design, engineering and marketing research. Training programmes for lecturers training scientists and technologists in advanced research institutions in different countries throughout the world will also need to be developed, and systems giving appropriate rewards, incentives and recognition to scientists and technologists will need to be instituted (see para. 16.44). Conditions of service will also need to be improved at the national level in developing countries to encourage and nurture trained manpower with a view to retaining that manpower locally. Society should be informed of the social and cultural impact of the development and application of biotechnology.

(d) Capacity-building

16.45. Biotechnology research and development is undertaken both under highly sophisticated conditions and at the practical level in many countries. Efforts will be needed to ensure that the necessary infrastructure facilities for research, extension and technology activities are available on a decentralized basis. Global and regional collaboration for basic and applied research and development will also need to be further enhanced and every effort should be made to ensure that existing national and regional facilities are fully utilized. Such institutions already exist in some countries and it should be possible to make use of them for training purposes and joint research projects. Strengthening of universities, technical schools and local research institutions for the development of biotechnologies and extension services for their application will need to be developed, especially in developing countries.

# Agenda 21 – Chapter 17
## PROTECTION OF THE OCEANS, ALL KINDS OF SEAS, INCLUDING ENCLOSED AND SEMI-ENCLOSED SEAS, AND COASTAL AREAS AND THE PROTECTION, RATIONAL USE AND DEVELOPMENT OF THEIR LIVING RESOURCES

17.1. The marine environment - including the oceans and all seas and adjacent coastal areas - forms an integrated whole that is an essential component of the global life-support system and a positive asset that presents opportunities for sustainable development. International law, as reflected in the provisions of the United Nations Convention on the Law of the Sea 1/, 2/ referred to in this chapter of Agenda 21, sets forth rights and obligations of States and provides the international basis upon which to pursue the protection and sustainable development of the marine and coastal environment and its resources. This requires new approaches to marine and coastal area management and development, at the national, subregional, regional and global levels, approaches that are integrated in content and are precautionary and anticipatory in ambit, as reflected in the following programme areas: 3/

    a.   Integrated management and sustainable development of coastal areas, including exclusive economic zones;

    b.   Marine environmental protection;

    c.   Sustainable use and conservation of marine living resources of the high seas;

    d.   Sustainable use and conservation of marine living resources under national jurisdiction;

    e.   Addressing critical uncertainties for the management of the marine environment and climate change;

    f.   Strengthening international, including regional, cooperation and coordination;

    g.   Sustainable development of small islands.

17.2. The implementation by developing countries of the activities set forth below shall be commensurate with their individual technological and financial capacities and priorities in allocating resources for development needs and ultimately depends on the technology transfer and financial resources required and made available to them.

## PROGRAMME AREAS

### A. Integrated management and sustainable development of coastal and marine areas, including exclusive economic zones

**Basis for action**

17.3. The coastal area contains diverse and productive habitats important for human settlements, development and local subsistence. More than half the world's population lives within 60 km of the shoreline, and this could rise to three quarters by the year 2020. Many of the world's poor are crowded in coastal areas. Coastal resources are vital for many local communities and indigenous people. The exclusive economic zone (EEZ) is also an important marine area where the States manage the development and conservation of natural resources for the benefit of their people. For small island States or countries, these are the areas most available for development activities.

17.4. Despite national, subregional, regional and global efforts, current approaches to the management of marine and coastal resources have not always proved capable of achieving sustainable development, and coastal resources and the coastal environment are being rapidly degraded and eroded in many parts of the world.

**Objectives**

17.5. Coastal States commit themselves to integrated management and sustainable development of coastal areas and the marine environment under their national jurisdiction. To this end, it is necessary to, inter alia:

    a.   Provide for an integrated policy and decision-making process, including all involved sectors, to promote compatibility and a balance of uses;

b. Identify existing and projected uses of coastal areas and their interactions;

c. Concentrate on well-defined issues concerning coastal management;

d. Apply preventive and precautionary approaches in project planning and implementation, including prior assessment and systematic observation of the impacts of major projects;

e. Promote the development and application of methods, such as national resource and environmental accounting, that reflect changes in value resulting from uses of coastal and marine areas, including pollution, marine erosion, loss of resources and habitat destruction;

f. Provide access, as far as possible, for concerned individuals, groups and organizations to relevant information and opportunities for consultation and participation in planning and decision-making at appropriate levels.

## Activities

(a) Management-related activities

17.6. Each coastal State should consider establishing, or where necessary strengthening, appropriate coordinating mechanisms (such as a high-level policy planning body) for integrated management and sustainable development of coastal and marine areas and their resources, at both the local and national levels. Such mechanisms should include consultation, as appropriate, with the academic and private sectors, non-governmental organizations, local communities, resource user groups, and indigenous people. Such national coordinating mechanisms could provide, inter alia, for:

a. Preparation and implementation of land and water use and siting policies;

b. Implementation of integrated coastal and marine management and sustainable development plans and programmes at appropriate levels;

c. Preparation of coastal profiles identifying critical areas, including eroded zones, physical processes, development patterns, user conflicts and specific priorities for management;

d. Prior environmental impact assessment, systematic observation and follow-up of major projects, including the systematic incorporation of results in decision-making;

e. Contingency plans for human induced and natural disasters, including likely effects of potential climate change and sealevel rise, as well as contingency plans for degradation and pollution of anthropogenic origin, including spills of oil and other materials;

f. Improvement of coastal human settlements, especially in housing, drinking water and treatment and disposal of sewage, solid wastes and industrial effluents;

g. Periodic assessment of the impacts of external factors and phenomena to ensure that the objectives of integrated management and sustainable development of coastal areas and the marine environment are met;

h. Conservation and restoration of altered critical habitats;

i. Integration of sectoral programmes on sustainable development for settlements, agriculture, tourism, fishing, ports and industries affecting the coastal area;

j. Infrastructure adaptation and alternative employment;

k. Human resource development and training;

l. Public education, awareness and information programmes;

> m. Promoting environmentally sound technology and sustainable practices;
>
> n. Development and simultaneous implementation of environmental quality criteria.

17.7. Coastal States, with the support of international organizations, upon request, should undertake measures to maintain biological diversity and productivity of marine species and habitats under national jurisdiction. Inter alia, these measures might include: surveys of marine biodiversity, inventories of endangered species and critical coastal and marine habitats; establishment and management of protected areas; and support of scientific research and dissemination of its results.

(b) Data and information

17.8. Coastal States, where necessary, should improve their capacity to collect, analyse, assess and use information for sustainable use of resources, including environmental impacts of activities affecting the coastal and marine areas. Information for management purposes should receive priority support in view of the intensity and magnitude of the changes occurring in the coastal and marine areas. To this end, it is necessary to, inter alia:

> a. Develop and maintain databases for assessment and management of coastal areas and all seas and their resources;
>
> b. Develop socio-economic and environmental indicators;
>
> c. Conduct regular environmental assessment of the state of the environment of coastal and marine areas;
>
> d. Prepare and maintain profiles of coastal area resources, activities, uses, habitats and protected areas based on the criteria of sustainable development;
>
> e. Exchange information and data.

17.9. Cooperation with developing countries, and, where applicable, subregional and regional mechanisms, should be strengthened to improve their capacities to achieve the above.

(c) International and regional cooperation and coordination

17.10. The role of international cooperation and coordination on a bilateral basis and, where applicable, within a subregional, interregional, regional or global framework, is to support and supplement national efforts of coastal States to promote integrated management and sustainable development of coastal and marine areas.

17.11. States should cooperate, as appropriate, in the preparation of national guidelines for integrated coastal zone management and development, drawing on existing experience. A global conference to exchange experience in the field could be held before 1994.

**Means of implementation**

(a) Financing and cost evaluation

17.12. The Conference secretariat has estimated the average total annual cost (1993-2000) of implementing the activities of this programme to be about $6 billion including about $50 million from the international community on grant or concessional terms. These are indicative and order-of-magnitude estimates only and have not been reviewed by Governments. Actual costs and financial terms, including any that are non-concessional, will depend upon, inter alia, the specific strategies and programmes Governments decide upon for implementation.

(b) Scientific and technological means

17.13. States should cooperate in the development of necessary coastal systematic observation, research and information management systems. They should provide access to and transfer environmentally safe technologies and methodologies for sustainable development of coastal and marine areas to developing countries. They should also develop technologies and endogenous scientific and technological capacities.

17.14. International organizations, whether subregional, regional or global, as appropriate, should support coastal States, upon request, in these efforts, as indicated above, devoting special attention to developing countries.

(c) Human resource development

17.15. Coastal States should promote and facilitate the organization of education and training in integrated coastal and marine management and sustainable development for scientists, technologists, managers (including community-based managers) and users, leaders, indigenous peoples, fisherfolk, women and youth, among others. Management and development, as well as environmental protection concerns and local planning issues, should be incorporated in educational curricula and public awareness campaigns, with due regard to traditional ecological knowledge and socio-cultural values.

17.16. International organizations, whet her subregional, regional or global, as appropriate, should support coastal States, upon request, in the areas indicated above, devoting special attention to developing countries.

(d) Capacity-building

17.17. Full cooperation should be extended, upon request, to coastal States in their capacity-building efforts and, where appropriate, capacity-building should be included in bilateral and multilateral development cooperation. Coastal States may consider, inter alia:

    a.    Ensuring capacity-building at the local level;

    b.    Consulting on coastal and marine issues with local administrations, the business community, the academic sector, resource user groups and the general public;

    c.    Coordinating sectoral programmes while building capacity;

    d.    Identifying existing and potential capabilities, facilities and needs for human resources development and scientific and technological infrastructure;

    e.    Developing scientific and technological means and research;

    f.    Promoting and facilitating human resource development and education;

    g.    Supporting "centres of excellence" in integrated coastal and marine resource management;

    h.    Supporting pilot demonstration programmes and projects in integrated coastal and marine management.

## B. Marine environmental protection

**Basis for action**

17.18. Degradation of the marine environment can result from a wide range of sources. Land-based sources contribute 70 per cent of marine pollution, while maritime transport and dumping-at-sea activities contribute 10 per cent each. The contaminants that pose the greatest threat to the marine environment are, in variable order of importance and depending on differing national or regional situations, sewage, nutrients, synthetic organic compounds, sediments, litter and plastics, metals, radionuclides, oil/hydrocarbons and polycyclic aromatic hydrocarbons (PAHs). Many of the polluting substances originating from land-based sources are of particular concern to the marine environment since they exhibit at the same time toxicity, persistence and bioaccumulation in the food chain. There is currently no global scheme to address marine pollution from land-based sources.

17.19. Degradation of the marine environment can also result from a wide range of activities on land. Human settlements, land use, construction of coastal infrastructure, agriculture, forestry, urban development, tourism and industry can affect the marine environment. Coastal erosion and siltation are of particular concern.

17.20. Marine pollution is also caused by shipping and sea-based activities. Approximately 600,000 tons of oil enter the oceans each year as a result of normal shipping operations, accidents and illegal discharges. With respect to offshore oil and gas activities, currently machinery space discharges are regulated internationally and six regional conventions to control platform discharges have been under consideration. The nature and extent of environmental impacts from offshore oil exploration and production activities generally account for a very small proportion of marine pollution.

17.21. A precautionary and anticipatory rather than a reactive approach is necessary to prevent the degradation of the marine environment. This requires, inter alia, the adoption of precautionary measures, environmental impact assessments, clean production techniques, recycling, waste audits and minimization, construction and/or improvement of sewage treatment facilities, quality management criteria for the proper handling of hazardous substances, and a comprehensive approach to damaging impacts from air, land and water. Any management framework must include the improvement of coastal human settlements and the integrated management and development of coastal areas.

**Objectives**

17.22. States, in accordance with the provisions of the United Nations Convention on the Law of the Sea on protection and preservation of the marine environment, commit themselves, in accordance with their policies, priorities and resources, to prevent, reduce and control degradation of the marine environment so as to maintain and improve its life-support and productive capacities. To this end, it is necessary to:

    a. Apply preventive, precautionary and anticipatory approaches so as to avoid degradation of the marine environment, as well as to reduce the risk of long-term or irreversible adverse effects upon it;

    b. Ensure prior assessment of activities that may have significant adverse impacts upon the marine environment;

    c. Integrate protection of the marine environment into relevant general environmental, social and economic development policies;

    d. Develop economic incentives, where appropriate, to apply clean technologies and other means consistent with the internalization of environmental costs, such as the polluter pays principle, so as to avoid degradation of the marine environment;

    e. Improve the living standards of coastal populations, particularly in developing countries, so as to contribute to reducing the degradation of the coastal and marine environment.

17.23. States agree that provision of additional financial resources, through appropriate international mechanisms, as well as access to cleaner technologies and relevant research, would be necessary to support action by developing countries to implement this commitment.

**Activities**

(a) Management-related activities

Prevention, reduction and control of degradation of the marine environment from land-based activities

17.24. In carrying out their commitment to deal with degradation of the marine environment from land-based activities, States should take action at the national level and, where appropriate, at the regional and subregional levels, in concert with action to implement programme area A, and should take account of the Montreal Guidelines for the Protection of the Marine Environment from Land-Based Sources.

17.25. To this end, States, with the support of the relevant international environmental, scientific, technical and financial organizations, should cooperate, inter alia, to:

   a. Consider updating, strengthening and extending the Montreal Guidelines, as appropriate;

   b. Assess the effectiveness of existing regional agreements and action plans, where appropriate, with a view to identifying means of strengthening action, where necessary, to prevent, reduce and control marine degradation caused by land-based activities;

   c. Initiate and promote the development of new regional agreements, where appropriate;

   d. Develop means of providing guidance on technologies to deal with the major types of pollution of the marine environment from land-based sources, according to the best scientific evidence;

   e. Develop policy guidance for relevant global funding mechanisms;

   f. Identify additional steps requiring international cooperation.

17.26. The UNEP Governing Council is invited to convene, as soon as practicable, an intergovernmental meeting on protection of the marine environment from land-based activities.

17.27. As concerns sewage, priority actions to be considered by States may include:

   a. Incorporating sewage concerns when formulating or reviewing coastal development plans, including human settlement plans;

   b. Building and maintaining sewage treatment facilities in accordance with national policies and capacities and international cooperation available;

   c. Locating coastal outfalls so as to maintain an acceptable level of environmental quality and to avoid exposing shell fisheries, water intakes and bathing areas to pathogens;

   d. Promoting environmentally sound co-treatments of domestic and compatible industrial effluents, with the introduction, where practicable, of controls on the entry of effluents that are not compatible with the system;

   e. Promoting primary treatment of municipal sewage discharged to rivers, estuaries and the sea, or other solutions appropriate to specific sites;

   f. Establishing and improving local, national, subregional and regional, as necessary, regulatory and monitoring programmes to control effluent discharge, using minimum sewage effluent guidelines and water quality criteria and giving due consideration to the characteristics of receiving bodies and the volume and type of pollutants.

17.28.  As concerns other sources of pollution, priority actions to be considered by States may include:

a.  Establishing or improving, as necessary, regulatory and monitoring programmes to control effluent discharges and emissions, including the development and application of control and recycling technologies;

b.  Promoting risk and environmental impact assessments to help ensure an acceptable level of environmental quality;

c.  Promoting assessment and cooperation at the regional level, where appropriate, with respect to the input of point source pollutants from new installations;

d.  Eliminating the emission or discharge of organohalogen compounds that threaten to accumulate to dangerous levels in the marine environment;

e.  Reducing the emission or discharge of other synthetic organic compounds that threaten to accumulate to dangerous levels in the marine environment;

f.  Promoting controls over anthropogenic inputs of nitrogen and phosphorus that enter coastal waters where such problems as eutrophication threaten the marine environment or its resources;

g.  Cooperating with developing countries, through financial and technological support, to maximize the best practicable control and reduction of substances and wastes that are toxic, persistent or liable to bio-accumulate and to establish environmentally sound land-based waste disposal alternatives to sea dumping;

h.  Cooperating in the development and implementation of environmentally sound land-use techniques and practices to reduce run-off to water-courses and estuaries which would cause pollution or degradation of the marine environment;

i.  Promoting the use of environmentally less harmful pesticides and fertilizers and alternative methods for pest control, and considering the prohibition of those found to be environmentally unsound;

j.  Adopting new initiatives at national, subregional and regional levels for controlling the input of non-point source pollutants, which require broad changes in sewage and waste management, agricultural practices, mining, construction and transportation.

17.29. As concerns physical destruction of coastal and marine areas causing degradation of the marine environment, priority actions should include control and prevention of coastal erosion and siltation due to anthropogenic factors related to, inter alia, land-use and construction techniques and practices. Watershed management practices should be promoted so as to prevent, control and reduce degradation of the marine environment.

Prevention, reduction and control of degradation of the marine environment from sea-based activities

17.30. States, acting individually, bilaterally, regionally or multilaterally and within the framework of IMO and other relevant international organizations, whether subregional, regional or global, as appropriate, should assess the need for additional measures to address degradation of the marine environment:

a.  From shipping, by:

i.  Supporting wider ratification and implementation of relevant shipping conventions and protocols;

ii.  Facilitating the processes in (i), providing support to individual States upon request to help them overcome the obstacles identified by them;

iii. Cooperating in monitoring marine pollution from ships, especially from illegal discharges (e.g., aerial surveillance), and enforcing MARPOL discharge, provisions more rigorously;

iv. )Assessing the state of pollution caused by ships in particularly sensitive areas identified by IMO and taking action to implement applicable measures, where necessary, within such areas to ensure compliance with generally accepted international regulations;

v. Taking action to ensure respect of areas designated by coastal States, within their exclusive economic zones, consistent with international law, in order to protect and preserve rare or fragile ecosystems, such as coral reefs and mangroves;

vi. Considering the adoption of appropriate rules on ballast water discharge to prevent the spread of non-indigenous organisms;

vii. Promoting navigational safety by adequate charting of coasts and ship-routing, as appropriate;

viii. Assessing the need for stricter international regulations to further reduce the risk of accidents and pollution from cargo ships (including bulk carriers);

ix. Encouraging IMO and IAEA to work together to complete consideration of a code on the carriage of irradiated nuclear fuel in flasks on board ships;

x. Revising and updating the IMO Code of Safety for Nuclear Merchant Ships and considering how best to implement a revised code;

xi. Supporting the ongoing activity within IMO regarding development of appropriate measures for reducing air pollution from ships;

xii. Supporting the ongoing activity within IMO regarding the development of an international regime governing the transportation of hazardous and noxious substances carried by ships and further considering whether the compensation funds similar to the ones established under the Fund Convention would be appropriate in respect of pollution damage caused by substances other than oil;

b. From dumping, by:

i. Supporting wider ratification, implementation and participation in relevant Conventions on dumping at sea, including early conclusion of a future strategy for the London Dumping Convention;

ii. Encouraging the London Dumping Convention parties to take appropriate steps to stop ocean dumping and incineration of hazardous substances;

c. From offshore oil and gas platforms, by assessing existing regulatory measures to address discharges, emissions and safety and assessing the need for additional measures;

d. From ports, by facilitating establishment of port reception facilities for the collection of oily and chemical residues and garbage from ships, especially in MARPOL special areas, and promoting the establishment of smaller scale facilities in marinas and fishing harbours.

17.31. IMO and as appropriate, other competent United Nations organizations, when requested by the States concerned, should assess, where appropriate, the state of marine pollution in areas of congested shipping, such as heavily used international straits, with a view to ensuring compliance with generally accepted international regulations, particularly those related to illegal discharges from ships, in accordance with the provisions of Part III of the United Nations Convention on the Law of the Sea.

17.32. States should take measures to reduce water pollution caused by organotin compounds used in anti-fouling paints.

17.33. States should consider ratifying the Convention on Oil Pollution Preparedness, Response and Cooperation, which addresses, inter alia, the development of contingency plans on the national and international level, as appropriate, including provision of oil-spill response material and training of personnel, including its possible extension to chemical spill response.

17.34. States should intensify international cooperation to strengthen or establish, where necessary, regional oil/chemical-spill response centres and/or, as appropriate, mechanisms in cooperation with relevant subregional, regional or global intergovernmental organizations and, where appropriate, industry-based organizations.


(b) Data and information

17.35. States should, as appropriate, and in accordance with the means at their disposal and with due regard for their technical and scientific capacity and resources, make systematic observations on the state of the marine environment. To this end, States should, as appropriate, consider:

    a. Establishing systematic observation systems to measure marine environmental quality, including causes and effects of marine degradation, as a basis for management;

    b. Regularly exchanging information on marine degradation caused by land-based and sea-based activities and on actions to prevent, control and reduce such degradation;

    c. Supporting and expanding international programmes for systematic observations such as the mussel watch programme, building on existing facilities with special attention to developing countries;

    d. Establishing a clearing-house on marine pollution control information, including processes and technologies to address marine pollution control and to support their transfer to developing countries and other countries with demonstrated needs;

    e. Establishing a global profile and database providing information on the sources, types, amounts and effects of pollutants reaching the marine environment from land-based activities in coastal areas and sea-based sources;

    f. Allocating adequate funding for capacity-building and training programmes to ensure the full participation of developing countries, in particular, in any international scheme under the organs and organizations of the United Nations system for the collection, analysis and use of data and information.

**Means of implementation**

(a) Financing and cost evaluation

17.36. The Conference secretariat has estimated the average total annual cost (1993-2000) of implementing the activities of this programme to be about $200 million from the international community on grant or concessional terms. These are indicative and order-of-magnitude estimates only and have not been reviewed by Governments. Actual costs and financial terms, including any that are non-concessional, will depend upon, inter alia, the specific strategies and programmes Governments decide upon for implementation.

(b) Scientific and technological means

17.37. National, subregional and regional action programmes will, where appropriate, require technology transfer, in conformity with chapter 34, and financial resources, particularly where developing countries are concerned, including:

  a. Assistance to industries in identifying and adopting clean production or cost-effective pollution control technologies;

  b. Planning development and application of low-cost and low-maintenance sewage installation and treatment technologies for developing countries;

  c. Equipment of laboratories to observe systematically human and other impacts on the marine environment;

  d. Identification of appropriate oil- and chemical-spill control materials, including low-cost locally available materials and techniques, suitable for pollution emergencies in developing countries;

  e. Study of the use of persistent organohalogens that are liable to accumulate in the marine environment to identify those that cannot be adequately controlled and to provide a basis for a decision on a time schedule for phasing them out as soon as practicable;

  f. Establishment of a clearing-house for information on marine pollution control, including processes and technologies to address marine pollution control, and support for their transfer to developing and other countries with demonstrated needs.

(c) Human resource development

17.38. States individually or in cooperation with each other and with the support of international organizations, whether subregional, regional or global, as appropriate, should:

  a. Provide training for critical personnel required for the adequate protection of the marine environment as identified by training needs' surveys at the national, regional or subregional levels;

  b. Promote the introduction of marine environmental protection topics into the curriculum of marine studies programmes;

  c. Establish training courses for oil- and chemical-spill response personnel, in cooperation, where appropriate, with the oil and chemical industries;

  d. Conduct workshops on environmental aspects of port operations and development;

  e. Strengthen and provide secure financing for new and existing specialized international centres of professional maritime education;

  f. States should, through bilateral and multilateral cooperation, support and supplement the national efforts of developing countries as regards human resource development in relation to prevention and reduction of degradation of the marine environment.

(d) Capacity-building

17.39. National planning and coordinating bodies should be given the capacity and authority to review all land-based activities and sources of pollution for their impacts on the marine environment and to propose appropriate control measures.

17.40. Research facilities should be strengthened or, where appropriate, developed in developing countries for systematic observation of marine pollution, environmental impact assessment and development of control recommendations and should be managed and staffed by local experts.

17.41. Special arrangements will be needed to provide adequate financial and technical resources to assist developing countries in preventing and solving problems associated with activities that threaten the marine environment.

17.42. An international funding mechanism should be created for the application of appropriate sewage treatment technologies and building sewage treatment facilities, including grants or concessional loans from international agencies and appropriate regional funds, replenished at least in part on a revolving basis by user fees.

17.43. In carrying out these programme activities, particular attention needs to be given to the problems of developing countries that would bear an unequal burden because of their lack of facilities, expertise or technical capacities.

## C. Sustainable use and conservation of marine living resources of the high seas

### Basis for action

17.44. Over the last decade, fisheries on the high seas have considerably expanded and currently represent approximately 5 per cent of total world landings. The provisions of the United Nations Convention on the Law of the Sea on the marine living resources of the high seas sets forth rights and obligations of States with respect to conservation and utilization of those resources.

17.45. However, management of high seas fisheries, including the adoption, monitoring and enforcement of effective conservation measures, is inadequate in many areas and some resources are overutilized. There are problems of unregulated fishing, overcapitalization, excessive fleet size, vessel reflagging to escape controls, insufficiently selective gear, unreliable databases and lack of sufficient cooperation between States. Action by States whose nationals and vessels fish on the high seas, as well as cooperation at the bilateral, subregional, regional and global levels, is essential particularly for highly migratory species and straddling stocks. Such action and cooperation should address inadequacies in fishing practices, as well as in biological knowledge, fisheries statistics and improvement of systems for handling data. Emphasis should also be on multi-species management and other approaches that take into account the relationships among species, especially in addressing depleted species, but also in identifying the potential of underutilized or unutilized populations.

### Objectives

17.46. States commit themselves to the conservation and sustainable use of marine living resources on the high seas. To this end, it is necessary to:

    a.    Develop and increase the potential of marine living resources to meet human nutritional needs, as well as social, economic and development goals;

    b.    Maintain or restore populations of marine species at levels that can produce the maximum sustainable yield as qualified by relevant environmental and economic factors, taking into consideration relationships among species;

c. Promote the development and use of selective fishing gear and practices that minimize waste in the catch of target species and minimize by-catch of non-target species;

d. Ensure effective monitoring and enforcement with respect to fishing activities;

e. Protect and restore endangered marine species;

f. Preserve habitats and other ecologically sensitive areas;

g. Promote scientific research with respect to the marine living resources in the high seas.

17.47. Nothing in paragraph 17.46 above restricts the right of a State or the competence of an international organization, as appropriate, to prohibit, limit or regulate the exploitation of marine mammals on the high seas more strictly than provided for in that paragraph. States shall cooperate with a view to the conservation of marine mammals and, in the case of cetaceans, shall in particular work through the appropriate international organizations for their conservation, management and study.

17.48. The ability of developing countries to fulfil the above objectives is dependent upon their capabilities, including the financial, scientific and technological means at their disposal. Adequate financial, scientific and technological cooperation should be provided to support action by them to implement these objectives.


**Activities**

(a) Management-related activities

17.49. States should take effective action, including bilateral and multilateral cooperation, where appropriate at the subregional, regional and global levels, to ensure that high seas fisheries are managed in accordance with the provisions of the United Nations Convention on the Law of the Sea. In particular, they should:

a. Give full effect to these provisions with regard to fisheries populations whose ranges lie both within and beyond exclusive economic zones (straddling stocks);

b. Give full effect to these provisions with regard to highly migratory species;

c. Negotiate, where appropriate, international agreements for the effective management and conservation of fishery stocks;

d. Define and identify appropriate management units;

e. States should convene, as soon as possible, an intergovernmental conference under United Nations auspices, taking into account relevant activities at the subregional, regional and global levels, with a view to promoting effective implementation of the provisions of the United Nations

Convention on the Law of the Sea on straddling fish stocks and highly migratory fish stocks. The conference, drawing, inter alia, on scientific and technical studies by FAO, should identify and assess existing problems related to the conservation and management of such fish stocks, and consider means of improving cooperation on fisheries among States, and formulate appropriate recommendations. The work and the results of the conference should be fully consistent with the provisions of the United Nations Convention on the Law of the Sea, in particular the rights and obligations of coastal States and States fishing on the high seas.

17.50. States should ensure that fishing activities by vessels flying their flags on the high seas take place in a manner so as to minimize incidental catch.

17.51. States should take effective action consistent with international law to monitor and control fishing activities by vessels flying their flags on the high seas to ensure compliance with applicable conservation and management rules, including full, detailed, accurate and timely reporting of catches and effort.

17.52. States should take effective action, consistent with international law, to deter reflagging of vessels by their nationals as a means of avoiding compliance with applicable conservation and management rules for fishing activities on the high seas.

17.53. States should prohibit dynamiting, poisoning and other comparable destructive fishing practices.

17.54. States should fully implement General Assembly resolution 46/215 on large-scale pelagic drift-net fishing.

17.55. States should take measures to increase the availability of marine living resources as human food by reducing wastage, post-harvest losses and discards, and improving techniques of processing, distribution and transportation.

(b) Data and information

17.56. States, with the support of international organizations, whether subregional, regional or global, as appropriate, should cooperate to:

    a. Promote enhanced collection of data necessary for the conservation and sustainable use of the marine living resources of the high seas;

    b. Exchange on a regular basis up-to-date data and information adequate for fisheries assessment;

    c. Develop and share analytical and predictive tools, such as stock assessment and bioeconomic models;

    d. Establish or expand appropriate monitoring and assessment programmes.

(c) International and regional cooperation and coordination

17.57. States, through bilateral and multilateral cooperation and within the framework of subregional and regional fisheries bodies, as appropriate, and with the support of other international intergovernmental agencies, should assess high seas resource potentials and develop profiles of all stocks (target and non-target).

17.58. States should, where and as appropriate, ensure adequate coordination and cooperation in enclosed and semi-enclosed seas and between subregional, regional and global intergovernmental fisheries bodies.

17.59. Effective cooperation within existing subregional, regional or global fisheries bodies should be encouraged. Where such organizations do not exist, States should, as appropriate, cooperate to establish such organizations.

17.60. States with an interest in a high seas fishery regulated by an existing subregional and/or regional high seas fisheries organization of which they are not members should be encouraged to join that organization, where appropriate.

17.61.  States recognize:

   a.  The responsibility of the International Whaling Commission for the conservation and management of whale stocks and the regulation of whaling pursuant to the 1946 International Convention for the Regulation of Whaling;

   b.  The work of the International Whaling Commission Scientific Committee in carrying out studies of large whales in particular, as well as of other cetaceans;

   c.  The work of other organizations, such as the Inter-American Tropical Tuna Commission and the Agreement on Small Cetaceans in the Baltic and North Sea under the Bonn Convention, in the conservation, management and study of cetaceans and other marine mammals.

17.62.  States should cooperate for the conservation, management and study of cetaceans.

**Means of implementation**

(a) Financing and cost evaluation

17.63. The Conference secretariat has estimated the average total annual cost (1993-2000) of implementing the activities of this programme to be about $12 million from the international community on grant or concessional terms. These are indicative and order-of-magnitude estimates only and have not been reviewed by Governments. Actual costs and financial terms, including any that are non-concessional, will depend upon, inter alia, the specific strategies and programmes Governments decide upon for implementation.

(b) Scientific and technological means

17.64. States, with the support of relevant international organizations, where necessary, should develop collaborative technical and research programmes to improve understanding of the life cycles and migrations of species found on the high seas, including identifying critical areas and life stages.

17.65. States, with the support of relevant internat ional organizations, whether subregional, regional or global, as appropriate, should:

   a.  Develop databases on the high seas marine living resources and fisheries;

   b.  Collect and correlate marine environmental data with high seas marine living resources data, including the impacts of regional and global changes brought about by natural causes and by human activities;

   c.  Cooperate in coordinating research programmes to provide the knowledge necessary to manage high seas resources.

(c) Human resource development

17.66. Human resource development at the national level should be targeted at both development and management of high seas resources, including training in high seas fishing techniques and in high seas resource assessment, strengthening cadres of personnel to deal with high seas resource management and conservation and related environmental issues, and training observers and inspectors to be placed on fishing vessels.

(d) Capacity-building

17.67. States, with the support, where appropriate, of relevant international organizations, whether subregional, regional or global, should cooperate to develop or upgrade systems and institutional structures for monitoring, control and surveillance, as well as the research capacity for assessment of marine living resource populations.

17.68. Special support, including cooperation among States, will be needed to enhance the capacities of developing countries in the areas of data and information, scientific and technological means, and human resource development in order to participate effectively in the conservation and sustainable utilization of high seas marine living resources.

## D. Sustainable use and conservation of marine living resources under national jurisdiction

### Basis for action

17.69. Marine fisheries yield 80 to 90 million tons of fish and shellfish per year, 95 per cent of which is taken from waters under national jurisdiction. Yields have increased nearly fivefold over the past four decades. The provisions of the United Nations Convention on the Law of the Sea on marine living resources of the exclusive economic zone and other areas under national jurisdiction set forth rights and obligations of States with respect to conservation and utilization of those resources.

17.70. Marine living resources provide an important source of protein in many countries and their use is often of major importance to local communities and indigenous people. Such resources provide food and livelihoods to millions of people and, if sustainably utilized, offer increased potential to meet nutritional and social needs, particularly in developing countries. To realize this potential requires improved knowledge and identification of marine living resource stocks, particularly of underutilized and unutilized stocks and species, use of new technologies, better handling and processing facilities to avoid wastage, and improved quality and training of skilled personnel to manage and conserve effectively the marine living resources of the exclusive economic zone and other areas under national jurisdiction. Emphasis should also be on multi-species management and other approaches that take into account the relationships among species.

17.71. Fisheries in many areas under national jurisdiction face mounting problems, including local overfishing, unauthorized incursions by foreign fleets, ecosystem degradation, overcapitalization and excessive fleet sizes, underevaluation of catch, insufficiently selective gear, unreliable databases, and increasing competition between artisanal and large-scale fishing, and between fishing and other types of activities.

17.72. Problems extend beyond fisheries. Coral reefs and other marine and coastal habitats, such as mangroves and estuaries, are among the most highly diverse, integrated and productive of the Earth's ecosystems. They often serve import ant ecological functions, provide coastal protection, and are critical resources for food, energy, tourism and economic development. In many parts of the world, such marine and coastal systems are under stress or are threatened from a variety of sources, both human and natural.

### Objectives

17.73. Coastal States, particularly developing countries and States whose economies are overwhelmingly dependent on the exploitation of the marine living resources of their exclusive economic zones, should obtain the full social and economic benefits from sustainable utilization of marine living resources within their exclusive economic zones and other areas under national jurisdiction.

17.74. States commit themselves to the conservation and sustainable use of marine living resources under national jurisdiction. To this end, it is necessary to:

a.   Develop and increase the potential of marine living resources to meet human nutritional needs, as well as social, economic and development goals;

b.   Take into account traditional knowledge and interests of local communities, small-scale artisanal fisheries and indigenous people in development and management programmes;

c.   Maintain or restore populations of marine species at levels that can produce the maximum sustainable yield as qualified by relevant environmental and economic factors, taking into consideration relationships among species;

d.   Promote the development and use of selective fishing gear and practices that minimize waste in the catch of target species and minimize by-catch of non-target species;

e.   Protect and restore endangered marine species;

f.   Preserve rare or fragile ecosystems, as well as habitats and other ecologically sensitive areas.

17.75. Nothing in paragraph 17.74 above restricts the right of a coastal State or the competence of an international organization, as appropriate, to prohibit, limit or regulate the exploitation of marine mammals more strictly than provided for in that paragraph. States shall cooperate with a view to the conservation of marine mammals and in the case of cetaceans shall in particular work through the appropriate international organizations for their conservation, management and study.

17.76. The ability of developing countries to fulfil the above objectives is dependent upon their capabilities, including the financial, scientific and technological means at their disposal. Adequate financial, scientific and technological cooperation should be provided to support action by them to implement these objectives.


**Activities**

(a) Management-related activities

17.77. States should ensure that marine living resources of the exclusive economic zone and other areas under national jurisdiction are conserved and managed in accordance with the provisions of the United Nations Convention on the Law of the Sea.

17.78. States, in implementing the provisions of the United Nations Convention on the Law of the Sea, should address the issues of straddling stocks and highly migratory species, and, taking fully into account the objective set out in paragraph 17.73, access to the surplus of allowable catches.

17.79. Coastal States, individually or through bilateral and/or multilateral cooperation and with the support, as appropriate of international organizations, whether subregional, regional or global, should inter alia:

a.   Assess the potential of marine living resources, including underutilized or unutilized stocks and species, by developing inventories, where necessary, for their conservation and sustainable use;

b.   Implement strategies for the sustainable use of marine living resources, taking into account the special needs and interests of small-scale artisanal fisheries, local communities and indigenous people to meet human nutritional and other development needs;

c.   Implement, in particular in developing countries, mechanisms to develop mariculture, aquaculture and small-scale, deep-sea and oceanic fisheries within areas under national jurisdiction where assessments show that marine living resources are potentially available;

    d.    Strengthen their legal and regulatory frameworks, where appropriate, including management, enforcement and surveillance capabilities, to regulate activities related to the above strategies;

    e.    Take measures to increase the availability of marine living resources as human food by reducing wastage, post-harvest losses and discards, and improving techniques of processing, distribution and transportation;

    f.    Develop and promote the use of environmentally sound technology under criteria compatible with the sustainable use of marine living resources, including assessment of the environmental impact of major new fishery practices;

    g.    Enhance the productivity and utilization of their marine living resources for food and income.

17.80.    Coastal States should explore the scope for expanding recreational and tourist activities based on marine living resources , including those for providing alternative sources of income. Such activities should be compatible with conservation and sustainable development policies and plans.

17.81. Coastal States should support the sustainability of small-scale artisanal fisheries. To this end, they should, as appropriate:

    a.    Integrate small-scale artisanal fisheries development in marine and coastal planning, taking into account the interests and, where appropriate, encouraging representation of fishermen, small-scale fisherworkers, women, local communities and indigenous people;

    b.    Recognize the rights of small-scale fishworkers and the special situation of indigenous people and local communities, including their rights to utilization and protection of their habitats on a sustainable basis ;

    c.    Develop systems for the acquisition and recording of traditional knowledge concerning marine living resources and environment and promote the incorporation of such knowledge into management systems.

17.82. Coastal States should ensure that, in the negotiation and implementation of international agreements on the development or conservation of marine living resources, the interests of local communities and indigenous people are taken into account, in particular their right to subsistence.

17.83. Coastal States, with the support, as appropriate, of international organizations should conduct analyses of the potential for aquaculture in marine and coastal areas under national jurisdiction and apply appropriate safeguards as to the introduction of new species.

17.84.    States should prohibit dynamiting, poisoning and other comparable destructive fishing practices.

17.85. States should identify marine ecosystems exhibiting high levels of biodiversity and productivity and other critical habitat areas and should provide necessary limit ations on use in these areas, through, inter alia, designation of protected areas. Priority should be accorded, as appropriate, to:

    a.    Coral reef ecosystems;

    b.    Estuaries;

    c.    Temperate and tropical wetlands, including mangroves;

    d.    Seagrass beds;

e. Other spawning and nursery areas.

(b) Data and information

17.86. States, individually or through bilateral and multilateral cooperation and with the support, as appropriate, of international organizations, whether subregional, regional or global, should:

    a. Promote enhanced collection and exchange of data necessary for the conservation and sustainable use of the marine living resources under national jurisdiction;

    b. Exchange on a regular basis up-to-date data and information necessary for fisheries assessment;

    c. Develop and share analytical and predictive tools, such as stock assessment and bioeconomic models;

    d. Establish or expand appropriate monitoring and assessment programmes;

    e. Complete or update marine biodiversity, marine living resource and critical habitat profiles of exclusive economic zones and other areas under national jurisdiction, taking account of changes in the environment brought about by natural causes and human activities.

(c) International and regional cooperation and coordination

17.87. States, through bilateral and multilateral cooperation, and with the support of relevant United Nations and other international organizations, should cooperate to:

    a. Develop financial and technical cooperation to enhance the capacities of developing countries in small-scale and oceanic fisheries, as well as in coastal aquaculture and mariculture;

    b. Promote the contribution of marine living resources to eliminate malnutrition and to achieve food self-sufficiency in developing countries, inter alia, by minimizing post-harvest losses and managing stocks for guaranteed sustainable yields;

    c. Develop agreed criteria for the use of selective fishing gear and practices to minimize waste in the catch of target species and minimize by-catch of non-target species;

    d. Promote seafood quality, including through national quality assurance systems for seafood, in order to promote access to markets, improve consumer confidence and maximize economic returns.

17.88. States should, where and as appropriate, ensure adequate coordination and cooperation in enclosed and semi-enclosed seas and between subregional, regional and global intergovernmental fisheries bodies.

17.89. States recognize:

    a. The responsibility of the International Whaling Commission for the conservation and management of whale stocks and the regulation of whaling pursuant to the 1946 International Convention for the Regulation of Whaling;

    b. The work of the International Whaling Commission Scientific Committee in carrying out studies of large whales in particular, as well as of other cetaceans;

    c. The work of other organizations, such as the Inter-American Tropical Tuna Commission and the Agreement on Small Cetaceans in the Baltic and North Sea under the Bonn Convention, in the conservation, management and study of cetaceans and other marine mammals.

17.90.   States should cooperate for the conservation, management and study of cetaceans.

**Means of implementation**

(a) Financing and cost evaluation

17.91. The Conference secretariat has estimated the average total annual cost (1993-2000) of implementing the activities of this programme to be about $6 billion, including about $60 million from the international community on grant or concessional terms. These are indicative and order-of-magnitude estimates only and have not been reviewed by Governments. Actual costs will depend upon, inter alia, the specific strategies and programmes Governments decide upon for implementation.

(b) Scientific and technological means

17.92.   States, with the support of relevant intergovernmental organizations, as appropriate, should:

   a.   Provide for the transfer of environmentally sound technologies to develop fisheries, aquaculture and mariculture, particularly to developing countries;

   b.   Accord special attention to mechanisms for transferring resource information and improved fishing and aquaculture technologies to fishing communities at the local level;

   c.   Promote the study, scientific assessment and use of appropriate traditional management systems;

   d.   Consider observing, as appropriate, the FAO/ICES Code of Practice for Consideration of Transfer and Introduction of Marine and Freshwater Organisms;

   e.   Promote scientific research on marine areas of particular importance for marine living resources, such as areas of high diversity, endemism and productivity and migratory stopover points.

(c) Human resource development

17.93. States individually, or through bilateral and multilateral cooperation and with the support of relevant international organizations, whether subregional, regional or global, as appropriate, should encourage and provide support for developing countries, inter alia, to:

   a.   Expand multidisciplinary education, training and research on marine living resources, particularly in the social and economic sciences;

   b.   Create training opportunities at national and regional levels to support artisanal (including subsistence) fisheries, to develop small-scale use of marine living resources and to encourage equitable participation of local communities, small-scale fish workers, women and indigenous people;

   c.   Introduce topics relating to the importance of marine living res ources in educational curricula at all levels.

(d) Capacity-building

17.94. Coastal States, with the support of relevant subregional, regional and global agencies, where appropriate, should:

   a.   Develop research capacities for assessment of marine living resource populations and monitoring;

   b.   Provide support to local fishing communities, in particular those that rely on fishing for subsistence, indigenous people and women, including, as appropriate, the technical and financial assistance to organize, maintain, exchange and improve traditional knowledge of marine living resources and fishing techniques, and upgrade knowledge on marine ecosystems;

    c.    Establish sustainable aquaculture development strategies, including environmental management in support of rural fish-farming communities;

    d.    Develop and strengthen, where the need may arise, institutions capable of implementing the objectives and activities related to the conservation and management of marine living resources.

17.95. Special support, including cooperation among States, will be needed to enhance the capacities of developing countries in the areas of data and information, scientific and technological means and human resource development in order to enable them to participate effectively in the conservation and sustainable use of marine living resources under national jurisdiction.

### E. Addressing critical uncertainties for the management of the marine environment and climate change

**Basis for action**

17.96. The marine environment is vulnerable and sensitive to climate and atmospheric changes. Rational use and development of coastal areas, all seas and marine resources, as well as conservation of the marine environment, requires the ability to determine the present state of these systems and to predict future conditions. The high degree of uncertainty in present information inhibits effective management and limits the ability to make predictions and assess environmental change. Systematic collection of data on marine environmental parameters will be needed to apply integrated management approaches and to predict effects of global climate change and of atmospheric phenomena, such as ozone depletion, on living marine resources and the marine environment. In order to determine the role of the oceans and all seas in driving global systems and to predict natural and human-induced changes in marine and coastal environments, the mechanisms to collect, synthesize and disseminate information from research and systematic observation activities need to be restructured and reinforced considerably.

17.97. There are many uncertainties about climate change and particularly about sealevel rise. Small increases in sealevel have the potential of causing significant damage to small islands and low-lying coasts. Response strategies should be based on sound data. A long-term cooperative research commitment is needed to provide the data required for global climate models and to reduce uncertainty. Meanwhile, precautionary measures should be undertaken to diminish the risks and effects, particularly on small islands and on low-lying and coastal areas of the world.

17.98. Increased ultraviolet radiation derived from ozone depletion has been reported in some areas of the world. An assessment of its effects in the marine environment is needed to reduce uncertainty and to provide a basis for action.

**Objectives**

17.99. States, in accordance with provisions of the United Nations Convention on the Law of the Sea on marine scientific research, commit themselves to improve the understanding of the marine environment and its role on global processes. To this end, it is necessary to:

    a.    Promote scientific research on and systematic observation of the marine environment within the limits of national jurisdiction and high seas, including interactions with atmospheric phenomena, such as ozone depletion;

b. Promote exchange of data and information resulting from scientific research and systematic observation and from traditional ecological knowledge and ensure its availability to policy makers and the public at the national level;

c. Cooperate with a view to the development of standard inter-calibrated procedures, measuring techniques, data storage and management capabilities for scientific research on and systematic observation of the marine environment.

**Activities**

(a) Management-related activities

17.100.   States should consider, inter alia:

a. Coordinating national and regional observation programmes for coastal and near-shore phenomena related to climate change and for research parameters essential for marine and coastal management in all regions;

b. Providing improved forecasts of marine conditions for the safety of inhabitants of coastal areas and for the efficiency of maritime operations;

c. Cooperating with a view to adopting special measures to cope with and adapt to potential climate change and sealevel rise, including the development of globally accepted methodologies for coastal vulnerability assessment, modelling and response strategies particularly for priority areas, such as small islands and low-lying and critical coastal areas;

d. Identifying ongoing and planned programmes of systematic observation of the marine environment, with a view to integrating activities and establishing priorities to address critical uncertainties for oceans and all seas;

e. Initiating a programme of research to determine the marine biological effects of increased levels of ultraviolet rays due to the depletion of the stratospheric ozone layer and to evaluate the possible effects.

17.101.   Recognizing the important role that oceans and all seas play in attenuating potential climate change, IOC and other relevant competent United Nations bodies, with the support of countries having the resources and expertise, should carry out analysis, assessments and systematic observation of the role of oceans as a carbon sink.

(b) Data and information

17.102.   States should consider, inter alia:

a. Increasing international cooperation particularly with a view to strengthening national scientific and technological capabilities for analysing, assessing and predicting global climate and environmental change;

b. Supporting the role of the IOC in cooperation with WMO, UNEP and other international organizations in the collection, analysis and distribution of data and information from the oceans and all seas, including as appropriate, through the Global Ocean Observing System, giving special attention to the need for IOC to develop fully the strategy for providing training and technical assistance for developing countries through its Training, Education and Mutual Assistance (TEMA) programme;

c. Creating national multisectoral information bases, covering the results of research and systematic observation programmes;

d. Linking these databases to existing data and information services and mechanisms, such as World Weather Watch and Earthwatch;

e. Cooperating with a view to the exchange of data and information and its storage and archiving through the world and regional data centres;

f. Cooperating to ensure full participation of developing countries, in particular, in any international scheme under the organs and organizations of the United Nations system for the collection, analysis and use of data and information.

(c) International and regional cooperation and coordination

17.103.  States should consider bilaterally and multilaterally and in cooperation with international organizations, whether subregional, regional, interregional or global, where appropriate:

a. Providing technical cooperation in developing the capacity of coastal and island States for marine research and systematic observation and for using its results;

b. Strengthening existing national institutions and creating, where necessary, international analysis and prediction mechanisms in order to prepare and exchange regional and global oceanographic analyses and forecasts and to provide facilities for international research and training at national, subregional and regional levels, where applicable.

17.104.  In recognition of the value of Antarctica as an area for the conduct of scientific research, in particular research essential to understanding the global environment, States carrying out such research activities in Antarctica should, as provided for in Article III of the Antarctic Treaty, continue to:

a. Ensure that data and information resulting from such research are freely available to the international community;

b. Enhance access of the international scientific community and specialized agencies of the United Nations to such data and information, including the encouragement of periodic seminars and symposia.

17.105.  States should strengthen high-level inter-agency, subregional, regional and global coordination, as appropriate, and review mechanisms to develop and integrate systematic observation networks. This would include:

a. Review of existing regional and global databases;

b. Mechanisms to develop comparable and compatible techniques, validate methodologies and measurements, organize regular scientific reviews, develop options for corrective measures, agree on formats for presentation and storage, and communicate the information gathered to potential users;

c. Systematic observation of coastal habitats and sealevel changes, inventories of marine pollution sources and reviews of fisheries statistics;

d. Organization of periodic assessments of ocean and all seas and coastal area status and trends.

17.106.  International cooperation, through relevant organizations within the United Nations system, should support countries to develop and integrate regional systematic long-term observation programmes, when applicable, into the Regional Seas Programmes in a coordinated fashion to implement, where appropriate, subregional, regional and global observing systems based on the principle of exchange of data. One aim should be the predicting of the effects of climate-related emergencies on existing coastal physical and socio-economic infrastructure.

17.107.  Based on the results of research on the effects of the additional ultraviolet radiation reaching the Earth's surface, in the fields of human health, agriculture and marine environment, States and international organizations should consider taking appropriate remedial measures.

**Means of implementation**

(a) Financing and cost evaluation

17.108.  The Conference secretariat has estimated the average total annual cost (1993-2000) of implementing the activities of this programme to be about $750 million, including about $480 million from the international community on grant or concessional terms. These are indicative and order-of-magnitude estimates only and have not been reviewed by Governments. Actual costs and financial terms, including any that are non-concessional, will depend upon, inter alia, the specific strategies and programmes Governments decide upon for implementation.

17.109.  Developed countries should provide the financing for the further development and implementation of the Global Ocean Observing System.

(b) Scientific and technological means

17.110.  To address critical uncertainties through systematic coastal and marine observations and research, coastal States should cooperate in the development of procedures that allow for comparable analysis and soundness of data. They should also cooperate on a subregional and regional basis, through existing programmes where applicable, share infrastructure and expensive and sophisticated equipment, develop quality assurance procedures and develop human resources jointly. Special attention should be given to transfer of scientific and technological knowledge and means to support States, particularly developing countries, in the development of endogenous capabilities.

17.111.  International organizations should support, when requested, coastal countries in implementing research projects on the effects of additional ultraviolet radiation.

(c) Human resource development

17.112.  States, individually or through bilateral and multilateral cooperation and with the support, as appropriate, of international organizations whether subregional, regional or global, should develop and implement comprehensive programmes, particularly in developing countries, for a broad and coherent approach to meeting their core human resource needs in the marine sciences.

(d) Capacity-building

17.113.  States should strengthen or establish as necessary, national scientific and technological oceanographic commissions or equivalent bodies to develop, support and coordinate marine science activities and work closely with international organizations.

17.114.  States should use existing subregional and regional mechanisms, where applicable, to develop knowledge of the marine environment, exchange information, organize systematic observations and assessments, and make the most effective use of scientists, facilities and equipment. They should also cooperate in the promotion of endogenous research capabilities in developing countries.

### F. Strengthening international, including regional, cooperation and coordination

**Basis for action**

17.115. It is recognized that the role of international cooperation is to support and supplement national efforts. Implementation of strategies and activities under the programme areas relative to marine and coastal areas and seas requires effective institutional arrangements at national, subregional, regional and global levels, as appropriate. There are numerous national and international, including regional, institutions, both within and outside the United Nations system, with competence in marine issues, and there is a need to improve coordination and strengthen links among them. It is also important to ensure that an integrated and multisectoral approach to marine issues is pursued at all levels.

**Objectives**

17.116. States commit themselves, in accordance with their policies, priorities and resources, to promote institutional arrangements necessary to support the implementation of the programme areas in this chapter. To this end, it is necessary, as appropriate, to:

  a. Integrate relevant sectoral activities addressing environment and development in marine and coastal areas at national, subregional, regional and global levels, as appropriate;

  b. Promote effective information exchange and, where appropriate, institutional linkages between bilateral and multilateral national, regional, subregional and interregional institutions dealing with environment and development in marine and coastal areas;

  c. Promote within the United Nations system, regular intergovernmental review and consideration of environment and development issues with respect to marine and coastal areas;

  d. Promote the effective operation of coordinating mechanisms for the components of the United Nations system dealing with issues of environment and development in marine and coastal areas, as well as links with relevant international development bodies.

**Activities**

(a) Management-related activities

Global

17.117. The General Assembly should provide for regular consideration, within the United Nations system, at the intergovernmental level of general marine and coastal issues, including environment and development matters, and should request the Secretary -General and executive heads of United Nations agencies and organizations to:

  a. Strengthen coordination and develop improved arrangements among the relevant United Nations organizations with major marine and coastal responsibilities, including their subregional and regional components;

  b. Strengthen coordination between those organizations and other United Nations organizations, institutions and specialized agencies dealing with development, trade and other related economic issues, as appropriate;

  c. Improve representation of United Nations agencies dealing with the marine environment in United Nations system-wide coordination efforts;

  d. Promote, where necessary, greater collaboration between the United Nations agencies and subregional and regional coastal and marine programmes;

  e. Develop a centralized system to provide for information on legislation and advice on implementation of legal agreements on marine environmental and development issues.

17.118. States recognize that environmental policies should deal with the root causes of environmental degradation, thus preventing environmental measures from resulting in unnecessary restrictions to trade. Trade policy measures for environmental purposes should not constitute a means of arbitrary or unjustifiable discrimination or a disguised restriction on international trade. Unilateral actions to deal with environmental challenges outside the jurisdiction of the importing country should be avoided. Environmental measures addressing international environmental problems should, as far as possible, be based on an international consensus. Domestic measures targeted to achieve certain environmental objectives may need trade measures to render them effective. Should trade policy measures be found necessary for the enforcement of environmental policies, certain principles and rules should apply. These could include, inter alia, the principle of non-discrimination; the principle that the trade measure chosen should be the least trade-restrictive necessary to achieve the objectives; an obligation to ensure transparency in the use of trade measures related to the environment and to provide adequate notification of national regulations; and the need to give consideration to the special conditions and development requirements of developing countries as they move towards internationally agreed environmental objectives.

Subregional and regional

17.119. States should consider, as appropriate:

  a. Strengthening, and extending where necessary, intergovernmental regional cooperation, the Regional Seas Programmes of UNEP, regional and subregional fisheries organizations and regional commissions;

  b. Introduce, where necessary, coordination among relevant United Nations and other multilateral organizations at the subregional and regional levels, including consideration of co-location of their staff;

  c. Arrange for periodic intraregional consultations;

  d. Facilitate access to and use of expertise and technology through relevant national bodies to subregional and regional centres and networks, such as the Regional Centres for Marine Technology.

(b) Data and information

17.120. States should, where appropriate:

  a. Promote exchange of information on marine and coastal issues;

  b. Strengthen the capacity of international organizations to handle information and support the development of national, subregional and regional data and information systems, where appropriate. This could also include networks linking countries with comparable environmental problems;

  c. Further develop existing international mechanisms such as Earthwatch and GESAMP.

## Means of implementation

(a) Financing and cost evaluation

17.121. The Conference secretariat has estimated the average total annual cost (1993-2000) of implementing the activities of this programme to be about $50 million from the international community on grant or concessional terms. These are indicative and order-of-magnitude estimates only and have not been reviewed by Governments. Actual costs and financial terms, including any that are non-concessional, will depend upon, inter alia, the specific strategies and programmes Governments decide upon for implementation.

(b) Scientific and technological means, human resource development and capacity-building

17.122.   The means of implementation outlined in the other programme areas on marine and coastal issues, under the sections on Scientific and technological means, human resource development and capacity-building are entirely relevant for this programme area as well. Additionally, States should, through international cooperation, develop a comprehensive programme for meeting the core human resource needs in marine sciences at all levels.

## G. Sustainable development of small islands

**Basis for action**

17.123.   Small island developing States, and islands supporting small communities are a special case both for environment and development. They are ecologically fragile and vulnerable. Their small size, limited resources, geographic dispersion and isolation from markets, place them at a disadvantage economically and prevent economies of scale. For small island developing States the ocean and coastal environment is of strategic importance and constitutes a valuable development resource.

17.124.   Their geographic isolation has resulted in their habitation of a comparatively large number of unique species of flora and fauna, giving them a very high share of global biodiversity. They also have rich and diverse cultures with special adaptations to island environments and knowledge of the sound management of island resources.

17.125.   Small island developing States have all the environmental problems and challenges of the coastal zone concentrated in a limited land area. They are considered extremely vulnerable to global warming and sealevel rise, with certain small low-lying islands facing the increasing threat of the loss of their entire national territories. Most tropical islands are also now experiencing the more immediate impacts of increasing frequency of cyclones, storms and hurricanes associated with climate change. These are causing major set-backs to their socio-economic development.

17.126.   Because small island development options are limited, there are special challenges to planning for and implementing sustainable development. Small island developing States will be constrained in meeting these challenges without the cooperation and assistance of the international community.

**Objectives**

17.127.   States commit themselves to addressing the problems of sustainable development of small island developing States. To this end, it is necessary:

      a.  To adopt and implement plans and programmes to support the sustainable development and utilization of their marine and coastal resources, including meeting essential human needs, maintaining biodiversity and improving the quality of life for island people;

      b.  To adopt measures which will enable small island developing States to cope effectively, creatively and sustainably with environmental change and to mitigate impacts and reduce the threats posed to marine and coastal resources.

**Activi ties**

(a) Management-related activities

17.128.   Small island developing States, with the assistance as appropriate of the international community and on the basis of existing work of national and international organizations, should:

a. Study the special environmental and developmental characteristics of small islands, producing an environmental profile and inventory of their natural resources, critical marine habitats and biodiversity;

b. Develop techniques for determining and monitoring the carrying capacity of small islands under different development assumptions and resource constraints;

c. Prepare medium- and long-term plans for sustainable development that emphasize multiple use of resources, integrate environmental considerations with economic and sectoral planning and policies, define measures for maintaining cultural and biological diversity and conserve endangered species and critical marine habitats;

d. Adapt coastal area management techniques, such as planning, siting and environmental impact assessments, using Geographical Information Systems (GIS), suitable to the special characteristics of small islands, taking into account the traditional and cultural values of indigenous people of island countries;

e. Review the existing institutional arrangements and identify and undertake appropriate institutional reforms essential to the effective implementation of sustainable development plans, including intersectoral coordination and community participation in the planning process;

f. Implement sustainable development plans, including the review and modification of existing unsustainable policies and practices;

g. Based on precautionary and anticipatory approaches, design and implement rational response strategies to address the environmental, social and economic impacts of climate change and sealevel rise, and prepare appropriate contingency plans;

h. Promote environmentally sound technology for sustainable development within small island developing States and identify technologies that should be excluded because of their threats to essential island ecosystems.

(b) Data and information

17.129. Additional information on the geographic, environmental, cultural and socio-economic characteristics of islands should be compiled and assessed to assist in the planning process. Existing island databases should be expanded and geographic information systems developed and adapted to suit the special characteristics of islands.

(c) International and regional cooperation and coordination

17.130. Small island developing States, with the support, as appropriate, of international organizations, whether subregional, regional or global, should develop and strengthen inter-island, regional and interregional cooperation and information exchange, including periodic regional and global meetings on sustainable development of small island developing States with the first global conference on the sustainable development of small island developing States, to be held in 1993.

17.131. International organizations, whether subregional, regional or global, must recognize the special development requirements of small island developing States and give adequate priority in the provision of assistance, particularly with respect to the development and implementation of sustainable development plans.


**Means of implementation**

(a) Financing and cost evaluation

17.132.  The Conference secretariat has estimated the average total annual cost (1993-2000) of implementing the activities of this programme to be about $130 million, including about $50 million from the international community on grant or concessional terms. These are indicative and order-of-magnitude estimates only and have not been reviewed by Governments. Actual costs and financial terms, including any that are non-concessional, will depend upon, inter alia, the specific strategies and programmes Governments decide upon for implementation.

(b) Scientific and technical means

17.133.  Centres for the development and diffusion of scientific information and advice on technical means and technologies appropriate to small island developing States, especially with reference to the management of the coastal zone, the exclusive economic zone and marine resources, should be established or strengthened, as appropriate, on a regional basis.

(c) Human resource development

17.134.  Since populations of small island developing States cannot maintain all necessary specializations, training for integrated coastal management and development should aim to produce cadres of managers or scientists, engineers and coastal planners able to integrate the many factors that need to be considered in integrated coastal management. Resource users should be prepared to execute both management and protection functions and to apply the polluter pays principle and support the training of their personnel. Educational systems should be modified to meet these needs and special training programmes developed in integrated island management and development. Local planning should be integrated in educational curricula of all levels and public awareness campaigns developed with the assistance of non-governmental organizations and indigenous coastal populations.

(d) Capacity-building

17.135.  The total capacity of small island developing States will always be limited. Existing capacity must therefore be restructured to meet efficiently the immediate needs for sustainable development and integrated management. At the same time, adequate and appropriate assistance from the international community must be directed at strengthening the full range of human resources needed on a continuous basis to imp lement sustainable development plans.

17.136.  New technologies that can increase the output and range of capability of the limited human resources should be employed to increase the capacity of very small populations to meet their needs. The development and application of traditional knowledge to improve the capacity of countries to implement sustainable development should be fostered.


Notes

1/ References to the United Nations Convention on the Law of the Sea in this chapter of Agenda 21 do not prejudice the position of any State with respect to signature, ratification of or accession to the Convention.

2/ References to the United Nations Convention on the Law of the Sea in this chapter of Agenda 21 do not prejudice the position of States which view the Convention as having a unified character.

3/ Nothing in the programme areas of this chapter should be interpreted as prejudicing the rights of the States involved in a dispute of sovereignty or in the delimitation of the maritime areas concerned.

# Agenda 21 – Chapter 18
# PROTECTION OF THE QUALITY AND SUPPLY OF FRESHWATER RESOURCES: APPLICATION OF INTEGRATED APPROACHES TO THE DEVELOPMENT, MANAGEMENT AND USE OF WATER RESOURCES

18.1. Freshwater resources are an essential component of the Earth's hydrosphere and an indispensable part of all terrestrial ecosystems. The freshwater environment is characterized by the hydrological cycle, including floods and droughts, which in some regions have become more extreme and dramatic in their consequences. Global climate change and atmospheric pollution could also have an impact on freshwater resources and their availability and, through sea-level rise, threaten low-lying coastal areas and small island ecosystems.

18.2. Water is needed in all aspects of life. The general objective is to make certain that adequate supplies of water of good quality are maintained for the entire population of this planet, while preserving the hydrological, biological and chemical functions of ecosystems, adapting human activities within the capacity limits of nature and combating vectors of water-related diseases. Innovative technologies, including the improvement of indigenous technologies, are needed to fully utilize limited water resources and to safeguard those resources against pollution.

18.3. The widespread scarcity, gradual destruction and aggravated pollution of freshwater resources in many world regions, along with the progressive encroachment of incompatible activities, demand integrated water resources planning and management. Such integration must cover all types of interrelated freshwater bodies, including both surface water and groundwater, and duly consider water quantity and quality aspects. The multisectoral nature of water resources development in the context of socio-economic development must be recognized, as well as the multi-interest utilization of water resources for water supply and sanitation, agriculture, industry, urban development, hydropower generation, inland fisheries, transportation, recreation, low and flat lands management and other activities. Rational water utilization schemes for the development of surface and underground water-supply sources and other potential sources have to be supported by concurrent water conservation and wastage minimization measures. Priority, however, must be accorded to flood prevention and control measures, as well as sedimentation control, where required.

18.4. Transboundary water resources and their use are of great importance to riparian States. In this connection, cooperation among those States may be desirable in conformity with existing agreements and/or other relevant arrangements, taking into account the interests of all riparian States concerned.

18.5. The following programme areas are proposed for the freshwater sector:

    a.   Integrated water resources development and management;

    b.   Water resources assessment;

    c.   Protection of water resources, water quality and aquatic ecosystems;

    d.   Drinking-water supply and sanitation;

    e.   Water and sustainable urban development;

    f.   Water for sustainable food production and rural development;

    g.   Impacts of climate change on water resources.

## PROGRAMME AREAS
### A. Integrated water resources development and management

**Basis for action**

18.6. The extent to which water resources development contributes to economic productivity and social well-being is not usually appreciated, although all social and economic activities rely heavily on the supply and quality of freshwater. As populations and economic activities grow, many countries are rapidly reaching conditions of water scarcity or facing limits to economic development. Water demands are increasing rapidly, with 70-80 per cent required for irrigation, less than 20 per cent for industry and a mere 6 per cent for domestic consumption. The holistic management of freshwater as a finite and vulnerable resource, and the integration of sectoral water plans and programmes within the framework of national economic and social policy, are of paramount importance for action in the 1990s and beyond. The fragmentation of responsibilities for water resources development among sectoral agencies is proving, however, to be an even greater impediment to promoting integrated water management than had been anticipated. Effective implementation and coordination mechanisms are required.

**Objectives**

18.7.  The overall objective is to satisfy the freshwater needs of all countries for their sustainable development.

18.8.  Integrated water resources management is based on the perception of water as an integral part of the ecosystem, a natural resource and a social and economic good, whose quantity and quality determine the nature of its utilization. To this end, water resources have to be protected, taking into account the functioning of aquatic ecosystems and the perenniality of the resource, in order to satisfy and reconcile needs for water in human activities. In developing and using water resources, priority has to be given to the satisfaction of basic needs and the safeguarding of ecosystems. Beyond these requirements, however, water users should be charged appropriately.

18.9.  Integrated water resources management, including the integration of land- and water-related aspects, should be carried out at the level of the catchment basin or sub-basin. Four principal objectives should be pursued, as follows:

a.  To promote a dynamic, interactive, iterative and multisectoral approach to water resources management, including the identification and protection of potential sources of freshwater supply, that integrates technological, socio-economic, environmental and human health considerations;

b.  To plan for the sustainable and rational utilization, protection, conservation and management of water resources based on community needs and priorities within the framework of national economic development policy;

c.  To design, implement and evaluate projects and programmes that are both economically efficient and socially appropriate within clearly defined strategies, based on an approach of full public participation, including that of women, youth, indigenous people and local communities in water management policy-making and decision-making;

d.  To identify and strengthen or develop, as required, in particular in developing countries, the appropriate institutional, legal and financial mechanisms to ensure that water policy and its implementation are a catalyst for sustainable social progress and economic growth.

18.10.  In the case of transboundary water resources, there is a need for riparian States to formulate water resources strategies, prepare water resources action programmes and consider, where appropriate, the harmonization of those strategies and action programmes.

18.11.  All States, according to their capacity and available resources, and through bilateral or multilateral cooperation, including the United Nations and other relevant organizations as appropriate, could set the following targets:

a.  By the year 2000:

        i.      To have designed and initiated costed and targeted national action programmes, and to have put in place appropriate institutional structures and legal instruments;

        ii.     To have established efficient water-use programmes to attain sustainable resource utilization patterns;

   b.    By the year 2025:

        i.      To have achieved subsectoral targets of all freshwater programme areas.

It is understood that the fulfilment of the targets quantified in (i) and (ii) above will depend upon new and additional financial resources that will be made available to developing countries in accordance with the relevant provisions of General Assembly resolution 44/228.

**Activities**

18.12.   All States, according to their capacity and available resources, and through bilateral or multilateral cooperation, including the United Nations and other relevant organizations as appropriate, could implement the following activities to improve integrated water resources management:

    a.    Formulation of costed and targeted national action plans and investment programmes;

    b.    Integration of measures for the protection and conservation of potential sources of freshwater supply, including the inventorying of water resources, with land-use planning, forest resource utilization, protection of mountain slopes and riverbanks and other relevant development and conservation activities;

    c.    Development of interactive databases, forecasting models, economic planning models and methods for water management and planning, including environmental impact assessment methods;

    d.    Optimization of water resources allocation under physical and socio-economic constraints;

    e.    Implementation of allocation decisions through demand management, pricing mechanisms and regulatory measures;

    f.    Flood and drought management, including risk analysis and environmental and social impact assessment;

    g.    Promotion of schemes for rational water use through public awareness-raising, educational programmes and levying of water tariffs and other economic instruments;

    h.    Mobilization of water resources, particularly in arid and semi-arid areas;

    i.    Promotion of international scientific research cooperation on freshwater resources;

    j.    Development of new and alternative sources of water-supply such as sea-water desalination, artificial groundwater recharge, use of marginal-quality water, waste-water reuse and water recycling;

    k.    Integration of water (including surface and underground water resources) quantity and quality management;

    l.    Promotion of water conservation through improved water-use efficiency and wastage minimization schemes for all users, including the development of water-saving devices;

    m.   Support to water-users groups to optimize local water resources management;

n. Development of public participatory techniques and their implementation in decision-making, particularly the enhancement of the role of women in water resources planning and management;

o. Development and strengthening, as appropriate, of cooperation, including mechanisms where appropriate, at all levels concerned, namely:

   a. At the lowest appropriate level, delegation of water resources management, generally, to such a level, in accordance with national legislation, including decentralization of government services to local authorities, private enterprises and communities;

   b. At the national level, integrated water resources planning and management in the framework of the national planning process and, where appropriate, establishment of independent regulation and monitoring of freshwater, based on national legislation and economic measures;

   c. At the regional level, consideration, where appropriate, of the harmonization of national strategies and action programmes;

   d. At the global level, improved delineation of responsibilities, division of labour and coordination of international organizations and programmes, including facilitating discussions and sharing of experiences in areas related to water resources management;

p. Dissemination of information, including operational guidelines, and promotion of education for water users, including the consideration by the United Nations of a World Water Day.

## Means of implementation

(a) Financing and cost evaluation

18.13. The Conference secretariat has estimated the average total annual cost (1993-2000) of implementing the activities of this programme to be about $115 million from the international community on grant or concessional terms. These are indicative and order-of-magnitude estimates only and have not been reviewed by Governments. Actual costs and financial terms, including any that are non-concessional, will depend upon, inter alia, the specific strategies and programmes Governments decide upon for implementation.

(b) Scientific and technological means

18.14. The development of interactive databases, forecasting methods and economic planning models appropriate to the task of managing water resources in an efficient and sustainable manner will require the application of new techniques such as geographical information systems and expert systems to gather, assimilate, analyse and display multisectoral information and to optimize decision-making. In addition, the development of new and alternative sources of water-supply and low-cost water technologies will require innovative applied research. This will involve the transfer, adaptation and diffusion of new techniques and technology among developing countries, as well as the development of endogenous capacity, for the purpose of being able to deal with the added dimension of integrating engineering, economic, environmental and social aspects of water resources management and predicting the effects in terms of human impact.

18.15. Pursuant to the recognition of water as a social and economic good, the various available options for charging water users (including domestic, urban, industrial and agricultural water-user groups) have to be further evaluated and field-tested. Further development is required for economic instruments that take into account opportunity costs and environmental externalities. Field studies on the willingness to pay should be conducted in rural and urban situations.

18.16. Water resources development and management should be planned in an integrated manner, taking into account long-term planning needs as well as those with narrower horizons, that is to say, they should incorporate environmental, economic and social considerations based on the principle of sustainability; include the requirements of all users as well as those relating to the prevention and mitigation of water-related hazards; and constitute an integral part of the socio-economic development planning process. A prerequisite for the sustainable management of water as a scarce vulnerable resource is the obligation to acknowledge in all planning and development its full costs. Planning considerations should reflect benefits investment, environmental protection and operation costs, as well as the opportunity costs reflecting the most valuable alternative use of water. Actual charging need not necessarily burden all beneficiaries with the consequences of those considerations. Charging mechanisms should, however, reflect as far as possible both the true cost of water when used as an economic good and the ability of the communities to pay.

18.17. The role of water as a social, economic and life-sustaining good should be reflected in demand management mechanisms and implemented through water conservation and reuse, resource assessment and financial instruments.

18.18. The setting afresh of priorities for private and public investment strategies should take into account (a) maximum utilization of existing projects, through maintenance, rehabilitation and optimal operation; (b) new or alternative clean technologies; and (c) environmentally and socially benign hydropower.

(c) Human resources development

18.19. The delegation of water resources management to the lowest appropriate level necessitates educating and training water management staff at all levels and ensuring that women participate equally in the education and training programmes. Particular emphasis has to be placed on the introduction of public participatory techniques, including enhancement of the role of women, youth, indigenous people and local communities. Skills related to various water management functions have to be developed by municipal government and water authorities, as well as in the private sector, local/national non-governmental organizations, cooperatives, corporations and other water-user groups. Education of the public regarding the importance of water and its proper management is also needed.

18.20. To implement these principles, communities need to have adequate capacities. Those who establish the framework for water development and management at any level, whether international, national or local, need to ensure that the means exist to build those capacities. The means will vary from case to case. They usually include:

    a. Awareness-creation programmes, including mobilizing commitment and support at all levels and initiating global and local action to promote such programmes;

    b. Training of water managers at all levels so that they have an appropriate understanding of all the elements necessary for their decision-making;

    c. Strengthening of training capacities in developing countries;

    d. Appropriate training of the necessary professionals, including extension workers;

    e. Improvement of career struct ures;

f.  Sharing of appropriate knowledge and technology, both for the collection of data and for the implementation of planned development including non-polluting technologies and the knowledge needed to extract the best performance from the existing investment system.

(d) Capacity-building

18.21.   Institutional capacity for implementing integrated water management should be reviewed and developed when there is a clear demand. Existing administrative structures will often be quite capable of achieving local water resources management, but the need may arise for new institutions based upon the perspective, for example, of river catchment areas, district development councils and local community committees. Although water is managed at various levels in the socio-political system, demand-driven management requires the development of water-related institutions at appropriate levels, taking into account the need for integration with land-use management.

18.22.   In creating the enabling environment for lowest-appropriate-level management, the role of Government includes mobilization of financial and human resources, legislation, standard-setting and other regulatory functions, monitoring and assessment of the use of water and land resources, and creating of opportunities for public participation. International agencies and donors have an important role to play in providing support to developing countries in creating the required enabling environment for integrated water resources management. This should include, as appropriate, donor support to local levels in developing countries, including community-based institutions, non-governmental organizations and women's groups.

## B. Water resources assessment

**Basis for action**

18.23.   Water resources assessment, including the identification of potential sources of freshwater supply, comprises the continuing determination of sources, extent, dependability and quality of water resources and of the human activities that affect those resources. Such assessment constitutes the practical basis for their sustainable management and a prerequisite for evaluation of the possibilities for their development. There is, however, growing concern that at a time when more precise and reliable information is needed about water resources, hydrologic services and related bodies are less able than before to provide this information, especially information on groundwater and water quality. Major impediments are the lack of financial resources for water resources assessment, the fragmented nature of hydrologic services and the insufficient numbers of qualified staff. At the same time, the advancing technology for data capture and management is increasingly difficult to access for developing countries. Establishment of national databases is, however, vital to water resources assessment and to mitigation of the effects of floods, droughts, desertification and pollution.

**Objectives**

18.24.   Based upon the Mar del Plata Action Plan, this programme area has been extended into the 1990s and beyond with the overall objective of ensuring the assessment and forecasting of the quantity and quality of water resources, in order to estimate the total quantity of water resources available and their future supply potential, to determine their current quality status, to predict possible conflicts between supply and demand and to provide a scientific database for rational water resources utilization.

18.25.   Five specific objectives have been set accordingly, as follows:

a.  To make available to all countries water resources assessment technology that is appropriate to their needs, irrespective of their level of development, including methods for the impact assessment of climate change on freshwaters;

b.  To have all countries, according to their financial means, allocate to water resources assessment financial resources in line with the economic and social needs for water resources data;

c. To ensure that the assessment information is fully utilized in the development of water management policies;

   d. To have all countries establish the institutional arrangements needed to ensure the efficient collection, processing, storage, retrieval and dissemination to users of information about the quality and quantity of available water resources at the level of catchments and groundwater aquifers in an integrated manner;

   e. To have sufficient numbers of appropriately qualified and capable staff recruited and retained by water resources assessment agencies and provided with the training and retraining they will need to carry out their responsibilities successfully.

18.26.   All States , according to their capacity and available resources, and through bilateral or multilateral cooperation, including cooperation with the United Nations and other relevant organizations, as appropriate, could set the following targets:

   a. By the year 2000, to have studied in detail the feasibility of installing water resources assessment services;

   b. As a long-term target, to have fully operational services available based upon high-density hydrometric networks.

## Activities

18.27.   All States, according to their capacity and available resources, and through bilateral or multilateral cooperation, including the United Nations and other relevant organizations as appropriate, could undertake the following activities:

   a. Institutional framework:

      a. Establish appropriate policy frameworks and national priorities;

      b. Establish and strengthen the institutional capabilities of countries, including legislative and regulatory arrangements, that are required to ensure the adequate assessment of their water resources and the provision of flood and drought forecasting services;

      c. Establish and maintain effective cooperation at the national level between the various agencies responsible for the collection, storage and analysis of hydrologic data;

      d. Cooperate in the assessment of transboundary water resources, subject to the prior agreement of each riparian State concerned;

   b. Data systems:

      a. Review existing data-collection networks and assess their adequacy, including those that provide real-time data for flood and drought forecasting;

      b. Improve networks to meet accepted guidelines for the provision of data on water quantity and quality for surface and groundwater, as well as relevant land-use data;

      c. Apply standards and other means to ensure data compatibility;

      d. Upgrade facilities and procedures used to store, process and analyse hydrologic data and make such data and the forecasts derived from them available to potential users;

      e. Establish databases on the availability of all types of hydrologic data at the national level;

      f. Implement "data rescue" operations, for example, establishment of national archives of water resources;

g. Implement appropriate well-tried techniques for the processing of hydrologic data;

h. Derive area-related estimates from point hydrologic data;

i. Assimilate remotely sensed data and the use, where appropriate, of geographical information systems;

c. Data dissemination:

a. Identify the need for water resources data for various planning purposes;

b. Analyse and present data and information on water resources in the forms required for planning and management of countries' socio-economic development and for use in environmental protection strategies and in the design and operation of specific water-related projects;

c. Provide forecasts and warnings of flood and drought to the general public and civil defence;

d. Research and development:

a. Establish or strengthen research and development programmes at the national, subregional, regional and international levels in support of water resources assessment activities;

b. Monitor research and development activities to ensure that they make full use of local expertise and other local resources and that they are appropriate for the needs of the country or countries concerned.

**Means of implementation**

**(a) Financing and cost evaluation**

18.28. The Conference secretariat has estimated the everage total annual cost (1993-2000) of implementing the activities of this programme to be about $355 million, including about $145 million from the international community on grant or concessional terms. These are indicative and order-of-magnitude estimates only and have not been reviewed by Governments. Actual costs and financial terms, including any that are non-concessional will depend upon, inter alia, the specific strategies and programmes Governments decide upon for imp lementation.

(b) Scientific and technological means

18.29. Important research needs include (a) development of global hydrologic models in support of analysis of climate change impact and of macroscale water resources assessment; (b) closing of the gap between terrestrial hydrology and ecology at different scales, including the critical water-related processes behind loss of vegetation and land degradation and its restoration; and (c) study of the key processes in water-quality genesis, closing the gap between hydrologic flows and biogeochemical processes. The research models should build upon hydrologic balance studies and also include the consumptive use of water. This approach should also, when appropriate, be applied at the catchment level.

18.30. Water resources assessment necessitates the strengthening of existing systems for technology transfer, adaptation and diffusion, and the development of new technology for use under field conditions, as well as the development of endogenous capacity. Prior to inaugurating the above activities, it is necessary to prepare catalogues of the water resources information held by government services, the private sector, educational institutes, consultants, local water-use organizations and others.

(c) Human resource development

18.31.     Water resources assessment requires the establishment and maintenance of a body of well-trained and motivated staff sufficient in number to undertake the above activities. Education and training programmes designed to ensure an adequate supply of these trained personnel should be established or strengthened at the local, national, subregional or regional level. In addition, the provision of attractive terms of employment and career paths for professional and technical staff should be encouraged. Human resource needs should be monitored periodically, including all levels of employment. Plans have to be established to meet those needs through education and training opportunities and international programmes of courses and conferences.

18.32.     Because well-trained people are particularly important to water resources assessment and hydrologic forecasting, personnel matters should receive special attention in this area. The aim should be to attract and retain personnel to work on water resources assessment who are sufficient in number and adequate in their level of education to ensure the effective implementation of the activities that are planned. Education may be called for at both the national and the international level, with adequate terms of employment being a national responsibility.

18.33. Recommended actions include:

a.   Identifying education and training needs geared to the specific requirements of countries;

b.   Establishing and strengthening education and training programmes on water-related topics, within an environmental and developmental context, for all categories of staff involved in water resources assessment activities, using advanced educational technology, where appropriate, and involving both men and women;

c.   Developing sound recruitment, personnel and pay policies for staff of national and local water agencies.

(d) Capacity-building

18.34.     The conduct of water resources assessment on the basis of operational national hydrometric networks requires an enabling environment at all levels. The following national support action is necessary for enhanced national capacities:

a.   Review of the legislative and regulatory basis of water resources assessment;

b.   Facilitation of close collaboration among water sector agencies, particularly between information producers and users;

c.   Implementation of water management policies based upon realistic appraisals of water resources conditions and trends;

d.   Strengthening of the managerial capabilities of water-user groups, including women, youth, indigenous people and local communities, to improve water-use efficiency at the local level.

### C. Protection of water resources, water quality and aquatic ecosystems

**Basis for action**

18.35.     Freshwater is a unitary resource. Long-term development of global freshwater requires holistic management of resources and a recognition of the interconnectedness of the elements related to freshwater and freshwater quality. There are few regions of the world that are still exempt from problems of loss of potential sources of freshwater supply, degraded water quality and pollution of surface and groundwater sources. Major problems affecting the water quality of rivers and lakes arise, in variable order of importance according to different situations, from inadequately treated domestic sewage, inadequate controls on the discharges of industrial waste waters, loss and destruction of catchment areas, ill-considered siting of industrial plants, deforestation, uncontrolled shifting cultivation and poor agricultural practices. This gives rise to the leaching of nutrients and pesticides. Aquatic ecosystems are disturbed and living freshwater resources are threatened. Under certain circumstances, aquatic ecosystems are also affected by agricultural water resource development projects such as dams, river diversions, water installations and irrigation schemes. Erosion, sedimentation, deforestation and desertification have led to increased land degradation, and the creation of reservoirs has, in some cases, resulted in adverse effects on ecosystems. Many of these problems have arisen from a development model that is environmentally destructive and from a lack of public awareness and education about surface and groundwater resource protection. Ecological and human health effects are the measurable consequences, although the means to monitor them are inadequate or non-existent in many countries. There is a widespread lack of perception of the linkages between the development, management, use and treatment of water resources and aquatic ecosystems. A preventive approach, where appropriate, is crucial to the avoiding of costly subsequent measures to rehabilitate, treat and develop new water supplies.

**Objectives**

18.36.    The complex interconnectedness of freshwater systems demands that freshwater management be holistic (taking a catchment management approach) and based on a balanced consideration of the needs of people and the environment. The Mar del Plata Action Plan has already recognized the intrinsic linkage between water resource development projects and their significant physical, chemical, biological, health and socio-economic repercussions. The overall environmental health objective was set as follows: "to evaluate the consequences which the various users of water have on the environment, to support measures aimed at controlling water-related diseases, and to protect ecosystems". 1/

18.37.    The extent and severity of contamination of unsaturated zones and aquifers have long been underestimated owing to the relative inaccessibility of aquifers and the lack of reliable information on aquifer systems. The protection of groundwater is therefore an essential element of water resource management.

18.38.    Three objectives will have to be pursued concurrently to integrate water-quality elements into water resource management:

   a.    Maintenance of ecosystem integrity, according to a management principle of preserving aquatic ecosystems, including living resources, and of effectively protecting them from any form of degradation on a drainage basin basis;

   b.    Public health protection, a task requiring not only the provision of safe drinking-water but also the control of disease vectors in the aquatic environment;

   c.    Human resources development, a key to capacity-building and a prerequisite for implementing water-quality management.

18.39.    All States, according to their cap acity and available resources, through bilateral or multilateral cooperation, including the United Nations and other relevant organizations as appropriate, could set the following targets:

   a.    To identify the surface and groundwater resources that could be developed for use on a sustainable basis and other major developable water-dependent resources and, simultaneously, to initiate programmes for the protection, conservation and rational use of these resources on a sustainable basis;

   b.    To identify all potential sources of water-supply and prepared outlines for their protection, conservation and rational use;

c. To initiate effective water pollution prevention and control programmes, based on an appropriate mixture of pollution reduction-at-source strategies, environmental impact assessments and enforceable standards for major point-source discharges and high-risk non-point sources, commensurate with their socio-economic development;

d. To participate, as far as appropriate, in international water-quality monitoring and management programmes such as the Global Water Quality Monitoring Programme (GEMS/WATER), the UNEP Environmentally Sound Management of Inland Waters (EMINWA), the FAO regional inland fishery bodies, and the Convention on Wetlands of International Import ance Especially as Waterfowl Habitat (Ramsar Convention);

e. To reduce the prevalence of water-associated diseases, starting with the eradication of dracunculiasis (guinea worm disease) and onchocerciasis (river blindness) by the year 2000;

f. To establish, according to capacities and needs, biological, health, physical and chemical quality criteria for all water bodies (surface and groundwater), with a view to an ongoing improvement of water quality;

g. To adopt an integrated approach to environmentally sustainable management of water resources, including the protection of aquatic ecosystems and freshwater living resources;

h. To put in place strategies for the environmentally sound management of freshwaters and related coastal ecosystems, including consideration of fisheries, aquaculture, animal grazing, agricultural activities and biodiversity.

**Activities**

18.40. All States, according to their capacity and available resources, and through bilateral or multilateral cooperation, including United Nations and other relevant organizations as appropriate, could implement the following activities:

a. Water resources protection and conservation:

    i. Establishment and strengthening of technical and institutional capacities to identify and protect potential sources of water-supply within all sectors of society;

    ii. Identification of potential sources of water-supply and preparation of national profiles;

    iii. Preparation of national plans for water resources protection and conservation;

    iv. Rehabilitation of important, but degraded, catchment areas, particularly on small islands;

    v. Strengthening of administrative and legislative measures to prevent encroachment on existing and potentially usable catchment areas;

b. Water pollution prevention and control:

    i. Application of the "polluter pays" principle, where appropriate, to all kinds of sources, including on-site and off-site sanitation;

    ii. Promotion of the construction of treatment facilities for domestic sewage and industrial effluents and the development of appropriate technologies, taking into account sound traditional and indigenous practices;

    iii. Establishment of standards for the discharge of effluents and for the receiving waters;

iv.      Introduction of the precautionary approach in water-quality management, where appropriate, with a focus on pollution minimization and prevention through use of new technologies, product and process change, pollution reduction at source and effluent reuse, recycling and recovery, treatment and environmentally safe disposal;

v.      Mandatory environmental impact assessment of all major water resource development projects potentially impairing water quality and aquatic ecosystems, combined with the delineation of appropriate remedial measures and a strengthened control of new industrial installations, solid waste landfills and infrastructure development projects;

vi.      Use of risk assessment and risk management in reaching decisions in this area and ensuring compliance with those decisions;

vii.      Identification and application of best environmental practices at reasonable cost to avoid diffuse p ollution, namely, through a limited, rational and planned use of nitrogenous fertilizers and other agrochemicals (pesticides, herbicides) in agricultural practices;

viii.      Encouragement and promotion of the use of adequately treated and purified waste waters in agriculture, aquaculture, industry and other sectors;

c.      Development and application of clean technology:

     i.      Control of industrial waste discharges, including low-waste production technologies and water recirculation, in an integrated manner and through application of precautionary measures derived from a broad-based life-cycle analysis;

     ii.      Treatment of municipal waste water for safe reuse in agriculture and aquaculture;

     iii.      Development of biotechnology, inter alia, for waste treatment, production of biofertilizers and other activities;

     iv.      Development of appropriate methods for water pollution control, taking into account sound traditional and indigenous practices;

d.      Groundwater protection:

     i.      Development of agricultural practices that do not degrade groundwaters;

     ii.      Application of the necessary measures to mitigate saline intrusion into aquifers of small islands and coastal plains as a consequence of sealevel rise or overexploitation of coastal aquifers;

     iii.      Prevention of aquifer pollution through the regulation of toxic substances that permeate the ground and the establishment of protection zones in groundwater recharge and abstraction areas;

     iv.      Design and management of landfills based upon sound hydrogeologic information and impact assessment, using the best practicable and best available technology;

     v.      Promotion of measures to improve the safety and integrity of wells and well-head areas to reduce intrusion of biological pathogens and hazardous chemicals into aquifers at well sites;

     vi.      Water-quality monitoring, as needed, of surface and groundwaters potentially affected by sites storing toxic and hazardous materials;

 e. Protection of aquatic ecosystems:

  i. Rehabilitation of polluted and degraded water bodies to restore aquatic habitats and ecosystems;

  ii. Rehabilitation programmes for agricultural lands and for other users, taking into account equivalent action for the protection and use of groundwater resources important for agricultural productivity and for the biodiversity of the tropics;

  iii. Conservation and protection of wetlands (owing to their ecological and habitat importance for many species), taking into account social and economic factors;

  iv. Control of noxious aquatic species that may destroy some other water species;

 f. Protection of freshwater living resources:

  i. Control and monitoring of water quality to allow for the sustainable development of inland fisheries;

  ii. Protection of ecosystems from pollution and degradation for the development of freshwater aquaculture projects;

 g. Monitoring and surveillance of water resources and waters receiving wastes:

  i. Establishment of networks for the monitoring and continuous surveillance of waters receiving wastes and of point and diffuse sources of pollution;

  ii. Promotion and extension of the application of environmental impact assessments of geographical information systems;

  iii. Surveillance of pollution sources to improve compliance with standards and regulations and to regulate the issue of discharge permits;

  iv. Monitoring of the utilization of chemicals in agriculture that may have an adverse environmental effect;

  v. Rational land use to prevent land degradation, erosion and siltation of lakes and other water bodies;

 h. Development of national and international legal instruments that may be required to protect the quality of water resources, as appropriate, particularly for:

  i. Monitoring and control of pollution and its effects in national and transboundary waters;

  ii. Control of long-range atmospheric transport of pollutants;

  iii. Control of accidental and/or deliberate spills in national and/or transboundary water bodies;

  iv. Environmental impact assessment.

**Means of implementation**

(a) Financing and cost evaluation

18.41. The Conference secretariat has estimated the average total cost (1993-2000) of implementing the activities of this programme to be about $1 billion, including about $340 million from the international community on grant or concessional terms. These are indicative and order-of-magnitude estimates only and have not been reviewed by Governments. Actual costs and financial terms, including any that are non-concessional, will depend upon, inter alia, the specific strategies and programmes Governments decide upon for implementation.

(b) Scientific and technological means

18.42.   States should undertake cooperative research projects to develop solutions to technical problems that are appropriate for the conditions in each watershed or country. States should consider strengthening and developing national research centres linked through networks and supported by regional water research institutes. The North-South twinning of research centres and field studies by international water research institutions should be actively promoted. It is important that a minimum percentage of funds for water resource development projects is allocated to research and development, particularly in externally funded projects.

18.43.   Monitoring and assessment of complex aquatic systems often require multidisciplinary studies involving several institutions and scientists in a joint programme. International water-quality programmes, such as GEMS/WATER, should be oriented towards the water-quality of developing countries. User-friendly software and Geographical Information Systems (GIS) and Global Resource Information Database (GRID) methods should be developed for the handling, analysis and interpretation of monitoring data and for the preparation of management strategies.

(c) Human resource development

18.44.   Innovative approaches should be adopted for professional and managerial staff training in order to cope with changing needs and challenges. Flexibility and adaptability regarding emerging water pollution issues should be developed. Training activities should be undertaken periodically at all levels within the organizations responsible for water-quality management and innovative teaching techniques adopted for specific aspects of water-quality monitoring and control, including development of training skills, in-service training, problem-solving workshops and refresher training courses.

18.45.   Suitable approaches include the strengthening and improvement of the human resource capabilities of local Governments in managing water protection, treatment and use, particularly in urban areas, and the establishment of national and regional technical and engineering courses on the subjects of water-quality protection and control at existing schools and education/training courses on water resources protection and conservation for laboratory and field technicians, women and other water-user groups.

(d) Capacity-building

18.46.   The effective protection of water resources and ecosystems from pollution requires considerable upgrading of most countries' present capacities. Water-quality management programmes require a certain minimum infrastructure and staff to identify and implement technical solutions and to enforce regulatory action. One of the key problems today and for the future is the sustained operation and maintenance of these facilities. In order not to allow resources gained from previous investments to deteriorate further, immediate action is required in a number of areas.

### D. Drinking-water supply and sanitation

**Basis for action**

18.47.   Safe water-supplies and environmental sanitation are vital for protecting the environment, improving health and alleviating poverty. Safe water is also crucial to many traditional and cultural activities. An estimated 80 per cent of all diseases and over one third of deaths in developing countries are caused by the consumption of contaminated water, and on average as much as one tenth of each person's productive time is sacrificed to water-related diseases. Concerted efforts during the 1980s brought water and sanitation services to hundreds of millions of the world's poorest people.

The most outstanding of these efforts was the launching in 1981 of the International Drinking Water Supply and Sanitation Decade, which resulted from the Mar del Plata Action Plan adopted by the United Nations Water Conference in 1977. The commonly agreed premise was that "all peoples, whatever their stage of development and their social and economic conditions, have the right to have access to drinking water in quantities and of a quality equal to their basic needs". 2/ The target of the Decade was to provide safe drinking-water and sanitation to underserved urban and rural areas by 1990, but even the unprecedented progress achieved during the Decade was not enough. One in three people in the developing world still lacks these two most basic requirements for health and dignity. It is also recognized that human excreta and sewage are important causes of the deterioration of water-quality in developing countries, and the introduction of available technologies, including appropriate technologies, and the construction of sewage treatment facilities could bring significant improvement.

## Objectives

18.48.    The New Delhi Statement (adopted at the Global Consultation on Safe Water and Sanitation for the 1990s, which was held in New Delhi from 10 to 14 September 1990) formalized the need to provide, on a sustainable basis, access to safe water in sufficient quantities and proper sanitation for all, emphasizing the "some for all rather than more for some" approach. Four guiding principles provide for the programme objectives:

   a.   Protection of the environment and safeguarding of health through the integrated management of water resources and liquid and solid wastes;

   b.   Institutional reforms promoting an integrated approach and including changes in procedures, attitudes and behaviour, and the full participation of women at all levels in sector institutions;

   c.   Community management of services, backed by measures to strengthen local institutions in implementing and sustaining water and sanitation programmes;

   d.   Sound financial practices, achieved through better management of existing assets, and widespread use of appropriate technologies.

18.49.    Past experience has shown that specific targets should be set by each individual country. At the World Summit for Children, in September 1990, heads of State or Government called for both universal access to water-supply and sanitation and the eradication of guinea worm disease by 1995. Even for the more realistic target of achieving full coverage in water-supply by 2025, it is estimated that annual investments must reach double the current levels. One realistic strategy to meet present and future needs, therefore, is to develop lower-cost but adequate services that can be implemented and sustained at the community level.

## Activities

18.50.    All States, according to their capacity and available resources, and through bilateral or multilateral cooperation, including the United Nations and other relevant organizations as appropriate, could implement the following activities:

   a.   Environment and health:

      a.   Establishment of protected areas for sources of drinking-water supply;

      b.   Sanitary disposal of excreta and sewage, using appropriate systems to treat waste waters in urban and rural areas;

     c.    Expansion of urban and rural water-supply and development and expansion of rainwater catchment systems, particularly on small islands, in addition to the reticulated water-supply system;

     d.    Building and expansion, where appropriate, of sewage treatment facilities and drainage systems;

     e.    Treatment and safe reuse of domestic and industrial waste waters in urban and rural areas;

     f.    Control of water-associated diseases;

b.   People and institutions:

     i.    Strengthening of the functioning of Governments in water resources management and, at the same time, giving of full recognition to the role of local authorities;

     ii.    Encouragement of water development and management based on a participatory approach, involving users, planners and policy makers at all levels;

     iii.    Application of the principle that decisions are to be taken at the lowest appropriate level, with public consultation and involvement of users in the planning and implementation of water projects;

     iv.    Human resource development at all levels, including special programmes for women;

     v.    Broad-based education programmes, with particular emphasis on hygiene, local management and risk reduction;

     vi.    International support mechanisms for programme funding, implementation and follow-up;

c.   National and community management:

     .    Support and assistance to communities in managing their own systems on a sustainable basis;

     i.    Encouragement of the local population, especially women, youth, indigenous people and local communities, in water management;

     ii.    Linkages between national water plans and community management of local waters;

     iii.    Integration of community management of water within the context of overall planning;

     iv.    Promotion of primary health and environmental care at the local level, including training for local communities in appropriate water management techniques and primary health care;

     v.    Assistance to service agencies in becoming more cost-effective and responsive to consumer needs;

     vi.    Providing of more attention to underserved rural and low-income periurban areas;

      vii.     Rehabilitation of defective systems, reduction of wastage and safe reuse of water and waste water;

      viii.    Programmes for rational water use and ensured operation and maintenance;

      ix.     Research and development of appropriate technical solutions;

      x.     Substantially increase urban treatment capacity commensurate with increasing loads;

    d.   Awareness creation and public information/participation:

     .    Strengthening of sector monitoring and information management at subnational and national levels;

      i.     Annual processing, analysis and publication of monitoring results at national and local levels as a sector management and advocacy/awareness creation tool;

      ii.    Use of limited sector indicators at regional and global levels to promote the sector and raise funds;

      iii.   Improvement of sector coordination, planning and implementation, with the assistance of improved monitoring and information management, to increase the sector's absorptive capacity, particularly in community-based self-help projects.

**Means of implementation**

(a) Financing and cost evaluation

18.51.   The Conference secretariat has estimated the average total annual cost (1993-2000) of implementing the activities of this programme to be about $20 billion, including about $7.4 billion from the international community on grant or concessional terms. These are indicative and order-of-magnitude estimates only and have not been reviewed by Governments. Actual costs and financial terms, including any that are non-concessional, will depend upon, inter alia, the specific strategies and programmes Governments decide upon for implementation.

(b) Scientific and technological means

18.52.   To ensure the feasibility, acceptability and sustainability of planned water-supply services, adopted technologies should be responsive to the needs and constraints imposed by the conditions of the community concerned. Thus, design criteria will involve technical, health, social, economic, provincial, institutional and environmental factors that determine the characteristics, magnitude and cost of the planned system. Relevant international support programmes should address the developing countries concerning, inter alia:

    a.   Pursuit of low-cost scientific and technological means, as far as practicable;

    b.   Utilization of traditional and indigenous practices, as far as practicable, to maximize and sustain local involvement;

    c.   Assistance to country-level technical/scientific institutes to facilitate curricula development to support fields critical to the water and sanitation sector.

(c) Human resource development

18.53.   To effectively plan and manage water-supply and sanitation at the national, provincial, district and community level, and to utilize funds most effectively, trained professional and technical staff must be developed within each country in sufficient numbers. To do this, countries must establish manpower development plans, taking into consideration present requirements and planned developments. Subsequently, the development and performance of country-level training institutions should be enhanced so that they can play a pivotal role in capacity-building. It is also important that countries provide adequate training for women in the sustainable maintenance of equipment, water resources management and environmental sanitation.

(d) Capacity-building

18.54.    The implementation of water-supply and sanitation programmes is a national responsibility. To varying degrees, responsibility for the implementation of projects and the operating of systems should be delegated to all administrative levels down to the community and individual served. This also means that national authorities, together with the agencies and bodies of the United Nations system and other external support agencies providing support to national programmes, should develop mechanisms and procedures to collaborate at all levels. This is particularly important if full advantage is to be taken of community-based approaches and self-reliance as tools for sustainability. This will entail a high degree of community participation, involving women, in the conception, planning, decision-making, implementation and evaluation connected with projects for domestic water-supply and sanitation.

18.55.    Overall national capacity-building at all administrative levels, involving institutional development, coordination, human resources, community participation, health and hygiene education and literacy, has to be developed according to its fundamental connection both with any efforts to improve health and socio-economic development through water-supply and sanitation and with their impact on the human environment. Capacity-building should therefore be one of the underlying keys in implementation strategies. Institutional capacity-building should be considered to have an importance equal to that of the sector supplies and equip ment component so that funds can be directed to both. This can be undertaken at the planning or programme/project formulation stage, accompanied by a clear definition of objectives and targets. In this regard, technical cooperation among developing countries owing to their available wealth of information and experience and the need to avoid "reinventing the wheel", is crucial. Such a course has proved cost-effective in many country projects already.

### E. Water and sustainable urban development

**Basis for action**

18.56.    Early in the next century, more than half of the world's population will be living in urban areas. By the year 2025, that proportion will have risen to 60 per cent, comprising some 5 billion people. Rapid urban population growth and industrialization are putting severe strains on the water resources and environmental protection capabilities of many cities. Special attention needs to be given to the growing effects of urbanization on water demands and usage and to the critical role played by local and municipal authorities in managing the supply, use and overall treatment of water, particularly in developing countries for which special support is needed. Scarcity of freshwater resources and the escalating costs of developing new resources have a considerable impact on national industrial, agricultural and human settlement development and economic growth. Better management of urban water resources, including the elimination of unsustainable consumption patterns, can make a substantial contribution to the alleviation of poverty and improvement of the health and quality of life of the urban and rural poor. A high proportion of large urban agglomerations are located around estuaries and in coastal zones. Such an arrangement leads to pollution from municipal and industrial discharges combined with overexploitation of available water resources and threatens the marine environment and the supply of freshwater resources.

**Objectives**

18.57.    The development objective of this programme is to support local and central Governments' efforts and capacities to sustain national development and productivity through environmentally sound management of water resources for urban use. Supporting this objective is the identification and implementation of strategies and actions to ensure the continued supply of affordable water for present and future needs and to reverse current trends of resource degradation and depletion.

18.58.   All States, according to their capacity and available resources, and through bilateral or multilateral cooperation, including the United Nations and other relevant organizations as appropriate, could set the following targets:

    a.   By the year 2000, to have ensured that all urban residents have access to at least 40 litres per capita per day of safe water and that 75 per cent of the urban population are provided with on-site or community facilities for sanitation;

    b.   By the year 2000, to have established and applied quantitative and qualitative discharge standards for municipal and industrial effluents;

    c.   By the year 2000, to have ensured that 75 per cent of solid waste generated in urban areas are collected and recycled or disposed of in an environmentally safe way.

**Activities**

18.59.   All States, according to their capacity and available resources, and through bilateral or multilateral cooperation, including the United Nations and other relevant organizations as appropriate, could implement the following activities:

    a.   Protection of water resources from depletion, pollution and degradation:

        i.   Introduction of sanitary waste disposal facilities based on environmentally sound low-cost and upgradable technologies;

        ii.   Implementation of urban storm-water run-off and drainage programmes;

        iii.   Promotion of recycling and reuse of waste water and solid wastes;

        iv.   Control of industrial pollution sources to protect water resources;

        v.   Protection of watersheds with respect to depletion and degradation of their forest cover and from harmful upstream activities;

        vi.   Promotion of research into the contribution of forests to sustainable water resources development;

        vii.   Encouragement of the best management practices for the use of agrochemicals with a view to minimizing their impact on water resources;

    b.   Efficient and equitable allocation of water resources:

        i.   Reconciliation of city development planning with the availability and sustainability of water resources;

        ii.   Satisfaction of the basic water needs of the urban population;

        iii.   Introduction of water tariffs, taking into account the circumstances in each country and where affordable, that reflect the marginal and opportunity cost of water, especially for productive activities;

    c.   Institutional/legal/management reforms:

        i.   Adoption of a city-wide approach to the management of water resources;

        ii.   Promotion at the national and local level of the elaboration of land-use plans that give due consideration to water resources development;

      iii.     Utilization of the skills and potential of non-governmental organizations, the private sector and local people, taking into account the public's and strategic interests in water resources;

    d.  Promotion of public participation:

      i.     Initiation of public-awareness campaigns to encourage the public's move towards rational water utilization;

      ii.    Sensitization of the public to the issue of protecting water quality within the urban environment;

      iii.   Promotion of public participation in the collection, recycling and elimination of wastes;

    e.  Support to local capacity-building:

      i.     Development of legislation and policies to promote investments in urban water and waste management, reflecting the major contribution of cities to national economic development;

      ii.    Provision of seed money and technical support to the local handling of materials supply and services;

      iii.   Encouragement, to the extent possible, of autonomy and financial viability of city water, solid waste and sewerage utilities;

      iv.   Creation and maintenance of a cadre of professionals and semi-professionals, for water, waste-water and solid waste management;

    f.  Provision of enhanced access to sanitary services:

      i.     Implementation of water, sanitation and waste management programmes focused on the urban poor;

      ii.    Making available of low-cost water-supply and sanitation technology choices;

      iii.   Basing of choice of technology and service levels on user preferences and willingness to pay;

      iv.   Mobilization and facilitation of the active involvement of women in water management teams;

      v.    Encouragement and equipment of local water associations and water committees to manage community water-supply systems and communal latrines, with technical back-up available when required;

      vi.   Consideration of the merits and practicality of rehabilitating existing malfunctioning systems and of correcting operation and maintenance inadequacies.

**Means of implementation**

(a) Financing and cost evaluation

18.60.    The Conference secretariat has estimated the average total annual cost (1993-2000) of implementing the activities of this programme to be about $20 billion, including about $4.5 billion from the international community on grant or concessional terms. These are indicative and order-of-magnitude estimates only and have not been reviewed by Governments. Actual costs and financial

terms, including any that are non-concessional, will depend upon, inter alia, the specific strategies and programmes Governments decide upon for implementation.

(b) Scientific and technological means

18.61.  The 1980s saw considerable progress in the development and application of low-cost water-supply and sanitation technologies. The programme envisages continuation of this work, with particular emphasis on development of appropriate sanitation and waste disposal technologies for low-income high-density urban settlements. There should also be international information exchange, to ensure a widespread recognition among sector professionals of the availability and benefits of appropriate low-cost technologies. The public-awareness campaigns will also include components to overcome user resistance to second-class services by emphasizing the benefits of reliability and sustainability.

(c) Human resource development

18.62.  Implicit in virtually all elements of this programme is the need for progressive enhancement of the training and career development of personnel at all levels in sector institutions. Specific programme activities will involve the training and retention of staff with skills in community involvement, low-cost technology, financial management, and integrated planning of urban water resources management. Special provision should be made for mobilizing and facilitating the active participation of women, youth, indigenous people and local communities in water management teams and for supporting the development of water associations and water committees, with appropriate training of such personnel as treasurers, secretaries and caretakers. Special education and training programmes for women should be launched with regard to the protection of water resources and water-quality within urban areas.

(d) Capacity-building

18.63.  In combination with human resource development, strengthening of institutional, legislative and management structures are key elements of the programme. A prerequisite for progress in enhancing access to water and sanitation services is the establishment of an institutional framework that ensures that the real needs and potential contributions of currently unserved populations are reflected in urban development planning. The multisectoral approach, which is a vital part of urban water resources management, requires institutional linkages at the national and city levels, and the programme includes proposals for establishing intersectoral planning groups. Proposals for greater pollution control and prevention depend for their success on the right combination of economic and regulatory mechanisms, backed by adequate monitoring and surveillance and supported by enhanced capacity to address environmental issues on the part of local Governments.

18.64.  Establishment of appropriate design standards, water-quality objectives and discharge consents is therefore among the proposed activities. The programme also includes support for strengthening the capability of water and sewerage agencies and for developing their autonomy and financial viability. Operation and maintenance of existing water and sanitation facilities have been recognized as entailing a serious shortcoming in many countries. Technical and financial support are needed to help countries correct present inadequacies and build up the capacity to operate and maintain rehabilitated and new systems.

## F. Water for sustainable food production and rural development

**Basis for action**

18.65.  Sustainability of food production increasingly depends on sound and efficient water use and conservation practices consisting primarily of irrigation development and management, including water management with respect to rain-fed areas, livestock water-supply, inland fisheries and agroforestry. Achieving food security is a high priority in many countries, and agriculture must not only provide food for rising populations, but also save water for other uses. The challenge is to develop and apply water-saving technology and management methods and, through capacity-building, enable communities to introduce institutions and incentives for the rural population to adopt new approaches, for both rain-fed and irrigated agriculture. The rural population must also have better access to a p otable water-supply and to sanitation services. It is an immense task but not an impossible one, provided appropriate policies and programmes are adopted at all levels - local, national and international. While significant expansion of the area under rain-fed agriculture has been achieved during the past decade, the productivity response and sustainability of irrigation systems have been constrained by problems of waterlogging and salinization. Financial and market constraints are also a common problem. Soil erosion, mismanagement and overexploitation of natural resources and acute competition for water have all influenced the extent of poverty, hunger and famine in the developing countries. Soil erosion caused by overgrazing of livestock is also often responsible for the siltation of lakes. Most often, the development of irrigation schemes is supported neither by environmental impact assessments identifying hydrologic consequences within watersheds of interbasin transfers, nor by the assessment of social imp acts on peoples in river valleys.

18.66.    The non-availability of water-supplies of suitable quality is a significant limiting factor to livestock production in many countries, and improper disposal of animal wastes can in certain circumstances result in pollution of water-supplies for both humans and animals. The drinking-water requirements of livestock vary according to species and the environment in which they are kept. It is estimated that the current global livestock drinking-water requirement is about 60 billion litres per day and based on livestock population growth estimates, this daily requirement is predicted to increase by 0.4 billion litres per annum in the foreseeable future.

18.67.    Freshwater fisheries in lakes and streams are an important source of food and protein. Fisheries of inland waters should be so managed as to maximize the yield of aquatic food organisms in an environmentally sound manner. This requires the conservation of water-quality and quantity, as well as of the functional morphology of the aquatic environment. On the other hand, fishing and aquaculture may themselves damage the aquatic ecosystem; hence their development should conform to guidelines for impact limitation. Present levels of production from inland fisheries, from both fresh and brackish water, are about 7 million tons per year and could increase to 16 million tons per year by the year 2000; however, any increase in environmental stress could jeopardize this rise.

**Objectives**

18.68.    The key strategic principles for holistic and integrated environmentally sound management of water resources in the rural context may be set forth as follows:

   a.    Water should be regarded as a finite resource having an economic value with significant social and economic implications reflecting the importance of meeting basic needs;

   b.    Local communities must participate in all phases of water management, ensuring the full involvement of women in view of their crucial role in the practical day-t o-day supply, management and use of water;

   c.    Water resource management must be developed within a comprehensive set of policies for (i) human health; (ii) food production, preservation and distribution; (iii) disaster mitigation plans; (iv) environmental protection and conservation of the natural resource base;

   d.    It is necessary to recognize and actively support the role of rural populations, with particular emphasis on women.

18.69.    An International Action Programme on Water and Sustainable Agricultural Development (IAP-WASAD) has been initiated by FAO in cooperation with other int ernational organizations. The main objective of the Action Programme is to assist developing countries in planning, developing and managing water resources on an integrated basis to meet present and future needs for agricultural production, taking into account environmental considerations.

18.70. The Action Programme has developed a framework for sustainable water use in the agricultural sector and identified priority areas for action at national, regional and global levels. Quantitative targets for new irrigation development, improvement of existing irrigation schemes and reclamation of waterlogged and salinized lands through drainage for 130 developing countries are estimated on the basis of food requirements, agro-climatic zones and availability of water and land.

18.71. FAO global projections for irrigation, drainage and small-scale water programmes by the year 2000 for 130 developing countries are as follows: (a) 15.2 million hectares of new irrigation development; (b) 12 million hectares of improvement/modernization of existing schemes; (c) 7 million hectares installed with drainage and water control facilities; and (d) 10 million hectares of small-scale water programmes and conservation.

18.72. The development of new irrigation areas at the above-mentioned level may give rise to environmental concerns in so far as it implies the destruction of wetlands, water pollution, increased sedimentation and a reduction in biodiversity. Therefore, new irrigation schemes should be accompanied by an environmental impact assessment, depending upon the scale of the scheme, in case significant negative environmental impacts are expected. When considering proposals for new irrigation schemes, consideration should also be given to a more rational exploitation, and an increase in the efficiency or productivity, of any existing schemes capable of serving the same localities. Technologies for new irrigation schemes should be thoroughly evaluated, including their potential conflicts with other land uses. The active involvement of water-users groups is a supporting objective.

18.73. It should be ensured that rural communities of all countries, according to their capacities and available resources and taking advantage of international cooperation as appropriate, will have access to safe water in sufficient quantities and adequate sanitation to meet their health needs and maintain the essential qualities of their local environments.

18.74. The objectives with regard to water management for inland fisheries and aquaculture include conservation of water-quality and water-quantity requirements for optimum production and prevention of water pollution by aquacultural activities. The Action Programme seeks to assist member countries in managing the fisheries of inland waters through the promotion of sustainable management of capture fisheries as well as the development of environmentally sound approaches to intensification of aquaculture.

18.75. The objectives with regard to water management for livestock supply are twofold: provision of adequate amounts of drinking-wat er and safeguarding of drinking-water quality in accordance with the specific needs of different animal species. This entails maximum salinity tolerance levels and the absence of pathogenic organisms. No global targets can be set owing to large regional and intra-country variations.

**Activities**

18.76. All States, according to their capacity and available resources, and through bilateral or multilateral cooperation, including the United Nations and other relevant organizations as appropriate, could implement the following activities:

    a. Water-supply and sanitation for the unserved rural poor:

        i. Establish national policies and budget priorities with regard to increasing service coverage;

        ii. Promote appropriate technologies;

        iii. Introduce suitable cost-recovery mechanisms, taking into account efficiency and equity through demand management mechanisms;

    iv.      Promote community ownership and rights to water-supply and sanitation facilities;

    v.      Establish monitoring and evaluation systems;

    vi.      Strengthen the rural water-supply and sanitation sector with emphasis on institutional development, efficient management and an appropriate framework for financing of services;

    vii.      Increase hygiene education and eliminate disease transmission foci;

    viii.      Adopt appropriate technologies for water treatment;

    ix.      Adopt wide-scale environmental management measures to control disease vectors;

b.    Water-use efficiency:

    i.      Increase of efficiency and productivity in agricultural water use for better utilization of limited water resources;

    ii.      Strengthen water and soil management research under irrigation and rain-fed conditions;

    iii.      Monitor and evaluate irrigation project performance to ensure, inter alia, the optimal utilization and proper maintenance of the project;

    iv.      Support water-users groups with a view to improving management performance at the local level;

    v.      Support the appropriate use of relatively brackish water for irrigation;

c.    Waterlogging, salinity control and drainage:

    i.      Introduce surface drainage in rain-fed agriculture to prevent temporary waterlogging and flooding of lowlands;

    ii.      Introduce artificial drainage in irrigated and rain-fed agriculture;

    iii.      Encourage conjunctive use of surface and groundwaters, including monitoring and water-balance studies;

    iv.      Practise drainage in irrigated areas of arid and semi-arid regions;

d.    Water-quality management:

    i.      Establish and operate cost-effective water-quality monitoring systems for agricultural water uses;

    ii.      Prevent adverse effects of agricultural activities on water-quality for other social and economic activities and on wetlands, inter alia, through optimal use of on-farm input and the minimization of the use of external input in agricultural activities;

    iii.      Establish biological, physical and chemical water-quality criteria for agricultural water-users and for marine and riverine ecosystems;

    iv.      Minimize soil run-off and sedimentation;

    v.      Dispose properly of sewage from human settlements and of manure produced by intensive livestock breeding;

      vi.     Minimize adverse effects from agricultural chemicals by use of integrated pest management;

      vii.    Educate communities about the pollution-related impacts of the use of fertilizers and chemicals on water-quality, food safety and human health;

e.   Water resources development programmes:

      i.      Develop small-scale irrigation and water-supply for humans and livestock and for water and soil conservation;

      ii.     Formulate large-scale and long-term irrigation development programmes, taking into account their effects on the local level, the economy and the environment;

      iii.    Promote local initiatives for the integrated development and management of water resources;

      iv.    Provide adequate technical advice and support and enhancement of institutional collaboration at the local community level;

      v.     Promote a farming approach for land and water management that takes account of the level of education, the capacity to mobilize local communities and the ecosystem requirements of arid and semi-arid regions;

      vi.    Plan and develop multi-purpose hydroelectric power schemes, making sure that environmental concerns are duly taken into account;

f.   Scarce water resources management:

      i.      Develop long-term strategies and practical implementation programmes for agricultural water use under scarcity conditions with competing demands for water;

      ii.     Recognize water as a social, economic and strategic good in irrigation planning and management;

      iii.    Formulate specialized programmes focused on drought preparedness, with emphasis on food scarcity and environmental safeguards;

      iv.    Promote and enhance waste-water reuse in agriculture;

g.   Water-supply for livestock:

      i.      Improve quality of water available to livestock, taking into account their tolerance limits;

      ii.     Increase the quantity of water sources available to livestock, in particular those in extensive grazing systems, in order to both reduce the distance needed to travel for water and to prevent overgrazing around water sources;

      iii.    Prevent contamination of water sources with animal excrement in order to prevent the spread of diseases, in particular zoonosis;

      iv.    Encourage multiple use of water-supplies through promotion of integrated agro-livestock-fishery systems;

      v.     Encourage water spreading schemes for increasing water retention of extensive grasslands to stimulate forage production and prevent run-off;

h. Inland fisheries:

    i. Develop the sustainable management of fisheries as part of national water resources planning;

    ii. Study specific aspects of the hydrobiology and environmental requirements of key inland fish species in relation to varying water regimes;

    iii. Prevent or mitigate modification of aquatic environments by other users or rehabilitate environments subjected to such modification on behalf of the sustainable use and conservation of biological diversity of living aquatic resources;

    iv. Develop and disseminate environmentally sound water resources development and management methodologies for the intensification of fish yield from inland waters;

    v. Establish and maintain adequate systems for the collection and interpretation of data on water quality and quantity and channel morphology related to the state and management of living aquatic resources, including fisheries;

i. Aquaculture development:

    i. Develop environmentally sound aquaculture technologies that are compatible with local, regional and national water resources management plans and take into consideration social factors;

    ii. Introduce appropriate aquaculture techniques and related water development and management practices in countries not yet experienced in aquaculture;

    iii. Assess environmental impacts of aquaculture with specific reference to commercialized culture units and potential water pollution from processing centres;

    iv. Evaluate economic feasibility of aquaculture in relation to alternative use of water, taking into consideration the use of marginal-quality water and investment and operational requirements.

**Means of implementation**

(a) Financing and cost evaluation

18.77. The Conference secretariat has estimated the average total annual cost (1993-2000) of implementing the activities of this programme to be about $13.2 billion, including about $4.5 billion from the international community on grant or concessional terms. These are indicative and order-of-magnitude estimates only and have not been reviewed by Governments. Actual costs and financial terms, including any that are non-concessional, will depend upon, inter alia, the specific strategies and programmes Governments decide upon for implementation.

(b) Scientific and technological means

18.78. There is an urgent need for countries to monitor water resources and water-quality, water and land use and crop production; compile inventories of type and extent of agricultural water development and of present and future contributions to sustainable agricultural development; evaluate the potential for fisheries and aquaculture development; and improve the availability and dissemination of data to planners, technicians, farmers and fishermen. Priority requirements for research are as follows:

    a. Identification of critical areas for water-related adaptive research;

    b. Strengthening of the adaptive research capacities of institutions in developing countries;

     c.    Enhancement of translation of water-related farming and fishing systems research results into practical and accessible technologies and provision of the support needed for their rapid adoption at the field level.

18.79.    Transfer of technology, both horizontal and vertical, needs to be strengthened. Mechanisms to provide credit, input supplies, markets, appropriate pricing and transportation must be developed jointly by countries and external support agencies. Integrated rural water-supply infrastructure, including facilities for water-related education and training and support services for agriculture, should be expanded for multiple uses and should assist in developing the rural economy.

(c) Human resource development

18.80.    Education and training of human resources should be actively pursued at the national level through: (a) assessment of current and long-term human resources management and training needs; (b) establishment of a national policy for human resources development; and (c) initiation and implementation of training programmes for staff at all levels as well as for farmers. The necessary actions are as follows:

     a.    Assess training needs for agricultural water management;

     b.    Increase formal and informal training activities;

     c.    Develop practical training courses for improving the ability of extension services to disseminate technologies and strengthen farmers' capabilities, with special reference to small-scale producers;

     d.    Train staff at all levels, including farmers, fishermen and members of local communities, with particular reference to women;

     e.    Increase the opportunities for career development to enhance the capabilities of administrators and officers at all levels involved in land- and water-management programmes.

(d) Capacity-building

18.81.    The importance of a functional and coherent institutional framework at the national level to promote water and sustainable agricultural development has generally been fully recognized at present. In addition, an adequate legal framework of rules and regulations should be in place to facilitate actions on agricultural water-use, drainage, water-quality management, small-scale water programmes and the functioning of water-users' and fishermen's associations. Legislation specific to the needs of the agricultural water sector should be consistent with, and stem from, general legislation for the management of water resources. Actions should be pursued in the following areas:

     a.    Improvement of water-use policies related to agriculture, fisheries and rural development and of legal frameworks for implementing such policies;

     b.    Review, strengthening and restructuring, if required, of existing institutions in order to enhance their capacities in water-related activities, while recognizing the need to manage water resources at the lowest appropriate level;

     c.    Review and strengthening, where necessary, of organizational structure, functional relationships and linkages among ministries and departments within a given ministry;

     d.    Provision of specific measures that require support for institutional strengthening, inter alia, through long-term programme budgeting, staff training, incentives, mobility, equipment and coordination mechanisms;

     e.    Enhancement of involvement of the private sector, where appropriate, in human resource development and provision of infrastructure;

     f.    Transfer of existing and new water-use technologies by creating mechanisms for cooperation and information exchange among national and regional institutions.

## G. Impacts of climate change on water resources

**Basis for action**

18.82.    There is uncertainty with respect to the prediction of climate change at the global level. Although the uncertainties increase greatly at the regional, national and local levels, it is at the national level that the most important decisions would need to be made. Higher temperatures and decreased precipitation would lead to decreased water-supplies and increased water demands; they might cause deterioration in the quality of freshwater bodies, putting strains on the already fragile balance between supply and demand in many countries. Even where precipitation might increase, there is no guarantee that it would occur at the time of year when it could be used; in addition, there might be a likelihood of increased flooding. Any rise in sealevel will often cause the intrusion of salt water into estuaries, small islands and coastal aquifers and the flooding of low-lying coastal areas; this puts low-lying countries at great risk.

18.83.    The Ministerial Declaration of the Second World Climate Conference states that "the potential impact of such climate change could pose an environmental threat of an up to now unknown magnitude ... and could even threaten survival in some small island States and in low-lying coastal, arid and semi-arid areas". 3/ The Conference recognized that among the most important impacts of climate change were its effects on the hydrologic cycle and on water management systems and, through these, on socio-economic systems. Increase in incidence of extremes, such as floods and droughts, would cause increased frequency and severity of disasters. The Conference therefore called for a strengthening of the necessary research and monitoring programmes and the exchange of relevant data and information, these actions to be undertaken at the national, regional and international levels.

**Objectives**

18.84.    The very nature of this topic calls first and foremost for more information about and greater understanding of the threat being faced. This topic may be translated into the following objectives, consistent with the United Nations Framework Convention on Climate Change:

    i.    To understand and quantify the threat of the impact of climate change on freshwater resources;

    ii.    To facilitate the implementation of effective national countermeasures, as and when the threatening impact is seen as sufficiently confirmed to justify such action;

    iii.    To study the potential impacts of climate change on areas prone to droughts and floods.

**Activities**

18.85.    All States, according to their capacity and available resources, and through bilateral or multilateral cooperation, including the United Nations and other relevant organizations as appropriate, could implement the following activities:

    a.    Monitor the hydrologic regime, including soil moisture, groundwater balance, penetration and transpiration of water-quality, and related climate factors, especially in the regions and countries most likely to suffer from the adverse effects of climate change and where the localities vulnerable to these effects should therefore be defined;

    b.    Develop and apply techniques and methodologies for assessing the potential adverse effects of climate change, through changes in temperature, precipitation and sealevel rise, on freshwater resources and the flood risk;

    c.    Initiate case-studies to establish whether there are linkages between climate changes and the current occurrences of droughts and floods in certain regions;

d. Assess the resulting social, economic and environmental impacts;

e. Develop and initiate response strategies to counter the adverse effects that are identified, including changing groundwater levels and to mitigate saline intrusion into aquifers;

f. Develop agricultural activities based on brackish-water use;

g. Contribute to the research activities under way within the framework of current international programmes.

**Means of implementation**

(a) Financing and cost evaluation

18.86.    The Conference secretariat has estimated the average total annual cost (1993-2000) of implementing the activities of this programme to be about $100 million, including about $40 million from the international community on grant or concessional terms. These are indicative and order-of-magnitude estimates only and have not been reviewed by Governments. Actual costs and financial terms, including any that are non-concessional, will depend upon, inter alia, the specific strategies and programmes Governments decide upon for implementation.

(b) Scientific and technological means

18.87.    Monitoring of climate change and its impact on freshwater bodies must be closely integrated with national and international programmes for monitoring the environment, in particular those concerned with the atmosphere, as discussed under other sections of Agenda 21, and the hydrosphere, as discussed under programme area B above. The analysis of data for indication of climate change as a basis for developing remedial measures is a complex task. Extensive research is necessary in this area and due account has to be taken of the work of the Intergovernmental Panel on Climate Change (IPCC), the World Climate Programme, the International Geosphere-Biosphere Programme (IGBP) and other relevant international programmes.

18.88.    The development and implementation of response strategies requires innovative use of technological means and engineering solutions, including the installation of flood and drought warning systems and the construction of new water resource development projects such as dams, aqueducts, well fields, waste-water treatment plants, desalination works, levees, banks and drainage channels. There is also a need for coordinated research networks such as the International Geosphere-Biosphere Programme/Global Change System for Analysis, Research and Training (IGBP/START) network.

(c) Human resource development

18.89.    The developmental work and innovation depend for their success on good academic training and staff motivation. International projects can help by enumerating alternatives, but each country needs to establish and implement the necessary policies and to develop its own expertise in the scientific and engineering challenges to be faced, as well as a body of dedicated individuals who are able to interpret the complex issues concerned for those required to make policy decisions. Such specialized personnel need to be trained, hired and retained in service, so that they may serve their countries in these tasks.

(d) Capacity-building

18.90.    There is a need, however, to build a capacity at the national level to develop, review and implement response strategies. Construction of major engineering works and installation of forecasting systems will require significant strengthening of the agencies responsible, whether in the public or the private sector. Most critical is the requirement for a socio-economic mechanism that can review predictions of the impact of climate change and possible response strategies and make the necessary judgements and decisions.

## Notes

1/ Report of the United Nations Water Conference, Mar del Plata, 14-25 March 1977 (United Nations publication, Sales No. E.77.II.A.12), part one, chap. I, sect. C, para. 35.

2/ Ibid., part one, chap. I, resolution II.

3/ A/45/696/Add.1, annex III, preamble, para. 2.

# Agenda 21 – Chapter 19
## ENVIRONMENTALLY SOUND MANAGEMENT OF TOXIC CHEMICALS, INCLUDING PREVENTION OF ILLEGAL INTERNATIONAL TRAFFIC IN TOXIC AND DANGEROUS PRODUCTS

19.1. A substantial use of chemicals is essential to meet the social and economic goals of the world community and today's best practice demonstrates that they can be used widely in a cost-effective manner and with a high degree of safety. However, a great deal remains to be done to ensure the environmentally sound management of toxic chemicals, within the principles of sustainable development and improved quality of life for humankind. Two of the major problems, particularly in developing countries, are (a) lack of sufficient scientific information for the assessment of risks entailed by the use of a great number of chemicals, and (b) lack of resources for assessment of chemicals for which data are at hand.

19.2. Gross chemical contamination, with grave damage to human health, genetic structures and reproductive outcomes, and the environment, has in recent times been continuing within some of the world's most important industrial areas. Restoration will require major investment and development of new techniques. The long-range effects of pollution, extending even to the fundamental chemical and physical processes of the Earth's atmosphere and climate, are becoming understood only recently and the importance of those effects is becoming recognized only recently as well.

19.3. A considerable number of international bodies are involved in work on chemical safety. In many countries work programmes for the promotion of chemical safety are in place. Such work has international implications, as chemical risks do not respect national boundaries. However, a significant strengthening of both national and international efforts is needed to achieve an environmentally sound management of chemicals.

19.4. Six programme areas are proposed:

    a. Expanding and accelerating international assessment of chemical risks;

    b. Harmonizat ion of classification and labelling of chemicals;

    c. Information exchange on toxic chemicals and chemical risks;

    d. Establishment of risk reduction programmes;

    e. Strengthening of national capabilities and capacities for management of chemicals;

    f. Prevention of illegal international traffic in toxic and dangerous products.

In addition, the short final subsection G deals with the enhancement of cooperation related to several programme areas.

19.5. The six programme areas are together dependent for their successful imp lementation on intensive international work and improved coordination of current international activities, as well as on the identification and application of technical, scientific, educational and financial means, in particular for developing countries. To varying degrees, the programme areas involve hazard assessment (based on the intrinsic properties of chemicals), risk assessment (including assessment of exposure), risk acceptability and risk management.

19.6. Collaboration on chemical safety between the United Nations Environment Programme (UNEP), the International Labour Organisation (ILO) and the World Health Organization (WHO) in the International Programme on Chemical Safety (IPCS) should be the nucleus for international cooperation on environmentally sound management of toxic chemicals. All efforts should be made to strengthen this programme. Cooperation with other programmes, such as those of the Organisation for Economic Cooperation and Development (OECD) and the European Communities (EC) and other regional and governmental chemical programmes, should be promoted.

19.7. Increased coordination of United Nations bodies and other international organizations involved in chemicals assessment and management should be further promoted. Within the framework of IPCS, an intergovernmental meeting, convened by the Executive Director of UNEP, was held in London in December 1991 to further explore this matter (see paras. 19.75 and 19.76).

19.8. The broadest possible awareness of chemical risks is a prerequisite for achieving chemical safety. The principle of the right of the community and of workers to know those risks should be recognized. However, the right to know the identity of hazardous ingredients should be balanced with industry's right to protect confidential business information. (Industry, as referred to in this chapter, shall be taken to include large industrial enterprises and transnational corporations as well as domestic industries.) The industry initiative on responsible care and product stewardship should be developed and promoted. Industry should apply adequate standards of operation in all countries in order not to damage human health and the environment.

19.9. There is international concern that part of the international movement of toxic and dangerous products is being carried out in contravention of existing national legislation and international instruments, to the detriment of the environment and public health of all countries, particularly developing countries.

19.10. In resolution 44/226 of 22 December 1989, the General Assembly requested each regional commission, within existing resources, to contribute to the prevention of the illegal traffic in toxic and dangerous products and wastes by monitoring and making regional assessments of that illegal traffic and its environmental and health implications. The Assembly also requested the regional commissions to interact among themselves and to cooperate with the United Nations Environment Programme, with a view to maintaining efficient and coordinated monitoring and assessment of the illegal traffic in toxic and dangerous products and wastes.

PROGRAMME AREAS

### A. Expanding and accelerating international assessment of chemical risks

19.11. Assessing the risks to human health and the environment hazards that a chemical may cause is a prerequisite to planning for its safe and beneficial use. Among the approximately 100,000 chemical substances in commerce and the thousands of substances of natural origin with which human beings come into contact, many appear as pollutants and contaminants in food, commercial products and the various environmental media. Fortunately, exposure to most chemicals (some 1,500 cover over 95 per cent of total world production) is rather limited, as most are used in very small amounts. However, a serious problem is that even for a great number of chemicals characterized by high-volume production, crucial data for risk assessment are often lacking. Within the framework of the OECD chemicals programme such data are now being generated for a number of chemicals.

19.12. Risk assessment is resource-intensive. It could be made cost-effective by strengthening international cooperation and better coordination, thereby making the best use of available resources and avoiding unnecessary duplication of effort. However, each nation should have a critical mass of technical staff with experience in toxicity testing and exposure analysis, which are two important components of risk assessment.

**Objectives**

19.13. The objectives of this programme area are:

    a. To strengthen international risk assessment. Several hundred priority chemicals or groups of chemicals, including major pollutants and contaminants of global significance, should be assessed by the year 2000, using current selection and assessment criteria;

      b.    To produce guidelines for acceptable exposure for a greater number of toxic chemicals, based on peer review and scientific consensus distinguishing between health- or environment-based exposure limits and those relating to socio-economic factors.

**Activities**

(a) Management-related activities

19.14. Governments, through the cooperation of relevant international organizations and industry, where appropriate, should:

      a.    Strengthen and expand programmes on chemical risk assessment within the United Nations system IPCS (UNEP, ILO, WHO) and the Food and Agriculture Organization of the United Nations (FAO), together with other organizations, including the Organisation for Economic Cooperation and Development (OECD), based on an agreed approach to data-quality assurance, application of assessment criteria, peer review and linkages to risk management activities, taking into account the precautionary approach;

      b.    Promote mechanisms to increase collaboration among Governments, industry, academia and relevant non-governmental organizations involved in the various aspects of risk assessment of chemicals and related processes, in particular the promoting and coordinating of research activities to improve understanding of the mechanisms of action of toxic chemicals;

      c.    Encourage the development of procedures for the exchange by countries of their assessment reports on chemicals with other countries for use in national chemical assessment programmes.

(b) Data and information

19.15. Governments, through the cooperation of relevant international organizations and industry, where appropriate, should:

      a.    Give high priority to hazard assessment of chemicals, that is, of their intrinsic properties as the appropriate basis for risk assessment;

      b.    Generate data necessary for assessment, building, inter alia, on programmes of IPCS (UNEP, WHO, ILO), FAO, OECD and EC and on established programmes other regions and Governments. Industry should participate actively.

19.16. Industry should provide data for substances produced that are needed specifically for the assessment of potential risks to human health and the environment. Such data should be made available to relevant national competent authorities and international bodies and other interested parties involved in hazard and risk assessment, and to the greatest possible extent to the public also, taking into account legitimate claims of confidentiality.

(c) International and regional cooperation and coordination

19.17. Governments, through the cooperation of relevant international organizations and industry, where appropriate, should:

      a.    Develop criteria for priority-setting for chemicals of global concern with respect to assessment;

      b.    Review strategies for exposure assessment and environmental monitoring to allow for the best use of available resources, to ensure compatibility of data and to encourage coherent national and international strategies for that assessment.

**Means of implementation**

(a) Financial and cost evaluation

19.18. Most of the data and methods for chemical risk assessment are generated in the developed countries and an expansion and acceleration of the assessment work will call for a considerable increase in research and safety testing by industry and research institutions. The cost projections address the needs to strengthen the capacities of relevant United Nations bodies and are based on current experience in IPCS. It should be noted that there are considerable costs, often not possible to quantify, that are not included. These comprise costs to industry and Governments of generating the safety data underlying the assessments and costs to Governments of providing background documents and draft assessment statements to IPCS, the International Register of Potentially Toxic Chemicals (IRPTC) and OECD. They also include the cost of accelerated work in non-United Nations bodies such as OECD and EC.

19.19. The Conference secretariat has estimated the average total annual cost (1993-2000) of implementing the activities of this programme to be about $30 million from the international community on grant or concessional terms. These are indicative and order-of-magnitude estimates only and have not been reviewed by Governments. Actual costs and financial terms, including any that are non-concessional, will depend upon, inter alia, the specific strategies and programmes Governments decide upon for implementation.

(b) Scientific and technological means

19.20. Major research efforts should be launched in order to improve methods for assessment of chemicals as work towards a common framework for risk assessment and to improve procedures for using toxicological and epidemiological data to predict the effects of chemicals on human health and the environment, so as to enable decision makers to adopt adequate policies and measures to reduce risks posed by chemicals.

19.21. Activities include:

a. Strengthening res earch on safe/safer alternatives to toxic chemicals that pose an unreasonable and otherwise unmanageable risk to the environment or human health and to those that are toxic, persistent and bio-accumulative and that cannot be adequately controlled;

b. Promotion of research on, and validation of, methods constituting a replacement for those using test animals (thus reducing the use of animals for testing purposes);

c. Promotion of relevant epidemiological studies with a view to establishing a cause-and-effect relationship between exposure to chemicals and the occurrence of certain diseases;

d. Promotion of ecotoxicological studies with the aim of assessing the risks of chemicals to the environment.

(c) Human resource development

19.22. International organizations, with the participation of Governments and non-governmental organizations, should launch training and education projects involving women and children, who are at greatest risk, in order to enable countries, and particularly developing countries, to make maximum national use of international assessments of chemical risks.

(d) Capacity-building

19.23. International organizations, building on past, present and future assessment work, should support countries, particularly developing countries, in developing and strengthening risk assessment capabilities at national and regional levels to minimize, and as far as possible control and prevent, risk in the manufacturing and use of toxic and hazardous chemicals. Technical cooperation and financial support or other contributions should be given to activities aimed at expanding and accelerating the national and international assessment and control of chemical risks to enable the best choice of chemicals.

## B. Harmonization of classification and labelling of chemicals

**Basis for action**

19.24. Adequate labelling of chemicals and the dissemination of safety data sheets such as ICSCs (International Chemical Safety Cards) and similarly written materials, based on assessed hazards to health and environment, are the simplest and most efficient way of indicating how to handle and use chemicals safely.

19.25. For the safe transport of dangerous goods, including chemicals, a comprehensive scheme elaborated within the United Nations system is in current use. This scheme mainly takes into account the acute hazards of chemicals.

19.26. Globally harmonized hazard classification and labelling systems are not yet available to promote the safe use of chemicals, inter alia, at the workplace or in the home. Classification of chemicals can be made for different purposes and is a particularly important tool in establishing labelling systems. There is a need to develop harmonized hazard classification and labelling systems, building on ongoing work.

**Objectives**

19.27. A globally harmonized hazard classification and compat ible labelling system, including material safety data sheets and easily understandable symbols, should be available, if feasible, by the year 2000.

**Activities**

(a) Management-related activities

19.28. Governments, through the cooperation of relevant international organizations and industry, where appropriate, should launch a project with a view to establishing and elaborating a harmonized classification and compatible labelling system for chemicals for use in all United Nations official languages including adequate pictograms. Such a labelling system should not lead to the imposition of unjustified trade barriers. The new system should draw on current systems to the greatest extent possible; it should be developed in steps and should address the subject of comp atibility with labels of various applications.

(b) Data and information

19.29. International bodies including, inter alia, IPCS (UNEP, ILO, WHO), FAO, the International Maritime Organization (IMO), the United Nations Committee of Experts on the Transport of Dangerous Goods and OECD, in cooperation with regional and national authorities having existing classification and labelling and other information-dissemination systems, should establish a coordinating group to:

    a.    Evaluate and, if appropriate, undertake studies of existing hazard classification and information systems to establish general principles for a globally harmonized system;

    b.    Develop and implement a work plan for the establishment of a globally harmonized hazard classification system. The plan should include a description of the tasks to be completed, deadline for completion and assignment of tasks to the participants in the coordinating group;

    c.    Elaborate a harmonized hazard classification system;

d. Draft proposals for standardization of hazard communication terminology and symbols in order to enhance risk management of chemicals and facilitate both international trade and translation of information into the end-user's language;

e. Elaborate a harmonized labelling system.

**Means of implementation**

(a) Financial and cost evaluation

19.30. The Conference secretariat has included the technical assistance costs related to this programme in estimates provided in programme area E. They estimate the average total annual cost (1993-2000) for strengthening international organizations to be about $3 million from the international community on grant or concessional terms. These are indicative and order-of-magnitude estimates only and have not been reviewed by Governments. Actual costs and financial terms, including any that are non-concessional, will depend upon, inter alia, the specific strategies and programmes Governments decide upon for implementation.

(b) Human resource development

19.31. Governments and institutions and non-governmental organizations, with the collaboration of appropriate organizations and programmes of the United Nations, should launch training courses and information campaigns to facilitate the understanding and use of a new harmonized classification and compatible labelling system for chemicals.

(c) Capacity-building

19.32. In strengthening national capacities for management of chemicals, including development and implementation of, and adaptation to, new classification and labelling systems, the creation of trade barriers should be avoided and the limited capacities and resources of a large number of countries, particularly developing countries, for implementing such systems, should be taken into full account.

### C. Information exchange on toxic chemicals and chemical risks

**Basis for action**

19.33. The following activities, related to information exchange on the benefits as well as the risks associated with the use of chemicals, are aimed at enhancing the sound management of toxic chemicals through the exchange of scientific, technical, economic and legal information.

19.34. The London Guidelines for the Exchange of Information on Chemicals in International Trade are a set of guidelines adopted by Governments with a view to increasing chemical safety through the exchange of information on chemicals. Special provisions have been included in the guidelines with regard to the exchange of information on banned and severely restricted chemicals.

19.35. The export to developing countries of chemicals that have been banned in producing countries or whose use has been severely restricted in some industrialized countries has been the subject of concern, as some importing countries lack the ability to ensure safe use, owing to inadequate infrastructure for controlling the importation, distribution, storage, formulation and disposal of chemicals.

19.36. In order to address this issue, provisions for Prior Informed Consent (PIC) procedures were introduced in 1989 in the London Guidelines (UNEP) and in the International Code of Conduct on the Distribution and Use of Pesticides (FAO). In addition a joint FAO/UNEP programme has been launched for the operation of the PIC procedures for chemicals, including the selection of chemicals to be included in the PIC procedure and preparation of PIC decision guidance documents. The ILO chemicals convention calls for communication between exporting and importing countries when hazardous chemicals have been prohibited for reasons of safety and health at work. Within the General Agreement on Tariffs and Trade (GATT) framework, negotiations have been pursued with a view to creating a binding instrument on products banned or severely restricted in the domestic market. Further, the GATT Council has agreed, as stated in its decision contained in C/M/251, to extend the mandate of the working group for a period of three months, to begin from the date of the group's next meeting, and has authorized the Chairman to hold consultations on timing with respect to convening this meeting.

19.37. Notwithstanding the importance of the PIC procedure, information exchange on all chemicals is necessary.

## Objectives

19.38.   The objectives of this programme area are:

a.   To promote intensified exchange of information on chemical safety, use and emissions among all involved parties;

b.   To achieve by the year 2000, as feasible, full participation in and implementation of the PIC procedure, including possible mandatory applications through legally binding instruments contained in the Amended London Guidelines and in the FAO International Code of Conduct, taking into account the experience gained in the PIC procedure.

## Activities

(a) Management-related activities

19.39.   Governments and relevant international organizations with the cooperation of industry should:

a.   Strengthen national institutions responsible for information exchange on toxic chemicals and promote the creation of national centres where these centres do not exist;

b.   Strengthen international institutions and networks, such as IRPTC, responsible for information exchange on toxic chemicals;

c.   Establish technical cooperation with, and provide information to, other countries, especially those with shortages of technical expertise, including training in the interpretation of relevant technical data, such as Environmental Health Criteria Documents, Health and Safety Guides and International Chemical Safety Cards (published by IPCS); monographs on the Evaluation of Carcinogenic Risks of Chemicals to Humans (published by the International Agency for Research on Cancer (IARC)); and decision guidance documents (provided through the FAO/UNEP joint programme on PIC), as well as those submitted by industry and other sources;

d.   Implement the PIC procedures as soon as possible and, in the light of experience gained, invite relevant international organizations, such as UNEP, GATT, FAO, WHO and others, in their respective area of competence to consider working expeditiously towards the conclusion of legally binding instruments.

(b) Data and information

19.40.   Governments and relevant international organizations with the cooperation of industry should:

a.   Assist in the creation of national chemical information systems in developing countries and improve access to existing international systems;

b.   Improve databases and information systems on toxic chemicals, such as emission inventory programmes, through provision of training in the use of those systems as well as software, hardware and other facilities;

c. Provide knowledge and information on severely restricted or banned chemicals to importing countries to enable them to judge and take decisions on whether to import, and how to handle, those chemicals and establish joint responsibilities in trade of chemicals between importing and exporting countries;

d. Provide data necessary to assess risks to human health and the environment of possible alternatives to banned or severely restricted chemicals.

19.41. United Nations organizations should provide, as far as possible, all international information material on toxic chemicals in all United Nations official languages.

(c) International and regional cooperation and coordination

19.42. Governments and relevant international organizations with the cooperation of industry should cooperate in establishing, strengthening and expanding, as appropriate, the network of designated national authorities for exchange of information on chemicals and establish a technical exchange programme to produce a core of trained personnel within each participating country.

**Means of implementation**

Financing and cost evaluation

19.43. The Conference secretariat has estimated the average total annual cost (1993-2000) of implementing the activities of this programme to be about $10 million from the international community on grant or concessional terms. These are indicative and order-of-magnitude estimates only and have not been reviewed by Governments. Actual costs and financial terms, including any that are non-concessional, will depend upon, inter alia, the specific strategies and programmes Governments decide upon for implementation.

### D. Establishment of risk reduction programmes

**Basis for action**

19.44. There are often alternatives to toxic chemicals currently in use. Thus, risk reduction can sometimes be achieved by using other chemicals or even non-chemical technologies. The classic example of risk reduction is the substitution of harmless or less harmful substances for harmful ones. Establishment of pollution prevention procedures and setting standards for chemicals in each environmental medium, including food and water, and in consumer goods, constitute another example of risk reduction. In a wider context, risk reduction involves broad-based approaches to reducing the risks of toxic chemicals, taking into account the entire life cycle of the chemicals. Such approaches could encompass both regulatory and non-regulatory measures, such as promotion of the use of cleaner products and technologies, pollution prevention procedures and programmes, emission inventories, product labelling, use limitations, economic incentives, procedures for safe handling and exposure regulations, and the phasing out or banning of chemicals that pose unreasonable and otherwise unmanageable risks to human health and the environment and of those that are toxic, persistent and bio-accumulative and whose use cannot be adequately controlled.

19.45. In the agricultural area, integrated pest management, including the use of biological control agents as alternatives to toxic pesticides, is one approach to risk reduction.

19.46. Other areas of risk reduction encompass the prevention of chemical accidents, prevention of poisoning by chemicals and the undertaking of toxicovigilance and coordination of clean-up and rehabilitation of areas damaged by toxic chemicals.

19.47. The OECD Council has decided that OECD member countries should establish or strengthen national risk reduction programmes. The International Council of Chemical Associations (ICCA) has introduced initiatives regarding responsible care and product stewardship aimed at reduction of chemical risks. The Awareness and Preparedness for Emergencies at Local Level (APELL) programme of UNEP is designed to assist decision makers and technical personnel in improving community awareness of hazardous installations and in preparing response plans. ILO has published a Code of Practice on the prevention of major industrial accidents and is preparing an international instrument on the prevention of industrial disasters for eventual adoption in 1993.

## Objectives

19.48. The objective of the programme area is to eliminate unacceptable or unreasonable risks and, to the extent economically feasible, to reduce risks posed by toxic chemicals, by employing a broad-based approach involving a wide range of risk reduction options and by taking precautionary measures derived from a broad-based life-cycle analysis.

## Activities

(a) Management-related activities

19.49. Governments, through the cooperation of relevant international organizations and industry, where appropriate, should:

    a. Consider adopting policies based on accepted producer liability principles, where appropriate, as well as precautionary, anticipatory and life-cycle approaches to chemical management, covering manufacturing, trade, transport, use and disposal;

    b. Undertake concerted activities to reduce risks for toxic chemicals, taking into account the entire life cycle of the chemicals. These activities could encompass both regulatory and non-regulatory measures, such as promotion of the use of cleaner products and technologies; emission inventories; product labelling; use limitations; economic incentives; and the phasing out or banning of toxic chemicals that pose an unreasonable and otherwise unmanageable risk to the environment or human health and those that are toxic, persistent and bio-accumulative and whose use cannot be adequately controlled;

    c. Adopt policies and regulatory and non-regulatory measures to identify, and minimize exposure to, toxic chemicals by replacing them with less toxic substitutes and ultimately phasing out the chemicals that pose unreasonable and otherwise unmanageable risk to human health and the environment and those that are toxic, persistent and bio-accumulative and whose use cannot be adequately controlled;

    d. Increase efforts to identify national needs for standard setting and implementation in the context of the FAO/WHO Codex Alimentarius in order to minimize adverse effects of chemicals in food;

    e. Develop national policies and adopt the necessary regulatory framework for prevention of accidents, preparedness and response, inter alia, through land-use planning, permit systems and reporting requirements on accidents, and work with the OECD/UNEP international directory of regional response centres and the APELL programme;

    f. Promote establishment and strengthening, as appropriate, of national poison control centres to ensure prompt and adequate diagnosis and treatment of poisonings;

    g. Reduce overdependence on the use of agricultural chemicals through alternative farming practices, integrated pest management and other appropriate means;

    h. Require manufacturers, importers and others handling toxic chemicals to develop, with the cooperation of producers of such chemicals, where applicable, emergency response procedures and preparation of on-site and off-site emergency response plans;

i. Identify, assess, reduce and minimize, or eliminate as far as feasible by environmentally sound disposal practices, risks from storage of outdated chemicals.

19.50. Industry should be encouraged to:

    a. Develop an internationally agreed upon code of principles for the management of trade in chemicals, recognizing in particular the responsibility for making available information on potential risks and environmentally sound disposal practices if those chemicals become wastes, in cooperation with Governments and relevant international organizations and appropriate agencies of the United Nations system;

    b. Develop application of a "responsible care" approach by producers and manufacturers towards chemical products, taking into account the total life cycle of such products;

    c. Adopt, on a voluntary basis, community right-t o-know programmes based on international guidelines, including sharing of information on causes of accidental and potential releases and means of preventing them, and reporting on annual routine emissions of toxic chemicals to the environment in the absence of host country requirements.

## (b) Data and information

19.51. Governments, through the cooperat ion of relevant international organizations and industry, where appropriate, should:

    a. Promote exchange of information on national and regional activities to reduce the risks of toxic chemicals;

    b. Cooperate in the development of communication guidelines on chemical risks at the national level to promote information exchange with the public and the understanding of risks.

## (c) International and regional cooperation and coordination

19.52. Governments, through the cooperation of relevant international organizations and industry, where appropriate, should:

    a. Collaborate to develop common criteria to determine which chemicals are suitable candidates for concerted risk reduction activities;

    b. Coordinate concerted risk reduction activities;

    c. Develop guidelines and policies for the disclosure by manufacturers, importers and others using toxic chemicals of toxicity information declaring risks and emergency response arrangements;

    d. Encourage large industrial enterprises including transnational corporations and other enterprises wherever they operate to introduce policies demonstrating the commitment, with reference to the environmentally sound management of toxic chemicals, to adopt standards of operation equivalent to or not less stringent than those existing in the country of origin;

    e. Encourage and support the development and adoption by small- and medium-sized industries of relevant procedures for risk reduction in their activities;

    f. Develop regulatory and non-regulatory measures and procedures aimed at preventing the export of chemicals that are banned, severely restricted, withdrawn or not approved for health or environmental reasons, except when such export has received prior written consent from the importing country or is otherwise in accordance with the PIC procedure;

g.   Encourage national and regional work to harmonize evaluation of pesticides;

h.   Promote and develop mechanisms for the safe production, management and use of dangerous materials, formulating programmes to substitute for them safer alternatives, where appropriat e;

i.   Formalize networks of emergency response centres;

j.   Encourage industry, with the help of multilateral cooperation, to phase out as appropriate, and dispose of, any banned chemicals that are still in stock or in use in an environmentally sound manner, including safe reuse, where approved and appropriate.

## Means of implementation

### (a) Financial and cost evaluation

19.53. The Conference secretariat has included most costs related to this programme in estimates provided for programme areas A and E. They estimate other requirements for training and strengthening the emergency and poison control centres to be about $4 million annually from the international community on grant or concessional terms. These are indicative and order-of-magnitude estimates only and have not been reviewed by Governments. Actual costs and financial terms, including any that are non-concessional, will depend upon, inter alia, the specific strategies and programmes Governments decide upon for implementation.

### (b) Scientific and technological means

19.54.   Governments, in cooperation with relevant international organizations and programmes, should:

a.   Promote technology that would minimize release of, and exposure to, toxic chemicals in all countries;

b.   Carry out national reviews, as appropriate, of previously accepted pesticides whose acceptance was based on criteria now recognized as insufficient or outdated and of their possible replacement with other pest control methods, particularly in the case of pesticides that are toxic, persistent and/or bio-accumulative.

### E. Strengthening of national capabilities and capacities for management of chemicals

## Basis for action

19.55. Many countries lack national systems to cope with chemical risks. Most countries lack scientific means of collecting evidence of misuse and of judging the impact of toxic chemicals on the environment, because of the difficulties involved in the detection of many problematic chemicals and systematically tracking their flow. Significant new uses are among the potential hazards to human health and the environment in developing countries. In several countries with systems in place there is an urgent need to make those systems more efficient.

19.56. Basic elements for sound management of chemicals are: (a) adequate legislation, (b) information gathering and dissemination, (c) capacity for risk assessment and interpretation, (d) establishment of risk management policy, (e) capacity for implementation and enforcement, (f) capacity for rehabilitation of contaminated sites and poisoned persons, (g) effective education programmes and (h) capacity to respond to emergencies.

19.57. As management of chemicals takes place within a number of sectors related to various national ministries, experience suggests that a coordinating mechanism is essential.

## Objective

19.58. By the year 2000, national systems for environmentally sound management of chemicals, including legislation and provisions for implementation and enforcement, should be in place in all countries to the extent possible.

**Activities**

(a) Management-related activities

19.59. Governments, where appropriate and with the collaboration of relevant intergovernmental organizations, agencies and programmes of the United Nations system, should:

    a. Promote and support multidisciplinary approaches to chemical safety problems ;

    b. Consider the need to establish and strengthen, where appropriate, a national coordinating mechanism to provide a liaison for all parties involved in chemical safety activities (for example, agriculture, environment, education, industry, labour, health, transportation, police, civil defence, economic affairs, research institutions, and poison control centres);

    c. Develop institutional mechanisms for the management of chemicals, including effective means of enforcement;

    d. Establish and develop or strengthen, where appropriate, networks of emergency response centres, including poison control centres;

    e. Develop national and local capabilities to prepare for and respond to accidents by taking into account the UNEP APELL programme and similar programmes on accident prevention, preparedness and response, where appropriate, including regularly tested and updated emergency plans;

    f. Develop, in cooperation with industry, emergency response procedures, identifying means and equipment in industries and plants necessary to reduce impacts of accidents.

(b) Data and information

19.60. Governments should:

    a. Direct information campaigns such as programmes providing information about chemical stockpiles, environmentally safer alternatives and emission inventories that could also be a tool for risk reduction to the general public to increase the awareness of problems of chemical safety;

    b. Establish, in conjunction with IRPTC, national registers and databases, including safety information, for chemicals;

    c. Generate field monitoring data for toxic chemicals of high environmental importance;

    d. Cooperate with international organizations, where appropriate, to effectively monitor and control the generation, manufacturing, distribution, transportation and disposal activities relating to toxic chemicals, to foster preventive and precautionary approaches and ensure compliance with safety management rules, and provide accurate reporting of relevant data.

(c) International and regional cooperation and coordination

19.61. Governments, with the cooperation of international organizations, where appropriate, should:

    a. Prepare guidelines, where not already available, with advice and check-lists for enacting legislation in the chemical safety field;

b. Support countries, particularly developing countries, in developing and further strengthening national legislation and its implementation;

c. Consider adoption of community right -to-know or other public information-dissemination programmes, when appropriate, as possible risk reduction tools. Appropriate international organizations, in particular UNEP, OECD, the Economic Commission for Europe (ECE) and other interested parties, should consider the possibility of developing a guidance document on the establishment of such programmes for use by interested Governments. The document should build on existing work on accidents and include new guidance on toxic emission inventories and risk communication. Such guidance should include harmonization of requirements, definitions and data elements to promote uniformity and allow shar ing of data internationally;

d. Build on past, present and future risk assessment work at an international level, to support countries, particularly developing countries, in developing and strengthening risk assessment capabilities at national and regional levels to minimize risk in the manufacturing and use of toxic chemicals;

e. Promote implementation of UNEP's APELL programme and, in particular, use of an OECD/UNEP international directory of emergency response centres;

f. Cooperate with all countries, particularly developing countries, in the setting up of an institutional mechanism at the national level and the development of appropriate tools for management of chemicals;

g. Arrange information courses at all levels of production and use, aimed at staff working on chemical safety issues;

h. Develop mechanisms to make maximum use in countries of internationally available information;

i. Invite UNEP to promote principles for accident prevention, preparedness and response for Governments, industry and the public, building on ILO, OECD and ECE work in this area.

**Means of implementation**

(a) Financing and cost evaluation

19.62. The Conference secretariat has estimated the average total annual cost (1993-2000) of implementing the activities of this programme in developing countries to be about $600 million, including $150 million from the international community on grant or concessional terms. These are indicative and order-of-magnitude estimates only and have not been reviewed by Governments. Actual costs and financial terms, including any that are non-concessional, will depend upon, inter alia, the specific strategies and programmes Governments decide upon for implementation.

(b) Scientific and technological means

19.63. International organizations should:

a. Promote the establishment and strengthening of national laboratories to ensure the availability of adequate national control in all countries regarding the importation, manufacture and use of chemicals;

b. Promote translation, where feasible, of internationally prepared documents on chemical safety into local languages and support various levels of regional activities related to technology transfer and information exchange.

(c) Human resource development

19.64.    International organizations should:

    a.    Enhance technical training for developing countries in relation to risk management of chemicals;

    b.    Promote and increase support for research activities at the local level by providing grants and fellowships for studies at recognized research institutions active in disciplines of importance for chemical safety programmes.

19.65. Governments should organize, in collaboration with industry and trade unions, training programmes in the management of chemicals, including emergency response, targeted at all levels. In all countries basic elements of chemical safety principles should be included in the primary education curricula.

## F. Prevention of illegal international traffic in toxic and dangerous products

19.66. There is currently no global international agreement on traffic in toxic and dangerous products (toxic and dangerous products are those that are banned, severely restricted, withdrawn or not approved for use or sale by Governments in order to protect public health and the environment). However, there is international concern that illegal international traffic in these products is detrimental to public health and the environment, particularly in developing countries, as acknowledged by the General Assembly in resolutions 42/183 and 44/226. Illegal traffic refers to traffic that is carried out in contravention of a country's laws or relevant international legal instruments. The concern also relates to transboundary movements of those products that are not carried out in accordance with applicable internationally adopted guidelines and principles. Activities under this programme area are intended to improve detection and prevention of the traffic concerned.

19.67. Further strengthening of international and regional cooperation is needed to prevent illegal transboundary movement of toxic and dangerous products. Furthermore, capacity-building at the national level is needed to improve monitoring and enforcement capabilities involving recognition of the fact that appropriate penalties may need to be imposed under an effective enforcement programme. Other activities envisaged in the present chapter (for example, under paragraph 19.39 (d)) will also contribute to achieving these objectives.

**Objectives**

19.68.    The objectives of the programme are:

    a.    To reinforce national capacities to detect and halt any illegal attempt to introduce toxic and dangerous products into the territory of any State, in contravention of national legislation and relevant international legal instruments;

    b.    To assist all countries, particularly developing countries, in obtaining all appropriate information concerning illegal traffic in toxic and dangerous products.

**Activities**

(a) Management-related activities

19.69. Governments, according to their capacities and available resources and with the cooperation of the United Nations and other relevant organizations, as appropriate, should:

    a.    Adopt, where necessary, and implement legislation to prevent the illegal import and export of toxic and dangerous products;

b. Develop appropriate national enforcement programmes to monitor compliance with such legislation, and detect and deter violations through appropriate penalties.

**(b) Data and information**

19.70. Governments should develop, as appropriate, national alert systems to assist in detecting illegal traffic in toxic and dangerous products; local communities, and others could be involved in the operation of such a system.

19.71. Governments should cooperate in the exchange of information on illegal transboundary movements of toxic and dangerous products and should make such information available to appropriate United Nations bodies, such as UNEP and the regional commissions.

**(c) International and regional cooperation and coordination**

19.72. Further strengthening of international and regional cooperation is needed to prevent illegal transboundary movement of toxic and dangerous products.

19.73. The regional commissions, in cooperation with and relying upon expert support and advice from UNEP and other relevant bodies of the United Nations, should monitor, on the basis of data and information provided by Governments, and on a continuous basis make regional assessments of, the illegal traffic in toxic and dangerous products and its environmental, economic and health implications, in each region, drawing upon the results and experience gained in the joint UNEP/ESCAP preliminary assessment of illegal traffic, expected to be completed in August 1992.

19.74. Governments and international organizations, as appropriate, should cooperate with developing countries in strengthening their institutional and regulatory capacities in order to prevent illegal import and export of toxic and dangerous products.

### G. Enhancement of international cooperation relating to several of the programme areas

19.75. A meeting of government-designated experts, held in London in December 1991, made recommendations for increased coordination among United Nations bodies and other international organizations involved in chemical risk assessment and management. That meeting called for the taking of appropriate measures to enhance the role of IPCS and establish an intergovernmental forum on chemical risk assessment and management.

19.76. To further consider the recommendations of the London meeting and initiate action on them, as appropriate, the Executive Heads of WHO, ILO and UNEP are invited to convene an intergovernmental meeting within one year, which could constitute the first meeting of the intergovernmental forum.

# Agenda 21 – Chapter 20
# ENVIRONMENTALLY SOUND MANAGEMENT OF HAZARDOUS WASTES, INCLUDING PREVENTION OF ILLEGAL INTERNATIONAL TRAFFIC IN HAZARDOUS WASTES

20.1. Effective control of the generation, storage, treatment, recycling and reuse, transport, recovery and disposal of hazardous wastes is of paramount importance for proper health, environmental protection and natural resource management, and sustainable development. This will require the active cooperation and participation of the international community, Governments and industry. Industry, as referred to in this paper, shall include large industrial enterprises, including transnational corporations and domestic industry.

20.2. Prevention of the generation of hazardous wastes and the rehabilitation of contaminated sites are the key elements, and both require knowledge, experienced people, facilities, financial resources and technical and scientific capacities.

20.3. The activities outlined in the present chapter are very closely related to, and have implications for, many of the programme areas described in other chapters, so that an overall integrated approach to hazardous waste management is necessary.

20.4. There is international concern that part of the international movement of hazardous wastes is being carried out in contravention of existing national legislation and international instruments to the detriment of the environment and public health of all countries, particularly developing countries.

20.5. In section I of resolution 44/226 of 22 December 1989, the General Assembly requested each regional commission, within existing resources, to contribute to the prevention of the illegal traffic in toxic and dangerous products and wastes by monitoring and making regional assessments of that illegal traffic and its environmental and health implications. The Assembly also requested the regional commissions to interact among themselves and cooperate with the United Nations Environment Programme (UNEP), with a view to maintaining efficient and coordinated monitoring and assessment of the illegal traffic in toxic and dangerous products and wastes.

## Overall objective

20.6. Within the framework of integrated life-cycle management, the overall objective is to prevent to the extent possible, and minimize, the generation of hazardous wastes, as well as to manage those wastes in such a way that they do not cause harm to health and the environment.

## Overall targets

20.7. The overall targets are:

   a. Preventing or minimizing the generation of hazardous wastes as part of an overall integrated cleaner production approach; eliminating or reducing to a minimum transboundary movements of hazardous wastes, consistent with the environmentally sound and efficient management of those wastes; and ensuring that environmentally sound hazardous waste management options are pursued to the maximum extent possible within the country of origin (the self-sufficiency principle). The transboundary movements that take place should be on environmental and economic grounds and based upon agreements between the States concerned;

   b. Ratification of the Basel Convention on the Control of Transboundary Movements of Hazardous Wastes and their Disposal and the expeditious elaboration of related protocols, such as the protocol on liability and compensation, mechanisms and guidelines to facilitate the implementation of the Basel Convention;

c. Ratification and full implementation by the countries concerned of the Bamako Convention on the Ban on the Import into Africa and the Control of Transboundary Movement of Hazardous Wastes within Africa and the expeditious elaboration of a protocol on liability and compensation;

d. Elimination of the export of hazardous wastes to countries that, individually or through international agreements, prohibits the import of such wastes, such as, the contracting parties to the Bamako Convention, the fourth Lom Convention or other relevant conventions, where such prohibition is provided for.

20.8. The following programme areas are included in this chapter:

a. Promoting the prevention and minimization of hazardous waste;

b. Promoting and strengthening institutional capacities in hazardous waste management;

c. Promoting and strengthening international cooperation in the management of transboundary movements of hazardous wastes;

d. Preventing illegal international traffic in hazardous wastes.

## PROGRAMME AREAS

### A. Promoting the prevention and minimization of hazardous waste

**Basis for action**

20.9. Human health and environmental quality are undergoing continuous degradation by the increasing amount of hazardous wastes being produced. There are increasing direct and indirect costs to society and to individual citizens in connection with the generation, handling and disposal of such wastes. It is therefore crucial to enhance knowledge and information on the economics of prevention and management of hazardous wastes, including the impact in relation to the employment and environmental benefits, in order to ensure that the necessary capital investment is made available in development programmes through economic incentives. One of the first priorities in hazardous waste management is minimization, as part of a broader approach to changing industrial processes and consumer patterns through pollution prevention and cleaner production strategies.

20.10. Among the most important factors in these strategies is the recovery of hazardous wastes and their tranformation into useful material. Technology application, modification and development of new low-waste t echnologies are therefore currently a central focus of hazardous waste minimization.

**Objectives**

20.11. The objectives of this programme area are:

a. To reduce the generation of hazardous wastes, to the extent feasible, as part of an integrated cleaner production approach;

b. To optimize the use of materials by utilizing, where practicable and environmentally sound, the residues from production processes;

c. To enhance knowledge and information on the economics of prevention and management of hazardous wastes.

20.12. To achieve those objectives, and thereby reduce the impact and cost of industrial development, countries that can afford to adopt the requisite technologies without detriment to their development should establish policies that include:

a. Integration of cleaner production approaches and hazardous waste minimization in all planning, and the adoption of specific goals;

b. Promotion of the use of regulatory and market mechanisms;

c. Establishment of an intermediate goal for the stabilization of the quantity of hazardous waste generated;

d. Establishment of long-term programmes and policies including targets where appropriate for reducing the amount of hazardous waste produced per unit of manufacture;

e. Achievement of a qualitative improvement of waste streams, mainly through activities aimed at reducing their hazardous characteristics;

f. Facilitation of the establishment of cost-effective policies and approaches to hazardous waste prevention and management, taking into consideration the state of development of each country.

**Activities**

(a) Management-related activities

20.13.  The following activities should be undertaken:

a. Governments should establish or modify standards or purchasing specifications to avoid discrimination against recycled materials, provided that those materials are environmentally sound;

b. Governments, according to their possibilities and with the help of multilateral cooperation, should provide economic or regulatory incentives, where appropriate, to stimulate industrial innovation towards cleaner production methods, to encourage industry to invest in preventive and/or recycling technologies so as to ensure environmentally sound management of all hazardous wastes, including recyclable wastes, and to encourage waste minimization investments;

c. Governments should int ensify research and development activities on cost-effective alternatives for processes and substances that currently result in the generation of hazardous wastes that pose particular problems for environmentally sound disposal or treatment, the possibility of ultimate phase-out of those substances that present an unreasonable or otherwise unmanageable risk and are toxic, persistent and bio-accumulative to be considered as soon as practicable. Emphasis should be given to alternatives that could be economically accessible to developing countries;

d. Governments, according to their capacities and available resources and with the cooperation of the United Nations and other relevant organizations and industries, as appropriate, should support the establishment of domestic facilities to handle hazardous wastes of domestic origin;

e. Governments of developed countries should promote the transfer of environmentally sound technologies and know-how on clean technologies and low-waste production to developing countries in conformity with chapter 34, which will bring about changes to sustain innovation. Governments should cooperate with industry to develop guidelines and codes of conduct, where appropriate, leading to cleaner production through sectoral trade industry associations;

f. Governments should encourage industry to treat, recycle, reuse and dispose of wastes at the source of generation, or as close as possible thereto, whenever hazardous waste generation is unavoidable and when it is both economically and environmentally efficient for industry to do so;

g. Governments should encourage technology assessments, for example through the use of technology assessment centres;

h. Governments should promote cleaner production through the establishment of centres providing training and information on environmentally sound technologies;

i. Industry should establish environmental management systems, including environmental auditing of its production or distribution sites, in order to identify where the installation of cleaner production methods is needed;

j. A relevant and competent United Nations organization should take the lead, in cooperation with other organizations, to develop guidelines for estimating the costs and benefits of various approaches to the adoption of cleaner production and waste minimization and environmentally sound management of hazardous wastes, including rehabilitation of contaminated sites, taking into account, where appropriate, the report of the 1991 Nairobi meeting of government -designated experts on an international strategy and an action programme, including technical guidelines for the environmentally sound management of hazardous wastes; in particular in the context of the work of the Basel Convention, being developed under the UNEP secretariat;

k. Governments should establish regulations that lay down the ultimate responsibility of industries for environmentally sound disposal of the hazardous wastes their activities generate.

(b) Data and information

20.14. The following activities should be undertaken:

a. Governments, assisted by international organizations, should establish mechanisms for assessing the value of existing information systems;

b. Governments should establish nationwide and regional information collection and dissemination clearing-houses and networks that are easy for Government institutions and industry and other non-governmental organizations to access and use;

c. International organizations, through the UNEP Cleaner Production programme and ICPIC, should extend and strengthen existing systems for collection of cleaner production information;

d. All United Nations organs and organizations should promote the use and dissemination of information collected through the Cleaner Production network;

e. OECD should, in cooperation with other organizations, undertake a comprehensive survey of, and disseminate information on, experiences of member countries in adopting economic regulatory schemes and incentive mechanisms for hazardous waste management and for the use of clean technologies that prevent such waste from being generated;

f. Governments should encourage industries to be transparent in their operations and provide relevant information to the communities that might be affected by the generation, management and disposal of hazardous wastes.

(c) International and regional cooperation and coordination

20.15. International/regional cooperation should encourage the ratification by States of the Basel and Bamako Conventions and promote the implementation of those Conventions. Regional cooperation will be necessary for the development of similar conventions in regions other than Africa, if so required. In addition there is a need for effective coordination of international regional and national policies and instruments. Another activity proposed is cooperating in monitoring the effects of the management of hazardous wastes.

**Means of implementation**

(a) Financing and cost evaluation

20.16.    The Conference secretariat has estimated the average total annual cost (1993-2000) of implementing the activities of this programme to be about $750 million from the international community on grant or concessional terms. These are indicative and order-of-magnitude estimates only and have not been reviewed by Governments. Actual costs and financial terms, including any that are non-concessional, will depend upon, inter alia, the specific strategies and programmes Governments decide upon for implementation.

(b) Scientific and technological means

20.17.    The following activities related to technology development and research should be undertaken:

    a.   Governments, according to their capacities and available resources and with the cooperation of the United Nations and other relevant organizations, and industries, as appropriate, should significantly increase financial support for cleaner technology research and development programmes, including the use of biotechnologies;

    b.   States, with the cooperation of international organizations where appropriate, should encourage industry to promote and undertake research into the phase-out of the processes that pose the greatest environmental risk based on hazardous wastes generated;

    c.   States should encourage industry to develop schemes to integrate the cleaner production approach into design of products and management practices;

    d.   States should encourage industry to exercise environmentally responsible care through hazardous waste reduction and by ensuring the environmentally sound reuse, recycling and recovery of hazardous wastes, as well as their final disposal.

(c) Human resource development

20.18.    The following activities should be undertaken:

    a.   Governments, international organizations and industry should encourage industrial training programmes, incorporating hazardous waste prevention and minimization techniques and launching demonstration projects at the local level to develop "success stories" in cleaner production;

    b.   Industry should integrate cleaner production principles and case examples into training programmes and establish demonstration projects/networks by sector/country;

    c.   All sectors of society should develop cleaner production awareness campaigns and promote dialogue and partnership with industry and other actors.

(d) Capacity-building

20.19.    The following activities should be undertaken:

    a.   Governments of developing countries, in cooperation with industry and with the cooperation of appropriate international organizations, should develop inventories of hazardous waste production, in order to identify their needs with respect to technology transfer and implementation of measures for the sound management of hazardous wastes and their disposal;

b.  Governments should include in national planning and legislation an integrated approach to environmental protection, driven by prevention and source reduction criteria, taking into account the "polluter pays" principle, and adopt programmes for hazardous waste reduction, including targets and adequate environmental control;

c.  Governments should work with industry on sector-by-sector cleaner production and hazardous waste minimization campaigns, as well as on the reduction of such wastes and other emissions;

d.  Governments should take the lead in establishing and strengthening, as appropriate, national procedures for environmental impact assessment, taking into acount the cradle-to-grave approach to the management of hazardous wastes, in order to identify options for minimizing the generation of hazardous wastes, through safer handling, storage, disposal and destruction;

e.  Governments, in collaboration with industry and appropriate international organizations, should develop procedures for monitoring the application of the cradle to grave approach, including environmental audits;

f.  Bilateral and multilateral development assistance agencies should substantially increase funding for cleaner technology transfer to developing countries, including small- and medium-sized enterprises.

## B. Promoting and strengthening institutional capacities in hazardous waste management

### Basis for action

20.20.  Many countries lack the national capacity to handle and manage hazardous wastes. This is primarily due to inadequate infrastructure, deficiencies in regulatory frameworks, insufficient education and training programmes and lack of coordination between the different ministries and institutions involved in various aspects of waste management. In addition, there is a lack of knowledge about environmental contamination and pollution and the associated health risk from the exposure of populations, especially women and children, and ecosystems to hazardous wastes; assessment of risks; and the characteristics of wastes. Steps need to be taken immediately to identify populations at high risk and to take remedial measures, where necessary. One of the main priorities in ensuring environmentally sound management of hazardous wastes is to provide awareness, education and training programmes covering all levels of society. There is also a need to undertake research programmes to understand the nature of hazardous wastes, to identify their potential environmental effects and to develop technologies to safely handle those wastes. Finally, there is a need to strengthen the capacities of institutions that are responsible for the management of hazardous wastes.

### Objectives

20.21.  The objectives in this programme area are:

a.  To adopt appropriate coordinating, legislative and regulatory measures at the national level for the environmentally sound management of hazardous wastes, including the implementation of international and regional conventions;

b.  To establish public awareness and information programmes on hazardous waste issues and to ensure that basic education and training programmes are provided for industry and government workers in all countries;

c.  To establish comprehensive research programmes on hazardous wastes in countries;

d.  To strengthen service industries to enable them to handle hazardous wastes, and to build up international networking;

e. To develop endogenous capacities in all developing countries to educate and train staff at all levels in environmentally sound hazardous waste handling and monitoring and in environmentally sound management;

f. To promote human exposure assessment with respect to hazardous waste sites and identify the remedial measures required;

g. To facilitate the assessment of impacts and risks of hazardous wastes on human health and the environment by establishing appropriate procedures, methodologies, criteria and/or effluent-related guidelines and standards;

h. To improve knowledge regarding the effects of hazardous wastes on human health and the environment;

i. To make information available to Governments and to the general public on the effects of hazardous wastes, including infectious wastes, on human health and the environment.

**Activities**

(a) Management-related activities

20.22. The following activities should be undertaken:

a. Governments should establish and maintain inventories, including computerized inventories, of hazardous wastes and their treatment/disposal sites, as well as of contaminated sites that require rehabilitation, and assess exposure and risk to human health and the environment; they should also identify t he measures required to clean up the disposal sites. Industry should make the necessary information available;

b. Governments, industry and international organizations should collaborate in developing guidelines and easy-to-implement methods for the characterization and classification of hazardous wastes;

c. Governments should carry out exposure and health assessments of populations residing near uncontrolled hazardous waste sites and initiate remedial measures;

d. International organizations should develop improved health-based criteria, taking into account national decision-making processes, and assist in the preparation of practical technical guidelines for the prevention, minimization and safe handling and disposal of hazardous wastes;

e. Governments of developing countries should encourage interdisciplinary and intersectoral groups, in cooperation with international organizations and agencies, to implement training and research activities related to evaluation, prevention and control of hazardous waste health risks. Such groups should serve as models to develop similar regional programmes;

f. Governments, according to their capacities and available resources and with the cooperation of the United Nations and other relevant organizations as appropriate, should encourage as far as possible the establishment of combined treatment/disposal facilities for hazardous wastes in small- and medium-sized industries;

g. Governments should promote identification and clean-up of sites of hazardous wastes in collaboration with industry and international organizations. Technologies, expertise and financing should be available for this purpose, as far as possible and when appropriate with the application of the "polluter pays" principle;

h. Governments should ascertain that their military establishments conform to their nationally applicable environmental norms in the treatment and disposal of hazardous wastes.

(b) Data and information

20.23.    The following activities should be undertaken:

a. Governments, international and regional organizations and industry should facilitate and expand the dissemination of technical and scientific information dealing with the various health aspects of hazardous wastes, and promote its application;

b. Governments should establish notification systems and registries of exposed populations and of adverse health effects and databases on risk assessments of hazardous wastes;

c. Governments should endeavour to collect information on those who generate or dispose/recycle hazardous wastes and provide such information to the individuals and institutions concerned.

(c) International and regional cooperation and coordination

20.24.    Governments, according to their capacities and available resources and with the cooperation of the United Nations and other relevant organizations, as appropriate, should:

a. Promote and support the integration and operation, at the regional and local levels as appropriate, of institutional and interdisciplinary groups that collaborate, according to their capabilities, in activities oriented towards strengthening risk assessment, risk management and risk reduction with respect to hazardous wastes;

b. Support capacity-building and technological development and research in developing countries in connection with human resource development, with particular support to be given to consolidating networks;

c. Encourage self-sufficiency in hazardous waste disposal in the country of origin to the extent environmentally sound and feasible. The transboundary movements that take place should be on environmental and economic grounds and based upon agreements between all States concerned.

**Means of implementation**

(a) Financing and cost evaluation

20.25.    The Conference secretariat has estimated the average total annual cost (1993-2000) of implementing the activities of this programme to be about $18.5 billion on a global basis with about $3.5 billion related to developing countries, including about $500 million from the international community on grant or concessional terms. These are indicative and order-of-magnitude estimates only and have not been reviewed by Governments. Actual costs and financial terms, including any that are non-concessional, will depend upon, inter alia, the specific strategies and programmes Governments decide upon for implementation.

(b) Scientific and technological means

20.26.    The following activities should be undertaken:

a. Governments, according to their capacities and available resources and with the cooperation of the United Nations and other relevant organizations and industry as appropriate, should increas e support for hazardous waste research management in developing countries;

b.    Governments, in collaboration with international organizations, should conduct research on the health effects of hazardous wastes in developing countries, including the long-term effects on children and women;

c.    Governments should conduct research aimed at the needs of small and medium-sized industries;

d.    Governments and international organizations in cooperation with industry should expand technological research on environmentally sound hazardous waste handling, storage, transport, treatment and disposal and on hazardous waste assessment, management and remediation;

e.    International organizations should identify relevant and improved technologies for handling, storage, treatment and disposal of hazardous wastes.

(c) Human resource development

20.27.    Governments, according to their capacities and available resources and with the cooperation of the United Nations and other relevant organizations and industry as appropriate, should:

a.    Increase public awareness and information on hazardous waste issues and promote the development and dissemination of hazardous wastes information that the general public can understand;

b.    Increase participation in hazardous waste management programmes by the general public, particularly women, including participation at grass-roots levels;

c.    Develop training and education programmes for men and women in industry and Government aimed at specific real-life problems, for example, planning and implementing hazardous waste minimization programmes, conducting hazardous materials audits and establishing appropriate regulatory programmes;

d.    Promote the training of labour, industrial management and government regulatory staff in developing countries on technologies to minimize and manage hazardous wastes in an environmentally sound manner.

20.28.    The following activities should also be undertaken:

a.    Governments, according to their capacities and available resources and with the cooperation of the United Nations, other organizations and non-governmental organizations, should collaborate in developing and disseminating educational materials concerning hazardous wastes and their effects on environment and human health, for use in schools, by women's groups and by the general public;

b.    Governments, according to their capacities and available resources and with the cooperation of the United Nations and other organizations, should establish or strengthen programmes for the environmentally sound management of hazardous wastes in accordance with, as appropriate, health and environmental standards, and extend surveillance systems for the purpose of identifying adverse effects on populations and the environment of exposure to hazardous wastes;

c.    International organizations should provide assistance to member States in assessing the health and environmental risks resulting from exposure to hazardous wastes, and in identifying their priorities for controlling the various categories or classes of wastes;

d.    Governments, according to their capacities and available resources and with the cooperation of the United Nations and other relevant organizations, should promote centres of excellence for training in hazardous waste management, building on appropriate national institutions and encouraging international cooperation, inter alia, through institutional links between developed and developing countries.

(d) Capacity-building

20.29.    Wherever they operate, transnational corporations and other large-scale enterprises should be encouraged to introduce policies and make commitments to adopt standards of operation with reference to hazardous waste generation and disposal that are equivalent to or no less stringent than standards in the country of origin, and Governments are invited to make efforts to establish regulations requiring environmentally sound management of hazardous wastes.

20.30.    International organizations should provide assistance to member States in assessing the health and environmental risks resulting from exposure to hazardous wastes and in identifying their priorities for controlling the various categories or classes of wastes.

20.31.    Governments, according to their capacities and available resources and with the cooperation of the United Nations and other relevant organizations and industries, should:

a.    Support national institutions in dealing with hazardous wastes from the regulatory monitoring and enforcement perspectives, with such support including enabling of those institutions to implement international conventions;

b.    Develop industry-based institutions for dealing with hazardous wastes and service industries for handling hazardous wastes;

c.    Adopt technical guidelines for the environmentally sound management of hazardous wastes and support the implementation of regional and international conventions;

d.    Develop and expand international networking among professionals working in the area of hazardous wastes and maintain an information flow among countries;

e.    Assess the feasibility of establishing and operating national, subregional and regional hazardous wastes treatment centres. Such centres could be used for education and training, as well as for facilitation and promotion of the transfer of technologies for the environmentally sound management of hazardous wastes;

f.    Identify and strengthen relevant academic/research institutions or centres for excellence to enable them to carry out education and training activities in the environmentally sound management of hazardous wastes;

g.    Develop a programme for the establishment of national capacities and capabilities to educate and train staff at various levels in hazardous wastes management;

h.    Conduct environmental audits of existing industries to improve in-plant regimes for the management of hazardous wastes.

## C. Promoting and strengthening international cooperation in the management of transboundary movements of hazardous wastes

**Basis for action**

20.32.    In order to promote and strengthen international cooperation in the management, including control and monitoring, of transboundary movements of hazardous wastes, a precautionary approach should be applied. There is a need to harmonize the procedures and criteria used in various international and legal instruments. There is also a need to develop or harmonize existing criteria for identifying wastes dangerous to the environment and to build monitoring capacities.

**Objectives**

20.33.   The objectives of this programme area are:

    a.   To facilitate and strengthen international cooperation in the environmentally sound management of hazardous wastes, including control and monitoring of transboundary movements of such wastes, including wastes for recovery, by using internationally adopted criteria to identify and classify hazardous wastes and to harmonize relevant international legal instruments;

    b.   To adopt a ban on or prohibit, as appropriate, the export of hazardous wastes to countries that do not have the capacity to deal with those wastes in an environmentally sound way or that have banned the import of such wastes;

    c.   To promote the development of control procedures for the transboundary movement of hazardous wastes destined for recovery operations under the Basel Convention that encourage environmentally and economically sound recycling options.

**Activities**

(a) Management-related activities

Strengthening and harmonizing criteria and regulations

20.34.   Governments, according to their capacities and available resources and with the cooperation of United Nations and other relevant organizations, as appropriate, should:

    a.   Incorporate the notification procedure called for in the Basel Convention and relevant regional conventions, as well as in their annexes, into national legislation;

    b.   Formulate, where appropriate, regional agreements such as the Bamako Convention regulating the transboundary movement of hazardous wastes;

    c.   Help promote the compatibility and comp lementarity of such regional agreements with international conventions and protocols;

    d.   Strengthen national and regional capacities and capabilities to monitor and control the transboundary movement of hazardous wastes;

    e.   Promote the development of clear criteria and guidelines, within the framework of the Basel Convention and regional conventions, as appropriate, for environmentally and economically sound operation in resource recovery, recycling reclamation, direct use or alternative uses and for determination of acceptable recovery practices, including recovery levels where feasible and appropriate, with a view to preventing abuses and false presentation in the above operations;

    f.   Consider setting up, at national and regional levels, as appropriate, systems for monitoring and surveillance of the transboundary movements of hazardous wastes;

    g.   Develop guidelines for the assessment of environmentally sound treatment of hazardous wastes;

    h.   Develop guidelines for the identification of hazardous wastes at the national level, taking into account existing internationally - and, where appropriate, regionally - agreed criteria and prepare a list of hazard profiles for the hazardous wastes listed in national legislation;

    i.   Develop and use appropriate methods for testing, characterizing and classifying hazardous wastes and adopt or adapt safety standards and principles for managing hazardous wastes in an environmentally sound way.

Implementing existing agreements

20.35.    Governments are urged to ratify the Basel Convention and the Bamako Convention, as applicable, and to pursue the expeditious elaboration of related protocols, such as protocols on liability and compensation, and of mechanisms and guidelines to facilitate the implementation of the Conventions.

**Means of implementation**

(a) Financing and cost evaluation

20.36.    Because this programme area covers a relatively new field of operation and because of the lack so far of adequate studies on costing of activities under this programme, no cost estimate is available at present. However, the costs for some of the activities related to capacity-building that are presented under this programme could be considered to have been covered under the costing of programme area B above.

20.37.    The interim secretariat for the Basel Convention should undertake studies in order to arrive at a reasonable cost estimate for activities to be undertaken initially until the year 2000.

(b) Capacity-building

20.38.    Governments, according to their capacities and available resources and with the cooperation of United Nations and other relevant organizations, as appropriate, should:

    a.   Elaborate or adopt policies for the environmentally sound management of hazardous wastes, taking into account existing international instruments;

    b.   Make recommendations to the appropriate forums or establish or adapt norms, including the equitable implementation of the polluter pays principle, and regulatory measures to comply with obligations and principles of the Basel Convention, the Bamako Convention and other relevant existing or future agreements, including protocols, as appropriate, for setting appropriate rules and procedures in the field of liability and compensation for damage resulting from the transboundary movement and disposal of hazardous wastes;

    c.   Implement policies for the implementation of a ban or prohibition, as appropriate, of exports of hazardous wastes to countries that do not have the capacity to deal with those wastes in an environmentally sound way or that have banned the import of such wastes;

    d.   Study, in the context of the Basel Convention and relevant regional conventions, the feasibility of providing temporary financial assistance in the case of an emergency situation, in order to minimize damage from accidents arising from transboundary movements of hazardous wastes or during the disposal of those wastes.

### D. Preventing illegal international traffic in hazardous wastes
**Basis for action**

20.39.    The prevention of illegal traffic in hazardous wastes will benefit the environment and public health in all countries, particularly developing countries. It will also help to make the Basel Convention and regional international instruments, such as the Bamako Convention and the fourth Lom Convention, more effective by promoting compliance with the controls established in those agreements. Article IX of the Basel Convention specifically addresses the issue of illegal shipments of hazardous wastes. Illegal traffic of hazardous wastes may cause serious threats to human health and the environment and impose a special and abnormal burden on the countries that receive such shipments.

20.40.    Effective prevention requires action through effective monitoring and the enforcement and imposition of appropriate penalties.

**Objectives**

20.41.   The objectives of this programme area are:

  a.   To reinforce national capacities to detect and halt any illegal attempt to introduce hazardous wastes into the territory of any State in contravention of national legislation and relevant international legal instruments;

  b.   To assist all countries, particularly developing countries, in obtaining all appropriate information concerning illegal traffic in hazardous wastes;

  c.   To cooperate, within the framework of the Basel Convention, in assisting countries that suffer the consequences of illegal traffic.

**Activities**

(a) Management-related activities

20.42.   Governments, according to their capacities and available resources and with the cooperation of the United Nations and other relevant organizations, as appropriate, should:

  a.   Adopt, where necessary, and implement legislation to prevent the illegal import and export of hazardous wastes;

  b.   Develop appropriate national enforcement programmes to monitor compliance with such legislation, detect and deter violations through appropriate penalties and give special attention to those who are known to have conducted illegal traffic in hazardous wastes and to hazardous wastes that are particularly susceptible to illegal traffic.

(b) Data and information

20.43.   Governments should develop as appropriate, an information network and alert system to assist in detecting illegal traffic in hazardous wastes. Local communities and others could be involved in the operation of such a network and system.

20.44.   Governments should cooperate in the exchange of information on illegal transboundary movements of hazardous wastes and should make such information available to appropriate United Nations bodies such as UNEP and the regional commissions.

(c) International and regional cooperation

20.45.   The regional commissions, in cooperation with and relying upon expert support and advice from UNEP and other relevant bodies of the United Nations system, taking full account of the Basel Convention, shall continue to monitor and assess the illegal traffic in hazardous wastes, including its environmental, economic and health implications, on a continuing basis, drawing upon the results and experience gained in the joint UNEP/ESCAP preliminary assessment of illegal traffic.

20.46.   Countries and international organizations, as appropriate, should cooperate to strengthen the institutional and regulatory capacities, in particular of developing countries, in order to prevent the illegal import and export of hazardous wastes.

## Agenda 21 – Chapter 21
## ENVIRONMENTALLY SOUND MANAGEMENT OF SOLID WASTES AND SEWAGE-RELATED ISSUES

21.1. This chapter has been incorporated in Agenda 21 in response to General Assembly resolution 44/228, section I, paragraph 3, in which the Assembly affirmed that the Conference should elaborate strategies and measures to halt and reverse the effects of environmental degradation in the context of increased national and international efforts to promote sustainable and environmentally sound development in all countries, and to section I, paragraph 12 (g), of the same resolution, in which the Assembly affirmed that environmentally sound management of wastes was among the environmental issues of major concern in maintaining the quality of the Earth's environment and especially in achieving environmentally sound and sustainable development in all countries.

21.2. Programme areas included in the present chapter of Agenda 21 are closely related to the following programme areas of other chapters of Agenda 21:

   a. Protection of the quality and supply of freshwater resources: application of integrated approaches to the development, management and use of water resources (chapter 18);

   b. Promoting sustainable human settlement development (chapter 7);

   c. Protecting and promoting human health conditions (chapter 6);

   d. Changing consumption patterns (chapter 4).

21.3. Solid wastes, as defined in this chapter, include all domestic refuse and non-hazardous wastes such as commercial and institutional wastes, street sweepings and construction debris. In some countries, the solid wastes management system also handles human wastes such as night -soil, ashes from incinerators, septic tank sludge and sludge from sewage treatment plants. If these wastes manifest hazardous characteristics they should be treated as hazardous wastes.

21.4. Environmentally sound waste management must go beyond the mere safe disposal or recovery of wastes that are generated and seek to address the root cause of the problem by attempting to change unsustainable patterns of production and consumption. This implies the application of the integrated life cycle management concept, which presents a unique opportunity to reconcile development with environmental protection.

21.5. Accordingly, the framework for requisite action should be founded on a hierarchy of objectives and focused on the four major waste-related programme areas, as follows:

   a. Minimizing wastes;

   b. Maximiz ing environmentally sound waste reuse and recycling;

   c. Promoting environmentally sound waste disposal and treatment;

   d. Extending waste service coverage.

21.6. The four programme areas are interrelated and mutually supportive and must therefore be integrated in order to provide a comprehensive and environmentally responsive framework for managing municipal solid wastes. The mix and emphasis given to each of the four programme areas will vary according to the local socio-economic and physical conditions, rates of waste generation and waste composition. All sectors of society should participate in all the programme areas.

### PROGRAMME AREAS

### A. Minimizing wastes

**Basis for action**

21.7. Unsustainable patterns of production and consumption are increasing the quantities and variety of environmentally persistent wastes at unprecedented rates. The trend could significantly increase the quantities of wastes produced by the end of the century and increase quantities four to fivefold by the year 2025. A preventive waste management approach focused on changes in lifestyles and in production and consumption patterns offers the best chance for reversing current trends.

**Objectives**

21.8. The objectives in this area are:

    a. To stabilize or reduce the production of wastes destined for final disposal, over an agreed time-frame, by formulating goals based on waste weight, volume and composition and to induce separation to facilitate waste recycling and reuse;

    b. To strengthen procedures for assessing waste quantity and composition changes for the purpose of formulating operational waste minimization policies utilizing economic or other instruments to induce beneficial modifications of production and consumption patterns.

21.9. Governments, according to their capacities and available resources and with t he cooperation of the United Nations and other relevant organizations, as appropriate, should:

    a. By the year 2000, ensure sufficient national, regional and international capacity to access, process and monitor waste trend information and implement waste minimization policies;

    b. By the year 2000, have in place in all industrialized countries programmes to stabilize or reduce, if practicable, production of wastes destined for final disposal, including per capita wastes (where this concept applies), at the level prevailing at that date; developing countries as well should work towards that goal without jeopardizing their development prospects;

    c. Apply by the year 2000, in all countries, in particular in industrialized countries, programmes to reduce the production of agrochemical wastes, containers and packaging materials, which do not meet hazardous characteristics.

**Activities**

(a) Management-related activities

21.10. Governments should initiate programmes to achieve sustained minimization of waste generation. Non-governmental organizations and consumer groups should be encouraged to participate in such programmes, which could be drawn up with the cooperation of international organizations, where necessary. These programmes should, wherever possible, build upon existing or planned activities and should:

    a. Develop and strengthen national capacities in research and design of environmentally sound technologies, as well as adopt measures to reduce wastes to a minimum;

    b. Provide for incentives to reduce unsustainable patterns of production and consumption;

    c. Develop, where necessary, national plans to minimize waste generation as part of overall national development plans;

    d. Emphasize waste minimization considerations in procurement within the United Nations system.

(b) Data and information

21.11. Monitoring is a key prerequisite for keeping track of changes in waste quantity and quality and their resultant impact on health and the environment. Governments, with the support of international agencies, should:

    a. Develop and apply methodologies for country-level waste monitoring;

    b. Undertake data gathering and analysis, establish national goals and monitor progress;

    c. Utilize data to assess environmental soundness of national waste policies as a basis for corrective action;

    d. Input information into global information systems.

(c) International and regional cooperation and coordination

21.12. The United Nations and intergovernmental organizations, with the collaboration of Governments, should help promote waste minimization by facilitating greater exchange of information, know-how and experience. The following is a non-exhaustive list of specific activities that could be undertaken:

    a. Identifying, developing and harmonizing methodologies for waste monitoring and transferring such methodologies to countries;

    b. Identifying and further developing the activities of existing information networks on clean technologies and waste minimization;

    c. Undertaking periodic assessment, collating and analysing country data and reporting systematically, in an appropriate United Nations forum, to the countries concerned;

    d. Reviewing the effectiveness of all waste minimization instruments and identifying potential new instruments that could be used and techniques by which they could be made operational at the country level. Guidelines and codes of practice should be developed;

    e. Undertaking research on the social and economic impacts of waste minimization at the consumer level.

**Means of implementation**

(a) Financing and cost evaluation

21.13. The Conference secretariat suggests that industrialized countries should consider investing in waste minimization the equivalent of about 1 per cent of the expenditures on solid wastes and sewage disposal. At current levels, this would amount to about $6.5 billion annually, including about $1.8 billion related to minimizing municipal solid wastes. Actual amounts would be determined by relevant municipal, provincial and national budget authorities based on local circumstances.

(b) Scientific and technological means

21.14. Waste minimization technologies and procedures will need to be identified and widely disseminated. This work should be coordinated by national Governments, with the cooperation and collaboration of non-governmental organizations, research institutions and appropriate organizations of the United Nations, and could include the following:

    a. Undertaking a continuous review of the effectiveness of all waste minimization instruments and identifying potential new instruments that could be used and techniques by which instruments could be made operational at the country level. Guidelines and codes of practice should be developed;

    b. Promoting waste prevention and minimization as the principal objective of national waste management programmes;

    c.    Promoting public education and a range of regulatory and non-regulatory incentives to encourage industry to change product design and reduce industrial process wastes through cleaner production technologies and good housekeeping practices and to encourage industries and consumers to use types of packaging that can be safely reused;

    d.    Executing, in accordance with national capacities, demonstration and pilot programmes to optimize waste minimization instruments;

    e.    Establishing procedures for adequate transport, storage, conservation and management of agricultural products, foodstuffs and other perishable goods in order to reduce the loss of those products, which results in the production of solid waste;

    f.    Facilitating the transfer of waste-reduction technologies to industry, particularly in developing countries, and establishing concrete national standards for effluents and solid waste, taking into account, inter alia, raw material use and energy consumption.

(c) Human resource development

21.15. Human resource development for waste minimization not only should be targeted at professionals in the waste management sector but also should seek to obtain the support of citizens and industry. Human resource development programmes must therefore aim to raise consciousness and educate and inform concerned groups and the public in general. Countries should incorporate within school curricula, where appropriate, the principles and practices of preventing and minimizing wastes and material on the environmental impacts of waste.

### B. Maximizing environmentally sound waste reuse and recycling

**Basis for action**

21.16. The exhaustion of traditional disposal sites, stricter environmental controls governing waste disposal and increasing quantities of more persistent wastes, particularly in industrialized countries, have all contributed t o a rapid increase in the cost of waste disposal services. Costs could double or triple by the end of the decade. Some current disposal practices pose a threat to the environment. As the economics of waste disposal services change, waste recycling and resource recovery are becoming increasingly cost-effective. Future waste management programmes should take maximum advantage of resource-efficient approaches to the control of wastes. These activities should be carried out in conjunction with public education programmes. It is important that markets for products from reclaimed materials be identified in the development of reuse and recycling programmes.

**Objectives**

21.17.    The objectives in this area are:

    a.    To strengthen and increase national waste reuse and recycling systems;

    b.    To create a model internal waste reuse and recycling programme for waste streams, including paper, within the United Nations system;

    c.    To make available information, techniques and appropriate policy instruments to encourage and make operational waste reuse and recycling schemes.

21.18. Governments, according to their capacities and available resources and with the cooperation of the United Nations and other relevant organizations, as appropriate, should:

a. By the year 2000, promote sufficient financial and technological capacities at the regional, national and local levels, as appropriate, to implement waste reuse and recycling policies and actions;

b. By the year 2000, in all industrialized countries, and by the year 2010, in all developing countries, have a national programme, including, to the extent possible, targets for efficient waste reuse and recycling.

**Activities**

(a) Management-related activities

21.19. Governments and institutions and non-governmental organizations, including consumer, women's and youth groups, in collaboration with appropriate organizations of the United Nations system, should launch programmes to demonstrate and make operational enhanced waste reuse and recycling. These programmes should, wherever possible, build upon existing or planned activities and should:

a. Develop and strengthen national capacity to reuse and recycle an increasing proportion of wastes;

b. Review and reform national waste policies to provide incentives for waste reuse and recycling;

c. Develop and implement national plans for waste management that take advantage of, and give priority to, waste reuse and recycling;

d. Modify existing standards or purchase specifications to avoid discrimination against recycled materials, taking into account the saving in energy and raw materials;

e. Develop public education and awareness programmes to promote the use of recycled products.

(b) Data and information

21.20. Information and research is required to identify promising socially acceptable and cost-effective forms of waste reuse and recycling relevant to each country. For example, supporting activities undertaken by national and local governments in collaboration with the United Nations and other international organizations could include:

a. Undertaking an extensive review of options and techniques for reuse and recycling all forms of municipal solid wastes. Policies for reuse and recycling should be made an integral component of national and local waste management programmes;

b. Assessing the extent and practice of waste reuse and recycling operations currently undertaken and identifying ways by which these could be increased and supported;

c. Increasing funding for research pilot programmes to test various options for reuse and recycling, including the use of small-scale, cottage-based recycling industries; compost production; treated waste-water irrigation; and energy recovery from wastes;

d. Producing guidelines and best practices for waste reuse and recycling;

e. Intensifying efforts, at collecting, analysing and disseminating, to key target groups, relevant information on waste issues. Special research grants could be made available on a competitive basis for innovative research projects on recycling techniques;

f. Identifying potential markets for recycled products.

(c) International and regional cooperation and coordination

21.21. States, through bilateral and multilateral cooperation, including through the United Nations and other relevant international organizations, as appropriate, should:

    a. Undertake a periodic review of the extent to which countries reuse and recycle their wastes;

    b. Review the effectiveness of techniques for and approaches to waste reuse and recycling and ways of enhancing their application in countries;

    c. Review and update international guidelines for the safe reuse of wastes;

    d. Establish appropriate programmes to support small communities' waste reuse and recycling industries in developing countries.

**Means of implementation**

(a) Financing and cost evaluation

21.22. The Conference secretariat has estimated that if the equivalent of 1 per cent of waste-related municipal expenditures was devoted to safe waste reuse schemes, worldwide expenditures for this purpose would amount to $8 billion. The secretariat estimates the total annual cost (1993-2000) of implementing the activities of this programme area in developing countries to be about $850 million on grant or concessional terms. These are indicative and order-of-magnitude estimates only and have not been reviewed by Governments. Actual costs and financial terms, including any that are non-concessional, will depend upon, inter alia, the specific programmes proposed by international institutions and approved by their governing bodies.

(b) Scientific and technological means

21.23. The transfer of technology should support waste recycling and reuse by the following means:

    a. Including the transfer of recycling technologies, such as machinery for reusing plastics, rubber and paper, within bilateral and multilateral technical cooperation and aid programmes;

    b. Developing and improving existing technologies, especially indigenous technologies, and facilitating their transfer under ongoing regional and interregional technical assistance programmes;

    c. Facilitating the transfer of waste reuse and recycling technology.

21.24. Incentives for waste reuse and recycling are numerous. Countries could consider the following options to encourage industry, institutions, commercial establishments and individuals to recycle wastes instead of disposing of them:

    a. Offering incentives to local and municipal authorities that recycle the maximum proportion of their wastes;

    b. Providing technical assistance to informal waste reuse and recycling operations;

    c. Applying economic and regulatory instruments, including tax incentives, to support the principle that generators of wastes pay for their disposal;

    d. Providing legal and economic conditions conducive to investments in waste reuse and recycling;

    e. Implementing specific mechanisms such as deposit/refund systems as incentives for reuse and recycling;

    f. Promoting the separate collection of recyclable parts of household wastes;

g.   Providing incentives to improve the marketability of technically recyclable waste;

h.   Encouraging the use of recyclable materials, particularly in packaging, where feasible;

i.   Encouraging the development of markets for recycled goods by establishing programmes.

(c) Human resource development

21.25. Training will be required to reorient current waste management practices to include waste reuse and recycling. Governments, in collaboration with United Nations international and regional organizations, should undertake the following indicative list of actions:

a.   Including waste reuse and recycling in in-service training programmes as integral components of technical cooperation programmes on urban management and infrastructure development;

b.   Expanding training programmes on water supply and sanitation to incorporate techniques and policies for waste reuse and recycling;

c.   Including the advantages and civic obligations associated with waste reuse and recycling in school curricula and relevant general educational courses;

d.   Encouraging non-governmental organizations, community-based organizations and women's, youth and public interest group programmes, in collaboration with local municipal authorities, to mobilize community support for waste reuse and recycling through focused community-level campaigns.

(d) Capacity-building

21.26. Capacity-building to support increased waste reuse and recycling should focus on the following areas:

a.   Making operational national policies and incentives for waste management;

b.   Enabling local and municipal authorities to mobilize community support for waste reuse and recycling by involving and assisting informal sector waste reuse and recycling operations and undertaking waste management planning that incorporates resource recovery practices.

### C. Promoting environmentally sound waste disposal and treatment

**Basis for action**

21.27. Even when wastes are minimized, some wastes will still remain. Even after treatment, all discharges of wastes have some residual impact on the receiving environment. Consequently, there is scope for improving waste treatment and disposal practices such as, for example, avoiding the discharge of sludges at sea. In developing countries, the problem is of a more fundamental nature: less than 10 per cent of urban wastes receive some form of treatment and only a small proportion of treatment is in compliance with any acceptable quality standard. Faecal matter treatment and disposal should be accorded due priority given the potential threat of faeces to human health.

**Objectives**

21.28. The objective in this area is to treat and safely dispose of a progressively increasing proportion of the generated wastes.

21.29. Governments, according to their capacities and available resources and with the cooperation of the United Nations and other relevant organizations, as appropriate, should:

a.  By the year 2000, establish waste treatment and disposal quality criteria, objectives and standards based on the nature and assimilative capacity of the receiving environment;

b.  By the year 2000, establish sufficient capacity to undertake waste-related pollution impact monitoring and conduct regular surveillance, including epidemiological surveillance, where appropriate;

c.  By the year 1995, in industrialized countries, and by the year 2005, in developing countries, ensure that at least 50 per cent of all sewage, waste waters and solid wastes are treated or disposed of in conformity with national or international environmental and health quality guidelines;

d.  By the year 2025, dispose of all sewage, waste waters and solid wastes in conformity with national or international environmental quality guidelines.

**Activities**

(a) Management-related activities

21.30. Governments, institutions and non-governmental organizations, together with industries , in collaboration with appropriate organizations of the United Nations system, should launch programmes to improve the control and management of waste-related pollution. These programmes should, wherever possible, build upon existing or planned activities and should:

a.  Develop and strengthen national capacity to treat and safely dispose of wastes;

b.  Review and reform national waste management policies to gain control over waste-related pollution;

c.  Encourage countries to seek waste disposal solutions within their sovereign territory and as close as possible to the sources of origin that are compatible with environmentally sound and efficient management. In a number of countries, transboundary movements take place to ensure that wastes are managed in an environmentally sound and efficient way. Such movements observe the relevant conventions, including those that apply to areas that are not under national jurisdiction;

d.  Develop human wastes management plans, giving due attention to the development and application of appropriate technologies and the availability of resources for implementation.

(b) Data and information

21.31. Standard setting and monitoring are two key elements essential for gaining control over waste-related pollution. The following specific activities are indicative of the kind of supportive actions that could be taken by international bodies such as the United Nations Centre for Human Settlements (Habitat), the United Nations Environment Programme and the World Health Organization:

a.  Assembling and analysing the scientific evidence and pollution impacts of wastes in the environment in order to formulate and disseminate recommended scientific criteria and guidelines for the environmentally sound management of solid wastes;

b.  Recommending national and, where relevant, local environmental quality standards based on scientific criteria and guidelines;

c.  Including within technical cooperation programmes and agreements the provision for monitoring equipment and for the requisite training in its use;

d. Establishing an information clearing-house with extensive networks at the regional, national and local levels to collect and disseminate information on all aspects of waste management, including safe disposal.

(c) International and regional cooperation and coordination

21.32. States, through bilateral and multilateral cooperation, including through the United Nations and other relevant international organizations, as appropriate, should:

a. Identify, develop and harmonize methodologies and environmental quality and health guidelines for safe waste discharge and disposal;

b. Review and keep abreast of developments and disseminate information on the effectiveness of techniques and approaches to safe waste disposal and ways of supporting their application in countries.

**Means of implementation**

(a) Financing and cost evaluation

21.33. Safe waste disposal programmes are relevant to both developed and developing countries. In developed countries the focus is on improving facilities to meet higher environmental quality criteria, while in developing countries considerable investment is required to build new treatment facilities.

21.34. The Conference secretariat has estimated the average total annual cost (1993-2000) of implementing the activities of this programme in developing countries to be about $15 billion, including about $3.4 billion from the international community on grant or concessional terms. These are indicative and order-of-magnitude estimates only and have not been reviewed by Governments. Actual costs and financial terms, including any that are non-concessional, will depend upon, inter alia, the specific strategies and programmes Governments decide upon for implementation.

(b) Scientific and technological means

21.35. Scientific guidelines and research on various aspects of waste-related pollution control will be crucial for achieving the objectives of this programme. Governments, municipalities and local authorities, with appropriate international cooperation, should:

a. Prepare guidelines and technical reports on subjects such as the integration of land-use planning in human settlements with waste disposal, environmental quality criteria and standards, waste treatment and safe disposal options, industrial waste treatment and landfill operations;

b. Undertake research on critical subjects such as low-cost, low-maintenance waste-water treatment systems; safe sludge disposal options; industrial waste treatment; and low-technology, ecologically safe waste disposal options;

c. Transfer technologies, in conformity with the terms as well as the p rovisions of chapter 34 (Transfer of environmentally sound technology, cooperation and capacity-building), on industrial waste treatment processes through bilateral nad multilateral technical cooperation programmes and in cooperation with business and industry, including large and transnational corporations, as appropriate.

d. Focus on the rehabilitation, operation and maintenance of existing facilities and technical assistance on improved maintenance practices and techniques followed by the planning and construction of waste treatment facilities;

e. Establish programmes to maximize the source segregation and safe disposal of the hazardous components of municipal solid waste;

f.  Ensure the investment and provision of waste collection facilities with the concomitant provision of water services and with an equal and parallel investment and provision of waste treatment facilities.

## (c) Human resource development

21.36. Training would be required to improve current waste management practices to include safe collection and waste disposal. The following is an indicative list of actions that should be taken by Governments, in collaboration with international organizations:

a.  Providing both formal and in-service training, focused on pollution control, waste treatment and disposal technologies, and operating and maintaining waste-related infrastructure. Intercountry staff exchange programmes should also be established;

b.  Undertaking the requisite training for waste-related pollution monitoring and control enforcement.

## (d) Capacity-building

21.37. Institutional reforms and capacity-building will be indispensable if countries are to be able to quantify and mitigate waste-related pollution. Activities to achieve this objective should include:

a.  Creating and strengthening independent environmental control bodies at the national and local levels. International organizations and donors should support needed upgrading of manpower skills and provision of equipment;

b.  Empowering of pollution control agencies with the requisite legal mandate and financial capacities to carry out their duties effectively.

### D. Extending waste service coverage

**Basis for action**

21.38. By the end of the century, over 2.0 billion people will be without access to basic sanitation, and an estimated half of the urban population in developing countries will be without adequate solid waste disposal services. As many as 5.2 million people, including 4 million children under five years of age, die each year from waste-related diseases. The health impacts are particularly severe for the urban poor. The health and environmental impacts of inadequate waste management, however, go beyond the unserved settlements themselves and result in water, land and air contamination and pollution over a wider area. Extending and improving waste collection and safe disposal services are crucial to gaining control over this form of pollution.

**Objectives**

21.39. The overall objective of this programme is to provide health-protecting, environmentally safe waste collection and disposal services to all people. Governments, according to their capacities and available resources and with the cooperation of the United Nations and other relevant organizations, as appropriate, should:

a.  By the year 2000, have the necessary technical, financial and human resource capacity to provide waste collection services commensurate with needs;

b.  By the year 2025, provide all urban populations with adequate waste services;

c.  By the year 2025, ensure that full urban waste service coverage is maintained and sanitation coverage achieved in all rural areas.

**Activities**

(a) Management-related activities

21.40. Governments, according to their capacities and available resources and with the cooperation of the United Nations and other relevant organizations, as appropriate, should:

    a. Establish financing mechanisms for waste management service development in deprived areas, including appropriate modes of revenue generation;

    b. Apply the "polluter pays" principle, where appropriate, by setting waste management charges at rates that reflect the costs of providing the service and ensure that those who generate the wastes pay the full cost of disposal in an environmentally safe way;

    c. Encourage institutionalization of communities' participation in planning and implementation procedures for solid waste management.

**(b) Data and information**

21.41. Governments, in collaboration with the United Nations and international organizations, should undertake the following:

    a. Developing and applying methodologies for waste monitoring;

    b. Data gathering and analysis to establish goals and monitor progress;

    c. Inputting information into a global information system building upon existing systems;

    d. Strengthening the activities of existing information networks in order to disseminate focused information on the application of innovative and low-cost alternatives for waste disposal to targeted audiences.

(c) International and regional cooperation and coordination

21.42. Many United Nations and bilateral programmes exist that seek to provide water supply and sanitation services to the unserved. The Water and Sanitation Collaborative Council, a global forum, currently acts to coordinate development and encourage cooperation. Even so, given the ever-increasing numbers of unserved urban poor populations and the need to address, in addition, the problem of solid waste disposal, additional mechanisms are essential to ensure accelerated coverage of urban waste disposal services. The international community in general and selected United Nations organizations in particular should:

    a. Launch a settlement infrastructure and environment programme following the United Nations Conference on Environment and Development to coordinate the activities of all organizations of the United Nations system involved in this area and include a clearing-house for information dissemination on all waste management issues;

    b. Undertake and systematically report on progress in providing waste services to those without such services;

    c. Review the effectiveness of techniques for and approaches to increasing coverage and identify innovative ways of accelerating the process.

**Means of implementation**

(a) Financing and cost evaluation

21.43. The Conference secretariat has estimated the average total annual cost (1993-2000) of implementing the activities of this programme to be about $7.5 billion, including about $2.6 billion from the international community on grant or concessional terms. These are indicative and order-of-magnitude estimates only and have not been reviewed by Governments. Actual costs and financial

terms, including any that are non-concessional, will depend upon, inter alia, the specific strategies and programmes Governments decide upon for implementation.

(b) Scientific and technological means

21.44. Governments and institutions, together with non-governmental organizations, should, in collaboration with appropriate organizations of the United Nations system, launch programmes in different parts of the developing world to extend waste services to the unserved populations. These programmes should, wherever possible, build upon and reorient existing or planned activities.

21.45. Policy changes at the national and local levels could enhance the rate of waste service coverage extension. These changes should include the following:

a. Giving full recognition to and using the full range of low-cost options for waste management, including, where appropriate, their institutionalization and incorporation within codes of practice and regulation;

b. Assigning high priority to the extension of waste management services, as necessary and appropriate, to all settlements irrespective of their legal status, giving due emphasis to meeting the waste disposal needs of the unserved, especially the unserved urban poor;

c. Integrating the provision and maintenance of waste management services with other basic services such as water-supply and storm-water drainage.

21.46. Research activities could be enhanced. Countries, in cooperation with appropriate international organizations and non-governmental organizations, should, for instance:

a. Find solutions and equipment for managing wastes in areas of concentrated populations and on small islands. In particular, there is a need for appropriate refuse storage and collection systems and cost-effective and hygienic human waste disposal options;

b. Prepare and disseminate guidelines, case-studies, policy reviews and technical reports on appropriate solutions and modes of service delivery to unserved low-income areas;

c. Launch campaigns to encourage active community participation involving women's and youth groups in the management of waste, particularly household waste;

d. Promote intercountry transfer of relevant technologies, especially technologies for high-density settlements.

(c) Human resource development

21.47. International organizations and national and local Governments, in collaboration with non-governmental organizations, should provide focused training on low-cost waste collection and disposal options, particularly techniques for their planning and delivery. Intercountry staff exchange programmes among developing countries could form part of such training. Particular attention should be given to upgrading the status and skills of management -level personnel in waste management agencies.

21.48. Improvements in management techniques are likely to yield the greatest returns in terms of improving waste management service efficiency. The United Nations, international organizations and financial institutions should, in collaboration with national and local Governments, develop and render operational management information systems for municipal record keeping and accounting and for efficiency and effectiveness assessment.

(d) Capacity-building

21.49. Governments, institutions and non-governmental organizations, with the collaboration of appropriate organizations of the United Nations system, should develop capacities to implement programmes to provide waste collection and disposal services to the unserved populations. Some activities under the programmes should include the following:

    a.    Establishing a special unit within current institutional arrangements to plan and deliver services to the unserved poor communities, with their involvement and participation;

    b.    Making revisions to existing codes and regulations to permit the use of the full range of low-cost alternative technologies for waste disposal;

    c.    Building institutional capacity and developing procedures for undertaking service planning and delivery.

## Agenda 21 – Chapter 22
# SAFE AND ENVIRONMENTALLY SOUND MANAGEMENT OF RADIOACTIVE WASTES

## PROGRAMME AREA

### Promoting the safe and environmentally sound management of radioactive wastes

### Basis for action

22.1. Radioactive wastes are generated in the nuclear fuel cycle as well as in nuclear applications (the use of radionuclides in medicine, research and industry). The radiological and safety risk from radioactive wastes varies from very low in short-lived, low-level wastes up to very large for high-level wastes. Annually about 200,000 m3 of low-level and intermediate-level waste and 10,000 m3 of high-level waste (as well as spent nuclear fuel destined for final disposal) is generated world wide from nuclear power production. These volumes are increasing as more nuclear power units are taken into operation, nuclear facilities are decommissioned and the use of radionuclides increases. The high-level waste contains about 99 per cent of the radionuclides and thus represents the largest radiological risk. The waste volumes from nuclear applications are generally much smaller, typically some tens of cubic metres or less per year and country. However, the activity concentration, especially in sealed radiation sources, might be high, thus justifying very stringent radiological protection measures. The growth of waste volumes should continue to be kept under close review.

22.2. The safe and environmentally sound management of radioactive wastes, including their minimization, transportation and disposal, is important, given their characteristics. In most countries with a substantial nuclear power programme, technical and administrative measures have been taken to implement a waste management system. In many other countries still only in preparation for a national nuclear programme or having only nuclear applications, such systems are still needed.

### Objective

22.3. The objective of this programme area is to ensure that radioactive wastes are safely managed, transported, stored and disposed of, with a view to protecting human health and the environment, within a wider framework of an interactive and integrated approach to radioactive waste management and safety.

### Activities

(a) Management-related activities

22.4. States, in cooperation with relevant international organizations, where appropriate, should:

   a. Promote policies and practical measures to minimize and limit, where appropriate, the generation of radioactive wastes and provide for their safe processing, conditioning, transportation and disposal;

   b. Support efforts within IAEA to develop and promulgate radioactive waste safety standards or guidelines and codes of practice as an internationally accepted basis for the safe and environmentally sound management and disposal of radioactive wastes;

   c. Promote safe storage, transportation and disposal of radioactive wastes, as well as spent radiation sources and spent fuel from nuclear reactors destined for final disposal, in all countries, in particular in developing countries, by facilitating the transfer of relevant technologies to those countries and/or the return to the supplier of radiation sources after their use, in accordance with relevant international regulations or guidelines;

d. Promote proper planning, including environmental impact assessment where appropriate, of safe and environmentally sound management of radioactive waste, including emergency procedures, storage, transportation and disposal, prior to and after activities that generate such waste.

(b) International and regional cooperation and coordination

22.5. States, in cooperation with relevant international organizations, where appropriate, should:

a. Strengthen their efforts to implement the Code of Practice on the Transboundary Movements of Radioactive Waste and, under the auspices of IAEA, in cooperation with relevant international organizations dealing with different modes of transport, keep the question of such movements under active review, including the desirability of concluding a legally binding instrument;

b. Encourage the London Dumping Convention to expedite work to complete studies on replacing the current voluntary moratorium on disposal of low-level radioactive wastes at sea by a ban, taking into account the precautionary approach, with a view to taking a well informed and timely decision on the issue;

c. Not promote or allow the storage or disposal of high-level, intermediate-level and low-level radioactive wastes near the marine environment unless they determine that scientific evidence, consistent with the applicable internationally agreed principles and guidelines, shows that such storage or disposal poses no unacceptable risk to people and the marine environment or does not interfere with other legitimate uses of the sea, making, in the process of consideration, appropriate use of the concept of the precautionary approach;

d. Not export radioactive wastes to countries that, individually or through international agreements, prohibit the import of such wastes, such as the contracting parties to the Bamako Convention on the Ban of the Import into Africa and the Control of Transboundary Movement of Hazardous Wastes within Africa, the fourth Lom Convention or other relevant conventions, where such prohibition is provided for;

e. Respect, in accordance with international law, the decisions, as far as applicable to them, taken by parties to other relevant regional environmental conventions dealing with other aspects of safe and environmentally sound management of radioactive wastes.

**Means of implementation**

(a) Financing and cost evaluation

22.6. The costs at the national level of managing and disposing of radioactive wastes are considerable and will vary, depending on the technology used for disposal.

22.7. The Conference secretariat has estimated the average total annual cost (1993-2000) to international organizations to implement the activities of this programme to be about $8 million. Actual costs and financial terms, including any that are non-concessional, will depend upon, inter alia, the specific strategies and programmes Governments decide upon for implementation.

(b) Scientific and technological means

22.8. States, in cooperation with international organizations, where appropriate, should:

a. Promote research and development of methods for the safe and environmentally sound treatment, processing and disposal, including deep geological disposal, of high-level radioactive waste;

b. Conduct research and assessment programmes concerned with evaluating the health and environmental impact of radioactive waste disposal.

(c) Capacity-building, including human resource development

22.9. States, in cooperation with relevant international organizations, should provide, as appropriate, assistance to developing countries to establish and/or strengthen radioactive waste management infrastructures, including legislation, organizations, trained manpower and facilities for the handling, processing, storage and disposal of wastes generated from nuclear applications.

# Agenda 21 – Chapter 23
## STRENGTHENING THE ROLE OF MAJOR GROUPS

### PREAMBLE

23.1. Critical to the effective implementation of the objectives, policies and mechanisms agreed to by Governments in all programme areas of Agenda 21 will be the commitment and genuine involvement of all social groups.

23.2. One of the fundamental prerequisites for the achievement of sustainable development is broad public participation in decision-making. Furthermore, in the more specific context of environment and development, the need for new forms of participation has emerged. This includes the need of individuals, groups and organizations to participate in environmental impact assessment procedures and to know about and participate in decisions, particularly those which potentially affect the communities in which they live and work. Individuals, groups and organizations should have access to information relevant to environment and development held by national authorities, including information on products and activities that have or are likely to have a significant impact on the environment, and information on environmental protection measures.

23.3. Any policies, definitions or rules affecting access to and participation by non-governmental organizations in the work of United Nations institutions or agencies associated with the implementation of Agenda 21 must apply equally to all major groups.

23.4. The programme areas set out below address the means for moving towards real social partnership in support of common efforts for sustainable development.

# Agenda 21 – Chapter 24
## GLOBAL ACTION FOR WOMEN TOWARDS SUSTAINABLE AND EQUITABLE DEVELOPMENT
### PROGRAMME AREA

**Basis for action**

24.1. The international community has endorsed several plans of action and conventions for the full, equal and beneficial integration of women in all development activities, in particular the Nairobi Forward-looking Strategies for the Advancement of Women, 1/ which emphasize women's participation in national and international ecosystem management and control of environment degradation. Several conventions, including the Convention on the Elimination of All Forms of Discrimination against Women (General Assembly resolution 34/180, annex) and conventions of ILO and UNESCO have also been adopted to end gender-based discrimination and ensure women access to land and other resources, education and safe and equal employment. Also relevant are the 1990 World Declaration on the Survival, Protection and Development of Children and the Plan of Action for implementing the Declaration (A/45/625, annex). Effective implementation of these programmes will depend on the active involvement of women in economic and political decision-making and will be critical to the successful implementation of Agenda 21.

**Objectives**

24.2. The following objectives are proposed for national Governments:

    a. To implement the Nairobi Forward-looking Strategies for the Advancement of Women, particularly with regard to women's participation in national ecosystem management and control of environment degradation;

    b. To increase the proportion of women decision makers, planners, technical advisers, managers and extension workers in environment and development fields;

    c. To consider developing and issuing by the year 2000 a strategy of changes necessary to eliminate constitutional, legal, administrative, cultural, behavioural, social and economic obstacles to women's full participation in sustainable development and in public life;

    d. To establish by the year 1995 mechanisms at the national, regional and international levels to assess the implementation and impact of development and environment policies and programmes on women and to ensure their contributions and benefits;

    e. To assess, review, revise and implement, where appropriate, curricula and other educational material, with a view to promoting the dissemination to both men and women of gender-relevant knowledge and valuation of women's roles through formal and non-formal education, as well as through training institutions, in collaboration with non-governmental organizations;

    f. To formulate and implement clear governmental policies and national guidelines, strategies and plans for the achievement of equality in all aspects of society, including the promotion of women's literacy, education, training, nutrition and health and their participation in key decision-making positions and in management of the environment, particularly as it pertains to their access to resources, by facilitating better access to all forms of credit, particularly in the informal sector, taking measures towards ensuring women's access to property rights as well as agricultural inputs and implements;

    g. To implement, as a matter of urgency, in accordance with country-specific conditions, measures to ensure that women and men have the same right to decide freely and responsibly the number and spacing of their children and have access to information, education and means, as appropriate, to enable them to exercise this right in keeping with their freedom, dignity and personally held values;

h. To consider adopting, strengthening and enforcing legislation prohibiting violence against women and to take all necessary administrative, social and educational measures to eliminate violence against women in all its forms.

**Activities**

24.3. Governments should take active steps to implement the following:

a. Measures to review policies and establish plans to increase the proportion of women involved as decision makers, planners, managers, scientists and technical advisers in the design, development and implementation of policies and programmes for sustainable development;

b. Measures to strengthen and empower women's bureaux, women's non-governmental organizations and women's groups in enhancing capacity-building for sustainable development;

c. Measures to eliminate illiteracy among females and to expand the enrolment of women and girls in educational institutions, to promote the goal of universal access to primary and secondary education for girl children and for women, and to increase educational and training opportunities for women and girls in sciences and technology, particularly at the post-secondary level;

d. Programmes to promote the reduction of the heavy workload of women and girl children at home and outside through the establishment of more and affordable nurseries and kindergartens by Governments, local authorities, employers and other relevant organizations and the sharing of household tasks by men and women on an equal basis, and to promote the provision of environmentally sound technologies which have been designed, developed and improved in consultation with women, accessible and clean water, an efficient fuel supply and adequate sanitation facilities;

e. Programmes to establish and strengthen preventive and curative health facilities, which include women-centred, women-managed, safe and effective reproductive health care and affordable, accessible, responsible planning of family size and services, as appropriate, in keeping with freedom, dignity and personally held values. Programmes should focus on providing comprehensive health care, including pre-natal care, education and information on health and responsible parenthood, and should provide the opportunity for all women to fully breastfeed at least during the first four months post-partum. Programmes should fully support women's productive and reproductive roles and well-being and should pay special attention to the need to provide equal and improved health care for all children and to reduce the risk of maternal and child mortality and sickness;

f. Programmes to support and strengthen equal employment opportunities and equitable remuneration for women in the formal and informal sectors with adequate economic, political and social support systems and services, including child care, particularly day-care facilities and parental leave, and equal access to credit, land and other natural resources;

g. Programmes to establish rural banking systems with a view to facilitating and increasing rural women's access to credit and to agricultural inputs and implements;

h. Programmes to develop consumer awareness and the active participation of women, emphasizing their crucial role in achieving changes necessary to reduce or eliminate unsustainable patterns of consumption and production, particularly in industrialized countries, in order to encourage investment in environmentally sound productive activities and induce environmentally and socially friendly industrial development;

    i. Programmes to eliminate persistent negative images, stereotypes, attitudes and prejudices against women through changes in socialization patterns, the media, advertising, and formal and non-formal education;

    j. Measures to review progress made in these areas, including the preparation of a review and appraisal report which includes recommendations to be submitted to the 1995 world conference on women.

24.4. Governments are urged to ratify all relevant conventions pertaining to women if they have not already done so. Those that have ratified conventions should enforce and establish legal, constitut ional and administrative procedures to transform agreed rights into domestic legislation and should adopt measures to implement them in order to strengthen the legal capacity of women for full and equal participation in issues and decisions on sustainable development.

24.5. States parties to the Convention on the Elimination of All Forms of Discrimination against Women should review and suggest amendments to it by the year 2000, with a view to strengthening those elements of the Convention related to environment and development, giving special attention to the issue of access and entitlements to natural resources, technology, creative banking facilities and low-cost housing, and the control of pollution and toxicity in the home and workplace. States parties should also clarify the extent of the Convention's scope with respect to the issues of environment and development and request the Committee on the Elimination of Discrimination against Women to develop guidelines regarding the nature of reporting such issues, required under particular articles of the Convention.

(a) Areas requiring urgent action

24.6. Countries should take urgent measures to avert the ongoing rapid environmental and economic degradation in developing countries that generally affects the lives of women and children in rural areas suffering drought, desertification and deforestation, armed hostilities, natural disasters, toxic waste and the aftermath of the use of unsuitable agro-chemical products.

24.7. In order to reach these goals, women should be fully involved in decision-making and in the implementation of sustainable development activities.

(b) Research, data collection and dissemination of information

24.8. Countries should develop gender-sensitive databases, information systems and participatory action-oriented research and policy analyses with the collaboration of academic institutions and local women researchers on the following:

    a. Knowledge and experience on the part of women of the management and conservation of natural resources for incorporation in the databases and information systems for sustainable development;

    b. The impact of structural adjustment programmes on women. In research done on structural adjustment programmes, special attention should be given to the differential impact of those programmes on women, especially in terms of cut-backs in social services, education and health and in the removal of subsidies on food and fuel;

    c. The impact on women of environmental degradation, particularly drought, desertification, toxic chemicals and armed hostilities;

    d. Analysis of the structural linkages between gender relations, environment and development;

e. The integration of the value of unpaid work, including work that is currently designated "domestic", in resource accounting mechanisms in order better to represent the true value of the contribution of women to the economy, using revised guidelines for the United Nations System of National Accounts, to be issued in 1993;

f. Measures to develop and include environmental, social and gender impact analyses as an essential step in the development and monitoring of programmes and policies;

g. Programmes to create rural and urban training, research and resource centres in developing and developed countries that will serve to disseminate environmentally sound technologies to women.

(c) International and regional cooperation and coordination

24.9. The Secretary-General of the United Nations should review the adequacy of all United Nations institutions, including those with a special focus on the role of women, in meeting development and environment objectives, and make recommendations for strengthening their capacities. Institutions that require special attention in this area include the Division for the Advancement of Women (Centre for Social Development and Humanit arian Affairs, United Nations Office at Vienna), the United Nations Development Fund for Women (UNIFEM), the International Research and Training Institute for the Advancement of Women (INSTRAW) and the women's programmes of regional commissions. The review should consider how the environment and development programmes of each body of the United Nations system could be strengthened to implement Agenda 21 and how to incorporate the role of women in programmes and decisions related to sustainable development.

24.10. Each body of the United Nations system should review the number of women in senior policy-level and decision-making posts and, where appropriate, adopt programmes to increase that number, in accordance with Economic and Social Council resolution 1991/17 on the improvement of the status of women in the Secretariat.

24.11. UNIFEM should establish regular consultations with donors in collaboration with UNICEF, with a view to promoting operational programmes and projects on sustainable development that will strengthen the participation of women, especially low-income women, in sustainable development and in decision-making. UNDP should establish a women's focal point on development and environment in each of its resident representative offices to provide information and promote exchange of experience and information in these fields. Bodies of the United Nations system, governments and non-governmental organizations involved in the follow-up to the Conference and the implementation of Agenda 21 should ensure that gender considerations are fully integrated into all the policies, programmes and activities.

**Means of implementation**

Financing and cost evaluation

24.12. The Conference secretariat has estimated the average total annual cost (1993-2000) of implementing the activities of this chapter to be about $40 million from the international community on grant or concessional terms. These are indicative and order-of-magnitude estimates only and have not been reviewed by Governments. Actual costs and financial terms, including any that are non-concessional, will depend upon, inter alia, the specific strategies and programmes Governments decide upon for implementation.

**Notes**

1/ Report of the World Conference to Review and Appraise the Achievements of the United Nations Decade for Women: Equality, Development and Peace, Nairobi, 15-26 July 1985 (United Nations publication, Sales No. E.85.IV.10), chap. I, sect. A.

# Agenda 21 – Chapter 25
## CHILDREN AND YOUTH IN SUSTAINABLE DEVELOPMENT

25.1. Youth comprise nearly 30 per cent of the world's population. The involvement of today's youth in environment and development decision-making and in the implementation of programmes is critical to the long-term success of Agenda 21.

## PROGRAMME AREAS

### A. Advancing the role of youth and actively involving them in the protection of the environment and the promotion of economic and social development

**Basis for action**

25.2. It is imperative that youth from all parts of the world participate actively in all relevant levels of decision-making processes because it affects their lives today and has implications for their futures. In addition to their intellectual contribution and their ability to mobilize support, they bring unique perspectives that need to be taken into account.

25.3. Numerous actions and recommendations within the international community have been proposed to ensure that youth are provided a secure and healthy future, including an environment of quality, improved standards of living and access to education and employment. These issues need to be addressed in development planning.

**Objectives**

25.4. Each country should, in consultation with its youth communities, establish a process to promote dialogue between the youth community and Government at all levels and to establish mechanisms that permit youth access to information and provide them with the opportunity to present their perspectives on government decisions, including the implementation of Agenda 21.

25.5. Each country, by the year 2000, should ensure that more than 50 per cent of its youth, gender balanced, are enrolled in or have access to appropriate secondary education or equivalent educational or vocational training programmes by increasing participation and access rates on an annual basis.

25.6. Each country should undertake initiatives aimed at reducing current levels of youth unemployment, particularly where they are disproportionately high in comparison to the overall unemployment rate.

25.7. Each country and the United Nations should support the promotion and creation of mechanisms to involve youth representation in all United Nations processes in order to influence those processes.

25.8. Each country should combat human rights abuses against young people, particularly young women and girls, and should consider providing all youth with legal protection, skills, opportunities and the support necessary for them to fulfil their personal, economic and social aspirations and potentials.

**Activities**

25.9. Governments, according to their strategies, should take measures to:

    a. Establish procedures allowing for consultation and possible participation of youth of both genders, by 1993, in decision-making processes with regard to the environment, involving youth at the local, national and regional levels;

    b. Promote dialogue with youth organizations regarding the drafting and evaluation of environment plans and programmes or questions on development;

  c. Consider for incorporation into relevant policies the recommendations of international, regional and local youth conferences and other forums that offer youth perspectives on social and economic development and resource management;

  d. Ensure access for all youth to all types of education, wherever appropriate, providing alternative learning structures, ensure that education reflects the economic and social needs of youth and incorporates the concepts of environmental awareness and sustainable development throughout the curricula; and expand vocational training, implementing innovative methods aimed at increasing practical skills, such as environmental scouting;

  e. In cooperation with relevant ministries and organizations, including representatives of youth, develop and implement strategies for creating alternative employment opportunities and provide required training to young men and women;

  f. Establish task forces that include youth and youth non-governmental organizations to develop educational and awareness programmes specifically targeted to the youth population on critical issues pertaining to youth. These task forces should use formal and non-formal educational methods to reach a maximum audience. National and local media, non-governmental organizations, businesses and other organizations should assist in these task forces;

  g. Give support to programmes, projects, networks, national organizations and youth non-governmental organizations to examine the integration of programmes in relation to their project requirements, encouraging the involvement of youth in project identification, design, implementation and follow-up;

  h. Include youth representatives in their delegations to international meetings, in accordance with the relevant General Assembly resolutions adopted in 1968, 1977, 1985 and 1989.

25.10. The United Nations and international organizations with youth programmes should take measures to:

  a. Review their youth programmes and consider how coordination between them can be enhanced;

  b. Improve the dissemination of relevant information to governments, youth organizations and other non-governmental organizations on current youth positions and activities, and monitor and evaluate the application of Agenda 21;

  c. Promote the United Nations Trust Fund for the International Youth Year and collaborate with youth representatives in the administration of it, focusing particularly on the needs of youth from developing countries.

**Means of implementation**

Financing and cost evaluation

25.11. The Conference secretariat has estimated the average total annual cost (1993-2000) of implementing the activities of this programme to be about $1.5 million on grant or concessional terms. These are indicative and order-of-magnitude estimates only and have not been reviewed by Governments. Actual costs and financial terms, including any that are non-concessional, will depend upon, inter alia, the specific strategies and programmes Governments decide upon for implementation.

**B. Children in sustainable development**

**Basis for action**

25.12.   Children not only will inherit the responsibility of looking after the Earth, but in many developing countries they comprise nearly half the population. Furthermore, children in both developing and industrialized countries are highly vulnerable to the effects of environmental degradation. They are also highly aware supporters of environmental thinking. The specific interests of children need to be taken fully into account in the participatory process on environment and development in order to safeguard the future sustainability of any actions taken to improve the environment.

## Objectives

25.13.   National governments, according to their policies, should take measures to:

  a. Ensure the survival, protection and development of children, in accordance with the goals endorsed by the 1990 World Summit for Children (A/45/625, annex);

  b. Ensure that the interests of children are taken fully into account in the participatory process for sustainable development and environmental improvement.

## Activities

25.14.   Governments should take active steps to:

  a. Implement programmes for children designed to reach the child-related goals of the 1990s in the areas of environment and development, especially health, nutrition, education, literacy and poverty alleviation;

  b. Ratify the Convention on the Rights of the Child (General Assembly resolution 44/25 of 20 November 1989, annex), at the earliest moment and implement it by addressing the basic needs of youth and children;

  c. Promote primary environmental care activities that address the basic needs of communities, improve the environment for children at the household and community level and encourage the participation and empowerment of local populations, including women, youth, children and indigenous people, towards the objective of integrated community management of resources, especially in developing countries;

  d. Expand educational opportunities for children and youth, including education for environmental and developmental responsibility, with overriding attention to the education of the girl child;

  e. Mobilize communities through schools and local health centres so that children and their parents become effective focal points for sensitization of communities to environmental issues;

  f. Establish procedures to incorporate children's concerns into all relevant policies and strategies for environment and development at the local, regional and national levels, including those concerning allocation of and entitlement to natural resources, housing and recreation needs, and control of pollution and toxicity in both rural and urban areas.

25.15.   International and regional organizations should cooperate and coordinate in the proposed areas. UNICEF should maintain cooperation and collaboration with other organizations of the United Nations, Governments and non-governmental organizations to develop programmes for children and programmes to mobilize children in the activities outlined above.

## Means of implementation

(a) Financing and cost evaluation

25.16.   Financing requirements for most of the activities are included in estimates for other programmes.

(b) Human resource development and capacity-building

25.17.   The activities should facilitate capacity-building and training activities already contained in other chapters of Agenda 21.

# RECOGNIZING AND STRENGTHENING THE ROLE OF INDIGENOUS PEOPLE AND THEIR COMMUNITIES

## PROGRAMME AREA

**Basis for action**

26.1. Indigenous people and their communities have an historical relationship with their lands and are generally descendants of the original inhabitants of such lands. In the context of this chapter the term "lands" is understood to include the environment of the areas which the people concerned traditionally occupy. Indigenous people and their communities represent a significant percentage of the global population. They have developed over many generations a holistic traditional scientific knowledge of their lands, natural resources and environment. Indigenous people and their communities shall enjoy the full measure of human rights and fundamental freedoms without hindrance or discrimination. Their ability to participate fully in sustainable development practices on their lands has tended to be limited as a result of factors of an economic, social and historical nature. In view of the interrelationship between the natural environment and its sustainable development and the cultural, social, economic and physical well-being of indigenous people, national and international efforts to implement environmentally sound and sustainable development should recognize, accommodate, promote and strengthen the role of indigenous people and their communities.

26.2. Some of the goals inherent in the objectives and activities of this programme area are already contained in such international legal instruments as the ILO Indigenous and Tribal Peoples Convention (No. 169) and are being incorporated into the draft universal declaration on indigenous rights, being prepared by the United Nations working group on indigenous populations. The International Year for the World's Indigenous People (1993), proclaimed by the General Assembly in its resolution 45/164 of 18 December 1990, presents a timely opportunity to mobilize further international technical and financial cooperation.

**Objectives**

26.3. In full partnership with indigenous people and their communities, Governments and, where appropriate, intergovernmental organizations should aim at fulfilling the following objectives:

    a. Establishment of a process to empower indigenous people and their communities through measures that include:

        i. Adoption or strengthening of appropriate policies and/or legal instruments at the national level;

        ii. Recognition that the lands of indigenous people and their communities should be protected from activities that are environmentally unsound or that the indigenous people concerned consider to be socially and culturally inappropriate;

        iii. Recognition of their values, traditional knowledge and resource management practices with a view to promoting environmentally sound and sustainable development;

        iv. Recognition that traditional and direct dependence on renewable resources and ecosystems, including sustainable harvesting, continues to be essential to the cultural, economic and physical well-being of indigenous people and their communities;

        v. Development and strengthening of national dispute-resolution arrangements in relation to settlement of land and resource-management concerns;

      vi.     Support for alternative environmentally sound means of production to ensure a range of choices on how to improve their quality of life so that they effectively participate in sustainable development;

      vii.    Enhancement of capacity-building for indigenous communities, based on the adaptation and exchange of traditional experience, knowledge and resource-management practices, to ensure their sustainable development;

    b.    Establishment, where appropriate, of arrangements to strengthen the active participation of indigenous people and their communities in the national formulation of policies, laws and programmes relating to resource management and other development processes that may affect them, and their initiation of proposals for such policies and programmes;

    c.    Involvement of indigenous people and their communities at the national and local levels in resource management and conservation strategies and other relevant programmes established to support and review sustainable development strategies, such as those suggested in other programme areas of Agenda 21.

## Activities

26.4. Some indigenous people and their communities may require, in accordance with national legislation, greater control over their lands, self-management of their resources, participation in development decisions affecting them, including, where appropriate, participation in the establishment or management of protected areas. The following are some of the specific measures which Governments could take:

    a.    Consider the ratification and application of existing international conventions relevant to indigenous people and their communities (where not y et done) and provide support for the adoption by the General Assembly of a declaration on indigenous rights;

    b.    Adopt or strengthen appropriate policies and/or legal instruments that will protect indigenous intellectual and cultural property and the right to preserve customary and administrative systems and practices.

26.5. United Nations organizations and other international development and finance organizations and Governments should, drawing on the active participation of indigenous people and their communities, as appropriate, take the following measures, inter alia, to incorporate their values, views and knowledge, including the unique contribution of indigenous women, in resource management and other policies and programmes that may affect them:

    a.    Appoint a special focal point within each international organization, and organize annual interorganizational coordination meetings in consultation with Governments and indigenous organizations, as appropriate, and develop a procedure within and between operational agencies for assisting Governments in ensuring the coherent and coordinated incorporation of the views of indigenous people in the design and implementation of policies and programmes. Under this procedure, indigenous people and their communities should be informed and consulted and allowed to participate in national decision-making, in particular regarding regional and international cooperative efforts. In addition, these policies and programmes should take fully into account strategies based on local indigenous initiatives;

    b.    Provide technical and financial assistance for capacity-building programmes to support the sustainable self-development of indigenous people and their communities;

    c.    Strengthen research and education programmes aimed at:

        i.      Achieving a better understanding of indigenous people's knowledge and management experience related to the environment, and applying this to contemporary development challenges;

        ii.     Increasing the efficiency of indigenous people's resource management systems, for example, by promoting the adaptation and dissemination of suitable technological innovations;

   d.   Contribute to the endeavours of indigenous people and their communities in resource management and conservation strategies (such as those that may be developed under appropriate projects funded through the Global Environment Facility and the Tropical Forestry Action Plan) and other programme areas of Agenda 21, including programmes to collect, analyse and use data and other information in support of sustainable development projects.

26.6. Governments, in full partnership with indigenous people and their communities should, where appropriate:

   a.   Develop or strengthen national arrangements to consult with indigenous people and their communities with a view to reflecting their needs and incorporating their values and traditional and other knowledge and practices in national policies and programmes in the field of natural resource management and conservation and other development programmes affecting them;

   b.   Cooperate at the regional level, where appropriate, to address common indigenous issues with a view to recognizing and strengthening their participation in sustainable development.

**Means of implementation**

(a) Financing and cost evaluation

26.7. The Conference secretariat has estimated the average total annual cost (1993-2000) of implementing the activities of this programme to be about $3 million on grant or concessional terms. These are indicative and order-of-magnitude estimates only and have not been reviewed by Governments. Actual costs and financial terms, including any that are non-concessional, will depend upon, inter alia, the specific strategies and programmes Governments decide upon for implementation.

(b) Legal and administrative frameworks

26.8. Governments should incorporate, in collaboration with the indigenous people affected, the rights and responsibilities of indigenous people and their communities in the legislation of each country, suitable to the country's specific situation. Developing countries may require technical assistance to implement these activities.

(c) Human resource development

26.9. International development agencies and Governments should commit financial and other resources to education and training for indigenous people and their communities to develop their capacities to achieve their sustainable self-development, and to contribute to and participate in sustainable and equitable development at the national level. Particular attention should be given to strengthening the role of indigenous women.

# Agenda 21 – Chapter 27
## STRENGTHENING THE ROLE OF NON-GOVERNMENTAL ORGANIZATIONS: PARTNERS FOR SUSTAINABLE DEVELOPMENT

### PROGRAMME AREA

**Basis for action**

27.1. Non-governmental organizations play a vital role in the shaping and implementation of participatory democracy. Their credibility lies in the responsible and constructive role they play in society. Formal and informal organizations, as well as grass-roots movements, should be recognized as partners in the implementation of Agenda 21. The nature of the independent role played by non-governmental organizations within a society calls for real participation; therefore, independence is a major attribute of non-governmental organizations and is the precondition of real participation.

27.2. One of the major challenges facing t he world community as it seeks to replace unsustainable development patterns with environmentally sound and sustainable development is the need to activate a sense of common purpose on behalf of all sectors of society. The chances of forging such a sense of purpose will depend on the willingness of all sectors to participate in genuine social partnership and dialogue, while recognizing the independent roles, responsibilities and special capacities of each.

27.3. Non-governmental organizations, including those non-profit organizations representing groups addressed in the present section of Agenda 21, possess well-established and diverse experience, expertise and capacity in fields which will be of particular importance to the implementation and review of environmentally sound and socially responsible sustainable development, as envisaged throughout Agenda 21. The community of non-governmental organizations, therefore, offers a global network that should be tapped, enabled and strengthened in support of efforts to achieve these common goals.

27.4. To ensure that the full potential contribution of non-governmental organizations is realized, the fullest possible communication and cooperation between international organizations, national and local governments and non-governmental organizations should be promoted in institutions mandated, and programmes designed to carry out Agenda 21. Non-governmental organizations will also need to foster cooperation and communication among themselves to reinforce their effectiveness as actors in the implementation of sustainable development.

**Objectives**

27.5. Society, Governments and international bodies should develop mechanisms to allow non-governmental organizations to play their partnership role responsibly and effectively in the process of environmentally sound and sustainable development.

27.6. With a view to strengthening the role of non-governmental organizations as social partners, the United Nations system and Governments should initiate a process, in consultation with non-governmental organizations, to review formal procedures and mechanisms for the involvement of these organizations at all levels from policy-making and decision-making to implementation.

27.7. By 1995, a mutually productive dialogue should be established at the national level between all Governments and non-governmental organizations and their self-organized networks to recognize and strengthen their respective roles in implementing environmentally sound and sustainable development.

27.8. Governments and international bodies should promote and allow the participation of non-governmental organizations in the conception, establishment and evaluation of official mechanisms and formal procedures designed to review the implementation of Agenda 21 at all levels.

**Activities**

27.9. The United Nations system, including international finance and development agencies, and all intergovernmental organizations and forums should, in consultation with non-governmental organizations, take measures to:

    a. Review and report on ways of enhancing existing procedures and mechanisms by which non-governmental organizations contribute to policy design, decision-making, implementation and evaluation at the individual agency level, in inter-agency discussions and in United Nations conferences;

    b. On the basis of subp aragraph (a) above, enhance existing or, where they do not exist, establish, mechanisms and procedures within each agency to draw on the expertise and views of non-governmental organizations in policy and programme design, implementation and evaluation;

    c. Review levels of financial and administrative support for non-governmental organizations and the extent and effectiveness of their involvement in project and programme implementation, with a view to augmenting their role as social partners;

    d. Design open and effective means of achieving the participation of non-governmental organizations in the processes established to review and evaluate the implementation of Agenda 21 at all levels;

    e. Promote and allow non-governmental organizations and their self-organized networks to contribute to the review and evaluation of policies and programmes designed to implement Agenda 21, including support for developing country non-governmental organizations and their self-organized networks;

    f. Take into account the findings of non-governmental review systems and evaluation processes in relevant reports of the Secretary-General to the General Assembly, and of all pertinent United Nations organizations and other intergovernmental organizations and forums concerning implementation of Agenda 21, in accordance with the review process for Agenda 21;

    g. Provide access for non-governmental organizations to accurate and timely data and information to promote the effectiveness of their programmes and activities and their roles in support of sustainable development.

27.10. Governments should take measures to:

    a. Establish or enhance an existing dialogue with non-governmental organizations and their self-organized networks representing various sectors, which could serve to: (i) consider the rights and responsibilities of these organizations; (ii) efficiently channel integrated non-governmental inputs to the governmental policy development process; and (iii) facilitate non-governmental coordination in implementing national policies at the programme level;

    b. Encourage and enable partnership and dialogue between local non-governmental organizations and local authorities in activities aimed at sustainable development;

    c. Involve non-governmental organizations in national mechanisms or procedures established to carry out Agenda 21, making the best use of their particular capacities, especially in the fields of education, poverty alleviation and environmental protection and rehabilitation;

d. Take into account the findings of non-governmental monitoring and review mechanisms in the design and evaluation of policies concerning the implementation of Agenda 21 at all levels;

e. Review government education systems to identify ways to include and expand the involvement of non-governmental organizations in the field of formal and informal education and of public awareness;

f. Make available and accessible to non-governmental organizations the data and information necessary for their effective contribution to research and to the design, implementation and evaluation of programmes.

**Means of implementation**

(a) Financing and cost evaluation

27.11.    Depending on the outcome of review processes and the evolution of views as to how best to build partnership and dialogue between official organizations and groups of non-governmental organizations, relatively limited but unpredictable, costs will be involved at the international and national levels in enhancing consultative procedures and mechanisms. Non-governmental organizations will also require additional funding in support of their establishment of, improvement of or contributions to Agenda 21 monitoring systems. These costs will be significant but cannot be reliably estimated on the basis of existing information.

(b) Capacity-building

27.12.    The organizations of the United Nations system and other intergovernmental organizations and forums, bilateral programmes and the private sector, as appropriate, will need to provide increased financial and administrative support for non-governmental organizations and their self-organized networks, in part icular those based in developing countries, that contribute to the monitoring and evaluation of Agenda 21 programmes, and provide training for non-governmental organizations (and assist them to develop their own training programmes) at the international and regional levels to enhance their partnership role in programme design and implementation.

27.13.    Governments will need to promulgate or strengthen, subject to country-specific conditions, any legislative measures necessary to enable the establishment by non-governmental organizations of consultative groups, and to ensure the right of non-governmental organizations to protect the public interest through legal action.

# Agenda 21 – Chapter 28
# LOCAL AUTHORITIES' INITIATIVES IN SUPPORT OF AGENDA 21

## PROGRAMME AREA

**Basis for action**

28.1. Because so many of the problems and solutions being addressed by Agenda 21 have their roots in local activities, the participation and cooperation of local authorities will be a determining factor in fulfilling its objectives. Local authorities construct, operate and maintain economic, social and environmental infrastructure, oversee planning processes, establish local environmental policies and regulations, and assist in implementing national and subnational environmental policies. As the level of governance closest to the people, they play a vital role in educating, mobilizing and responding to the public to promote sustainable development.

**Objectives**

28.2. The following objectives are proposed for this programme area:

    a. By 1996, most local authorities in each country should have undertaken a consultative process with their populations and achieved a consensus on "a local Agenda 21" for the community;

    b. By 1993, the international community should have initiated a consultative process aimed at increasing cooperation between local authorities;

    c. By 1994, representatives of associations of cities and other local authorities should have increased levels of cooperation and coordination with the goal of enhancing the exchange of information and experience among local authorities;

    d. All local authorities in each country should be encouraged to implement and monitor programmes which aim at ensuring that women and youth are represented in decision-making, planning and implementation processes.

**Activities**

28.3. Each local authority should enter into a dialogue with its citizens, local organizations and private enterprises and adopt "a local Agenda 21". Through consultation and consensus-building, local authorities would learn from citizens and from local, civic, community, business and industrial organizations and acquire the information needed for formulating the best strategies. The process of consultation would increase household awareness of sustainable development issues. Local authority programmes, policies, laws and regulations to achieve Agenda 21 objectives would be assessed and modified, based on local programmes adopted. Strategies could also be used in supporting proposals for local, national, regional and international funding.

28.4. Partnerships should be fostered among relevant organs and organizations such as UNDP, the United Nations Centre for Human Settlements (Habitat) and UNEP, the World Bank, regional banks, the International Union of Local Authorities, the World Association of the Major Metropolises, Summit of Great Cities of the World, the United Towns Organization and other relevant partners, with a view to mobilizing increased international support for local authority programmes. An important goal would be to support, extend and improve existing institutions working in the field of local authority capacity-building and local environment management. For this purpose:

    a. Habitat and other relevant organs and organizations of the United Nations system are called upon to strengthen services in collecting information on strategies of local authorities, in particular for those that need international support;

    b. Periodic consultations involving both international partners and developing countries could review strategies and consider how such international support could best be mobilized. Such a sectoral consultation would complement concurrent country-focused consultations, such as those taking place in consultative groups and round tables.

28.5. Representatives of associations of local aut horities are encouraged to establish processes to increase the exchange of information, experience and mutual technical assistance among local authorities.

**Means of implementation**

(a) Financing and cost evaluation

28.6. It is recommended that all parties reassess funding needs in this area. The Conference secretariat has estimated the average total annual cost (1993-2000) for strengthening international secretariat services for implementing the activities in this chapter to be about $1 million on grant or concessional terms. These are indicative and order-of-magnitude estimates only and have not been reviewed by Governments.

(b) Human resource development and capacity-building

28.7. This programme should facilitate the capacity-building and training activities already contained in other chapters of Agenda 21.

# STRENGTHENING THE ROLE OF WORKERS AND THEIR TRADE UNIONS

## PROGRAMME AREA

**Basis for action**

29.1. Efforts to implement sustainable development will involve adjustments and opportunities at the national and enterprise levels, with workers foremost among those concerned. As their representatives, trade unions are vital actors in facilitating the achievement of sustainable development in view of their experience in addressing industrial change, the extremely high priority they give to protection of the working environment and the related natural environment, and their promotion of socially responsible and economic development. The existing network of collaboration among trade unions and their extensive membership provide important channels through which the concepts and practices of sustainable development can be supported. The established principles of tripartism provide a basis for strengthened collaboration between workers and their representatives, Governments and employers in the implementation of sustainable development.

## Objectives

29.2. The overall objective is poverty alleviation and full and sustainable employment, which contribute to safe, clean and healthy environments - the working environment, the community and the physical environment. Workers should be full participants in the implementation and evaluation of activities related to Agenda 21.

29.3. To that end the following objectives are proposed for accomplishment by the year 2000:

    a.    To promote ratification of relevant conventions of ILO and the enactment of legislation in support of those conventions;

    b.    To establish bipartite and tripartite mechanisms on safety, health and sustainable development;

    c.    To increase the number of environmental collective agreements aimed at achieving sustainable development;

    d.    To reduce occupational accidents, injuries and diseases according to recognized statistical reporting procedures;

    e.    To increase the provision of workers' education, training and retraining, particularly in the area of occupational health and safety and environment.

## Activities

(a) Promoting freedom of association

29.4. For workers and their trade unions to play a full and informed role in support of sustainable development, Governments and employers should promote the rights of individual workers to freedom of association and the protection of the right to organize as laid down in ILO conventions. Governments should consider ratifying and implementing those conventions, if they have not already done so.

(b) Strengthening participation and consultation

29.5. Governments, business and industry should promote the active participation of workers and their trade unions in decisions on the design, implementation and evaluation of national and international policies and programmes on environment and development, including employment policies, industrial strategies, labour adjustment programmes and technology transfers.

29.6. Trade unions, employers and Governments should cooperate to ensure that the concept of sustainable development is equitably implemented.

29.7. Joint (employer/worker) or tripartite (employer/worker/Government) collaborative mechanisms at the workplace, community and national levels should be established to deal with safety, health and environment, including special reference to the rights and status of women in the workplace.

29.8. Governments and employers should ensure that workers and their representatives are provided with all relevant information to enable effective participation in these decision-making processes.

29.9. Trade unions should continue to define, develop and promote policies on all aspects of sustainable development.

29.10. Trade unions and employers should establish the framework for a joint environmental policy, and set priorities to improve the working environment and the overall environmental performance of enterprise.

29.11. Trade unions should:

    a. Seek to ensure that workers are able to participate in environmental audits at the workplace and in environmental impact assessments;

    b. Participate in environment and development activities within the local community and promote joint action on potential problems of common concern;

    c. Play an active role in the sustainable development activities of international and regional organizations, particularly within the United Nations system.

(c) Provide adequate training

29.12. Workers and their representatives should have access to adequate training to augment environmental awareness, ensure their safety and health, and improve their economic and social welfare. Such training should ensure that the necessary skills are available to promote sustainable livelihoods and improve the working environment. Trade unions, employers, Governments and international agencies should cooperate in assessing training needs within their respective spheres of activity. Workers and their representatives should be involved in the design and implementation of worker training programmes conducted by employers and Governments.

**Means of implementation**

(a) Financing and cost evaluation

29.13. The Conference secretariat has estimated the average total annual cost (1993-2000) of implementing the activities of this programme to be about $300 million from the international community on grant or concessional t erms. These are indicative and order-of-magnitude estimates only and have not been reviewed by Governments. Actual costs and financial terms, including any that are non-concessional, will depend upon, inter alia, the specific strategies and programmes Governments decide upon for implementation.

(b) Capacity-building

29.14. Particular attention should be given to strengthening the capacity of each of the tripartite social partners (Governments and employers' and workers' organizations) to facilitate greater collaboration towards sustainable development.

# Agenda 21 – Chapter 30
## STRENGTHENING THE ROLE OF BUSINESS AND INDUSTRY

### INTRODUCTION

30.1. Business and industry, including transnational corporations, play a crucial role in the social and economic development of a country. A stable policy regime enables and encourages business and industry to operate responsibly and efficiently and to implement longer-term policies. Increasing prosperity, a major goal of the development process, is contributed primarily by the activities of business and industry. Business enterprises, large and small, formal and informal, provide major trading, employment and livelihood opportunities. Business opportunities available to women are contributing towards their professional development, strengthening their economic role and transforming social systems. Business and industry, including transnational corporations, and their representative organizations should be full participants in the implementation and evaluation of activities related to Agenda 21.

30.2. Through more efficient production processes, preventive strategies, cleaner production technologies and procedures throughout the product life cycle, hence minimizing or avoiding wastes, the policies and operations of business and industry, including transnational corporations, can play a major role in reducing impacts on resource use and the environment. Technological innovations, development, applications, transfer and the more comprehensive aspects of partnership and cooperation are to a very large extent within the province of business and industry.

30.3. Business and industry, including transnational corporations, should recognize environmental management as among the highest corporate priorities and as a key determinant to sustainable development. Some enlightened leaders of enterprises are already implementing "responsible care" and product stewardship policies and programmes, fostering openness and dialogue with employees and the public and carrying out environmental audits and assessments of compliance. These leaders in business and industry, including transnational corporations, are increasingly taking voluntary initiatives, promoting and implementing self-regulations and greater responsibilities in ensuring their activities have minimal imp acts on human health and the environment. The regulatory regimes introduced in many countries and the growing consciousness of consumers and the general public and enlightened leaders of business and industry, including transnational corporations, have all contributed to this. A positive contribution of business and industry, including transnational corporations, to sustainable development can increasingly be achieved by using economic instruments such as free market mechanisms in which the prices of goods and services should increasingly reflect the environmental costs of their input, production, use, recycling and disposal subject to country-specific conditions.

30.4. The improvement of production systems through technologies and processes that utilize resources more efficiently and at the same time produce less wastes - achieving more with less - is an important pathway towards sustainability for business and industry. Similarly, facilitating and encouraging inventiveness, competitiveness and voluntary initiatives are necessary for stimulating more varied, efficient and effective options. To address these major requirements and strengthen further the role of business and industry, including transnational corporations, the following two programmes are proposed.

### PROGRAMME AREAS

#### A. Promoting cleaner production

**Basis for action**

30.5. There is increasing recognition that production, technology and management that use resources inefficiently form residues that are not reused, discharge wastes that have adverse impacts on human health and the environment and manufacture products that when used have further impacts and are difficult to recycle, need to be replaced with technologies, good engineering and management practices and know-how that would minimize waste throughout the product life cycle. The concept of cleaner production implies striving for optimal efficiencies at every stage of the product life cycle. A result would be the improvement of the overall competitiveness of the enterprise. The need for a transition towards cleaner production policies was recognized at the UNIDO-organized ministerial-level Conference on Ecologically Sustainable Industrial Development, held at Copenhagen in October 1991. 1/

## Objectives

30.6. Governments, business and industry, including transnational corporations, should aim to increase the efficiency of resource utilization, including increasing the reuse and recycling of residues, and to reduce the quantity of waste discharge per unit of economic output.

## Activities

30.7. Governments, business and industry, including transnational corporations, should strengthen partnerships to implement the principles and criteria for sustainable development.

30.8. Governments should identify and implement an appropriate mix of economic instruments and normative measures such as laws, legislations and standards, in consultation with business and industry, including transnational corporations, that will promote the use of cleaner production, with special consideration for small and medium-sized enterprises. Voluntary private initiatives should also be encouraged.

30.9. Governments, business and industry, including transnational corporations, academia and international organizations, should work towards the development and implementation of concepts and methodologies for the internalization of environmental costs into accounting and pricing mechanisms.

30.10. Business and industry, including transnational corporations, should be encouraged:

a. To report annually on their environmental records, as well as on their use of energy and natural resources;

b. To adopt and report on the implementation of codes of conduct promoting the best environmental practice, such as the Business Charter on Sustainable Development of the International Chamber of Commerce (ICC) and the chemical industry's responsible care initiative.

30.11. Governments should promote technological and know-how cooperation between enterprises, encompassing identification, assessment, research and development, management marketing and application of cleaner production.

30.12. Industry should incorporate cleaner production policies in its operations and investments, taking also into account its influence on suppliers and consumers.

30.13. Industry and business associations should cooperate with workers and trade unions to continuously improve the knowledge and skills for implementing sustainable development operations.

30.14. Industry and business associations should encourage individual companies to undertake programmes for improved environmental awareness and responsibility at all levels to make these enterprises dedicated to the task of improving environmental performance based on internationally accepted management practices.

30.15.   International organizations should increase education, training and awareness activities relating to cleaner production, in collaboration with industry, academia and relevant national and local authorities.

30.16.   International and non-governmental organizations, including trade and scientific associations, should strengthen cleaner production information dissemination by expanding existing databases, such as the UNEP International Cleaner Production Clearing House (ICPIC), the UNIDO Industrial and Technological Information Bank (INTIB) and the ICC International Environment Bureau (IEB), and should forge networking of national and international information systems.

## B. Promoting responsible entrepreneurship

**Basis for action**

30.17.   Entrepreneurship is one of the most important driving forces for innovations, increasing market efficiencies and responding to challenges and opportunities. Small and medium-sized entrepreneurs, in particular, play a very important role in the social and economic development of a country. Often, they are the major means for rural development, increasing off-farm employment and providing the transitional means for improving the livelihoods of women. Responsible entrepreneurship can play a major role in improving the efficiency of resource use, reducing risks and hazards, minimizing wastes and safeguarding environmental qualities.

**Objectives**

30.18.   The following objectives are proposed:

    a.   To encourage the concept of stewardship in the management and utilization of natural resources by entrepreneurs;

    b.   To increase the number of entrepreneurs engaged in enterprises that subscribe to and implement sustainable development policies.

**Activities**

30.19.   Governments should encourage the establishment and operations of sustainably managed enterprises. The mix would include regulatory measures, economic incentives and streamlining of administrative procedures to assure maximum efficiency in dealing with applications for approval in order to facilitate investment decisions, advice and assistance with information, infrastructural support and stewardship responsibilities.

30.20.   Governments should encourage, in cooperation with the private sector, the establishment of venture capital funds for sustainable development projects and programmes.

30.21.   In collaboration with business, industry, academia and international organizations, Governments should support training in the environmental aspects of enterprise management. Attention should also be directed towards apprenticeship schemes for youth.

30.22.   Business and industry, including transnational corporations, should be encouraged to establish world-wide corporate policies on sustainable development, arrange for environmentally sound technologies to be available to affiliates owned substantially by their parent company in developing countries without extra external charges, encourage overseas affiliates to modify procedures in order to reflect local ecological conditions and share experiences with local authorities, national Governments and international organizations.

30.23.   Large business and industry, including transnational corporations, should consider establishing partnership schemes with small and medium-sized enterprises to help facilitate the exchange of experience in managerial skills, market development and technological know-how, where appropriate, with the assistance of international organizations.

30.24.   Business and industry should establish national councils for sustainable development and help promote entrepreneurship in the formal and informal sectors. The inclusion of women entrepreneurs should be facilitated.

30.25.   Business and industry, including transnational corporations, should increase research and development of environmentally sound technologies and environmental management systems, in collaboration with academia and the scientific/engineering establishments, drawing upon indigenous knowledge, where appropriate.

30.26.   Business and industry, including transnational corporations, should ensure responsible and ethical management of products and processes from the point of view of health, safety and environmental aspects. Towards this end, business and industry should increase self-regulation, guided by appropriate codes, charters and initiatives integrated into all elements of business planning and decision-making, and fostering openness and dialogue with employees and the public.

30.27.   Multilateral and bilateral financial aid institutions should continue to encourage and support small- and medium-scale entrepreneurs engaged in sustainable development activities.

30.28.   United Nations organizations and agencies should improve mechanisms for business and industry inputs, policy and strategy formulation processes, to ensure that environmental aspects are strengthened in foreign investment.

30.29.   International organizations should increase support for research and development on improving the technological and managerial requirements for sustainable development, in particular for small and medium-sized enterprises in developing countries.

**Means of implementation**

Financing and cost evaluation

30.30.   The activities included under this programme area are mostly changes in the orientation of existing activities and additional costs are not expected to be significant. The cost of activities by Governments and international organizations are already included in other programme areas.

# Agenda 21 – Chapter 31
## SCIENTIFIC AND TECHNOLOGICAL COMMUNITY

31.1. The pres ent chapter focuses on how to enable the scientific and technological community, which includes, among others, engineers, architects, industrial designers, urban planners and other professionals and policy makers, to make a more open and effective contribution to the decision-making processes concerning environment and development. It is important that the role of science and technology in human affairs be more widely known and better understood, both by decision makers who help determine public policy and by the general public. The cooperative relationship existing between the scientific and technological community and the general public should be extended and deepened into a full partnership. Improved communication and cooperation between the scientific and technological community and decision makers will facilitate greater use of scientific and technical information and knowledge in policies and programme implementation. Decision makers should create more favourable conditions for improving training and independent research in sustainable development. Existing multidisciplinary approaches will have to be strengthened and more interdisciplinary studies developed between the scientific and technological community and policy makers and with the general public to provide leadership and practical know-how to the concept of sustainable development. The public should be assisted in communicating their sentiments to the scientific and technological community concerning how science and technology might be better managed to affect their lives in a beneficial way. By the same token, the independence of the scientific and technological community to investigate and publish without restriction and to exchange their findings freely must be assured. The adoption and implementation of ethical principles and codes of practice for the scientific and technological community that are internationally accepted could enhance professionalism and may improve and hasten recognition of the value of its contributions to environment and development, recognizing the continuing evolution and uncertainty of scientific knowledge.

## PROGRAMME AREAS

### A. Improving communication and cooperation among the scientific and technological community, decision makers and the public

**Basis for action**

31.2. The scientific and technological community and policy makers should increase their interaction in order to implement strategies for sustainable development on the basis of the best available knowledge. This implies that decision makers should provide the necessary framework for rigorous research and for full and open communication of the findings of the scientific and technological community, and develop with it ways in which research results and the concerns stemming from the findings can be communicated to decision-making bodies so as to better link scientific and technical knowledge with strategic policy and programme formulation. At the same time, this dialogue would assist the scientific and technological community in developing priorities for research and proposing actions for constructive solutions.

**Objectives**

31.3. The following objectives are proposed:

    a. To extend and open up the decision-making process and broaden the range of developmental and environmental issues where cooperation at all levels between the scientific and technological community and decision makers can take place;

    b. To improve the exchange of knowledge and concerns between the scientific and technological community and the general public in order to enable policies and programmes to be better formulated, understood and supported.

**Activities**

31.4. Governments should undertake the following activities:

    a.    Review how national scientific and technological activities could be more responsive to sustainable development needs as part of an overall effort to strengthen national research and development systems, including through strengthening and widening the membership of national scientific and technological advisory councils, organizations and committees to ensure that:

            i.    The full range of national needs for scientific and technological programmes are communicated to Governments and the public;

            ii.    The various strands of public opinion are represented;

    b.    Promote regional cooperative mechanisms to address regional needs for sustainable development. Such regional cooperative mechanisms could be facilitated through public/private partnerships and provide support to Governments, industry, non-governmental educational institutions and other domestic and international organizations, and by strengthening global professional networks;

    c.    Improve and expand scientific and technical inputs through appropriate mechanisms to intergovernmental consultative, cooperative and negotiating processes towards international and regional agreements;

    d.    Strengthen science and technology advice to the highest levels of the United Nations, and other international institutions, in order to ensure the inclusion of science and technology know-how in sustainable development policies and strategies;

    e.    Improve and strengthen programmes for disseminating research results of universities and research institutions. This requires recognition of and greater support to the scientists, technologists and teachers who are engaged in communicating and interpreting scientific and technological information to policy makers, professionals in other fields and the general public. Such support should focus on the transfer of skills and the transfer and adaptation of planning techniques. This requires full and open sharing of data and information among scientists and decision makers. The publication of national scientific research reports and technical reports that are understandable and relevant to local sustainable development needs would also improve the interface between science and decision-making, as well as the implementation of scientific results;

    f.    Improve links between the official and independent research sectors and industry so that research may become an important element of industrial strategy;

    g.    Promote and strengthen the role of women as full partners in the science and technology disciplines;

    h.    Develop and implement information technologies to enhance the dissemination of information for sustainable development.

**Means of implementation**

(a) Financing and cost evaluation

31.5. The Conferense secretariat has estimated the average total annual cost (1993-2000) of implementing the activities of this programme to be about $15 million from the international community on grant or concessional terms. These are indicative and order-of-magnitude estimates only and have not been reviewed by Governments. Actual costs and financial terms, including any that are non-concessional, will depend upon, inter alia, the specific strategies and programmes Governments decide upon for implementation.

(b) Capacity-building

31.6. Int ergovernmental panels on development and environmental issues should be organized, with emphasis on their scientific and technical aspects, and studies of responsiveness and adaptability included in subsequent programmes of action.

## B. Promoting codes of practice and guidelines related to science and technology

**Basis for action**

31.7. Scientists and technologists have a special set of responsibilities which belong to them both as inheritors of a tradition and as professionals and members of disciplines devot ed to the search for knowledge and to the need to protect the biosphere in the context of sustainable development.

31.8. Increased ethical awareness in environmental and developmental decision-making should help to place appropriate priorities for the maintenance and enhancement of life-support systems for their own sake, and in so doing ensure that the functioning of viable natural processes is properly valued by present and future societies. Therefore, a strengthening of the codes of practice and guidelines for the scientific and technological community would increase environmental awareness and contribute to sustainable development. It would build up the level of esteem and regard for the scientific and technological community and facilitate the "accountability" of science and technology.

**Objectives**

31.9. The objective should be to develop, improve and promote international acceptance of codes of practice and guidelines relating to science and technology in which the integrity of life-support systems is comprehensively accounted for and where the important role of science and technology in reconciling the needs of environment and development is accepted. To be effective in the decision-making process, such principles, codes of practice and guidelines must not only be agreed upon by the scientific and technological community, but also recognized by the society as a whole.

**Activities**

31.10. The following activities could be undertaken:

a. Strengthening national and international cooperation, including the non-governmental sector, to develop codes of practice and guidelines regarding environmentally sound and sustainable development, taking into account the Rio Declaration and existing codes of practice and guidelines;

b. Strengthening and establishing national advisory groups on environmental and developmental ethics, in order to develop a common value framework between the scientific and technological community and society as a whole, and promote continuous dialogue;

c. Extending education and training in developmental and environmental ethical issues to integrate such objectives into education curricula and research priorities;

d. Reviewing and amending relevant national and international environment and development legal instruments to ensure appropriate codes of practice and guidelines are incorporated into such regulatory machinery.

**Means of implementation**

(a) Financing and cost evaluation

31.11. The Conferense secretariat has estimated the average total annual cost (1993-2000) of implementing the activities of this programme to be about $5 million from the international community on grant or concessional terms. These are indicative and order-of-magnitude estimates only and have not been reviewed by Governments. Actual costs and financial terms, including any that are non-concessional, will depend upon, inter alia, the specific strategies and programmes Governments decide upon for implementation.

(b) Capacity-building

31.12. Codes of practice and guidelines, including on appropriate principles, should be developed for and by the scientific and technological community in the pursuit of its research activities and implementation of programmes aimed at sustainable development.

# STRENGTHENING THE ROLE OF FARMERS*

## PROGRAMME AREA

**Basis for action**

32.1. Agriculture occupies one third of the land surface of the Earth, and is the central activity for much of the world's population. Rural activities take place in close contact with nature, adding value to it by producing renewable resources, while at the same time becoming vulnerable to overexploitation and improper management.

32.2. The rural household, indigenous people and their communities, and the family farmer, a substantial number of whom are women, have been the stewards of much of the Earth's resources. Farmers must conserve their physical environment as they depend on it for their sustenance. Over the past 20 years there has been impressive increase in aggregate agricultural production. Yet, in some regions, this increase has been outstripped by population growth or international debt or falling commodity prices. Further, the natural resources that sustain farming activity need proper care, and there is a growing concern about the sustainability of agricultural production systems.

32.3. A farmer-centred approach is the key to the attainment of sustainability in both developed and developing countries and many of the programme areas in Agenda 21 address this objective. A significant number of the rural population in developing countries depend primarily upon small-scale, subsistence-oriented agriculture based on family labour. However, they have limited access to resources, technology, alternative livelihood and means of production. As a result, they are engaged in the overexploitation of natural resources, including marginal lands.

32.4. The sustainable development of people in marginal and fragile ecosystems is also addressed in Agenda 21. The key to the successful implementation of these programmes lies in the motivation and attitudes of individual farmers and government policies that would provide incentives to farmers to manage their natural resources efficiently and in a sustainable way. Farmers, particularly women, face a high degree of economic, legal and institutional uncertainties when investing in their land and other resources. The decentralization of decision-making towards local and community organizations is the key in changing people's behaviour and implementing sustainable farming strategies. This programme area deals with activities which can contribute to this end.

**Objectives**

32.5. The following objectives are proposed:

    a. To encourage a decentralized decision-making process through the creation and strengthening of local and village organizations that would delegate power and responsibility to primary users of natural resources;

    b. To support and enhance the legal capacity of women and vulnerable groups with regard to access, use and tenure of land;

    c. To promote and encourage sustainable farming practices and technologies;

    d. To introduce or strengthen policies that would encourage self-sufficiency in low-input and low-energy technologies, including indigenous practices, and pricing mechanisms that internalize environmental costs;

    e. To develop a policy framework that provides incentives and motivation among farmers for sustainable and efficient farming practices;

f.    To enhance the participation of farmers, men and women, in the design and implementation of policies directed towards these ends, through their representative organizations.

**Activities**

(a) Management-related activities

32.6.  National Governments should:

    a.    Ensure the implementation of the programmes on sustainable livelihoods, agriculture and rural development, managing fragile ecosystems, water use in agriculture, and integrated management of natural resources;

    b.    Promote pricing mechanisms, trade policies, fiscal incentives and other policy instruments that positively affect individual farmer's decisions about an efficient and sustainable use of natural resources, and take full account of the impact of these decisions on household food security, farm incomes, employment and the environment;

    c.    Involve farmers and their representative organizations in the formulation of policy;

    d.    Protect, recognize and formalize women's access to tenure and use of land, as well as rights to land, access to credit, technology, inputs and training;

    e.    Support the formation of farmers' organizations by providing adequate legal and social conditions.

32.7.  Support for farmers' organizations could be arranged as follows:

    a.    National and international research centres should cooperate with farmers' organizations in developing location-specific environment-friendly farming techniques;

    b.    National Governments, multilateral and bilateral development agencies and non-governmental organizations should collaborate with farmers' organizations in formulating agricultural development projects to specific agro-ecological zones.

(b) Data and information

32.8.  Governments and farmers' organizations should:

    a.    Initiate mechanisms to document, synthesize and disseminate local knowledge, practices and project experiences so that they will make use of the lessons of the past when formulating and implementing policies affecting farming, forest and fishing populations;

    b.    Establish networks for t he exchange of experiences with regard to farming that help to conserve land, water and forest resources, minimize the use of chemicals and reduce or reutilize farm wastes;

    c.    Develop pilot projects and extension services that would seek to build on the needs and knowledge base of women farmers.

(c) International and regional cooperation

32.9.  FAO, IFAD, WFP, the World Bank, the regional development banks and other international organizations involved in rural development should involve farmers and their representatives in their deliberations, as appropriate.

32.10. Representative organizations of farmers should establish programmes for the development and support of farmers' organizations, particularly in developing countries.

**Means of implementation**

(a) Financing and cost evaluation

32.11. The financing needed for this programme area is estimated in chapter 14 (Promoting sustainable agriculture and rural development), particularly in the programme area entitled "Ensuring people's participation and promoting human res ource development for sustainable agriculture". The costs shown under chapters 3 (Combating poverty), 12 (Managing fragile ecosystems: combating desertification and drought), and 13 (Managing fragile ecosystems: sustainable mountain development) are also relevant to this programme area.

(b) Scientific and technological means

32.12. Governments and appropriate international organizations, in collaboration with national research organizations and non-governmental organizations should, as appropriate:

    a. Develop environmentally sound farming technologies that enhance crop yields, maintain land quality, recycle nutrients, conserve water and energy and control pests and weeds;

    b. Conduct studies of high-resource and low-resource agriculture to compare their productivity and sustainability. The research should preferably be conducted under various environmental and sociological settings;

    c. Support research on mechanization that would optimize human labour and animal power and hand-held and animal-drawn equipment that can be easily operated and maintained. The development of farm technologies should take into account farmers' available resources and the role of animals in farming households and the ecology.

(c) Human resource development

32.13. Governments, with the support of multilateral and bilateral development agencies and scientific organizations, should develop curricula for agricultural colleges and training institutions that would integrate ecology into agricultural science. Interdisciplinary programmes in agricultural ecology are essential to the training of a new generation of agricultural scientists and field-level extension agents.

(d) Capacity-building

32.14. Governments should, in the light of each country's specific situation:

    a. Create the institutional and legal mechanisms to ensure effective land tenure to farmers. The absence of legislation indicating land rights has been an obstacle in taking action against land degradation in many farming communities in developing countries;

    b. Strengthen rural institutions that would enhance sustainability through locally managed credit systems and technical assistance, local production and distribution facilities for inputs, appropriate equipment and small-scale processing units, and marketing and distribution systems;

    c. Establish mechanisms to increase access of farmers, in particular women and farmers from indigenous groups, to agricultural training, credit and use of improved technology for ensuring food security.

\* \* \* \*

\* In this chapter, all references to "farmers" include all rural people who derive their livelihood from activities such as farming, fishing and forest harvesting. The term "farming" also includes fishing and forest harvesting.

# Agenda 21 – Chapter 33
## FINANCIAL RESOURCES AND MECHANISMS

33.1. The General Assembly, in resolution 44/228 of 22 December 1989, inter alia, decided that the United Nations Conference on Environment and Development should:

> Identify ways and means of providing new and additional financial resources, particularly to developing countries, for environmentally sound development programmes and projects in accordance with national development objectives, priorities and plans and to consider ways of effectively monitoring the provision of such new and additional financial resources, particularly to developing countries, so as to enable the international community to take further appropriate action on the basis of accurate and reliable data;

> Identify ways and means of providing additional financial resources for measures directed towards solving major environmental problems of global concern and especially of supporting those countries, in particular developing countries, for which the implementation of such measures would entail a special or abnormal burden, owing, in particular, to their lack of financial resources, expertise or technical capacity;

> Consider various funding mechanisms, including voluntary ones, and examine the possibility of a special international fund and other innovative approaches, with a view to ensuring, on a favourable basis, the most effective and expeditious transfer of environmentally sound technologies to developing countries;

> Quantify the financial requirements for the successful implementation of Conference decisions and recommendations and identify possible sources, including innovative ones, of additional resources.

33.2. This chapter deals with the financing of the implementation of Agenda 21, which reflects a global consensus integrating environmental considerations into an accelerated development process. For each of t he other chapters, the secretariat of the Conference has provided indicative estimates of the total costs of implementation for developing countries and the requirements for grant or other concessional financing needed from the international community. These reflect the need for a substantially increased effort, both by countries themselves and by the international community.

### BASIS FOR ACTION

33.3. Economic growth, social development and poverty eradication are the first and overriding priorities in developing countries and are themselves essential to meeting national and global sustainability objectives. In the light of the global benefits to be realized by the implementation of Agenda 21 as a whole, the provision to developing countries of effective means, inter alia, financial resources and technology, without which it will be difficult for them to fully implement their commitments, will serve the common interests of developed and developing countries and of humankind in general, including future generations.

33.4. The cost of inaction could outweigh the financial costs of implementing Agenda 21. Inaction will narrow the choices of future generations.

33.5. For dealing with environmental issues, special efforts will be required. Global and local environmental issues are interrelated. The United Nations Framework Convention on Climate Change and the Convention on Biological Diversity address two of the most important global issues.

33.6. Economic conditions, both domestic and international, that encourage free trade and access to markets will help make economic growth and environmental protection mutually supportive for all countries, particularly for developing countries and countries undergoing the process of transition to a market economy (see chapter 2 for a fuller discussion of these issues).

33.7. International cooperation for sustainable development should also be strengthened in order to support and complement the efforts of developing countries, particularly the least developed countries.

33.8. All countries should assess how to translate Agenda 21 into national policies and programmes through a process that will integrate environment and development considerations. National and local priorities should be established by means that include public participation and community involvement, promoting equal opportunity for men and women.

33.9. For an evolving partnership among all countries of the world, including, in particular, between developed and developing countries, sustainable development strategies and enhanced and predictable levels of funding in support of longer term objectives are required. For that purpose, developing countries should articulate their own priority actions and needs for support and developed countries should commit themselves to addressing these priorities. In this respect, consultative groups and round tables and other nationally based mechanisms can play a facilitative role.

33.10. The implementation of the huge sustainable development programmes of Agenda 21 will require the provision to developing countries of substantial new and additional financial resources. Grant or concessional financing should be provided according to sound and equitable criteria and indicators. The progressive implementation of Agenda 21 should be matched by the provision of such necessary financial resources. The initial phase will be accelerated by substantial early commitments of concessional funding.

## OBJECTIVES

33.11. The objectives are as follows:

    a. To establish measures concerning financial resources and mechanisms for the implementation of Agenda 21;

    b. To provide new and additional financial resources that are both adequate and predictable;

    c. To seek full use and continuing qualitative improvement of funding mechanisms to be utilized for the implementation of Agenda 21.

## ACTIVITIES

33.12. Fundamentally, the activities of this chapter are related to the implementation of all the other chapters of Agenda 21.

## MEANS OF IMPLEMENTATION

33.13. In general, the financing for the implementation of Agenda 21 will come from a country's own public and private sectors. For developing countries, particularly the least developed countries, ODA is a main source of external funding, and substantial new and additional funding for sustainable development and implementation of Agenda 21 will be required. Developed countries reaffirm their commitments to reach the accepted United Nations target of 0.7 per cent of GNP for ODA and, to the extent that they have not yet achieved that target, agree to augment their aid programmes in order to reach that target as soon as possible and to ensure prompt and effective implementation of Agenda 21. Some countries have agreed to reach the target by the year 2000. It was decided that the Commission on Sustainable Development would regularly review and monitor progress towards this target. This review process should systematically combine the monitoring of the implementation of Agenda 21 with a review of the financial resources available. Those countries that have already reached the target are to be commended and encouraged to continue to contribute to the common effort to make available the substantial additional resources that have to be mobilized. Other developed countries, in line with their support for reform efforts in developing countries, agree to make their best efforts to increase their level of ODA. In this context, the importance of equitable burden-sharing among developed countries is recognized. Other countries, including those undergoing the process of transition to a market economy, may voluntarily augment the contributions of the developed countries.

33.14. Funding for Agenda 21 and other outcomes of the Conference should be provided in a way that maximizes the availability of new and additional resources and uses all available funding sources and mechanisms. These include, among others:

    a. The multilateral development banks and funds:

        i. The International Development Association (IDA). Among the various issues and options that IDA deputies will examine in connection with the forthcoming tenth replenishment of IDA, the statement made by the President of the World Bank at the United Nations Conference on Environment and Development should be given special consideration in order to help the poorest countries meet their sustainable development objectives as contained in Agenda 21;

        ii. Regional and subregional development banks. The regional and subregional development banks and funds should play an increased and more effective role in providing resources on concessional or other favourable terms needed to implement Agenda 21;

        iii. The Global Environment Facility, managed jointly by the World Bank, UNDP and UNEP, whose additional grant and concessional funding is designed to achieve global environmental benefits, should cover the agreed incremental costs of relevant activities under Agenda 21, in particular for developing countries. Therefore, it should be restructured so as to, inter alia:

        Encourage universal participation;

        Have sufficient flexibility to expand its scope and coverage to relevant programme areas of Agenda 21, with global environmental benefits, as agreed;

        Ensure a governance that is transparent and democratic in nature, including in terms of decision-making and operations, by guaranteeing a balanced and equitable representation of the interests of developing countries and giving due weight to the funding efforts of donor countries;

        Ensure new and additional financial resources on grant and concessional terms, in particular to developing countries;

        Ensure predictability in the flow of funds by contributions from developed countries, taking into account the importance of equitable burden-sharing;

        Ensure access to and disbursement of the funds under mutually agreed criteria without introducing new forms of conditionality;

    b. The relevant specialized agencies, other United Nations bodies and other international organizations, which have designated roles to play in supporting national Governments in implementing Agenda 21;

    c. Multilateral institutions for capacity-building and technical cooperation. Necessary financial resources should be provided to UNDP to use its network of field offices and its broad mandate and experience in the field of technical cooperation for facilitating capacity-building at the country level, making full use of the expertise of the specialized agencies and other United Nations bodies within their respective areas of competence, in particular UNEP and including the multilateral and regional development banks;

d. Bilateral assistance programmes. These programmes will need to be strengthened in order to promote sustainable development;

e. Debt relief. It is important to achieve durable solutions to the debt problems of low- and middle-income developing countries in order to provide them with the needed means for sustainable development. Measures to address the continuing debt problems of low- and middle-income countries should be kept under review. All creditors in the Paris Club should promptly implement the agreement of December 1991 to provide debt relief for the poorest heavily indebted countries pursuing structural adjustment; debt relief measures should be kept under review so as to address the continuing difficulties of those countries;

f. Private funding. Voluntary contributions through non-governmental channels, which have been running at about 10 per cent of ODA, might be increased.

33.15. Investment. Mobilization of higher levels of foreign direct investment and technology transfers should be encouraged through national policies that promote investment and through joint ventures and other modalities.

33.16. Innovative financing. New ways of generating new public and private financial resources should be explored, in particular:

a. Various forms of debt relief, apart from official or Paris Club debt, including greater use of debt swaps;

b. The use of economic and fiscal incentives and mechanisms;

c. The feasibility of tradeable permits;

d. New schemes for fund-raising and voluntary contributions through private channels, including non-governmental organizations;

e. The reallocation of resources at present committed to military purposes.

33.17. A supportive international and domestic economic climate conducive to sustained economic growth and development is important, particularly for developing countries, in order to achieve sustainability.

33.18. The secretariat of the Conference has estimated the average annual costs (1993-2000) of implementing in developing countries the activities in Agenda 21 to be over $600 billion, including about $125 billion on grant or concessional terms from the international community. These are indicative and order-of-magnitude estimates only, and have not been reviewed by Governments. Actual costs will depend upon, inter alia, the specific strategies and programmes Governments decide upon for implementation.

33.19. Developed countries and others in a position to do so should make initial financial commitments to give effect to the decisions of the Conference. They should report on such plans and commitments to the United Nations General Assembly at its forty-seventh session, in 1992.

33.20. Developing countries should also begin to draw up national plans for sustainable development to give effect to the decisions of the Conference.

33.21. Review and monitoring of the financing of Agenda 21 is essential. Questions related to the effective follow-up of the Conference are discussed in chapter 38 (International institutional arrangements). It will be important to review on a regular basis the adequacy of funding and mechanisms, including efforts to reach agreed objectives of the present chapter, including targets where applicable.

# TRANSFER OF ENVIRONMENTALLY SOUND TECHNOLOGY, COOPERATION AND CAPACITY-BUILDING

34.1.  Environmentally sound technologies protect the environment, are less polluting, use all resources in a more sustainable manner, recycle more of their wastes and products, and handle residual wastes in a more acceptable manner than the technologies for which they were substitutes.

34.2.  Environmentally sound technologies in the context of pollution are "process and product technologies" that generate low or no waste, for the prevention of pollution. They also cover "end of the pipe" technologies for treatment of pollution after it has been generated.

34.3.  Environmentally sound technologies are not just individual technologies, but total systems which include know-how, procedures, goods and services, and equipment as well as organizational and managerial procedures. This implies that when discussing transfer of technologies, the human resource development and local capacity-building aspects of technology choices, including gender-relevant aspects, should also be addressed. Environmentally sound technologies should be compatible with nationally determined socio-economic, cultural and environmental priorities.

34.4.  There is a need for favourable access to and transfer of environmentally sound technologies, in particular to developing countries, through supportive measures that promote technology cooperation and that should enable transfer of necessary technological know-how as well as building up of economic, technical, and managerial capabilities for the efficient use and further development of transferred technology. Technology cooperation involves joint efforts by enterprises and Governments, both suppliers of technology and its recipients. Therefore, such cooperation entails an iterative process involving government, the private sector, and research and development facilities to ensure the best possible results from transfer of technology. Successful long-term partnerships in technology cooperation necessarily require continuing systematic training and capacity-building at all levels over an extended period of time.

34.5.  The activities proposed in this chapter aim at improving conditions and processes on information, access to and transfer of technology (including the state-of-the-art technology and related know-how), in particular to developing countries, as well as on capacity-building and cooperative arrangements and partnerships in the field of technology, in order to promote sustainable development. New and efficient technologies will be essential to increase the capabilities, in particular of developing countries, to achieve sustainable development, sustain the world's economy, protect the environment, and alleviate poverty and human suffering. Inherent in these activities is the need to address the improvement of technology currently used and its replacement, when appropriate, with more accessible and more environmentally sound technology.

## BASIS FOR ACTION

34.6.  This chapter of Agenda 21 is without prejudice to specific commitments and arrangements on transfer of technology to be adopted in specific international instruments.

34.7.  The availability of scientific and technological information and access to and transfer of environmentally sound technology are essential requirements for sustainable development. Providing adequate information on the environmental aspects of present technologies consists of two interrelated components: upgrading information on present and state-of-the-art technologies, including their environmental risks, and improving access to environmentally sound technologies.

34.8. The primary goal of improved access to technology information is to enable informed choices, leading to access to and transfer of such technologies and the strengthening of countries' own technological capabilities.

34.9. A large body of useful technological knowledge lies in the public domain. There is a need for the access of developing countries to such technologies as are not covered by patents or lie in the public domain. Developing countries would also need to have access to the know-how and expertise required for the effective utilization of the aforesaid technologies.

34.10. Consideration must be given to the role of patent protection and intellectual property rights along with an examination of their impact on the access to and transfer of environmentally sound technology, in particular to developing countries, as well as to further exploring efficiently the concept of assured access for developing countries to environmentally sound technology in its relation to proprietary rights with a view to developing effective responses to the needs of developing countries in this area.

34.11. Proprietary technology is available through commercial channels, and international business is an important vehicle for t echnology transfer. Tapping this pool of knowledge and recombining it with local innovations to generate alternative technologies should be pursued. At the same time that concepts and modalities for assured access to environmentally sound technologies, including state-of-the-art technologies, in particular by developing countries, continued to be explored, enhanced access to environmentally sound technologies should be promoted, facilitated and financed as appropriate, while providing fair incentives to innovators that promote research and development of new environmentally sound technologies.

34.12. Recipient countries require technology and strengthened support to help further develop their scientific, technological, professional and related capacities, taking into account existing technologies and capacities. This support would enable countries, in particular developing countries, to make more rational technology choices. These countries could then better assess environmentally sound technologies prior to their transfer and properly apply and manage them, as well as improve upon already existing technologies and adapt them to suit their specific development needs and priorities.

34.13. A critical mass of research and development capacity is crucial to the effective dissemination and use of environmentally sound technologies and their generation locally. Education and training programmes should reflect the needs of specific goal-oriented research activities and should work to produce specialists literate in environment ally sound technology and with an interdisciplinary outlook. Achieving this critical mass involves building the capabilities of craftspersons, technicians and middle-level managers, scientists, engineers and educators, as well as developing their corresponding social or managerial support systems. Transferring environmentally sound technologies also involves innovatively adapting and incorporating them into the local or national culture.

## OBJECTIVES

34.14. The following objectives are proposed:

   a. To help to ensure the access, in particular of developing countries, to scientific and technological information, including information on state-of-the-art technologies;

   b. To promote, facilitate, and finance, as appropriate, the access to and the transfer of environmentally sound technologies and corresponding know-how, in particular to developing countries, on favourable terms, including on concessional and preferential terms, as mutually agreed, taking into account the need to protect intellectual property rights as well as the special needs of developing countries for the implementation of Agenda 21;

c.  To facilitate the maintenance and promotion of environmentally sound indigenous technologies that may have been neglected or displaced, in particular in developing countries, paying particular attention to their priority needs and taking into account the complementary roles of men and women;

d.  To support endogenous capacity-building, in particular in developing countries, so they can assess, adopt, manage and apply environmentally sound technologies. This could be achieved through inter alia:

    i.  Human resource development;

    ii.  Strengthening of institutional capacities for research and development and programme implementation;

    iii.  Integrated sector assessments of technology needs, in accordance with countries' plans, objectives and priorities as foreseen in the implementation of Agenda 21 at the national level;

    iv.  To promote long-term technological partnerships between holders of environmentally sound technologies and potential users.

### ACTIVITIES

(a) Development of international information networks which link national, subregional, regional and international systems

34.15.  Existing national, subregional, regional and international information systems should be developed and linked through regional clearing-houses covering broad-based sectors of the economy such as agriculture, industry and energy. Such a network might, inter alia, include national, subregional and regional patent offices that are equipped to produce reports on state-of-the-art technology. The clearing-house networks would disseminate information on available technologies, their sources, their environmental risks, and the broad terms under which they may be acquired. They would operate on an information-demand basis and focus on the information needs of the end-users. They would take into account the positive roles and contributions of international, regional and subregional organizations, business communities, trade associations, non-governmental organizations, national Governments, and newly established or strengthened national networks.

34.16.  The international and regional clearing-houses would take the initiative, where necessary, in helping users to identify their needs and in disseminating information that meets those needs, including the use of existing news, public information, and communication systems. The disseminated information would highlight and detail concrete cases where environmentally sound technologies were successfully developed and implemented. In order to be effective, the clearing-houses need to provide not only information, but also referrals to other services, including sources of advice, training, technologies and technology assessment. The clearing-houses would thus facilitate the establishment of joint ventures and partnerships of various kinds.

34.17.  An inventory of existing and international or regional clearing-houses or information exchange systems should be undertaken by the relevant United Nations bodies. The existing structure should be strengthened and improved when necessary. Additional information systems should be developed, if necessary, in order to fill identified gaps in this international network.

(b) Support of and promotion of access to transfer of technology

34.18.  Governments and international organizations should promote, and encourage the private sector to promote, effective modalities for the access and transfer, in particular to developing countries, of environmentally sound technologies by means of activities, including the following:

a. Formulation of policies and programmes for the effective transfer of environmentally sound technologies that are publicly owned or in the public domain;

b. Creation of favourable conditions to encourage the private and public sectors to innovate, market and use environmentally sound technologies;

c. Examination by Governments and, where appropriate, by relevant organizations of existing policies, including subsidies and tax policies, and regulations to determine whether they encourage or impede the access to, transfer of and introduction of environmentally sound technologies;

d. Addressing, in a framework which fully integrates environment and development, barriers to the transfer of privately owned environmentally sound technologies and adoption of appropriate general measures to reduce such barriers while creating specific incentives, fiscal or otherwise, for the transfer of such technologies;

e. In the case of privately owned technologies, the adoption of the following measures, in particular for developing countries:

   i. Creation and enhancement by developed countries, as well as other countries which might be in a position to do so, of appropriate incentives, fiscal or otherwise, to stimulate the transfer of environmentally sound technology by companies, in particular to developing countries, as integral to sustainable development;

   ii. Enhancement of the access to and transfer of patent protected environmentally sound technologies, in particular to developing countries;

   iii. Purchase of patents and licences on commercial terms for their transfer to developing countries on non-commercial terms as part of development cooperation for sustainable development, taking into account the need to protect intellectual property rights;

   iv. In compliance with and under the specific circumstances recognized by the relevant international conventions adhered to by States, the undertaking of measures to prevent the abuse of intellectual property rights, including rules with respect to their acquisition through compulsory licensing, with the provision of equitable and adequate compensation;

   v. Provision of financial resources to acquire environmentally sound technologies in order to enable in particular developing countries to implement measures to promote sustainable development that would entail a special or abnormal burden to them;

   vi. Development of mechanisms for the access to and transfer of environmentally sound technologies, in particular to developing countries, while taking into account development in the process of negotiating an international code of conduct on transfer of technology, as decided by UNCTAD at its eighth session, held at Cartagena de Indias, Colombia, in February 1992.

f. Improvement of the capacity to develop and manage environmentally sound technologies

34.19. Frameworks at subregional, regional and international levels should be established and/or strengthened for the development, transfer and application of environmentally sound technologies and corresponding technical know-how with a special focus on developing countries' needs, by adding such functions to already existing bodies. Such frameworks would facilitate initiatives from both developing and developed countries to stimulate the research, development and transfer of environmentally sound technologies, often through partnerships within and among countries and between the scientific and technological community, industry and Governments.

34.20.    National capacities to assess, develop, manage and apply new technologies should be developed. This will require strengthening existing institutions, training of personnel at all levels, and education of the end-user of the technology.

(d) Establishment of a collaborative network of research centres

34.21.    A collaborative network of national, subregional, regional and international research centres on environmentally sound technology should be established to enhance the access to and development, management and transfer of environmentally sound technologies, including transfer and cooperation among developing countries and between developed and developing countries, primarily based on existing subregional or regional research, development and demonstration centres which are linked with the national institutions, in close cooperation with the private sector.

(e) Support for programmes of cooperation and assistance

34.22.    Support should be provided for programmes of cooperation and assistance, including those provided by United Nations agencies, international organizations, and other appropriate public and private organizations, in particular to developing countries, in the areas of research and development, technological and human resources capacity-building in the fields of training, maintenance, national technology needs assessments, environmental impact assessments, and sustainable development planning.

34.23.    Support should also be provided for national, subregional, regional, multilateral and bilateral programmes of scientific research, dissemination of information and technology development among developing countries, including through the involvement of both public and private enterprises and research facilities, as well as funding for technical cooperation among developing countries' programmes in this area. This should include developing links among these facilities to maximize their efficiency in understanding, disseminating and implementing technologies for sustainable development.

34.24.    The development of global, regional and subregional programmes should include identification and evaluation of regional, subregional and national need-based priorities. Plans and studies supporting these programmes should provide the basis for potential financing by multilateral development banks, bilateral organizations, private sector interests and non-governmental organizations.

34.25.    Visits should be sponsored and, on a voluntary basis, the return of qualified experts from developing countries in the field of environmentally sound technologies who are currently working in developed country institutions should be facilitated.

(f) Technology assessment in support of the management of environmentally sound technology

34.26.    The international community, in particular United Nations agencies, international organizations, and other appropriate and private organizations should help exchange experiences and develop capacity for technology needs assessment, in particular in developing countries, to enable them to make choices based on environmentally sound technologies. They should:

        a.   Build up technology assessment capacity for the management of environmentally sound technology, including environmental impact and risk assessment, with due regard to appropriate safeguards on the transfer of technologies subject to prohibition on environmental or health grounds;

b. Strengthen the international network of regional, subregional or national environmentally sound technology assessment centres, coupled with clearing-houses, to tap the technology assessment sources mentioned above for the benefit of all nations. These centres could, in principle, provide advice and training for specific national situations and promote the building up of national capacity in environmentally sound technology assessment. The possibility of assigning this activity to already existing regional organizations should be fully explored before creating entirely new institutions, and funding of this activity through public-private partnerships should also be explored, as appropriate.

(g) Collaborative arrangements and partnerships

34.27.    Long-term collaborative arrangements should be promoted between enterprises of developed and developing countries for the development of environmentally sound technologies. Multinational companies, as repositories of scarce technical skills needed for the protection and enhancement of the environment, have a special role and interest in promoting cooperation in and related to technology transfer, as they are important channels for such transfer, and for building a trained human resource pool and infrastructure.

34.28.    Joint ventures should be promoted between suppliers and recipients of technologies, taking into account developing countries' policy priorities and objectives. Together with direct foreign investment, these ventures could constitute important channels of transferring environmentally sound technologies. Through such joint ventures and direct investment, sound environmental management practices could be transferred and maintained.

## MEANS OF IMPLEMENTATION

Financing and cost evaluation

34.29.    The Conference secretariat has estimated the average total annual cost (1993-2000) of implementing the activities of this chapter to be between $450 million and $600 million from the international community on grant or concessional terms. These are indicative and order-of-magnitude estimates only and have not been reviewed by Governments. Actual costs and financial terms, including any that are non-concessional, will depend upon, inter alia, the specific strategies and programmes Governments decide upon for implementation.

# Agenda 21 – Chapter 35
## SCIENCE FOR SUSTAINABLE DEVELOPMENT

35.1. This chapter focuses on the role and the use of the sciences in supporting the prudent management of the environment and development for the daily survival and future development of humanity. The programme areas proposed herein are intended to be over-arching, in order to support the specific scientific requirements identified in the other Agenda 21 chapters. One role of the sciences should be to provide information to better enable formulation and selection of environment and development policies in the decision-making process. In order to fulfil this requirement, it will be essential to enhance scientific understanding, improve long-term scientific assessments, strengthen scientific capacities in all countries and ensure that the sciences are responsive to emerging needs.

35.2. Scientists are improving their understanding in areas such as climatic change, growth in rates of resource consumption, demographic trends, and environmental degradation. Changes in those and other areas need to be taken into account in working out long-term strategies for development. A first step towards improving the scientific basis for these strategies is a better understanding of land, oceans, atmosphere and their interlocking water, nutrient and biogeochemical cycles and energy flows which all form part of the Earth system. This is essential if a more accurate estimate is to be provided of the carrying capacity of the planet Earth and of its resilience under the many stresses placed upon it by human activities. The sciences can provide this understanding through increased research into the underlying ecological processes and through the application of modern, effective and efficient tools that are now available, such as remote-sensing devices, robotic monitoring instruments and computing and modelling capabilities. The sciences are playing an important role in linking the fundamental significance of the Earth system as life support to appropriate strategies for development which build on its continued functioning. The sciences should continue to play an increasing role in providing for an improvement in the efficiency of resource utilization and in finding new development practices, resources, and alternatives. There is a need for the sciences constantly to reassess and promote less intensive trends in resource utilization, including less intensive utilization of energy in industry, agriculture, and transportation. Thus, the sciences are increasingly being understood as an essential component in the search for feasible pathways towards sustainable development.

35.3. Scientific knowledge should be applied to articulate and support the goals of sustainable development, through scientific assessments of current conditions and future prospects for the Earth system. Such assessments, based on existing and emerging innovations within the sciences, should be used in the decision-making process and in the interactive processes between the sciences and policy-making. There needs to be an increased output from the sciences in order to enhance understanding and facilitate interaction between science and society. An increase in the scientific capacity and capability to achieve these goals will also be required, particularly in developing countries. Of crucial importance is the need for scientists in developing countries to participate fully in international scientific research programmes dealing with the global problems of environment and development so as to allow all countries to participate on equal footing in negotiations on global environmental and developmental issues. In the face of threats of irreversible environmental damage, lack of full scientific understanding should not be an excuse for postponing actions which are justified in their own right. The precautionary approach could provide a basis for policies relating to complex systems that are not yet fully understood and whose consequences of disturbances cannot yet be predicted.

35.4. The programme areas, which are in harmony with the conclusions and recommendations of the International Conference on an Agenda of Science for Environment and Development into the 21st Century (ASCEND 21) are:

      a. Strengthening the scientific basis for sustainable management;

      b. Enhancing scientific understanding;

      c. Improving long-term scientific assessment;

d. Building up scientific capacity and capability.

## PROGRAMME AREAS

### A. Strengthening the scientific basis for sustainable management

**Basis for action**

35.5. Sustainable development requires taking longer-term perspectives, integrating local and regional effects of global change into the development process, and using the best scientific and traditional knowledge available. The development process should be constantly re-evaluated, in light of the findings of scientific research, to ensure that resource utilization has reduced impacts on the Earth system. Even so, the future is uncertain, and there will be surprises. Good environmental and developmental management policies must therefore be scientifically robust, seeking to keep open a range of options to ensure flexibility of response. The precautionary approach is important. Often, there is a communication gap among scientists, policy makers, and the public at large, whose interests are articulated by both governmental and non-governmental organizations. Better communication is required among scientists, decision makers, and the general public.

**Objectives**

35.6. The primary objective is for each country with the support of international organizations, as requested, to identify the state of its scientific knowledge and its research needs and priorities in order to achieve, as soon as possible, substantial improvements in:

    a. Large-scale widening of the scientific base and strengthening of scientific and research capacities and capabilities - in particular, those of developing countries - in areas relevant to environment and development;

    b. Environmental and developmental policy formulation, building upon the best scientific knowledge and assessments, and taking into account the need to enhance international cooperation and the relative uncertainties of the various processes and options involved;

    c. The interaction between the sciences and decision-making, using the precautionary approach, where appropriate, to change the existing patterns of production and consumption and to gain time for reducing uncertainty with respect to the selection of policy options;

    d. The generation and application of knowledge, especially indigenous and local knowledge, to the capacities of different environments and cultures, to achieve sustained levels of development, taking into account interrelations at the national, regional and international levels;

    e. Improving cooperation between scientists by promoting interdisciplinary research programmes and activities;

    f. Participation of people in setting priorities and in decision-making relating to sustainable development.

**Activities**

35.7. Countries, with the assistance of international organizations, where required, should:

    a. Prepare an inventory of their natural and social science data holdings relevant to the promotion of sustainable development;

    b. Identify their research needs and priorities in the context of international research efforts;

c. Strengthen and design appropriate institutional mechanisms at the highest appropriate local, national, subregional and regional levels and within the United Nations system for developing a stronger scientific basis for the improvement of environmental and developmental policy formulation consistent with long-term goals of sustainable development. Current research in this area should be broadened to include more involvement of the public in establishing long-term societal goals for formulating the sustainable development scenarios;

d. Develop, apply and institute the necessary tools for sustainable development, with regard to:

   i. Quality-of-life indicators covering, for example, health, education, social welfare, state of the environment, and the economy;

   ii. Economic approaches to environmentally sound development and new and improved incentive structures for better resource management;

   iii. Long-term environmental policy formulation, risk management and environmentally sound technology assessment;

e. Collect, analyse and integrate data on the linkages between the state of ecosystems and the health of human communities in order to improve knowledge of the cost and benefit of different development policies and strategies in relation to health and the environment, particularly in developing countries;

f. Conduct scientific studies of national and regional pathways to sustainable development, using comparable and complementary methodologies. Such studies, coordinated by an international science effort, should to a large extent involve local expertise and be conducted by multidisciplinary teams from regional networks and/or research centres, as appropriate and according to national capacities and the available resources;

g. Improve capabilities for determining scientific research priorities at the national, regional and global levels to meet the needs of sustainable development. This is a process that involves scientific judgements regarding short-term and long-term benefits and possible long-term costs and risks. It should be adaptive and responsive to perceived needs and be carried out via transparent, "user-friendly", risk-evaluation methodologies;

h. Develop methods to link the findings of the established sciences with the indigenous knowledge of different cultures. The methods should be tested using pilot studies. They should be developed at the local level and should concentrate on the links between the traditional knowledge of indigenous groups and corresponding, current "advanced science", with particular focus on disseminating and applying the results to environmental protection and sustainable development.

**Means of implementation**

(a) Financing and cost evaluation

35.8. The Conference secretariat has estimated the average total annual cost (1993-2000) of implementing the activities of this programme to be about $150 million, including about $30 million from the international community on grant or concessional terms. These are indicative and order-of-magnitude estimates only and have not been reviewed by Governments. Actual costs and financial terms, including any that are non-concessional, will depend upon, inter alia, the specific strategies and programmes Governments decide upon for implementation.

(b) Scientific and technological means

35.9. The scientific and technological means include the following:

    a. Supporting new scientific research programmes, including their socio-economic and human aspects, at the community, national, subregional, regional and global levels, to complement and encourage synergies between traditional and conventional scientific knowledge and practices and strengthening interdisciplinary research related to environmental degradation and rehabilitation;

    b. Setting up demonstration models of different types (e.g., socio-economic, environmental conditions) to study methodologies and formulate guidelines;

    c. Supporting research by developing relative-risk evaluation methods to assist policy makers in ranking scientific research priorities.

## B. Enhancing scientific understanding

**Basis for action**

35.10. In order to promote sustainable development, more extensive knowledge is required of the Earth's carrying capacity, including the processes that could either impair or enhance its ability to support life. The global environment is changing more rapidly than at any time in recent centuries; as a result, surprises may be expected, and the next century could see significant environmental changes. At the same time, the human consumption of energy, water and non-renewable resources is increasing, on both a total and a per capita basis, and shortages may ensue in many parts of the world even if environmental conditions were to remain unchanged. Social processes are subject to multiple variations across time and space, regions and culture. They both affect and are influenced by changing environmental conditions. Human factors are key driving forces in these intricate sets of relationships and exert their influence directly on global change. Therefore, study of the human dimensions of the causes and consequences of environmental change and of more sustainable development paths is essential.

**Objectives**

35.11. One key objective is to improve and increase the fundamental understanding of the linkages between human and natural environmental systems and improve the analytical and predictive tools required to better understand the environmental impacts of development options by:

    a. Carrying out research programmes in order better to understand the carrying capacity of the Earth as conditioned by its natural systems, such as the biogeochemical cycles, the atmosphere/hydrosphere/lithosphere/cryosphere system, the biosphere and biodiversity, the agro-ecosystem and other terrestrial and aquatic ecosystems;

    b. Developing and applying new analytical and predictive tools in order to assess more accurately the ways in which the Earth's natural systems are being increasingly influenced by human actions, both deliberate and inadvertent, and demographic trends, and the impact and consequences of those actions and trends;

    c. Integrating physical, economic and social sciences in order better to understand the impacts of economic and social behaviour on the environment and of environmental degradation on local and global economies.

**Activities**

35.12. The following activities should be undertaken:

    a. Support development of an expanded monitoring network to describe cycles (for example, global, biogeochemical and hydrological cycles) and test hypotheses regarding their behaviour, and improve research into the interactions among the various global cycles and their consequences at national, subregional, regional and global levels as guides to tolerance and vulnerability;

b. Support national, subregional, regional and international observation and research programmes in global atmospheric chemistry and the sources and sinks of greenhouse gases, and ensure that the results are presented in a publicly accessible and understandable form;

c. Support national, subregional, regional and international research programmes on marine and terrestrial systems, strengthen global terrestrial databases of their components, expand corresponding systems for monitoring their changing states and enhance predictive modelling of the Earth system and its subsystems, including modelling of the functioning of these systems assuming different intensities of human impact. The research programmes should include the programmes mentioned in other Agenda 21 chapters which support mechanisms for cooperation and coherence of research programmes on global change;

d. Encourage coordination of satellite missions, the networks, systems and procedures for processing and disseminating their data; and develop the interface with the research users of Earth observation data and with the United Nations EARTHWATCH system;

e. Develop the capacity for predicting the responses of terrestrial, freshwater, coastal and marine ecosystems and biodiversity to short- and long-term perturbations of the environment, and develop further restoration ecology;

f. Study the role of biodiversity and the loss of species in the functioning of ecosystems and the global life-support system;

g. Initiate a global observing system of parameters needed for the rational management of coastal and mountain zones and significantly expand freshwater quantity/quality monitoring systems, particularly in developing countries;

h. In order to understand the Earth as a system, develop Earth observation systems from space which will provide integrated, continuous and long-term measurements of the interactions of the atmosphere, hydrosphere and lithosphere, and develop a distribution system for data which will facilitate the utilization of data obtained through observation;

i. Develop and apply systems and technology that automatically collect, record and transmit data and information to data and analysis centres, in order to monitor marine, terrestrial and atmospheric processes and provide advance warning of natural disasters;

j. Enhance the contribution of the engineering sciences to multidisciplinary research programmes on the Earth system, in particular with regard to increasing emergency preparedness and reducing the negative effects of major natural disasters;

k. Intensify research to integrate the physical, economic and social sciences to better understand the impacts of economic and social behaviour on the environment and of environmental degradation on local and global economies and, in particular:

    a. Develop research on human attitudes and behaviour as driving forces central to an understanding of the causes and consequences of environmental change and resource use;

    b. Promote research on human, economic and social responses to global change;

l. Support development of new user-friendly technologies and systems that facilitate the integration of multidisciplinary, physical, chemical, biological and social/human processes which, in turn, provide information and knowledge for decision makers and the general public.

**Means of implementation**

(a) Financing and cost evaluation

35.13. The Conference secretariat has estimated the average total annual cost (1993-2000) of implementing the activities of this programme to be about $2 billion, including about $1.5 billion from the international community on grant or concessional terms. These are indicative and order-of-magnitude estimates only and have not been reviewed by Governments. Actual costs and financial terms, including any that are non-concessional, will depend upon, inter alia, the specific strategies and programmes Governments decide upon for implementation.

(b) Scientific and technological means

35.14. The scientific and technological means include the following:

    a. Supporting and using the relevant national research activities of academia, research institutes and governmental and non-governmental organizations, and promoting their active participation in regional and global programmes, particularly in developing countries;

    b. Increasing the use of appropriate enabling systems and technologies, such as supercomputers, space-based observational technology, Earth- and ocean-based observational technologies, data management and database technologies and, in particular, developing and expanding the Global Climate Observing System.

### C. Improving long-term scientific assessment

**Basis for action**

35.15. Meeting scientific research needs in the environment/development field is only the first step in the support that the sciences can provide for the sustainable development process. The knowledge acquired may then be used to provide scientific assessments (audits) of the current status and for a range of possible future conditions. This implies that the biosphere must be maintained in a healthy state and that losses in biodiversity must be slowed down. Although many of the long-term environmental changes that are likely to affect people and the biosphere are global in scale, key changes can often be made at the national and local levels. At the same time, human activities at the local and regional levels often contribute to global threats - e.g., stratospheric ozone depletion. Thus scientific assessments and projections are required at the global, regional and local levels. Many countries and organizations already prepare reports on the environment and development which review current conditions and indicate future trends. Regional and global assessments could make full use of such reports but should be broader in scope and include the results of detailed studies of future conditions for a range of assumptions about possible future human responses, using the best available models. Such assessments should be designed to map out manageable development pathways within the environmental and socio-economic carrying capacity of each region. Full use should be made of traditional knowledge of the local environment.

**Objectives**

35.16. The primary objective is to provide assessments of the current status and trends in major developmental and environmental issues at the national, subregional, regional and global levels on the basis of the best available scientific knowledge in order to develop alternative strategies, including indigenous approaches, for the different scales of time and space required for long-term policy formulation.

**Activities**

35.17. The following activities should be undertaken:

a. Coordinate existing data- and statistics-gathering systems relevant to developmental and environmental issues so as to support preparation of long-term scientific assessments - for example, data on resource depletion, import/export flows, energy use, health impacts and demographic trends; apply the data obtained through the activities identified in programme area B to environment/development assessments at the global, regional and local levels; and promote the wide distribution of the assessments in a form that is responsive to public needs and can be widely understood;

b. Develop a methodology to carry out national and regional audits and a five-year global audit on an integrated basis. The standardized audits should help to refine the pattern and character of development, examining in particular the capacities of global and regional life-supporting systems to meet the needs of human and non-human life forms and identifying areas and resources vulnerable to further degradation. This task would involve the integration of all relevant sciences at the national, regional, and global levels, and would be organized by governmental agencies, non-governmental organizations, universities and research institutions, assisted by international governmental and non-governmental organizations and United Nations bodies, when necessary and as appropriate. These audits should then be made available to the general public.

**Means of implementation**

Financing and cost evaluation

35.18. The Conference secretariat has estimated the average total annual cost (1993-2000) of implementing the activities of this programme to be about $35 million, including about $18 million from the international community on grant or concessional terms. These are indicative and order-of-magnitude estimates only and have not been reviewed by Governments. Actual costs and financial terms, including any that are non-concessional, will depend upon, inter alia, the specific strategies and programmes Governments decide upon for implementation.

35.19. With regard to the existing data requirements under programme area A, support should be provided for national data collection and warning systems. This would involve setting up database, information and reporting systems, including data assessment and information dissemination in each region.

### D. Building up scientific capacity and capability

**Basis for action**

35.20. In view of the increasing role the sciences have to play in dealing with the issues of environment and development, it is necessary to build up scientific capacity and strengthen such capacity in all countries - particularly in developing countries - to enable them to participate fully in the generation and application of the results of scientific research and development concerning sustainable development. There are many ways to build up scientific and technological capacity. Some of the most important of them are the following: education and training in science and technology; assistance to developing countries to improve infrastructures for research and development which could enable scientists to work more productively; development of incentives to encourage research and development; and greater utilization of their results in the productive sectors of the economy. Such capacity-building would also form the basis for improving public awareness and understanding of the sciences. Special emphasis must be put on the need to assist developing countries to strengthen their capacities to study their own resource bases and ecological systems and manage them better in order to meet national, regional and global challenges. Furthermore, in view of the size and complexity of global environmental problems, a need for more specialists in several disciplines has become evident world wide.

**Objectives**

35.21.    The primary objective is to improve the scientific capacities of all countries - in particular, those of developing countries - with specific regard to:

a.    Education, training and facilities for local research and development and human resource development in basic scientific disciplines and in environment-related sciences, utilizing where appropriate traditional and local knowledge of sustainability;

b.    A substantial increase by the year 2000 in the number of scientists - particularly women scientists - in those developing countries where their number is at present insufficient;

c.    Reducing significantly the exodus of scientists from developing countries and encouraging those who have left to return;

d.    Improving access to relevant information for scientists and decision makers, with the aim of improving public awareness and participation in decision-making;

e.    Involvement of scientists in national, regional and global environmental and developmental research programmes, including multidisciplinary research;

f.    Periodic academic update of scientists from developing countries in their respective fields of knowledge.

**Activities**

35.22.    The following activities should be undertaken:

a.    Promote the education and training of scientists, not only in their disciplines but also in their ability to identify, manage and incorporate environmental considerations into research and development projects; ensure that a sound base in natural systems, ecology and resource management is provided; and develop specialists capable of working in interdisciplinary programmes related to environment and development, including the field of applied social sciences;

b.    Strengthen the scientific infrastructure in schools, universities and research institutions - particularly those in developing countries - by the provision of adequate scientific equipment and access to current scientific literature, for the purpose of achieving and sustaining a critical mass of highly qualified scientists in these countries;

c.    Develop and expand national scientific and technological databases, processing data in unified formats and systems, and allowing full and open access to the depository libraries of regional scientific and technological information networks. Promote submission of scientific and technological information and databases to global or regional data centres and network systems;

d.    Develop and expand regional and global scientific and technological information networks which are based on and linked to national scientific and technological databases; collect, process and disseminate information from regional and global scientific programmes; expand activities to reduce information barriers due to language differences. Increase the applications - particularly in developing countries - of computer-based retrieval systems in order to cope with the growth of scientific literature;

e.    Develop, strengthen and forge new partnerships among national, regional and global capacities to promote the full and open exchange of scientific and technological data and information and to facilitate technical assistance related to environmentally sound and sustainable development. This should be done through the development of mechanisms for the sharing of basic research, data and information, and the improvement and development of international networks and centres, including regional linking with national scientific databases, for research, training and monitoring. Such mechanisms should be designed so as to enhance professional cooperation among scientists in all countries and to establish strong national and regional alliances between industry and research institutions;

   f. Improve and develop new links between existing networks of natural and social scientists and universities at the international level in order to strengthen national capacities in the formulation of policy options in the field of environment and development;

   g. Compile, analyse and publish information on indigenous environmental and developmental knowledge, and assist the communities that possess such knowledge to benefit from them.

**Means of implementation**

(a) Financing and cost evaluation

35.23. The Conference secretariat has estimated the average total annual cost (1993-2000) of implementing the activities of this programme to be about $750 million, including about $470 million from the international community on grant or concessional terms. These are indicative and order-of-magnitude estimates only and have not been reviewed by Governments. Actual costs and financial terms, including any that are non-concessional, will depend upon, inter alia, the specific strategies and programmes Governments decide upon for implementation.

(b) Scientific and technological means

35.24. Such means include increasing and strengthening regional multidisciplinary research and training networks and centres making optimal use of existing facilities and associated sustainable development and technology support systems in developing regions. Promote and use the potential of independent initiatives and indigenous innovations and entrepreneurship. The function of such networks and centres could include, for example:

   a. Support and coordination of scientific cooperation among all nations in the region;

   b. Linking with monitoring centres and carrying out assessment of environmental and developmental conditions;

   c. Support and coordination of national studies of pathways towards sustainable development;

   d. Organization of science education and training;

   e. Establishment and maintenance of information, monitoring and assessment systems and databases.

(c) Capacity-building

35.25.   Capacity-building includes the following:

   a. Creating conditions (e.g., salaries, equipment, libraries) to ensure that the scientists will work effectively in their home countries;

   b. Enhancing national, regional and global capacities for carrying out scientific research and applying scientific and technological information to environmentally sound and sustainable development. This includes a need to increase financial resources for global and regional scientific and technological information networks, as may be appropriate, so that they will be able to function effectively and efficiently in satisfying the scientific needs of developing countries. Ensure the capacity-building of women by recruiting more women in research and research training.

# Agenda 21 – Chapter 36
# PROMOTING EDUCATION, PUBLIC AWARENESS AND TRAINING

36.1. Education, raising of public awareness and training are linked to virtually all areas in Agenda 21, and even more closely to the ones on meeting basic needs, capacity-building, data and information, science, and the role of major groups. This chapter sets out broad proposals, while specific suggestions related to sectoral issues are contained in other chapters. The Declaration and Recommendations of the Tbilisi Intergovernmental Conference on Environmental Education 1/ organized by UNESCO and UNEP and held in 1977, have provided the fundamental principles for the proposals in this document.

36.2. Programme areas described in the present chapter are:

    a. Reorienting education towards sustainable development;

    b. Increasing public awareness;

    c. Promoting training.

## PROGRAMME AREAS

A. Reorienting education towards sustainable development

Basis for action

36.3. Education, including formal education, public awareness and training should be recognized as a process by which human beings and societies can reach their fullest potential. Education is critical for promoting sustainable development and improving the capacity of the people to address environment and development issues. While basic education provides the underpinning for any environmental and development education, the latter needs to be incorporated as an essential part of learning. Both formal and non-formal education are indispensable to changing people's attitudes so that they have the capacity to assess and address their sustainable development concerns. It is also critical for achieving environmental and ethical awareness, values and attitudes, skills and behaviour consistent with sustainable development and for effective public participation in decision-making. To be effective, environment and development education should deal with the dynamics of both the physical/biological and socio-economic environment and human (which may include spiritual) development, should be integrated in all disciplines, and should employ formal and non-formal methods and effective means of communication.

**Objectives**

36.4. Recognizing that countries, regional and international organizations will develop their own priorities and schedules for implementation in accordance with their needs, policies and programmes, the following objectives are proposed:

    o To endorse the recommendations arising from the World Conference on Education for All: Meeting Basic Learning Needs 2/ (Jomtien, Thailand, 5-9 March 1990) and to strive to ensure universal access to basic education, and to achieve primary education for at least 80 per cent of girls and 80 per cent of boys of primary school age through formal schooling or non-formal education and to reduce the adult illiteracy rate to at least half of its 1990 level. Efforts should focus on reducing the high illiteracy levels and redressing the lack of basic education among women and should bring their literacy levels into line with those of men;

    o To achieve environmental and development awareness in all sectors of society on a world-wide scale as soon as possible;

o To strive to achieve the accessibility of environmental and development education, linked to social education, from primary school age through adulthood to all groups of people;

o To promote integration of environment and development concepts, including demography, in all educational programmes, in particular the analysis of the causes of major environment and development issues in a local context, drawing on the best available scientific evidence and other appropriate sources of knowledge, and giving special emphasis to the further training of decision makers at all levels.

**Activities**

36.5. Recognizing that countries and regional and international organizations will develop their own priorities and schedules for implementation in accordance with their needs, policies and programmes, the following activities are proposed:

a. All countries are encouraged to endorse the recommendations of the Jomtien Conference and strive to ensure its Framework for Action. This would encompass the preparation of national strategies and actions for meeting basic learning needs, universalizing access and promoting equity, broadening the means and scope of education, developing a supporting policy context, mobilizing resources and strengthening international cooperation to redress existing economic, social and gender disparities which interfere with these aims. Non-governmental organizations can make an important contribution in designing and implementing educational programmes and should be recognized;

b. Governments should strive to update or prepare strategies aimed at integrating environment and development as a cross-cutting issue into education at all levels within the next three years. This should be done in cooperation with all sectors of society. The strategies should set out policies and activities, and identify needs, cost, means and schedules for their implementation, evaluation and review. A thorough review of curricula should be undertaken to ensure a multidisciplinary approach, with environment and development issues and their socio-cultural and demographic aspects and linkages. Due respect should be given to community-defined needs and diverse knowledge systems, including science, cultural and social sensitivities;

c. Countries are encouraged to set up national advisory environmental education coordinating bodies or round tables representative of various environmental, developmental, educational, gender and other interests, including non-governmental organizations, to encourage partnerships, help mobilize resources, and provide a source of information and focal point for international ties. These bodies would help mobilize and facilitate different population groups and communities to assess their own needs and to develop the necessary skills to create and implement their own environment and development initiatives;

d. Educational authorities, with the appropriate assistance from community groups or non-governmental organizations, are recommended to assist or set up pre-service and in-service training programmes for all teachers, administrators, and educational planners, as well as non-formal educators in all sectors, addressing the nature and methods of environmental and development education and making use of relevant experience of non-governmental organizations;

e.  Relevant authorities should ensure that every school is assisted in designing environmental activity work plans, with the participation of students and staff. Schools should involve schoolchildren in local and regional studies on environmental health, including safe drinking water, sanitation and food and ecosystems and in relevant activities, linking these studies with services and research in national parks, wildlife reserves, ecological heritage sites etc.;

f.  Educational authorities should promote proven educational methods and the development of innovative teaching methods for educational settings. They should also recognize appropriate traditional education systems in local communities;

g.  Within two years the United Nations system should undertake a comprehensive review of its educational programmes, encompassing training and public awareness, to reassess priorities and reallocate resources. The UNESCO/UNEP International Environmental Education Programme should, in cooperation with the appropriate bodies of the United Nations system, Governments, non-governmental organizations and others, establish a programme within two years to integrate the decisions of the Conference into the existing United Nations framework adapted to the needs of educators at different levels and circumstances. Regional organizations and national authorities should be encouraged to elaborate similar parallel programmes and opportunities by conducting an analysis of how to mobilize different sectors of the population in order to assess and address their environmental and development education needs;

h.  There is a need to strengthen, within five years, information exchange by enhancing technologies and capacities necessary to promote environment and development education and public awareness. Countries should cooperate with each other and with the various social sectors and population groups to prepare educational tools that include regional environment and development issues and initiatives, using learning materials and resources suited to their own requirements;

i.  Countries could support university and other tertiary activities and networks for environmental and development education. Cross-disciplinary courses could be made available to all students. Existing regional networks and activities and national university actions which promote research and common teaching approaches on sustainable development should be built upon, and new partnerships and bridges created with the business and other independent sectors, as well as with all countries for technology, know-how, and knowledge exchange;

j.  Countries, assisted by international organizations, non-governmental organizations and other sectors, could strengthen or establish national or regional centres of excellence in interdisciplinary research and education in environmental and developmental sciences, law and the management of specific environmental problems. Such centres could be universities or existing networks in each country or region, promoting cooperative research and information sharing and dissemination. At the global level these functions should be performed by appropriate institutions;

k.  Countries should facilitate and promote non-formal education activities at the local, regional and national levels by cooperating with and supporting the efforts of non-formal educators and other community-based organizations. The appropriate bodies of the United Nations system in cooperation with non-governmental organizations should encourage the development of an international network for the achievement of global educational aims. At the national and local levels, public and scholastic forums should discuss environmental and development issues, and suggest sustainable alternatives to policy makers;

l.  Educational authorities, with appropriate assistance of non-governmental organizations, including women's and indigenous peoples' organizations, should promote all kinds of adult education programmes for continuing education in environment and development, basing activities around elementary/secondary schools and local problems. These authorities and industry should encourage business, industrial and agricultural schools to include such topics in their curricula. The corporate sector could include sustainable development in their education and training programmes. Programmes at a post-graduate level should include specific courses aiming at the further training of decision makers;

m.  Governments and educational authorities should foster opportunities for women in non-traditional fields and eliminate gender stereotyping in curricula. This could be done by improving enrolment opportunities, including females in advanced programmes as students and instructors, reforming entrance and teacher staffing policies and providing incentives for establishing child-care facilities, as appropriate. Priority should be given to education of young females and to programmes promoting literacy among women;

n.  Governments should affirm the rights of indigenous peoples, by legislation if necessary, to use their experience and understanding of sustainable development to play a part in education and training;

o.  The United Nations could maintain a monitoring and evaluative role regarding decisions of the United Nations Conference on Environment and Development on education and awareness, through the relevant United Nations agencies. With Governments and non-governmental organizations, as appropriate, it should present and disseminate decisions in a variety of forms, and should ensure the continuous implementation and review of the educational implications of Conference decisions, in particular through relevant events and conferences.

### Means of implementation Financing and cost evaluation

36.6. The Conference secretariat has estimated the average total annual cost (1993-2000) of implementing the activities of this programme to be about $8 billion to $9 billion, including about $3.5 billion to $4.5 billion from the international community on grant or concessional terms. These are indicative and order-of-magnitude estimates only and have not been reviewed by Governments. Actual costs and financial terms, including any that are non-concessional, will depend upon, inter alia, the specific strategies and programmes Governments decide upon for implementation.

36.7. In the light of country -specific situations, more support for education, training and public awareness activities related to environment and development could be provided, in appropriate cases, through measures such as the following:

    a. Giving higher priority to those sectors in budget allocations, protecting them from structural cutting requirements;

    b. Shifting allocations within existing education budgets in favour of primary education, with focus on environment and development;

    c. Promoting conditions where a larger share of the cost is borne by local communities, with rich communities assisting poorer ones;

    d. Obtaining additional funds from private donors concentrating on the poorest countries, and those with rates of literacy below 40 per cent;

    e. Encouraging debt for education swaps;

    f. Lifting restrictions on private schooling and increasing the flow of funds from and to non-governmental organizations, including small-scale grass-roots organizations;

    g. Promoting the effective use of existing facilities, for example, multiple school shifts, fuller development of open universities and other long-distance teaching;

    h. Facilitating low-cost or no-cost use of mass media for the purposes of education;

    i. Encouraging twinning of universities in developed and developing countries.

### B.  Increasing public awareness

**Basis for action**

36.8. There is still a considerable lack of awareness of the interrelated nature of all human activities and the environment, due to inaccurate or insufficient information. Developing countries in particular lack relevant technologies and expertise. There is a need to increase public sensitivity to environment and development problems and involvement in their solutions and foster a sense of personal environmental responsibility and greater motivation and commitment towards sustainable development.

**Objective**

36.9. The objective is to promote broad public awareness as an essential part of a global education effort to strengthen attitudes, values and actions which are compatible with sustainable development. It is important to stress the principle of devolving authority, accountability and resources to the most appropriate level with preference given to local responsibility and control over awareness-building activities.

**Activities**

36.10.    Recognizing that countries, regional and international organizations will develop their own priorities and schedules for implementat ion in accordance with their needs, policies and programmes, the following activities are proposed:

a. Countries should strengthen existing advisory bodies or establish new ones for public environment and development information, and should coordinate activities with, among others, the United Nations, non-governmental organizations and important media. They should encourage public participation in discussions of environmental policies and assessments. Governments should also facilitate and support national to local networking of information through existing networks;

b. The United Nations system should improve its outreach in the course of a review of its education and public awareness activities to promote greater involvement and coordination of all parts of the system, especially its information bodies and regional and country operations. Systematic surveys of the impact of awareness programmes should be conducted, recognizing the needs and contributions of specific community groups;

c. Countries and regional organizations should be encouraged, as appropriate, to provide public environmental and development information services for raising the awareness of all groups, the private sector and particularly decision makers;

d. Countries should stimulate educational establishments in all sectors, especially the tertiary sector, to contribute more to awareness building. Educational materials of all kinds and for all audiences should be based on the best available scientific information, including the natural, behavioural and social sciences, and taking into account aesthetic and ethical dimensions;

e. Countries and the United Nations system should promote a cooperative relationship with the media, popular theatre groups, and entertainment and advertising industries by initiat ing discussions to mobilize their experience in shaping public behaviour and consumption patterns and making wide use of their methods. Such cooperation would also increase the active public participation in the debate on the environment. UNICEF should make child-oriented material available to media as an educational tool, ensuring close cooperation between the out-of-school public information sector and the school curriculum, for the primary level. UNESCO, UNEP and universities should enrich pre-service curricula for journalists on environment and development topics;

f. Countries, in cooperation with the scientific community, should establish ways of employing modern communication technologies for effective public outreach. National and local educational authorities and relevant United Nations agencies should expand, as appropriate, the use of audio-visual methods, especially in rural areas in mobile units, by producing television and radio programmes for developing countries, involving local participation, employing interactive multimedia methods and integrating advanced methods with folk media;

g. Countries should promote, as appropriate, environmentally sound leisure and tourism activities, building on The Hague Declaration of Tourism (1989) and the current programmes of the World Tourism Organization and UNEP, making suitable use of museums, heritage sites, zoos, botanical gardens, national parks, and other protected areas;

h. Countries should encourage non-governmental organizations to increase their involvement in environmental and development problems, through joint awareness initiatives and improved interchange with other constituencies in society;

i. Countries and the United Nations system should increase their interaction with and include, as appropriate, indigenous people in the management, planning and development of their local environment, and should promote dissemination of traditional and socially learned knowledge through means based on local customs, especially in rural areas, integrating these efforts with the electronic media, whenever appropriate;

j. UNICEF, UNESCO, UNDP and non-governmental organizations should develop support programmes to involve young people and children in environment and development issues, such as children's and youth hearings and building on decisions of the World Summit for Children (A/45/625, annex);

k. Countries, the United Nations and non-governmental organizations should encourage mobilization of both men and women in awareness campaigns, stressing the role of the family in environmental activities, women's contribution to transmission of knowledge and social values and the development of human resources;

l. Public awareness should be heightened regarding the impacts of violence in society.

**Means of implementation Financing and cost evaluation**

36.11. The Conference secretariat has estimated the average total annual cost (1993-2000) of implementing the activities of this programme to be about $1.2 billion, including about $110 million from the international community on grant or concessional terms. These are indicative and order-of-magnitude estimates only and have not been reviewed by Governments. Actual costs and financial terms, including any that are non-concessional, will depend upon, inter alia, the specific strategies and programmes Governments decide upon for implementation.

### C. Promoting training

**Basis for action**

36.12.   Training is one of the most important tools to develop human resources and facilitate the transition to a more sustainable world. It should have a job-specific focus, aimed at filling gaps in knowledge and skill that would help individuals find employment and be involved in environmental and development work. At the same time, training programmes should promote a greater awareness of environment and development issues as a two-way learning process.

**Objectives**

36.13.   The following objectives are proposed:

    a.   To establish or strengthen vocational training programmes that meet the needs of environment and development with ensured access to training opportunities, regardless of social status, age, gender, race or religion;

    b.   To promote a flexible and adaptable workforce of various ages equipped to meet growing environment and development problems and changes arising from the transition to a sustainable society;

    c.   To strengthen national capacities, particularly in scientific education and training, to enable Governments, employers and workers to meet their environmental and development objectives and to facilitate the transfer and assimilation of new environmentally sound, socially acceptable and appropriate technology and know-how;

    d.   To ensure that environmental and human ecological considerations are integrated at all managerial levels and in all functional management areas, such as marketing, production and finance.

**Activities**

36.14.   Countries with the support of the United Nations system should identify workforce training needs and assess measures to be taken to meet those needs. A review of progress in this area could be undertaken by the United Nations system in 1995.

36.15.   National professional associations are encouraged to develop and review their codes of ethics and conduct to strengthen environmental connections and commitment. The training and personal development components of programmes sponsored by professional bodies should ensure incorporation of skills and information on the implementation of sustainable development at all points of policy- and decision-making.

36.16.   Countries and educational institutions should integrate environmental and developmental issues into existing training curricula and promote the exchange of their methodologies and evaluations.

36.17.   Countries should encourage all sectors of society, such as industry, universities, government officials and employees, non-governmental organizations and community organizations, to include an environmental management component in all relevant training activities, with emphasis on meeting immediate skill requirements through short-term formal and in-plant vocational and management training. Environmental management training capacities should be strengthened, and specialized "training of trainers" programmes should be established to support training at the national and enterprise levels. New training approaches for existing environmentally sound practices should be developed that create employment opportunities and make maximum use of local resource-based methods.

36.18. Countries should strengthen or establish practical training programmes for graduates from vocational schools, high schools and universities, in all countries, to enable them to meet labour market requirements and to achieve sustainable livelihoods. Training and retraining programmes should be established to meet structural adjustments which have an impact on employment and skill qualifications.

36.19. Governments are encouraged to consult with people in isolated situations, whether geographically, culturally or socially, to ascertain their needs for training to enable them to contribute more fully to developing sustainable work practices and lifestyles.

36.20. Governments, industry, trade unions, and consumers should promote an understanding of the interrelationship between good environment and good business practices.

36.21. Countries should develop a service of locally trained and recruited environmental technicians able to provide local people and communities, particularly in deprived urban and rural areas, with the services they require, starting from primary environmental care.

36.22. Countries should enhance the ability to gain access to, analyse and effectively use information and knowledge available on environment and development. Existing or established special training programmes should be strengthened to support information needs of special groups. The impact of these programmes on productivity, health, safety and employment should be evaluated. National and regional environmental labour-market information systems should be developed that would supply, on a continuing basis, data on environmental job and training opportunities. Environment and development training resource-guides should be prepared and updated, with information on training programmes, curricula, methodologies and evaluation results at the local, national, regional and international levels.

36.23. Aid agencies should strengthen the training component in all development projects, emphasizing a multidisciplinary approach, promoting awareness and providing the necessary skills for transition to a sustainable society. The environmental management guidelines of UNDP for operational activities of the United Nations system may contribute to t his end.

36.24. Existing networks of employers' and workers' organizations, industry associations and non-governmental organizations should facilitate the exchange of experience concerning training and awareness programmes.

36.25. Governments, in cooperation with relevant international organizations, should develop and implement strategies to deal with national, regional and local environmental threats and emergencies, emphasizing urgent practical training and awareness programmes for increasing public preparedness.

36.26. The United Nations system, as appropriate, should extend its training programmes, particularly its environmental training and support activities for employers' and workers' organizations.

**Means of implementation Financing and cost evaluation**

36.27. The Conference secretariat has estimated the average total annual cost (1993-2000) of implementing the activities of this programme to be about $5 billion, including about $2 billion from the international community on grant or concessional terms. These are indicative and order-of-magnitude estimates only and have not been reviewed by Governments. Actual costs and financial terms, including any that are non-concessional, will depend upon, inter alia, the specific strategies and programmes Governments decide upon for implementation.

## Notes

1. Intergovernmental Conference on Environmental Education: Final Report (Paris, UNESCO, 1978), chap. III.

2. Final Report of the World Conference on Education for All: Meeting Basic Learning Needs, Jomtien, Thailand, 5-9 March 1990 (New York, Inter-Agency Commission (UNDP, UNESCO, UNICEF, World Bank) for the World Conference on Education for All, 1990).

## Agenda 21 – Chapter 37
## NATIONAL MECHANISMS AND INTERNATIONAL COOPERATION FOR CAPACITY-BUILDING IN DEVELOPING COUNTRIES

**PROGRAMME AREA**

**Basis for action**

37.1. The ability of a country to follow sustainable development paths is determined to a large extent by the capacity of its people and its institutions as well as by its ecological and geographical conditions. Specifically, capacity-building encompasses the country's human, scientific, technological, organizational, institutional and resource capabilities. A fundamental goal of capacity-building is to enhance the ability to evaluate and address the crucial questions related to policy choices and modes of implementation among development options, based on an understanding of environmental potentials and limits and of needs as perceived by the people of the country concerned. As a result, the need to strengthen national capacities is shared by all countries.

37.2. Building endogenous capacity to implement Agenda 21 will require the efforts of the countries themselves in partnership with relevant United Nations organizations, as well as with developed countries. The international community at the national, subregional and regional levels, municipalities, non-governmental organizations, universities and research centres, and business and other private institutions and organizations could also assist in these efforts. It is essential for individual countries to identify priorities and determine the means for building the capacity and capability to implement Agenda 21, taking into account their environmental and economic needs. Skills, knowledge and technical know-how at the individual and institutional levels are necessary for institution-building, policy analysis and development management, including the assessment of alternative courses of action with a view to enhancing access to and tranfer of technology and promoting economic development. Technical cooperation, including that related to technology transfer and know-how, encompasses the whole range of activities to develop or strengthen individual and group capacities and capabilities. It should serve the purpose of long-term capacity-building and needs to be managed and coordinated by the countries themselves. Technical cooperation, including that related to technology transfer and know-how, is effective only when it is derived from and related to a country's own strategies and priorities on environment and development and when development agencies and Governments define improved and consistent policies and procedures to support this process.

**Objectives**

37.3. The overall objectives of endogenous capacity-building in this programme area are to develop and improve national and related subregional and regional capacities and capabilities for sustainable development, with the involvement of the non-governmental sectors. The programme should assist by:

    a.   Promoting an ongoing participatory process to define country needs and priorities in promoting Agenda 21 and to give importance to technical and professional human resource development and development of institutional capacities and capabilities on the agenda of countries, with due recognition of the potential for optimum use of existing human resources as well as enhancement of the efficiency of existing institutions and non-governmental organizations, including scientific and technological institutions;

    b.   Reorienting technical cooperation and, in that process, setting new priorities in the field, including that related to transfer of technology and know-how processes, while giving due attention to the specific conditions and individual needs of recipients, and improving coordination among providers of assistance for support to countries' own programmes of action. This coordination should also include non-governmental organizations and scientific and technological institutions, as well as business and industry whenever appropriate;

c.  Shifting time horizons in programme planning and implementation for the development and strengthening of institutional structures to permit an enhancement of their ability to respond to new longer-term challenges rather than concentrating only on immediate problems;

d.  Improving and reorienting existing international multilateral institutions with responsibilities for environment and/or development matters to ensure that those institutions have the capability and capacity to integrate environment and development;

e.  Improving institutional capacity and capability, both public and private, in order to evaluate the environmental impact of all development projects.

37.4.  Specific objectives include the following:

a.  Each country should aim to complete, as soon as practicable, if possible by 1994, a review of capacity- and capability-building requirements for devising national sustainable development strategies, including those for generating and implementing its own Agenda 21 action programme;

b.  By 1997, the Secretary-General should submit to the General Assembly a report on the achievement of improved policies, coordination systems and procedures for strengthening the implementation of technical cooperation programmes for sustainable development, as well as on additional measures required to strengthen such cooperation. That report should be prepared on the basis of information provided by countries, international organizations, environment and development institutions, donor agencies and non-governmental partners.

**Activities**

a.  Building a national consensus and formulating capacity-building strategies for implementing Agenda 21

37.5.  As an important aspect of overall planning, each country should seek internal consensus at all levels of society on policies and programmes needed for short- and long-term capacity-building to implement its Agenda 21 programme. This consensus should result from a participatory dialogue of relevant interest groups and lead to an identification of skill gaps, institutional capacities and capabilities, technological and scientific requirements and resource needs to enhance environmental knowledge and administration to integrate environment and development. UNDP in partnership with relevant specialized agencies and other international intergovernmental and non-governmental organizations could assist, upon request of Governments, in the identification of the requirements for technical cooperation, including those related to technology transfer and know-how and development assistance for the implementation of Agenda 21. The national planning process together, where appropriate, with national sustainable development action plans or strategies should provide the framework for such cooperation and assistance. UNDP should use and further improve its network of field offices and its broad mandate to provide assistance, using its experience in the field of technical cooperation for facilitating capacity-building at the country and regional levels and making full use of the expertise of other bodies, in particular UNEP, the World Bank and regional commissions and development banks, as well as relevant international intergovernmental and non-governmental organizations.

b.  Identification of national sources and presentation of requests for technical cooperation, including that related to technology transfer and know-how in the framework of sector strategies

37.6.  Countries desiring arrangements for technical cooperation, including that related to transfer of technology and know-how, with international organizations and donor institutions should formulate requests in the framework of long-term sector or subsector capacity-building strategies. Strategies should, as appropriate, address policy adjustments to be implemented, budgetary issues, cooperation and coordination among institutions, human resource requirements, and technology and scientific equipment requirements. They should cover public and private sector needs and consider strengthening scientific training and educational and research programmes, including such training in the developed countries and the strengthening of centres of excellence in developing countries. Countries could designate and strengthen a central unit to organize and coordinate technical cooperation, linking it with the priority-setting and the resource allocation process.

c. Establishment of a review mechanism of technical cooperation in and related to technology transfer and know-how

37.7. Donors and recipients, the organizations and institutions of the United Nations system, and international public and private organizations should review the development of the cooperation process as it relates to technical cooperation, including that related to activities for the transfer of technology and know-how linked to sustainable development. To facilitate this process the Secretary-General could undertake, taking into account work carried out by UNDP and other organizations in preparation for the United Nations Conference on Environment and Development, consultations with developing countries, regional organizations, organizations and institutions of the United Nations system, including regional commissions, and multilateral and bilateral aid and environment agencies, with a view to further strengthening the endogenous capacities of countries and improving technical cooperation, including that related to the technology transfer and know-how process. The following aspects should be reviewed:

a. Evaluation of existing capacity and capability for the integrated management of environment and development, including technical, technological and institutional capacities and capabilities, and facilities to assess the environmental impact of development projects; and evaluation of abilities to respond to and link up with needs for technical cooperation, including that related to technology transfer and know-how, of Agenda 21 and the global conventions on climate change and biological diversity;

b. Assessment of the contribution of existing activities in technical cooperation, including that related to transfer of technology and know-how, towards strengthening and building national capacity and capability for integrated environment and development management and an assessment of the means of improving the quality of international technical cooperation, including that related to transfer of technolgy and know-how;

c. A strategy for shifting to a capacity- and capability-building thrust that recognizes the need for the operational integration of environment and development with longer-term commitments, having as a basis the set of national programmes established by each country, through a participatory process;

d. Consideration of greater use of long-term cooperative arrangements between municipalities, non-governmental organizations, universities, training and research centres and business, public and private institutions with counterparts in other countries or within countries or regions. Programmes such as the Sustainable Development Networks of UNDP should be assessed in this regard;

e. Strengthening of the sustainability of projects by including in the original project design consideration of environmental impacts, the costs of institution-building, human resource development and technology needs, as well as financial and organizational requirements for operation and maintenance;

f. Improvement of technical cooperation, including that related to transfer of technology and know-how and management processes, by giving greater attention to capacity- and capability-building as an integral part of sustainable development strategies for environment and development programmes both in country-related coordination processes, such as consultative groups and round tables, and in sectoral coordination mechanisms to enable developing countries to participate actively in obtaining assistance from different sources.

d.  Enhancement of the expertise and collective contribution of the United Nations system for capacity- and capability-building initiatives

37.8.  Organizations, organs, bodies and institutions of the United Nations system, together with other international and regional organizations and the public and private sectors, could, as appropriate, strengthen their joint activities in technical cooperation, including that related to transfer of technology and know-how, in order to address linked environment and development issues and to promote coherence and consistency of action. Organizations could assist and reinforce countries, particularly least developed countries, upon request, on matters relating to national environmental and developmental policies, human resource development and fielding of experts, legislation, natural resources and environmental data.

37.9.  UNDP, the World Bank and regional multilateral development banks, as part of their participation in national and regional coordination mechanisms, should assist in facilitating capacity- and capability-building at the country level, drawing upon the special expertise and operational capacity of UNEP in the environmental field as well as of the specialized agencies, organizations of the United Nations system and regional and subregional organizations in their respective areas of competence. For this purpose UNDP should mobilize funding for capacity- and capability-building, utilizing its network of field offices and its broad mandate and experience in the field of technical cooperation, including that related to transfer of technology and know-how. UNDP, together with these international organizations, should at the same time continue to develop consultative processes to enhance the mobilization and coordination of funds from the international community for capacity- and capability-building, including the establishment of an appropriate database. These responsibilities may need to be accompanied by strengthening of the capacities of UNDP.

37.10. The national entity in charge of technical cooperation, with the assistance of the UNDP resident representatives and the UNEP representatives, should establish a small group of key actors to steer the process, giving priority to the country's own strategies and priorities. The experience gained through existing planning exercises such as the national reports for the United Nations Conference on Environment and Development, national conservation strategies and environment action plans should be fully used and incorporated into a country-driven, participatory and sustainable development strategy. This should be complemented with information networks and consultations with donor organizations in order to improve coordination, as well as access to the existing body of scientific and technical knowledge and information available in institutions elsewhere.

e.  Harmonization of the delivery of assistance at the regional level

37.11. At the regional level, existing organizations should consider the desirability of improved regional and subregional consultative processes and round-table meetings to facilitate the exchange of data, information and experience in the implementation of Agenda 21. UNDP, building on the results of the regional surveys on capacity-building that those regional organizations carried out on the United Nations Conference on Environment and Development initiative, and in collaboration with existing regional, subregional or national organizations with potential for regional coordination, should provide a significant input for this purpose. The relevant national unit should establish a steering mechanism. A periodic review mechanism should be established among the countries of the region with the assistance of the appropriate relevant regional organizations and the participation of development banks, bilateral aid agencies and non-governmental organizations. Other possibilities are to develop national and regional research and training facilities building on existing regional and subregional institutions.

**Means of implementation**

Financing and cost evaluation

37.12. The cost of bilateral expenditures to developing countries for technical cooperation, including that related to transfer of technology and know-how, is about $15 billion or about 25 per cent of total official development assistance. The implementation of Agenda 21 will require a more effective use of these funds and additional funding in key areas.

37.13. The Conference secretariat has estimated the average total annual cost (1993-2000) of implementing the activities of this chapter to be between $300 million and $1 billion from the international community on grant or concessional terms. These are indicative and order-of-magnitude estimates only and have not been reviewed by Governments. Actual costs and financial terms, including any that are non-concessional, will depend upon, inter alia, the specific strategies and programmes Governments decide upon for implementation.

# Agenda 21 – Chapter 38
## INTERNATIONAL INSTITUTIONAL ARRANGEMENTS

**BASIS FOR ACTION**

38.1. The mandate of the United Nations Conference on Environment and Development emanates from General Assembly resolution 44/228, in which the Assembly, inter alia, affirmed that the Conference should elaborate strategies and measures to halt and reverse the effects of environmental degradation in the context of increased national and international efforts to promote sustainable and environmentally sound development in all countries and that the promotion of economic growth in developing countries is essential to address problems of environmental degradation. The intergovernmental follow-up to the Conference process shall be within the framework of the United Nations system, with the General Assembly being the supreme policy-making forum that would provide overall guidance to Governments, the United Nations system and relevant treaty bodies. At the same time, Governments, as well as regional economic and technical cooperation organizations, have a responsibility to play an important role in the follow-up to the Conference. Their commitments and actions should be adequately supported by the United Nations system and multilateral financial institutions. Thus, national and international efforts would mutually benefit from one another.

38.2. In fulfilling the mandate of the Conference, there is a need for institutional arrangements within the United Nations system in conformity with, and providing input into, the restructuring and revitalization of the United Nations in the economic, social and related fields, and the overall reform of the United Nations, including ongoing changes in the Secretariat. In the spirit of reform and revitalization of the United Nations system, implementation of Agenda 21 and other conclusions of the Conference shall be based on an action- and result-oriented approach and consistent wit h the principles of universality, democracy, transparency, cost-effectiveness and accountability.

38.3. The United Nations system, with its multisectoral capacity and the extensive experience of a number of specialized agencies in various spheres of international cooperation in the field of environment and development, is uniquely positioned to assist Governments to establish more effective patterns of economic and social development with a view to achieving the objectives of Agenda 21 and sustainable development.

38.4. All agencies of the United Nations system have a key role to play in the implementation of Agenda 21 within their respective competence. To ensure proper coordination and avoid duplication in the implementation of Agenda 21, there should be an effective division of labour between various parts of the United Nations system based on their terms of reference and comparative advantages. Member States, through relevant governing bodies, are in a position to ensure that these tasks are carried out properly. In order to facilitate evaluation of agencies' performance and promote knowledge of their activities, all bodies of the United Nations system should be required to elaborate and publish reports of their activities concerning the implementation of Agenda 21 on a regular basis. Serious and continuous reviews of their policies, programmes, budgets and activities will also be required.

38.5. The continued active and effective participation of non-governmental organizations, the scientific community and the private sector, as well as local groups and communities, are important in the implementation of Agenda 21.

38.6. The institutional structure envisaged below will be based on agreement on financial resources and mechanisms, technology transfer, the Rio Declaration and Agenda 21. In addition, there has to be an effective link between substantive action and financial support, and this requires close and effective cooperation and exchange of information between the United Nations system and the multilateral financial institutions for the follow-up of Agenda 21 within the institutional arrangement.

**OBJECTIVES**

38.7. The overall objective is the integration of environment and development issues at national, subregional, regional and international levels, including in the United Nations system institutional arrangements.

38.8. Specific objectives shall be:

    a. To ensure and review the implementation of Agenda 21 so as to achieve sustainable development in all countries;

    b. To enhance the role and functioning of the United Nations system in the field of environment and development. All relevant agencies, organizations and programmes of the United Nations system should adopt concrete programmes for the implementation of Agenda 21 and also provide policy guidance for United Nations activities or advice to Governments, upon request, within their areas of competence;

    c. To strengthen cooperation and coordination on environment and development in the United Nations system;

    d. To encourage interaction and cooperation between the United Nations system and other intergovernmental and non-governmental subregional, regional and global institutions and non-governmental organizations in the field of environment and development;

    e. To strengthen institutional capabilities and arrangements required for the effective implementation, follow-up and review of Agenda 21;

    f. To assist in the strengthening and coordination of national, subregional and regional capacities and actions in the areas of environment and development;

    g. To establish effective cooperation and exchange of information between United Nations organs, organizations, programmes and the multilateral financial bodies, within the institutional arrangements for the follow-up of Agenda 21;

    h. To respond to continuing and emerging issues relating to environment and development;

    i. To ensure that any new institutional arrangements would support revitalization, clear division of responsibilities and the avoidance of duplication in the United Nations system and depend to the maximum extent possible upon existing resources.

## INSTITUTIONAL STRUCTURE

### A. General Assembly

38.9. The General Assembly, as the highest intergovernmental mechanism, is the principal policy-making and appraisal organ on matters relating to the follow-up of the Conference. The Assembly would organize a regular review of the implementation of Agenda 21. In fulfilling this task, the Assembly could consider the timing, format and organizational aspects of such a review. In particular, the Assembly could consider holding a special session not later than 1997 for the overall review and appraisal of Agenda 21, with adequate preparations at a high level.

### B. Economic and Social Council

38.10. The Economic and Social Council, in the context of its role under the Charter vis-a-vis the General Assembly and the ongoing restructuring and revitalization of the United Nations in the economic, social and related fields, would assist the General Assembly by overseeing system-wide coordination in the implementation of Agenda 21 and making recommendations in this regard. In addition, the Council would undertake the task of directing system-wide coordination and integration of environmental and developmental aspects of United Nations policies and programmes and would make appropriate recommendations to the General Assembly, specialized agencies concerned and Member States. Appropriate steps should be taken to obtain regular reports from specialized agencies on their plans and programmes related to the implementation of Agenda 21, pursuant to Article 64 of the Charter of the United Nations. The Economic and Social Council should organize a periodic review of the work of the Commission on Sustainable Development envisaged in paragraph 38.11, as well as of system-wide activities to integrate environment and development, making full use of its high-level and coordination segments.

## C. Commission on Sustainable Development

38.11. In order to ensure the effective follow-up of the Conference, as well as to enhance international cooperation and rationalize the intergovernmental decision-making capacity for the integration of environment and development issues and to examine the progress in the implementation of Agenda 21 at the national, regional and international levels, a high-level Commission on Sustainable Development should be established in accordance with Article 68 of the Charter of the United Nations. This Commission would report to the Economic and Social Council in the context of the Council's role under the Charter vis--vis the General Assembly. It would consist of representatives of States elected as members with due regard to equitable geographical distribution. Representatives of non-member States of the Commission would have observer status. The Commission should provide for the active involvement of organs, programmes and organizations of the United Nations system, international financial institutions and other relevant intergovernmental organizations, and encourage the participation of non-governmental organizations, including industry and the business and scientific communities. The first meeting of the Commission should be convened no later than 1993. The Commission should be supported by the secretariat envisaged in paragraph 38.19. Meanwhile the Secretary-General of the United Nations is requested to ensure adequate interim administrative secretariat arrangements.

38.12. The General Assembly, at its forty-seventh session, should determine specific organizational modalities for the work of this Commission, such as its membership, its relationship with other intergovernmental United Nations bodies dealing with matters related to environment and development, and the frequency, duration and venue of its meetings. These modalities should take into account the ongoing process of revitalization and restructuring of the work of the United Nations in the economic, social and related fields, in particular measures recommended by the General Assembly in resolutions 45/264 of 13 May 1991 and 46/235 of 13 April 1992 and other relevant Assembly resolutions. In this respect, the Secretary-General of the United Nations, with the assistance of the Secretary -General of the United Nations Conference on Environment and Development, is requested to prepare for the Assembly a report with appropriate recommendations and proposals.

38.13.  The Commission on Sustainable Development should have the following functions:

a. To monitor progress in the implementation of Agenda 21 and activities related to the integration of environmental and developmental goals throughout the United Nations system through analysis and evaluation of reports from all relevant organs, organizations, programmes and institutions of the United Nations system dealing with various issues of environment and development, including those related to finance;

b. To consider information provided by Governments, including, for example, information in the form of periodic communications or national reports regarding the activities they undertake to implement Agenda 21, the problems they face, such as problems related to financial resources and technology transfer, and other environment and development issues they find relevant;

c. To review the progress in the implementation of the commitments contained in Agenda 21, including those related to provision of financial resources and transfer of technology;

d. To receive and analyse relevant input from competent non-governmental organizations, including the scientific and private sectors, in the context of the overall implementation of Agenda 21;

e. To enhance the dialogue, within the framework of the United Nations, with non-governmental organizations and the independent sector, as well as other entities outside the United Nations system;

f. To consider, where appropriate, information regarding the progress made in the implementation of environmental conventions, which could be made available by the relevant Conferences of Parties;

g. To provide appropriate recommendations to the General Assembly through the Economic and Social Council on the basis of an integrated consideration of the reports and issues related to the implementation of Agenda 21;

h. To consider, at an appropriate time, the results of the review to be conducted expeditiously by the Secretary-General of all recommendations of the Conference for capacity-building programmes, information networks, task forces and other mechanisms to support the integration of environment and development at regional and subregional levels.

38.14. Within the intergovernmental framework, consideration should be given to allowing non-governmental organizations, including those related to major groups, particularly women's groups, committed to the implementation of Agenda 21 to have relevant information available to them, including information, reports and other data produced within the United Nations system.

## D. The Secretary-General

38.15. Strong and effective leadership on the part of the Secretary-General is crucial, since he/she would be the focal point of the institutional arrangements within the United Nations system for the successful follow-up to the Conference and for the implementation of Agenda 21.

## E. High-level inter-agency coordination mechanism

38.16. Agenda 21, as the basis for action by the international community to integrate environment and development, should provide the principal framework for coordination of relevant activities within the United Nations system. To ensure effective monitoring, coordination and supervision of the involvement of the United Nations system in the follow-up to the Conference, there is a need for a coordination mechanism under the direct leadership of the Secretary-General.

38.17. This task should be given to the Administrative Committee on Coordination (ACC), headed by the Secretary-General. ACC would thus provide a vital link and interface between the multilateral financial institutions and other United Nations bodies at the highest administrative level. The Secretary-General should continue to revitalize the functioning of the Committee. All heads of agencies and institutions of the United Nations system shall be expected to cooperate with the Secretary-General fully in order to make ACC work effectively in fulfilling its crucial role and ensure successful implementation of Agenda 21. ACC should consider establishing a special task force, subcommittee or sustainable development board, taking into account the experience of the Designated Officials for Environmental Matters (DOEM) and the Committee of International Development Institutions on Environment (CIDIE), as well as the respective roles of UNEP and UNDP. Its report should be submitted to the relevant intergovernmental bodies.

## F. High-level advisory body

38.18. Intergovernmental bodies, the Secretary-General and the United Nations system as a whole may also benefit from the expertise of a high-level advisory board consisting of eminent persons knowledgeable about environment and development, including relevant sciences, appointed by the Secretary-General in their personal capacity. In this regard, the Secretary-General should make appropriate recommendations to the General Assembly at its forty-seventh session.

## G. Secretariat support structure

38.19. A highly qualified and competent secretariat support structure within the United Nations Secretariat, drawing, inter alia, on the expertise gained in the Conference preparatory process is essential for the follow-up to the Conference and the implementation of Agenda 21. This secretariat support structure should provide support to the work of both intergovernmental and inter-agency coordination mechanisms. Concrete organizational decisions fall within the competence of t he Secretary-General as the chief administrative officer of the Organization, who is requested to report on the provisions to be made, covering staffing implications, as soon as practicable, taking into account gender balance as defined in Article 8 of the Charter of the United Nations and the need for the best use of existing resources in the context of the current and ongoing restructuring of the United Nations Secretariat.

## H. Organs, programmes and organizations of the United Nations system

38.20. In the follow-up to the Conference, in particular the implementation of Agenda 21, all relevant organs, programmes and organizations of the United Nations system will have an important role within their respective areas of expertise and mandates in supporting and supplementing national efforts. Coordination and mutual complementarity of their efforts to promote integration of environment and development can be enhanced by encouraging countries to maintain consistent positions in the various governing bodies.

1.   United Nations Environment Programme

38.21. In the follow-up to the Conference, there will be a need for an enhanced and strengthened role for UNEP and its Governing Council. The Governing Council should, within its mandate, continue to play its role with regard to policy guidance and coordination in the field of the environment, taking into account the development perspective.

38.22.   Priority areas on which UNEP should concentrate include the following:

  a.   Strengthening its catalytic role in stimulating and promoting environmental activities and considerations throughout the United Nations system;

  b.   Promoting international cooperation in the field of environment and recommending, as appropriate, policies to this end;

  c.   Developing and promoting the use of such techniques as natural resource accounting and environmental economics;

  d.   Environmental monitoring and assessment, both through improved participation by the United Nations system agencies in the Earthwatch programme and expanded relations with private scientific and non-governmental research institutes; strengthening and making operational its early-warning function;

  e.   Coordination and promotion of relevant scientific research with a view to providing a consolidated basis for decision-making;

f. Dissemination of environmental information and data to Governments and to organs, programmes and organizations of the United Nations system;

g. Raising general awareness and action in the area of environmental protection through collaboration with the general public, non-governmental entities and intergovernmental institutions;

h. Further development of international environmental law, in particular conventions and guidelines, promotion of its implementation, and coordinating functions arising from an increasing number of international legal agreements, inter alia, the functioning of the secretariats of the Conventions, taking into account the need for the most efficient use of resources, including possible co-location of secretariats established in the future;

i. Further development and promotion of the widest possible use of environmental impact assessments, including activities carried out under the auspices of specialized agencies of the United Nations system, and in connection with every significant economic development project or activity;

j. Facilitation of information exchange on environmentally sound technologies, including legal aspects, and provision of training;

k. Promotion of subregional and regional cooperation and support to relevant initiatives and programmes for environmental protection, including playing a major contributing and coordinating role in the regional mechanisms in the field of environment identified for the follow-up to the Conference;

l. Provision of technical, legal and institutional advice to Governments, upon request, in establishing and enhancing their national legal and institutional frameworks, in particular, in cooperation with UNDP capacity-building efforts;

m. Support to Governments, upon request, and development agencies and organs in the integration of environmental aspects into their development policies and programmes, in particular through provision of environmental, technical and policy advice during programme formulation and implementation;

n. Further developing assessment and assistance in cases of environmental emergencies.

38.23. In order to perform all of these functions, while retaining its role as the principal body within the United Nations system in the field of environment and taking into account the development aspects of environmental questions, UNEP would require access to greater expertise and provision of adequate financial resources and it would require closer cooperation and collaboration with development organs and other relevant organs of the United Nations system. Furthermore, the regional offices of UNEP should be strengthened without weakening its headquarters in Nairobi, and UNEP should take steps to reinforce and intensify its liaison and interaction with UNDP and the World Bank.

2. United Nations Development Programme

38.24. UNDP, like UNEP, also has a crucial role in the follow-up to the United Nations Conference on Environment and Development. Through its network of field offices it would foster the United Nations system's collective thrust in support of the implementation of Agenda 21, at the country, regional, interregional and global levels, drawing on the expertise of the specialized agencies and other United Nations organizations and bodies involved in operational activities. The role of the resident representative/resident coordinator of UNDP needs to be strengthened in order to coordinate the field-level activities of the United Nations operational activities.

38.25. Its role should include the following:

a. Acting as the lead agency in organizing United Nations system efforts towards capacity-building at the local, national and regional levels;

b. Mobilizing donor resources on behalf of Governments for capacity-building in recipient countries and, where appropriate, through the use of the UNDP donor round-table mechanisms;

c. Strengthening its own programmes in support of follow-up to the Conference without prejudice to the fifth programming cycle;

d. Assisting recipient countries, upon request, in the establishment and strengthening of national coordination mechanisms and networks related to activities for the follow-up to the Conference;

e. Assisting recipient countries, upon request, in coordinating the mobilization of domestic financial resources;

f. Promoting and strengthening the role and involvement of women, youth and other major groups in recipient countries in t he implementation of Agenda 21.

3. United Nations Conference on Trade and Development

38.26. UNCTAD should play an important role in the implementation of Agenda 21 as extended at its eighth session, taking into account the importance of the interrelationships between development, international trade and the environment and in accordance with its mandate in the area of sustainable development.

4. United Nations Sudano-Sahelian Office

38.27. The role of the United Nations Sudano-Sahelian Office (UNSO), with added resources that may become available, operating under the umbrella of UNDP and with the support of UNEP, should be strengthened so that it can assume an appropriate major advisory role and participate effectively in the implementation of Agenda 21 provisions related to combating drought and desertification and to land resource management. In this context, the experience gained could be used by all other countries affected by drought and desertification, in particular those in Africa, with special attention to countries most affected or classified as least developed countries.

5. Specialized agencies of the United Nations system and related organizations and other relevant intergovernmental organizations

38.28. All specialized agencies of the United Nations system, related organizations and other relevant intergovernmental organizations within their respective fields of competence have an important role to play in the implementation of relevant parts of Agenda 21 and other decisions of the Conference. Their governing bodies may consider ways of strengthening and adjusting activities and programmes in line with Agenda 21, in particular, regarding projects for promoting sustainable development. Furthermore, they may consider establishing special arrangements with donors and financial institutions for project implementation that may require additional resources.

**I. Regional and subregional cooperation and implementation**

38.29. Regional and subregional cooperation will be an important part of the outcome of the Conference. The regional commissions, regional development banks and regional economic and technical cooperation organizations, within their respective agreed mandates, can contribute to this process by:

a. Promoting regional and subregional capacity-building;

b. Promoting the integrat ion of environmental concerns in regional and subregional development policies;

c. Promoting regional and subregional cooperation, where appropriate, regarding transboundary issues related to sustainable development.

38.30. The regional commissions, as appropriate, should play a leading role in coordinating regional and subregional activities by sectoral and other United Nations bodies and shall assist countries in achieving sustainable development. The commissions and regional programmes within the United Nations system, as well as other regional organizations, should review the need for modification of ongoing activities, as appropriate, in light of Agenda 21.

38.31. There must be active cooperation and collaboration among the regional commissions and other relevant organizations, regional development banks, non-governmental organizations and other institutions at the regional level. UNEP and UNDP, together with the regional commissions, would have a crucial role to play, especially in providing the necessary assistance, with particular emphasis on building and strengthening the national capacity of Member States.

38.32. There is a need for closer cooperation between UNEP and UNDP, together with other relevant institutions, in the implementation of projects to halt environmental degradation or its impact and to support training programmes in environmental planning and management for sustainable development at the regional level.

38.33. Regional intergovernmental technical and economic organizations have an important role to play in helping Governments to take coordinated action in solving environment issues of regional significance.

38.34. Regional and subregional organizations should play a major role in the implementation of the provisions of Agenda 21 related to combating drought and desertification. UNEP, UNDP and UNSO should assist and cooperate with those relevant organizations.

38.35. Cooperation between regional and subregional organizations and relevant organizations of the United Nations system should be encouraged, where appropriate, in other sectoral areas.

## J. National implementation

38.36. States have an important role to play in the follow-up of the Conference and the implementation of Agenda 21. National level efforts should be undertaken by all countries in an integrated manner so that both environment and development concerns can be dealt with in a coherent manner.

38.37. Policy decisions and activities at the national level, tailored to support and implement Agenda 21, should be supported by the United Nations system upon request.

38.38. Furthermore, States could consider the preparation of national reports. In this context, the organs of the United Nations system should, upon request, assist countries, in particular developing countries. Countries could also consider the preparation of national action plans for the implementation of Agenda 21.

38.39. Existing assistance consortia, consultative groups and round tables should make greater efforts to integrate environmental considerations and related development objectives into their development assistance strategies and should consider reorienting and appropriately adjusting their memberships and operations to facilitate this process and better support national efforts to integrate environment and development.

38.40. States may wish to consider setting up a national coordination structure responsible for the follow-up of Agenda 21. Within this structure, which would benefit from the expertise of non-governmental organizations, submissions and other relevant information could be made to the United Nations.

## K. Cooperation between United Nations bodies and international financial organizations

38.41. The success of the follow-up to the Conference is dependent upon an effective link between substantive action and financial support, and this requires close and effective cooperation between United Nations bodies and the multilateral financial organizations. The Secretary-General and heads of United Nations programmes, organizations and the multilateral financial organizations have a special responsibility in forging such cooperation, not only through the United Nations high-level coordination mechanism (Administrative Committee on Coordination) but also at regional and national levels. In particular, representatives of multilateral financial institutions and mechanisms, as well as IFAD, should actively be associated with deliberations of the intergovernmental structure responsible for the follow-up to Agenda 21.

## L. Non-governmental organizations

38.42. Non-governmental organizations and major groups are important partners in the implementation of Agenda 21. Relevant non-governmental organizations, including the scientific community, the private sector and women's groups, should be given opportunities to make their contributions and establish appropriate relationships with the United Nations system. Support should be provided for developing countries' non-governmental organizations and their self-organized networks.

38.43. The United Nations system, including international finance and development agencies, and all intergovernment al organizations and forums should, in consultation with non-governmental organizations, take measures to:

    a. Design open and effective means to achieve the participation of non-governmental organizations, including those related to major groups, in the process established to review and evaluate the implementation of Agenda 21 at all levels and promote their contribution to it;

    b. Take into account the findings of review systems and evaluation processes of non-governmental organizations in relevant reports of the Secretary-General to the General Assembly and all pertinent United Nations agencies and intergovernmental organizations and forums concerning implementation of Agenda 21 in accordance with the review process.

38.44. Procedures should be established for an exp anded role for non-governmental organizations, including those related to major groups, with accreditation based on the procedures used in the Conference. Such organizations should have access to reports and other information produced by the United Nations system. The General Assembly, at an early stage, should examine ways of enhancing the involvement of non-governmental organizations within the United Nations system in relation to the follow-up process of the Conference.

38.45. The Conference takes note of other institutional initiatives for the implementation of Agenda 21, such as the proposal to establish a non-governmental Earth Council and the proposal to appoint a guardian for future generations, as well as other initiatives taken by local governments and business sectors.

# INTERNATIONAL LEGAL INSTRUMENTS AND MECHANISMS

**Basis for action**

39.1.  The recognition that the following vital aspects of the universal, multilateral and bilateral treaty-making process should be taken into account:

a.  The further development of international law on sustainable development, giving special attention to the delicate balance between environmental and developmental concerns;

b.  The need to clarify and strengthen the relationship between existing international instruments or agreements in the field of environment and relevant social and economic agreements or instruments, taking into account the special needs of developing countries;

c.  At the global level, the essential importance of the participation in and the contribution of all countries, including the developing countries, to treaty making in the field of international law on sustainable development. Many of the existing international legal instruments and agreements in the field of environment have been developed without adequate participation and contribution of developing countries, and thus may require review in order to reflect the concerns and interests of developing countries and to ensure a balanced governance of such instruments and agreements;

d.  Developing countries should also be provided with technical assistance in their attempts to enhance their national legislative capabilities in the field of environmental law;

e.  Future projects for the progressive development and codification of internat ional law on sustainable development should take into account the ongoing work of the International Law Commission;

f.  Any negotiations for the progressive development and codification of international law concerning sustainable development should, in general, be conducted on a universal basis, taking into account special circumstances in the various regions.

**Objectives**

39.2.  The overall objective of the review and development of international environmental law should be to evaluate and to promote the efficacy of that law and to promote the integration of environment and development policies through effective international agreements or instruments taking into account both universal principles and the particular and differentiated needs and concerns of all countries.

39.3.  Specific objectives are:

a.  To identify and address difficulties which prevent some States, in particular developing countries, from participating in or duly implementing international agreements or instruments and, where appropriate, to review and revise them with the purposes of integrating environmental and developmental concerns and laying down a sound basis for the implementation of these agreements or instruments;

b.  To set priorities for future law-making on sustainable development at the global, regional or subregional level, with a view to enhancing the efficacy of international law in this field through, in particular, the integration of environmental and developmental concerns;

c.  To promote and support the effective participation of all countries concerned, in particular developing countries, in the negotiation, implementation, review and governance of international agreements or instruments, including appropriate provision of technical and financial assistance and other available mechanisms for this purpose, as well as the use of differential obligations where appropriate;

d. To promote, through the gradual development of universally and multilaterally negotiated agreements or instruments, international standards for the protection of the environment that take into account the different situations and capabilities of countries. States recognize that environmental policies should deal with the root causes of environmental degradation, thus preventing environmental measures from resulting in unnecessary restrictions to trade. Trade policy measures for environmental purposes should not constitute a means of arbitrary or unjustifiable discrimination or a disguised restriction on international trade. Unilateral actions to deal with environmental challenges outside the jurisdiction of the importing country should be avoided. Environmental measures addressing international environmental problems should, as far as possible, be based on an international consensus. Domestic measures targeted to achieve certain environmental objectives may need trade measures to render them effective. Should trade policy measures be found necessary for the enforcement of environmental policies, certain principles and rules should apply. These could include, inter alia, the principle of non-discrimination; the principle that the trade measure chosen should be the least trade-restrictive necessary to achieve the objectives; an obligation to ensure transparency in the use of trade measures related to the environment and to provide adequate notification of national regulations; and the need to give consideration to the special conditions and development requirements of developing countries as they move towards internationally agreed environmental objectives;

e. To ensure the effective, full and prompt implementation of legally binding instruments and to facilitate timely review and adjustment of agreements or instruments by the parties concerned, taking into account the special needs and concerns of all countries, in particular developing countries;

f. To improve the effectiveness of institutions, mechanisms and procedures for the administration of agreements and instruments;

g. To identify and prevent actual or potential conflicts, particularly between environmental and social/economic agreements or instruments, with a view to ensuring that such agreements or instruments are consistent. Where conflicts arise they should be appropriately resolved;

h. To study and consider the broadening and strengthening of the capacity of mechanisms, inter alia, in the United Nations system, to facilitate, where appropriate and agreed to by the parties concerned, the identification, avoidance and settlement of international disputes in the field of sustainable development, duly taking into account existing bilateral and multilateral agreements for the settlement of such disputes.

## Activities

39.4. Activities and means of implementation should be considered in the light of the above basis for action and objectives, without prejudice to the right of every State to put forward suggestions in this regard in the General Assembly. These suggestions could be reproduced in a separate compilation on sustainable development.

### A. Review, assessment and fields of action in international law for sustainable development

39.5. While ensuring the effective participation of all countries concerned, Parties should at periodic intervals review and assess both the past performance and effectiveness of existing international agreements or instruments as well as the priorities for future law making on sustainable development. This may include an examination of the feasibility of elaborating general rights and obligations of States, as appropriate, in the field of sustainable development, as provided by General Assembly resolution 44/228. In certain cases, attention should be given to the possibility of taking into account varying circumstances through differential obligations or gradual application. As an option for carrying out this task, earlier UNEP practice may be followed whereby legal experts designated by

Governments could meet at suitable intervals, to be decided later, with a broader environmental and developmental perspective.

39.6. Measures in accordance with international law should be considered to address, in times of armed conflict, large-scale destruction of the environment that cannot be justified under international law. The General Assembly and its Sixth Committee are the appropriate forums to deal with this subject. The specific competence and role of the International Committee of the Red Cross should be taken into account.

39.7. In view of the vital necessity of ensuring safe and environmentally sound nuclear power, and in order to strengthen international cooperation in this field, efforts should be made to conclude the ongoing negotiations for a nuclear safety convention in the framework of the International Atomic Energy Agency.

**B. Implementation mechanisms**

39.8. The parties to international agreements should consider procedures and mechanisms to promote and review their effective, full and prompt implementation. To that effect, States could, inter alia:

       a.   Establish efficient and practical reporting systems on the effective, full and prompt implementation of international legal instruments;

       b.   Consider appropriate ways in which relevant international bodies, such as UNEP, might contribute towards the further development of such mechanisms.

**C. Effective participation in international law making**

39.9. In all these activities and others that may be pursued in the future, based on the above basis for action and objectives, the effective participation of all countries, in particular developing countries, should be ensured through appropriate provision of technical assistance and/or financial assistance. Developing countries should be given "headstart" support not only in their national efforts to implement international agreements or instruments, but also to participate effectively in the negotiation of new or revised agreements or instruments and in the actual international operation of such agreements or instruments. Support should include assistance in building up expertise in international law particularly in relation to sustainable development, and in assuring access to the necessary reference information and scientific/technical expertise.

**D. Disputes in the field of sustainable development**

39.10. In the area of avoidance and settlement of disputes, States should further study and consider methods to broaden and make more effective the range of techniques available at present, taking into account, among others, relevant experience under existing international agreements, instruments or institutions and, where appropriate, their implementing mechanisms such as modalities for dispute avoidance and settlement. This may include mechanisms and procedures for the exchange of data and information, notification and consultation regarding situations that might lead to disputes with other States in the field of sustainable development and for effective peaceful means of dispute settlement in accordance with the Charter of the United Nations, including, where appropriate, recourse to the International Court of Justice, and their inclusion in treaties relating to sustainable development.

# Agenda 21 – Chapter 40
## INFORMATION FOR DECISION-MAKING

40.1. In sustainable development, everyone is a user and provider of information considered in the broad sense. That includes data, information, appropriately packaged experience and knowledge. The need for information arises at all levels, from that of senior decision makers at the national and international levels to the grass-roots and individual levels. The following two programme areas need to be implemented to ensure that decisions are based increasingly on sound information:

    a. Bridging the data gap;

    b. Improving information availability.

### PROGRAMME AREAS

## A. Bridging the data gap

Basis for action

40.2. While considerable data already exist, as the various sectoral chapters of Agenda 21 indicate, more and different types of data need to be collected, at the local, provincial, national and international levels, indicating the status and trends of the planet's ecosystem, natural resource, pollution and socio-economic variables. The gap in the availability, quality, coherence, standardization and accessibility of data between the developed and the developing world has been increasing, seriously impairing the capacities of countries to make informed decisions concerning environment and development.

40.3. There is a general lack of capacity, particularly in developing countries, and in many areas at the international level, for the collection and assessment of data, for their transformation into useful information and for their dissemination. There is also need for improved coordination among environmental, demographic, social and developmental data and information activities.

40.4. Commonly used indicators such as the gross national product (GNP) and measurements of individual resource or pollution flows do not provide adequate indications of sustainability. Methods for assessing interactions between different sectoral environmental, demographic, social and developmental parameters are not sufficiently developed or applied. Indicators of sustainable development need to be developed to provide solid bases for decision-making at all levels and to contribute to a self-regulating sustainability of integrated environment and development systems.

## Objectives

40.5. The following objectives are important:

    a. To achieve more cost-effective and relevant data collection and assessment by better identification of users, in both the public and private sectors, and of their information needs at the local, provincial, national and international levels;

    b. To strengthen local, provincial, national and international capacity to collect and use multisectoral information in decision-making processes and to enhance capacities to collect and analyse data and information for decision-making, particularly in developing countries;

    c. To develop or strengthen local, provincial, national and international means of ensuring that planning for sustainable development in all sectors is based on timely, reliable and usable information;

    d. To make relevant information accessible in the form and at the time required to facilitate its use. Activities

a. Development of indicators of sustainable development

40.6. Countries at the national level and international governmental and non-governmental organizations at the international level should develop the concept of indicators of sustainable development in order to identify such indicators. In order to promote the increasing use of some of those indicators in satellite accounts, and eventually in national accounts, the development of indicators needs to be pursued by the Statistical Office of the United Nations Secretariat, as it draws upon evolving experience in this regard.

b. Promotion of global use of indicators of sustainable development

40.7. Relevant organs and organizations of the United Nations system, in cooperation with other international governmental, intergovernmental and non-governmental organizations, should use a suitable set of sustainable development indicators and indicators related to areas outside of national jurisdiction, such as the high seas, the upper atmosphere and outer space. The organs and organizations of the United Nations system, in coordination with other relevant international organizations, could provide recommendations for harmonized development of indicators at the national, regional and global levels, and for incorporation of a suitable set of these indicators in common, regularly updated, and widely accessible reports and databases, for use at the international level, subject to national sovereignty considerations.

c. Improvement of data collection and use

40.8. Countries and, upon request, international organizations should carry out inventories of environmental, resource and developmental data, based on national/global priorities for the management of sustainable development. They should determine the gaps and organize activities to fill those gaps. Within the organs and organizations of the United Nations system and relevant international organizations, data-collection activities, including those of Earthwatch and World Weather Watch, need to be strengthened, especially in the areas of urban air, freshwater, land resources (including forests and rangelands), desertification, other habitats, soil degradation, biodiversity, the high seas and the upper atmosphere. Countries and international organizations should make use of new techniques of data collection, including satellite-based remote sensing. In addition to the strengthening of existing development-related data collection, special attention needs to be paid to such areas as demographic factors, urbanization, poverty, health and rights of access to resources, as well as special groups, including women, indigenous peoples, youth, children and the disabled, and their relationships with environment issues.

d. Improvement of methods of data assessment and analysis

40.9. Relevant international organizations should develop practical recommendations for coordinated, harmonized collection and assessment of data at the national and international levels. National and international data and information centres should set up continuous and accurate data-collection systems and make use of geographic information systems, expert systems, models and a variety of other techniques for the assessment and analysis of data. These steps will be particularly relevant, as large quantities of data from satellite sources will need to be processed in the future. Developed countries and international organizations, as well as the private sector, should cooperate, in particular with developing countries, upon request, to facilitate their acquiring these technologies and this know-how.

e. Establishment of a comprehensive information framework

40.10. Governments should consider undertaking the necessary institutional changes at the national level to achieve the integration of environmental and developmental information. At the international level, environmental assessment activities need to be strengthened and coordinated with efforts to assess development trends.

f.    Strengthening of the capacity for traditional information

40.11.    Countries, with the cooperation of international organizations, should establish supporting mechanisms to provide local communities and resource users with the information and know-how they need to manage their environment and resources sustainably, applying traditional and indigenous knowledge and approaches when appropriate. This is particularly relevant for rural and urban populations and indigenous, women's and youth groups.

**Means of implementation**

a.    Financing and cost evaluation

40.12.    The secretariat of the Conference has estimated the average total annual cost (1993-2000) of implementing the activities of this programme to be about $1.9 billion from the international community on grant or concessional terms. These are indicative and order-of-magnitude estimates only and have not been reviewed by Governments. Actual costs and financial terms, including any that are non-concessional, will depend upon, inter alia, the specific strategies and programmes Governments decide upon for implementation.

b.    (b) Institutional means

40.13.    Institutional capacity to integrate environment and development and to develop relevant indicators is lacking at both the national and international levels. Existing institutions and programmes such as the Global Environmental Monitoring System (GEMS) and the Global Resource Information Database (GRID) within UNEP and different entities within the systemwide Earthwatch will need to be considerably strengthened. Earthwatch has been an essential element for environment -related data. While programmes related to development data exist in a number of agencies, there is insufficient coordination between them. The activities related to development data of agencies and institutions of the United Nations system should be more effectively coordinated, perhaps through an equivalent and complementary "Development Watch", which with the existing Earthwatch should be coordinated through an appropriate office within the United Nations to ensure the full integration of environment and development concerns.

c.    Scientific and technological means

d.

40.14.    Regarding transfer of technology, with the rapid evolution of data-collection and information technologies it is necessary to develop guidelines and mechanisms for the rapid and continuous transfer of those technologies, particularly to developing countries, in conformity with chapter 34 (Transfer of environmentally sound technology, cooperation and capacity-building), and for the training of personnel in their utilization.

e.    Human resource development

40.15.    International cooperation for training in all areas and at all levels will be required, particularly in developing countries. That training will have to include technical training of those involved in data collection, assessment and transformation, as well as assistance to decision makers concerning how to use such information.

f.    Capacity-building

40.16.    All countries, particularly developing countries, with the support of international cooperation, should strengthen their capacity to collect, store, organize, assess and use data in decision-making more effectively.

## B. Improving availability of information

Basis for action

40.17.   There already exists a wealth of data and information that could be used for the management of sustainable development. Finding the appropriate information at the required time and at the relevant scale of aggregation is a difficult task.

40.18.   Information within many countries is not adequately managed, because of shortages of financial resources and trained manpower, lack of awareness of the value and availability of such information and other immediate or pressing problems, especially in developing countries. Even where information is available, it may not be easily accessible, either because of the lack of technology for effective access or because of associated costs, especially for information held outside the country and available commercially.

## Objectives

40.19.   Existing national and international mechanisms of information processing and exchange, and of related technical assistance, should be strengthened to ensure effective and equitable availability of information generated at the local, provincial, national and international levels, subject to national sovereignty and relevant intellectual property rights.

40.20.   National capacities should be strengthened, as should capacities within Governments, non-governmental organizations and the private sector, in information handling and communication, particularly within developing countries.

40.21.   Full participation of, in particular, developing countries should be ensured in any international scheme under the organs and organizations of the United Nations system for the collection, analysis and use of data and information.

## Activities

a.   Production of information usable for decision-making

40.22.   Countries and international organizations should review and strengthen information systems and services in sectors related to sustainable development, at the local, provincial, national and international levels. Special emphasis should be placed on the transformation of existing information into forms more useful for decision-making and on targeting information at different user groups. Mechanisms should be strengthened or established for transforming scientific and socio-economic assessments into information suitable for both planning and public information. Electronic and non-electronic formats should be used.

b.   Establishment of standards and methods for handling information

40.23.   Governments should consider supporting the efforts of governmental as well as non-governmental organizations to develop mechanisms for efficient and harmonized exchange of information at the local, national, provincial and international levels, including revision and establishment of data, access and dissemination formats, and communication interfaces.

c.   Development of documentation about information

40.24.   The organs and organizations of the United Nations system, as well as other governmental and non-governmental organizations, should document and share information about the sources of available information in their respective organizations. Existing programmes, such as those of the Advisory Committee for the Coordination of Information Systems (ACCIS) and the International Environmental Information System (INFOTERRA), should be reviewed and strengthened as required. Networking and coordinating mechanisms should be encouraged between the wide variety of other actors, including arrangements with non-governmental organizations for information sharing and donor activities for sharing information on sustainable development projects. The private sector should be encouraged to strengthen the mechanisms of sharing its experience and information on sustainable development.

    d.   Establishment and strengthening of electronic networking capabilities

40.25.   Countries, international organizations, including organs and organizations of the United Nations system, and non-governmental organizations should exploit various initiatives for electronic links to support information sharing, to provide access to databases and other information sources, to facilitate communication for meeting broader objectives, such as the implementation of Agenda 21, to facilitate intergovernmental negotiations, to monitor conventions and efforts for sustainable development to transmit environmental alerts, and to transfer technical data. These organizations should also facilitate the linkage of different electronic networks and the use of appropriate standards and communication protocols for the transparent interchange of electronic communications. Where necessary, new technology should be developed and its use encouraged to permit participation of those not served at present by existing infrastructure and methods. Mechanisms should also be established to carry out the necessary transfer of information to and from non-electronic systems to ensure the involvement of those not able to participate in this way.

    e.   Making use of commercial information sources

40.26.   Countries and international organizations should consider undertaking surveys of information available in the private sector on sustainable development and of present dissemination arrangements to determine gaps and how those gaps could be filled by commercial or quasi-commercial activity, particularly activities in and/or involving developing countries where feasible. Whenever economic or other constraints on supplying and accessing information arise, particularly in developing countries, innovative schemes for subsidizing such information-related access or removing the non-economic constraints should be considered.

**Means of implementation**

    a.   Financing and cost evaluation

40.27.   The secretariat of the Conference has estimated the average total annual cost (1993-2000) of implementing the activities of this programme to be about $165 million from the international community on grant or concessional terms. These are indicative and order-of-magnitude estimates only and have not been reviewed by Governments. Actual costs and financial terms, including any that are non-concessional, will depend upon, inter alia, the specific strategies and programmes Governments decide upon for implementation.

    b.   Institutional means

40.28.   The institutional implications of this programme concern mostly the strengthening of already existing institutions, as well as the strengthening of cooperation with non-governmental organizations, and need to be consistent with the overall decisions on institutions made by the United Nations Conference on Environment and Development.

    c.   Capacity-building

40.29.   Developed countries and relevant international organizations should cooperate, in particular with developing countries, to expand their capacity to receive, store and retrieve, contribute, disseminate, use and provide appropriate public access to relevant environmental and developmental information, by providing technology and training to establish local information services and by supporting partnership and cooperative arrangements between countries and on the regional or subregional level.

    d.   Scientific and technological means

40.30.   Developed countries and relevant international organizations should support research and development in hardware, software and other aspects of information technology, in particular in developing countries, appropriate to their operations, national needs and environmental contexts.

Printed in Great Britain
by Amazon